"I ENCOUNTERED GOD!"

Series III. Original Studies, Composed in English

On the cover is a photograph of a stained glass window in the Church of St. John the Apostle in St. Louis, Missouri.

DAVID M. STANLEY, S.J.

"I ENCOUNTERED GOD!"

THE SPIRITUAL EXERCISES

WITH THE

GOSPEL OF SAINT JOHN

THE INSTITUTE OF JESUIT SOURCES

St. Louis, 1986

in cooperation with
Gujarat Sahitya Prakash
Anand Press
Anand, India

IMPRIMI POTEST: Very Reverend William M. Addley, S.J.
Provincial, Province of Upper Canada
August 16, 1984

IMPRIMATUR: G. Emmett Cardinal Carter
Archbishop of Toronto
August 22nd, 1984

This is the
First Edition, for the Americas, Western Europe,
Australia, and New Zealand

Note: There is a *Second Edition,* authórized for
sale only in Asia and Africa, which can be
orderd from Gujarat Sahitya Prakash,
Anand 388 001, India

©1986 The Institute of Jesuit Sources
Fusz Memorial, St. Louis, University
3700 West Pine Blvd.
St. Louis, Missouri 63108

Library of Congress Catalog Card Number: 84-82164
ISBN 0-912422-71-8 Smyth sewn paperbound
ISBN 0-912422-72-6 clothbound

CONTENTS

Father David M. Stanley, S.J., Professor of New Testament in Regis College, Toronto, Ontario, is well known to many of our readers from his earlier *A Modern Scriptural Approach to the Spiritual Exercises.* Published in 1967, it was the first book to appear in this Institute's Series III, Original Studies, Composed in English. Reprinted four times, and translated into Spanish and Polish, it was in heavy demand until our stock was exhausted in 1982. In it the author drew from all four Gospels the episodes from the life of Christ which in St. Ignatius' *Spiritual Exercises* reinforce the progress of thought toward ever growing love—as Ignatius himself had done before him.

In this present book, Number 6 in that same series, Father Stanley draws all these episodes from one Gospel, that commonly attributed to St. John. By this unifying procedure he brings out the remarkable similarity in the respective spiritual outlooks of St. John and of St. Ignatius. Each of them could truthfully say: "I encountered God." Stanley selects from John passages appropriate to an Ignatian retreat and interprets them in depth, aiming in this way to stimulate the prayerful reflection of retreatants; and they in turn can thus dispose themselves to let God move their affections. These movements in their minds and hearts can become deeper, firmer, and more habitual insofar as they are based on sound, insightful, and satisfying exegesis of Scripture.

In other words, the author offers help to a retreatant toward practicing the age-old and time-honored method of "prayerful reading" *(lectio divina),* which through reverent meditation leads a devout person toward contemplation. With approval Stanley quotes from the renowned Johannine specialist Donatien Mollat, S.J.: "The spirit of St. John consists totally in love and in bringing others to love" (page 2, below).

"I Encountered God" is therefore predominantly a book for deepening one's spiritual life. Its chapters can scarcely be regarded as ready-made points for a director to pass on with only a little change to his retreatants. Instead it presents profound and satisfying biblical theology. But this is a theology orientated to the heart, rather than to an understanding merely academic. Its chapters can bring rich spiritual benefits to retreat directors and retreatants alike. It will prove especially profitable to those who have previously made retreats of eight or more days with

the *Spiritual Exercises* of St. Ignatius, and who desire to nourish their prayer life through a better grasp of the inspiring message contained in the Fourth Gospel.

It is likely, in fact, that different classes of readers will find the book useful for their own particular needs. Retreat directors, for example, can deepen their personal appreciation of John's passages and of their places in his overall thought. Then, charged with his spirit, they can present these passages of his Gospel more effectively when they give directives or points to exercitants.

Retreatants, similarly, can peruse these chapters prayerfully, perhaps in small portions, and through this prayerful reading *(lectio divina)* prepare themselves for more fruitful contemplation. In this they will be especially helped by Father Stanley's earlier article which he has added as an Appendix: "A Suggested Approach to *Lectio Divina.*"

Persons less familiar with St. Ignatius' *Exercises*[1] can, by a prayerful reading of this work absorb directly from St. John much of the fruit of Ignatius' little book. The Fourth Gospel and the *Exercises* will be seen to complement each other in many ways. Each gives its own peculiar approach to the same habitual and intimate relationship with God.

In its manner of presentation, this book on St. John's Gospel is a companion volume to its author's earlier book, *The Call to Discipleship: The Spiritual Exercises with the Gospel of St. Mark* (London: *The Way,* 1982).

George E. Ganss, S.J.
Director and General Editor
The Institute of Jesuit Sources
Pentecost, May 26, 1985

[The term "Spiritual Exercises" gives rise to many editorial problems. Throughout this book, *Spiritual Exercises* (in italic type) is used when the reference is chiefly to St. Ignatius' book, and Spiritual Exercises (in roman type) when it is chiefly to the activities within a retreat. However, since the book usually envisages the activities and vice versa, there are overlappings of emphasis which sometimes make the choice of the typeface somewhat arbitrary.

For other similar editorial problems and their treatment, see the Editorial Note on page 328 below. Editor.]

It is now some thirty years since I first entertained the design of giving the Spiritual Exercises through the exclusive use of the Fourth Gospel. With the intention of one day publishing a book on the subject, I wrote a series of articles for *Worship* (1957-1961) on the liturgical use of a dozen Johannine pericopes. In 1982, *The Call to Discipleship: the Spiritual Exercises with the Gospel of St Mark* appeared as a double *Supplement* (43/44) to *The Way* from London, England. In an article which discussed the aids in making the Exercises offered by recent Gospel-criticism,[1] Father Joseph A. Fitzmyer suggested "that in an eight day retreat, in which a number of episodes from the life of Christ are to be used, they be taken entirely from one Gospel," as this would serve the Ignatian concern "that the retreatant acquire a thorough knowledge of the Christ . . . and it is difficult to think of a better way . . . than to follow and use as much as possible of the inspired portrait of one of the evangelists." The present study, like that in which the Marcan Gospel was used, will indicate my agreement with Fitzmyer, and indeed my own conviction that a single Gospel can be effectively adapted (with a few necessary transpositions) to the Four Weeks of the *Exercises*.

It is fortunate that my own implementation of the plan has remained in abeyance until now, as meanwhile a spate of magisterial commentaries on the Gospel of John have appeared—by Father Rudolph Schnackenburg, Father Raymond Brown, Doctor Rudolph Bultmann (in English), Doctor C. K. Barrett (in a second edition).[2] A series of less technical expositions of this Gospel have been published by Fathers George

---

1   Joseph A. Fitzmyer, S.J., "The Spiritual Exercises of St. Ignatius and Recent Gospel Study," *Woodstock Letters* 91 (1962), 246-274.

2   Rudolf Schnackenburg, *The Gospel according to St. John*, Vol. I, tr. Kevin Smyth (New York, London, Montreal, 1968); Vol. II, tr. C. Hastings, F. McDonagh, D. Smith, R. Foley, S.J. (New York: Seabury, 1980); Vol. III, tr. D. Smith, G. A. Kon (New York: Crossroad, 1982), (cited hereafter as Schnackenburg, *John*, I, II, or III); Raymond E. Brown, S.S., *The Gospel according to John I–XII* Anchor Bible 29; *The Gospel according to John XIII–XXI* Anchor Bible 29A (Garden City, N.Y., 1966, 1970); (cited hereafter as R. E. Brown, *John I–XII* or *John XIII–XXI*); Rudolph Bultmann, *The Gospel of John: A Commentary*, tr. G. R. Beasley-Murray, R. W. N. Hoare, J. K. Riches (Philadelphia: Fortress Press, 1975), (cited hereafter as Bultmann, *The Gospel of John*); C. K. Barrett, *The Gospel according to St. John*, 2nd ed. (Philadephia: Fortress Press, 1978), (cited hereafter as C. K. Barrett, *John*).

MacRae, James McPolin, and Joseph Blank, among others.[3]

Meanwhile also, two Jesuit New Testament scholars, the late, regretted Donatien Mollat and Carlo Martini, now cardinal-archbishop of Milano, have edited their reflections on the striking compatibility between the approach of the fourth evangelist and that of Ignatius of Loyola to the mystery of Jesus.[4] And to all these exegetes I gratefully acknowledge my indebtedness, which will become evident in the course of this work.

May I confess at the outset that such a project as this—the suggestion that the Spiritual Exercises may be made with the help of a single Gospel-writer—is inevitably confronted with certain stubborn realities, which resist the ingenuity of more creative minds than my own. Accordingly, I remain painfully aware that this modest endeavor displays, in its implementation, a number of unavoidable limitations. To mention only the principal problem—one faces the irresolvable incompatibility between the purpose of the fourth evangelist in structuring his book as he did, and that of an Ignatius of Loyola, who did not intend to author a book (in the usual literary sense), but to issue a practical guide for an exercitant of suitable qualities to a new spiritual experience of the person of the risen Jesus. Indeed it is for that reason considerably easier to account for Ignatius' creation of the *Spiritual Exercises* than to resolve satisfactorily the nagging question of John's complex aim in creating such an innovative, fourth example of the uniquely Christian genre *(Gattung)*, which goes by the name Gospel. Did this writer, with his impressive assimilation of the Old Testament and its symbolism, his acquaintance with certain rabbinic commentaries on those sacred books, intend to bring his Jewish contemporaries to accept Jesus and his message? Did he not rather propose to present the gospel in a mode compatible with Hellenistic (even Gnostic) religious sensibilities? Was he conversant with certain forms of Buddhism? While a case might be made for such varying opinions, for my part I concur with the balanced view of George MacRae, "John's message is that Jesus can be approached in many ways, but he can only be understood on Christian terms, not Jewish or Greek, or Gnostic. That is why the Fourth Gospel was ac-

3   George W. MacRae, S.J., *Invitation to John, Image Books* (Garden City, N.Y.: Doubleday, 1978); G. W. MacRae, S.J., *Faith in the Word: the Fourth Gospel* (Chicago: Franciscan Herald Press, 1973); J. McPolin, S.J., *John* (Wilmington: M. Glazier, 1980); J. J. Huckle and P. Visokay, *The Gospel According to St. John,* I; II, III, Josef Blank, tr. M. J. O'Connell (New York: Crossroads, 1981).
4   Donatien Mollat, S.J., "St. John's Gospel and the Exercises of St. Ignatius," *Communications,* no. 5 (Rome: Ignatian Center of Spirituality, 1974 and St. Louis: The Institute of Jesuit Sources, 1975); Carlo M. Martini, S.J., *The Spiritual Exercises in the Light of St. John* (Anand, India: Gujarat Sahitya Prakash, 1981).

cepted as a Christian book . . . because despite its gnosticizing trend it is the Christian gospel that is proclaims."[5]

One fairly recent development in Johannine studies deserves mention here, since it makes possible the discernment of significant parallels between the composition of John's Gospel and the genesis of the Spiritual Exercises, long acknowledged to be the fruit of Ignatius of Loyola's spiritual odyssey. I refer, of course, to the impressive attempts by scholars such as Doctor J. Louis Martyn and Father Raymond E. Brown to show how the Fourth Gospel reflects the religious experiences of the community for which it was composed.[6] We shall have occasion to return to this important insight in our reflections on the Gospel-text as the starting-point for the contemplations in the Exercises.

In addition, one of the well known achievements of the approach to the study of our Gospels called Redaction criticism has been of considerable aid to the prayerful consideration of these sacred books. It has been pointed out that one of the realities which presided over the structuring of each of the Gospels has been its author's personal image of Jesus, with the help of which each Gospel-writer articulated his own faith in a message relevant to the needs of his own contemporary community. So also St. Ignatius in the sixteenth century, after being graced with the profound mystical experience near the river Cardoner at Manresa, was endowed with his own vision of the risen Christ actively at work within the Church and in the world, which he presented to his own contemporaries through *The Spiritual Exercises.*

And again, just as our Gospels retain their relevance for each succeeding generation of believers, so the Ignatian Exercises, as the last four centuries' experience of them by countless women and men, who have met the somewhat exacting standards set out by their author, can testify, have led such exercitants "to seek and find God's will for the direction of their lives" (Annotation 1).

If I may be permitted an *apologia* for concentrating almost exclusively upon the explication of the Gospel-texts, it is out of a conviction that thereby the retreatant can be helped to assimilate these inspired writings. Such is the intent of that time-honored *lectio divina* ("divine reading"), which through meditation and prayer is calculated to lead to contemplation. For, in the traditions of western contemplation, which

5   G. W. MacRae, S.J., "The Fourth Gospel and *Religionsgeschichte,*" *Catholic Biblical Quarterly* 32 (1970), 13-24.
6   J. L. Martyn, *History and Theology in the Fourth Gospel* (New York: Harper & Row, 1968; rev. ed. Nashville, 1979); see also his *The Gospel of John in Christian History* (New York: Paulist, 1979); Raymond E. Brown, S.S., *The Community of the Beloved Disciple* (New York: Paulist, 1979).

come down to us from earliest times, such has always been the pattern of Christian prayer—that "keeping Jesus in mind," which (with the celebration of the Lord's Supper) forms the obedient response of the Church to the command, "Do this in memory of me" (1 Cor 11:24b). Accordingly, one will search in vain for anything like those "moral applications," which seventeenth century French Jesuits were led to make under the influence of St. Francis de Sales.

Hermeneutical issues arising from the text of *The Spiritual Exercises* have long been, and continue to be, a topic of debate amongst the professional interpreters. While a discussion of such questions lies beyond the scope of this small book (and beyond my own competence), I have restricted myself to the discussion of certain points where I judged it to be necessary and have cited those views which appeared to me to be solidly established.

The citations from the Fourth Gospel, in my own translation, are indicated in parentheses simply by chapter and verse, e.g., (3:5), while other scriptural references are given in the generally accepted manner, e.g. (1 Cor 3:4). The references to the text of *The Spiritual Exercises* are given within brackets (for example, [139]), to indicate the section or paragraph numbers which have become standard since their addition to Ignatius' text, in the edition of Turin in 1928.

I wish to thank two of my New Testament colleagues and friends, Raymond E. Brown, S.S. and George W. MacRae, S.J. for their gracious permission to use passages from their books, which I felt would help my own readers to an understanding of the Johannine Gospel. Indeed, they have, by their insights into this difficult book, enhanced my own appreciation of it. Father Brown, by his kind intervention with Doubleday, helped me with permission to quote from his Anchor Bible commentary. Father Mark Hegener, O.F.M., Managing Director of Franciscan Herald Press, has generously allowed me to cite some of the many helpful insights in Father MacRae's monograph, *Faith in the Word: The Fourth Gospel.*

There remains only the pleasant duty of acknowledging with gratitude the patient and efficient help of Mrs. Moira Hughes, whose expertise produced the final, "fair copy," from my own with its many glosses and emendations.

David M. Stanley, S.J.
Regis College
Toronto, Ontario, Canada
Holy Thursday, April 4, 1985

"I ENCOUNTERED GOD!"

DEDICATION

For Father James Walsh

of the British Province of the Society of Jesus,

founder-editor of The Way,

without whose friendship and repeated assistance

this book could never have been written.

Chapter 1

JOHN'S GOSPEL AND THE IGNATIAN EXERCISES

W hile the ultimate justification of this attempt to present the Exercises through a series of reflections on the Fourth Gospel will become evident only in the course of the reading of this book, I may be permitted at the outset to draw attention to certain remarkable affinities between Johannine and Ignatian spiritualities, which have led to my choice of John's Gospel as a vehicle for making an Ignatian retreat.

In the first place, the noteworthy compatibility between the religious thought of these two authors, which has left an indelible mark upon the prayer-life of the Church, is to be traced back to an extraordinarily privileged experience of the triune God granted to each of these saints through a mystical encounter with the risen Lord Jesus. One catches a hint of this in Ignatius' characteristic and repeated references to Christ as "our creator and Lord." Evidence of a similiar precious experience is attested by our evangelist's predilection—unusual elsewhere in the New Testament—for the title "the only Son" (3:16,18; see 1 Jn 4:9), or "only Son from the Father" (1:14), and the surprising (yet best attested) reading at 1:18, "God an only Son." The imperative demand by the Johannine Jesus from his Jewish disciples of a belief in himself at the very level of their monotheistic faith in the God of Israel, "You believe in God: believe also in me!" (14:1), appears explicable only in terms of John's specially graced prerogative as an inspired Gospel-writer. One catches a reflection of this in his formulation of Jesus' response to Philip, "How can you say, 'Show us the Father?' The person who has seen me has seen the Father!" (14:9).

"I Encountered God!"

The evidence for the divine origin of these two approaches to the Christian mystery will be reviewed shortly in some detail. For the moment, some comment of the selection of a title for the present work may illustrate the notable harmony between the Christological development in the Johannine Gospel and the Ignatian Exercises.

When he ranks Ignatius of Loyola with the great men of the Church,

Father Hugo Rahner remarks that "The connection between all these men is far beyond mere literary dependence, and hence is incapable of being fitted into the categories of history based directly on sources. The connection is, so to speak, meta-historical, founded on an identity of mystical insight which inspires them—removed from each other though they are in time and space and separated from one another as to historical sources—and on an identity of fundamental ideas, which in turn are then expressed in surprisingly parallel principles."[1]

Father Donatien Mollat, by way of introduction to a discussion of the relationships between Johannine and Ignatian spiritualities, recounts a vision of the sixteenth century Carmelite, Mary Magdalene de' Pazzi, during the first vespers for the feast of St. John, 26 December, 1599, in which the Florentine nun beheld in ecstasy the two saints in glory. She exclaimed repeatedly, "The spirit of John and of Ignatius is one and the same!" And she later explained her view by stating, "That spirit consists totally in love and in bringing others to love."[2]

The immediate source for the title, *I Encountered God,* derives from the reading of Father Karl Rahner's theological whimsey, *Ignatius of Loyola,* an interpretation in popular picture-book format of the message of the founder for the contemporary Society of Jesus. With what one can only characterize as serious theological facetiousness, the eminent German thinker assumes the person of the saint. He takes, as his point of departure for the monologue, that "so great illumination" by the river Cardoner at Manresa, which inaugurated the life of Ignatius as a mystic. "As you know my great desire was 'to help save people' *(salvare animas)* . . . to tell people about God and his grace, and about Jesus Christ, the Crucified and Risen, so that their freedom would become the freedom of God . . . to bring the same message the Church has always brought, and yet I felt . . . I could put the old message in new words. Why was this? I was convinced that first tentatively during my illness in Loyola, and then decisively . . . in Manresa, I had a direct encounter with God. This was the experience I longed to communicate to others." And Rahner adds, "All I say is I knew God, nameless and unfathomable, silent and yet near, bestowing himself upon me in his Trinity. I knew God beyond all

1 H. Rahner, S.J., *The Spirituality of St. Ignatius Loyola: an Account of its Historical Development,* tr. Francis John Smith, S.J. (Westminster, Md., 1953), pp. 58-59.
2 D. Mollat, S.J., "St. John's Gospel and the Exercises of St. Ignatius," *Communications,* no. 5, p. 2. This was a lecture given at the Ignatian Center of Spirituality, Rome, in January, 1974.

concrete imaginings, I knew him in such nearness and grace as is impossible to confound or mistake."[3] One finds in fact a breath-taking confidence manifest in the way both John and Ignatius reveal their aim in composing Gospel or Exercises.

Ignatius and John: Parallel Statements of Purpose

Each of these authors makes the startling pledge of leading the believer to the life-giving experience of intimacy with the tri-personal God through the contemplation of selected narratives of the life of Jesus. Ignatius, for his part, explains that "By the name Spiritual Exercises is to be understood every way . . . of readying and disposing a person to rid the self of all disordered affections, and once rid of them, *to seek and find God's will* for the direction of one's life, for the soul's salvation" (Annotation 1). "Two words recur frequently under Ignatius' pen," observes Maurice Giuliani, "revealing, so to speak, the interior oscillation of his prayer: to seek and to find. Man seeks by all the means in his power. God alone brings him to find his grace by revealing it at his own time."[4] Père Mollat in turn points out that the Ignatian expression "to seek the will of God" is found only once in the entire New Testament, where it is placed on the lips of the Johannine Jesus (5:30). Indeed, John frequently attaches special significance to the verbs "seek" and "find"; and he makes it clear that *that* Jesus lives his entire human life in absolute reference to the will of God (4:34; 6:38).

In this grand enterprise on which Ignatius proposes to direct the exercitant he warns that it is of the utmost importance to realize that it is "not knowing a great deal [that] can feed and fully gratify . . . but rather the acquiring of a deeply personal feeling and taste" (Annotation 2). The significance of attending to one's feelings (under grace) and to spiritual "taste" was crucial to the mind of Ignatius, and he clung to his view despite accusations of illuminism made by certain contemporary "intellectualist" guardians of orthodoxy in his age. Paradoxically many Jesuits were led, from the end of the seventeenth century (with the condemnation of Quietism) into the first decades of the twentieth century (with the witch-hunt against Modernism), to play down the capital role assigned in the *Exercises* to affectivity, thus providing grounds for charges (unfounded or not) of rationalism, voluntarism, moralism.

---

3   K. Rahner, S.J., *Ignatius of Loyola,* with an *Historical Introduction* by Paul Imhof, S.J., tr. Rosaleen Ockenden (Cleveland, New York, Toronto, 1979), p. 11.
4   Cited by Mollat from the Introduction, p. 18, in Saint Ignace, *Journal Spirituel: Traduit et commenté* par Maurice Giuliani (Paris, 1959).

Joseph Veale has astutely remarked that "It is ironical that the spirituality of many nineteenth- and twentieth-century Jesuits should have come to resemble the spirituality of Melchior Cano, the Society's fiercest opponent in its early years."[5]

Another aspect of Ignatian teaching deserves to be stressed in our day because of the almost neurotic preoccupation of so many earnest Christians with "what really happened" in Jesus' earthly existence. I refer to Ignatius' insistence, in this same Annotation 2, that the true object of contemplation can only be the story of Jesus *as it is narrated in our Gospels.* He asserts that "The person, who contemplates *the genuine grounds of the history* by ranging over it and reflecting upon it *for oneself,* will surely uncover something that clarifies that history and makes it deeply felt, whether by his own reflection or through the enlightenment of his understanding by the divine power." The phrase "for oneself" indicates what Pedro de Leturia describes as "one of the most salient traits of Ignatius' *Basque character* . . . his inner concentration and reflective individualism . . . he puts his whole soul into his ideas and pursues and diagnoses them *by himself* until he has extracted the vital sap from them. The key phrase is 'by himself.' "[6]

We might add that such a forthright claim also issues from Ignatius' conviction that Christ "the creator and Lord" is lovingly involved with the exercitant and intent upon making him the precious gift of Himself. "When a person is engaged in the Spiritual Exercises, it is more appropriate and much better, in the quest of the divine will, that the creator and Lord give himself to the open-hearted exercitant, inflame him with his love and praise, and ready him for the way in which he can best serve him in future. Consequently, the one who gives the Exercises . . . like a balance at equilibrium . . . is to leave room *for the creator to deal immediately* with his creature, and the creature *directly* with his creator and Lord" (Annotation 15). The astonishing certainty displayed here as to the immediacy of such an experience of God we find mirrored in the stated aim of the fourth evangelist. John's concluding statement turns out, upon reflection, to be not so much an *apologia* for the restricted number of narrated "signs" performed by Jesus, as an assured judgment regarding the supreme value of what he has related for leading the attentive reader to receive the divine gift of life. On this point Raymond

5   Joseph Veale, S.J., "Ignatian Prayer or Jesuit spirituality," *The Way: Supplement* no. 27 (1976), 4.
6   Pedro Leturia, S.J., *Iñigo de Loyola,* tr. Aloysius J. Owen, S.J. (Chicago, 1965), p. 98.

Brown is in agreement with Rudolf Bultmann, "that the primary purpose was to draw attention to the inexhaustible riches of what Jesus had done."[7] Here is how John terminated his Gospel in its original form.

"Actually Jesus performed many other signs in the presence of his disciples, which are not set down in this book. These have been recorded however in order that you may believe that Jesus is the Messiah, the Son of God, and that by believing you may possess life in his name" (20:30-31). While John does not exclude the possibility that a person of good will, not yet a believer, may be given faith in Jesus through the reading of his Gospel, his first concern is with readers already "his disciples." This inspired writer declares that he has set forth his interpretation of what Jesus said and did primarily for such as have become Christians — that "they may attain to a more profound and stable faith."[8] This faith is directed in the first place to Jesus, who as John has shown (especially at 10:22-30) transcends Jewish messianic expectations by actually being one with the Father. It is moreover, he asserts, an infallible means to the final goal, "life in his name." It is this last phrase which discloses John's consistent intention to focus upon the person of Jesus. It also provides grounds for Father Schnackenburg's view that "Johannine Christology is essentially ordained to soteriology."[9] The "life" (or, "eternal life") in question has been described by John as "to know You the only true God and the One You sent, Jesus Christ" (17:3). Here "to know," as frequently in biblical usage, denotes an immediate experience of communion with God Himself. Because John is aware that it is God in His triune personality Who becomes present to the believer through the human life of Jesus, Word become flesh, he has also drawn attention to the role of the Paraclete as divine artificer of this intimate relationship with God the Father. The Spirit of truth "unveils the meaning" of Jesus' life for each succeeding generation of Christians. "He will glorify me, because he will take what is mine and unveil its meaning for you" (16:14).

Accordingly, this bold claim by the fourth evangelist, as his Gospel draws to its close, is rightly seen as a promise to induct the believing reader into that mysterious "abiding" with Father, Son, and Spirit, in

---

7   R. E. Brown, *John XIII–XXI,* p. 1057. Excerpts are from *The Gospel According to John (Anchor Bible)* translated and edited by Raymond E. Brown. Copyright 1966, 1970 by Doubleday & Company, Inc. Reprinted by permission of Doubleday & Company, Inc.

8   Schnackenburg, *John,* I, 155.

9   Ibid.

which for him the fulness of Christian existence consists. Such was the lofty venture on which, John discreetly hinted as his Prologue reached its climax, he would conduct his reader. "Now the Law was a gift through Moses: this graciousness, this truth have become reality through Jesus Christ. No one has ever seen God. God an only Son, who (now) reposes on the Father's heart—He it is who revealed Him!" (1:17-18).

We may say then that John's purpose was to produce a spirituality which was more expressly trinitarian than that found in the earlier Gospels, and which centuries later would re-echo in the *Spiritual Exercises*. George MacRae thus comments on the evangelist's intention: "Aided by the Spirit of truth, the evangelist has written to do what Jesus' revealing word was meant to do: to elicit faith and thus make eternal life possible."[10] In his brief, yet deeply sensitive commentary, the same scholar remarks that "The Gospel of John reflects an understanding of God and the world in which everything is drawn in sharp lines. There are radical choices to be made within the framework of opposites in cosmic conflict. But the challenge is always personal, even individual. John serves to remind the Christian that underlying all the legitimate and necessary preoccupations of Christian life, there is the personal, existential attitude of faith, not as a decision to be made once and for all, but as an act that is always present when the believer realizes that God is encountered in the humanity of Jesus."[11] These words might aptly be applied to the *Exercises*, which in the intention of the author were simply to constitute an introduction to a life of contemplative prayer, as can be seen from a note for the Second Week. "If he wishes to shorten the Week, he may omit even some of the mysteries that have been assigned. For the intention is to provide an introduction and a way of contemplating *afterwards* in a better and fuller manner" ([162]).

Trinitarian Orientation of Ignatian Spirituality

In a lecture on "The Trinitarian Inspiration of the Ignatian charism" given in Rome 1980, the then Father General of the Society, Pedro Arrupe, insists that "Ignatius' entire mystical and trinitarian adventure is practically imposed on him; it is a divine initiative." He points out that in the third phase of Ignatius' time at Manresa, "God begins to make his presence felt with elemental, pictorial representations, acting with him 'as a schoolteacher deals with a child.' These representa-

10   MacRae, *Invitation to John*, p. 226.
11   Ibid., pp. 22-23.

tions have to to with subjects . . . dominant all the rest of his life: the creation of the world, the Eucharist, the humanity of Christ and, in the shape of very concrete images, the Trinity. The earlier mention of saints in his *Autobiography* now disappears. In their place, he bursts into a surprising paragraph about 'his great devotion to the most Holy Trinity,' which is becoming a dominant theme in his spiritual life.''[12]

When Arrupe discusses that "so great illumination," granted to Ignatius by the river Cardoner, he cites Nadal's testimony about its content. "There he received a penetrating knowledge of the Persons of the Trinity and of the divine Essence. Even more, he received not only a clear intelligence, but an interior vision of how God created the world, of how the Word became flesh."[13] The former General comments: "This trinitarian context will be clearly detectable in the *Exercises:* not only in Ignatius' presentation of the mystery of the Incarnation, but in the Principle and Foundation too, which he will write later—which the pilgrim at Manresa was not yet educated enough to compose."[14] In speaking of the thrust of the Second Week, Father Arrupe notes moreover that "Ignatius passes very logically from the Word, the trinitarian Person, to the historical Christ . . . and to the perennial Christ who acts in the world until the end of time. The trinitarian framework of the contemplation of the Incarnation is based on this approach . . . For Ignatius, Christ is above all the one sent by the Father, whose will he seeks and wants to accomplish in an indifference that extends even to the cross."[15] Surely to no other Gospel do these words apply so appositely as to that of John. The summary by Pedro de Leturia of Ignatius' mystical encounter at the river Cardoner is also couched in terms reminiscent of the Fourth Gospel. "The descent of creatures from God and their necessary reascent and reintegration into their ultimate end, God himself, is one of the most vivid experiences of the great enlightenment."[16]

A place of particular importance is assigned by Pedro Arrupe to the profound experience at La Storta in November 1537—the culmination of that year which Ignatius says he spent "preparing himself and asking the Virgin to be good enough to place him with her Son." Our Saint thus describes the happening which finally clarified once for all his hitherto

---

12   Pedro Arrupe, S.J., "The Trinitarian Inspiration of the Ignatian Charism," *Acta Romana Societatis Iesu,* 18 (1981), 116-118.
13   Ibid., p. 122.
14   Ibid., p. 122.
15   Ibid., p. 125.
16   Ibid., p. 122.

half-conscious design of founding the Society of Jesus. "On making a prayer, he felt such a change coming over his soul, and saw too clearly that God the Father was placing him with Christ his Son, that he could not doubt but that God the Father was indeed placing him with his Son."[17] The reader will have seen in all this the source of that threefold colloquy which plays a significant role in Two Standards.

Indeed, so vivid was the memory of this peak experience that, as Father Arrupe remarks, seven years later in the few precious pages of the Ignatian *Spiritual Diary,* which escaped destruction at the hands of its author, we read the entry for 23 February, 1544, "With these thoughts growing in intensity and seeming to be a confirmation, even though I received no consolations about this matter, and Jesus' showing himself, or letting himself be felt, seeming to me to be somehow the work of the most holy Trinity, and *remembering when the Father placed me with his Son . . .*"[18] This sampling of texts may serve to show the fundamentally trinitarian orientation of Ignatian spirituality, which exhibits in a remarkable degree an affinity with that of the Fourth Gospel.

In order better to assess certain similarities between the Ignatian and the Johannine approaches to the prayerful consideration of Jesus' earthly history, it is helpful to recall how each of these authors is at once a man of tradition and a creative contributor to the evolution of what is termed the "Jesus-tradition."

Ignatius, Heir to Traditions of Medieval Spirituality

Just as the fourth evangelist, notwithstanding his innovative re-interpretation of earlier evangelical traditions, stands perceptibly within the ranks of his predecessors the Synoptic Gospel-writers, so Ignatius of Loyola must be seen as legitimate heir to the spirituality of the Middle Ages, particularly the great inheritance bequeathed by the Cistercians and the Carthusians. An appreciation of the continuity that exists between the various ways of praying in the Exercises and what has been called "Western mysticism" will serve to throw light on the relationship between "meditation" and "contemplation" as proposed by Ignatius. This is all the more necessary, not only because some historians of spirituality appear to consider Ignatian contemplation as analogous to a biological sport, but also because Jesuit commentators on the *Exercises* have tended erroneously to reduce "contemplation" to "meditation."

17 Ibid., p. 123.
18 Ibid., p. 133.

Yet it is only when one realizes the indebtedness of Ignatius to the medieval practice of prayer that his own highly original contribution can be rightly evaluated.

Credit for the relatively recent recognition of the historical links between Ignatian spirituality and that of the twelfth-century monastic writers on prayer belongs to James Walsh, founder-editor of *The Way,* both for his own research into the Cistercian and Carthusian tradition, as well as for his considerable influence upon contemporary Jesuit spiritual writers in the English-speaking world. In collaboration with the Augustinian medievalist, Edmund College, Father Walsh produced a critical edition and translation of the work of a twelfth-century prior of the Grande Chartreuse, Guigo II (+ ca 1188), Guigo's letter on the interior life *(Scala Claustralium)* which is relevant to our discussion here.[19] It appears that Guigo is debtor to Augustine, as well as to his own contemporaries, the Cistercians, Bernard of Clairvaux and William of St. Thierry, and to the Victorines, Hugh and Richard. Yet, in Walsh's judgment, Guigo made his own contribution to the teaching on contemplation as "the first to apply to it the classical teaching about grace and free will, and to work out precisely what are the roles of these two forces as man climbs the traditional ladder towards the heights." There are four "rungs" to Guigo's "ladder": *lectio,* the attentive, reverent reading of Scripture, *meditatio,* the diligent mental reflection upon the truth hidden in the reading, *oratio,* persevering appeal for divine help in achieving communion with God, and *contemplatio,* the fruit of God's compassionate response by which the devout heart is raised to Himself through consolation.

When it is remembered that the ancients habitually read aloud to themselves (a custom which appears to have persisted into the Middle Ages), it becomes clear that this exercise aimed at impressing the scriptural word upon the two senses, hearing and sight, which most effectively aid the memory. In the *Holy Rule,* St. Benedict ranks the reading of the Bible with the *opus Dei* (the sacred liturgy) and manual labor as an essential monastic occupation, and prescribes its practice particularly for sacred times, Sundays and Lent (chs. 48,49). He underscores its ruminative character by making it synonymous with meditation *(meditare aut legere)* and its affective character by associating it with *compunctio cordis* (heartfelt sorrow).

Dom Jean Leclercq remarks that "The *meditatio* consists in apply-

---

19   See the English version by James Walsh, S.J., *The Way* 5 (1965), 333-344.

ing oneself with attention to this exercise in total memorization . . . it is what inscribes, so to speak, the sacred text in the body and the soul . . . this deep impregnation with the words of Scripture that explains the extremely important phenomenon of reminiscence."[20] Guigo observes that "When meditation busily applies itself to this work, it does not remain on the outside . . . it goes to the heart of the matter . . . When the soul is set alight by this kindling . . . it deduces how sweet it would be to know by experience . . . yet it can find no means of its own to have what it longs for."

"So the soul, seeing that by itself it cannot attain to that sweetness of knowing and feeling for which it longs . . . humbles itself and betakes itself to *prayer*." The divine response to this cry for help, Guigo assures his reader, forestalls, even interrupts the petition. "The Lord, whose eyes are upon the just . . . whose ears can catch . . . the very meaning of their prayers, does not wait . . . but breaks in upon . . . the prayer," by bestowing the precious gift of *contemplation*.

Godfrey O'Donnell has shown how this classic description of progress in the spiritual life was taken over by another Carthusian, Guiges du Pont (+ 1297), and later plundered without acknowledgement (as was the freebooting practice in pre-copyright times) by a Tuscan Franciscan, the pseudo-Bonaventure, John de Caulibus ("of the cabbages"), and still later plagiarized by Ludolf the Saxon Carthusian in his Prologue to the *Life of Christ compiled from the four Gospels and certain orthodox Christian writers.*[21] It was this voluminous work, rendered into Castilian by the Franciscan Ambrosio Montesino, that Ignatius read in the castle of Loyola during his convalescence (1521-1522) from the wound received in the siege of Pamplona. The many echoes of Ludolf in the *Exercises* attest beyond doubt how much the author, unbeknownst to himself no doubt, owed to the Cistercian and Carthusian traditions regarding prayer.

This Ignatian indebtedness to medieval spirituality is of paramount importance, in my opinion, for a proper appreciation of the genetic con-

---

20   Dom Jean Leclercq, *The Love of Learning and the Desire for God,* tr. Catherine Misralie (New York, 1961), p. 90.

21.   Godfrey O'Donnell, S.J., "Contemplation," *The Way: Supplement* no. 27 (1976), 27-34. See also J. P. Grausem, S.J., "Le *De Contemplatione* du chartreux Guiges du Pont (+ 1297)," *Revue d'Ascétique et Mystique* 10 (1924), 259-289. L. W. Rigollot published what is regarded as the standard edition of Ludolf's work (Rome, 1870): see Emmerich Raitz von Frentz, S.J., "Ludolphe le Chartreux et les Exercices de S. Ignace de Loyola," *Revue d'Ascétique et Mystique* 25 (1949), 375-388; Walter Baier, "Ludolphe de Saxe," *Dictionnaire de Spiritualité,* Vol. 9, cols. 1130-1138.

nection between "meditation," "contemplation," and "application of the senses." And since failure to see how in the *Spiritual Exercises* "meditation" was presumed to develop spontaneously into "contemplation" has sometimes led to unfounded criticisms of rigidity and insensitivity to liberty of spirit on the part of Ignatius, it may be helpful to review certain Ignatian texts which clearly demonstrate that such an evolution was expected to occur.

The Advance to "Contemplation" from "Meditation"

It is unfortunate that so many translators of the text of the *Exercises* have rendered the expression "ways of praying" *(modos)* by "methods," a word that suggests the strictures of technique and a rigid compartmentalization, totally alien to the mind of Ignatius. Lambert Classen has made a perceptive remark. "Ignatius himself does not speak in the little book of methods. We never meet the word."[22] Disregard of this point can jeopardize the exercitant's growth in prayer. Nineteenth-century Jesuits appear to have tended, in giving the Exercises, to speak almost exclusively of "meditation" to the neglect of the abundant variety of "ways of praying" indicated in the Ignatian text itself.

John Philip Roothaan, second general of the restored Society (1829-1853), has been blamed—somewhat unfairly in my judgment—for this unfortunate concentration upon "meditation." It may not be sufficiently known that his little treatise on prayer, *De ratione meditandi,* was a tract, composed in his youth for junior Jesuits in the Russia of 1812. This distinguished commentator on the *Spiritual Exercises* during his lengthy generalate recalled the Society to the genuinely traditional use of the book (by retrieving as far as he was able the authentic text and insisting upon its study) and to the practice of what are now known as "directed retreats" (by urging French Jesuits to abandon their misguided custom of "preaching" the Exercises, and by emphasizing, as an essential, the procedure of discernment).[23] He can scarcely be held responsible for the widespread adoption by Jesuit novice-masters of his youthful essay on the art of meditation.

That a distinction is made in the text of the *Exercises* between

---

22   Lambert Classen, S.J., "The 'Exercise with the Three Powers of the Soul' in the Exercises as a Whole," in *Ignatius of Loyola: his Personality and Spiritual Heritage, 1556-1956: Studies on the 400th Anniversary of his Death,* tr. Louis W. Roberts (St. Louis: 1977), 237-271: see p. 260.

23   H. Bernard-Maitre, S.J., "Le Pére Jean-Philippe Roothaan et la Vulgata latine des Exercices de Saint-Ignace," *Revue d'Ascétique et Mystique* 37 (1961), 193-212.

"meditation" and "contemplation" is beyond cavil. However, account is to be taken of their author's presupposition that contemplation inevitably emerges from meditation. One sees this from the explanation of the term "resumption," which designates the fourth exercise of the First Week: "because the understanding, without digressing, carefully ranges over the recall of what was *contemplated* in the exercises already made" ([64]). It is a question here of two meditations and one repetition of these in combination, "by taking account of, and dwelling on, the points where one felt greater consolation or desolation, or greater spiritual feeling" ([62]). Ignatius takes it for granted that contemplation will regularly occur even in the First Week. "When I awake, without yielding to irrelevant thoughts, [I should] attend at once to what I am about to *contemplate* in the first exercise" ([74]). Father William Peters would appear to be right in observing that "as soon as there is true consolation, meditation turns into contemplation, even though the subject matter remains the same."[24]

A still more arresting example of the Ignatian sensitivity to this genetic development appears in a note appended to Three Classes, where "I will employ the same three colloquies that were made in the preceding *contemplation* on Two Standards" ([156]), designated earlier ([136]) as "a meditation." Thus Ignatius presumes that the experience of consolation will occur from the prayerful reflection on this powerful, panoramic presentation of the forces of good and evil at work in history, in which one finds oneself to be actually involved.

Can one discover a reason in Ignatius' own life for this curious switch in terminology with reference to Two Standards? An explanation presents itself when one recalls the main purpose he had in writing his book. "In the mind of St. Ignatius, the Exercises to which suitable candidates were invited to devote a whole month, were intended to reproduce for them the Saint's own experience of his conversion to God. They propose in universalized form a sequence of acts similar to those through which God guided Ignatius himself, in the castle at Loyola, at Manresa . . . at the University of Paris. It is the Saint's purpose to make available to his neighbor . . . the opportunity at least of receiving the same great graces God had bestowed on him."[25] Stanislas Lyonnet in his turn points

---

24 William A. M. Peters, S.J., *The Spiritual Exercises of St. Ignatius: Exposition and Interpretation* (Jersey City, 1968), p. 38.

25 R. A. F. MacKenzie, S.J., "Biblical Theology and the Spiritual Exercises," in *Contemporary Thought and the Spiritual Exercises of St. Ignatius Loyola* (Chicago, 1963), pp. 68-69.

to "the meditation on Two Standards" as "one of those to which St. Ignatius attaches the greatest importance." He notes that "it belongs to the most primitive core of the *Exercises,* that is to say, it stems from the spiritual experience of Ignatius . . . incipient at Loyola, [which] unfolded itself during the six months' solitude he passed at Manresa . . . We reach then the heart of the spiritual experience of Saint Ignatius and the heart of the Exercises." [26] What began at Loyola as "a meditation" from the reading of Augustine's life in Fray Gauberto M. Vagad's *Flos Sanctorum* (a Castilian revision of the *Legenda Aurea* by Jacopo da Varazze) became immeasurably deepened through the mystical illumination at the Cardoner, by the singular grace of infused contemplation.

Consequently, it becomes clear that an essential part of Ignatian pedagogy is to lead the exercitant from "meditation" on those mysteries of faith (in the First Week, and in Two Standards), which inspired his own incipient essays in the spiritual life, to "contemplation." For it was this that constituted the goal towards which the monastic practice of prayer was designed to lead, under the grace of God. So far removed was Ignatius from inhibiting the freedom of a retreatant led by divine favor from relishing the delights of contemplation even in the First Week, that, as his text is seen to indicate, he left room for such privileged moments early in the thirty days. That he termed these inceptive exercises "meditations" however is, I suspect, consistent with his design to permit (without prejudice to the divine graciousness) the exercitant to share in his own spiritual odyssey.

At this point one may well ask, just what precisely is the distinction in the mind of Ignatius between "meditation" and "contemplation"? A first answer, as has been seen, lies in the experience of "consolation." This somewhat quaint word designates a reaction during prayer, which with its opposite, "desolation," and discernment of such "spirits," has been assessed by Laurence Murphy as "the lynch-pin of the Spiritual Exercises." He warns his readers moreover that, "the passages in which Ignatius deals with consolation are among the most difficult in the whole book of the *Exercises.*" [27] Two texts, in the same writer's words, "suggest a common unifying characteristic." "I call consolation each increase of hope, faith, and charity, with any interior joy that summons and draws one towards heavenly realities and towards one's own salvation by instil-

---

26 S. Lyonnet, S.J., "La Méditation des Deux Étendards et son fondement scripturaire," *Christus* 12 (1956), 435-456: see pp. 435-436.
27 Laurence Murphy, S.J., "Consolation," *The Way: Supplement* no. 27 (1976), 35-36.

ling repose and peace in his creator and Lord" ([316]). Three things are to be noticed: the prominence given hope, the awareness in one so favored of growth in communion with God, and (above all) the Christological orientation of such progress ("repose and peace in his creator and Lord"). A second text occurs in the fragmentary Ignatian directory where it is question of "the Elections." "The reality which is consolation is to be made clear by showing how it is like spiritual joy, love, hope, in the things from above *(de arriba)*, tears and any interior emotion *(movimiento)* that leaves one consoled in our Lord" ([377]). Once again we perceive the emphasis upon awareness of receiving the gifts, of their origin "from above," the resultant deeper union with the risen Christ.

Can one discover further clues to the distinction between "meditation" and "contemplation" from the text of the *Exercises*? I confess I find Peters' criterion "according to the subject-matter" somewhat imprecise ("the mysteries of Christ's life" as opposed to "facts or truths"). For then the Contemplation to Attain Love ([230-237]), where there is no question of praying on Jesus' earthly life, would appear to be misnamed. Likewise inadequate is Peters' norm for "meditation." "Mainly through the use of his natural faculties the exercitant tries to understand these truths and facts."[28] If by "natural faculties" he means "the three powers of the soul" ([45]), these, as Classen has shown, are necessarily employed in any way of praying. Indeed, they are expressly indicated in the Contemplation to Attain Love.

Furthermore, Peters' contention that the first exercise in the First Week is a "meditation *on* the three powers of the soul . . . on the exercitant's reactions to the three sins" (and *not* on accounts of the sins of the angels, the first parents, the tragic consequences of one "mortal," that is "capital" sin) is debatable, as it involves a point concerning the original reading of the so-called "autograph" text, which is not conceded by all experts in the *Exercises*.[29]

Despite the dubious validity of his argument, I feel that Peters has however hit upon an important insight into the nature of Ignatian "meditation." While in "contemplation" one makes use of the senses, imagination, memory, intellect, and will, to become personally involved with the risen Jesus, the work of "meditation" is meant to assist *in situating oneself* within the history of sin and grace, as revealed in scriptural or patristic sources. This profound realization that one is a member of

---

28 William Peters, *The Spiritual Exercises of St. Ignatius,* p. 38.
29 Ibid., pp. 57-60.

fallen humanity "under sentence of death" (2 Cor 1:9)—nowadays known as "self-definition"—will be lacunary, to the mind of Ignatius, unless account be also taken of the grace-filled relationships with God in Christ. This is clear from the colloquy which terminates the first exercise ([53]), where the exercitant is confronted with Christ on the cross (as the risen Lord who remains the Crucified even in glory), and is to begin "speaking as one friend converses with another" ([54]). The considerations in the second exercise are calculated ([60]) to evoke "a cry of wonder with ever deepening love" *(esclamación admirative, con crecido afecto)*. These texts indicate how connaturally the work of meditating is to lead to the joys of contemplation. Here I permit myself to cite from a letter of James Walsh. "I think one could argue that all Ignatian colloquies demand a measure of contemplation. Otherwise they will tend towards petitionary prayer in the narrow sense, and cease to be 'friend talking to friend.' The Victorines, Hugh and Richard, insist on the presence of wonder and admiration for 'contemplation,' as opposed to 'meditation.' I think that Ignatius would agree that reverence and affect (see Annotation 3) belong more strictly to contemplation than to meditation" (6 September, 1982).

To return to my own suggestion that "meditation" is basically orientated to self-definition—I suggest that this view is confirmed by a remark of Ignacio Iparraguirre concerning the history of the genesis of Ignatius' book. Three Classes ([149-157]), he asserts, was (with the first part of the "Rules for right judgment in the Church militant") inserted into the *Exercises* during the Paris period (1528-1535). This meditation "reflects the milieu of the Parisian church-dignitaries and university professors. The very designation 'pairs' *(binarios)*, employed in the dialectics of the day, appears to confirm its period of origin. The chief clue however lies in the internal, psychological framework; the typical reaction of the men betrays a mindset peculiar to personages of established position, caught up in affairs, full of complexes, as were so many of the French retreatants, by contrast with the simpler attitude of those hitherto directed by the Saint.''[30] For the sophisticated, worldly mentality of "the establishment," Ignatius' experience taught him that a further refinement in self-definition was a requirement. An observation of Laurence Murphy points in this same direction. "There is a nuance in this exercise we can easily miss. None of the groups actually gives up the sum of money. In fact, giving up the money is never in question directly . . .

---

30 *Obras completas de san Ignacio de Loyola,* ed. Ignacio Iparraguirre, S.J., 2 ed. (Madrid, 1963), p. 183; cf. 4 ed., p. 191; (hereafter abbreviated *Obras completas*).

This point is of considerable psychological significance and in fact constitutes the inner freedom both from inordinate attachment and compulsive detachment, both of which can prevent a person from *doing* God's will."[31] It is perhaps significant that "contemplation" is nowhere mentioned in connection with Three Classes (as it is with all the other meditations): it is the single instance in the *Exercises* of "meditation" pure and simple. And its aim is quite clearly to assist towards self-definition.

Actually, as regards the First Week, the intent of Ignatius is similar to that of Paul in the opening chapters of Romans, where Jew no less than Greek is bid confess his personal culpability, and yet realize that each is the object of God's totally free redemptive action in Christ. The Apostle makes effective use of symbol (notably at 3:11-18) to "draw up the accusation that Jew and Greek alike are all under the domination of Sin" (Rom 3:9), "for all have sinned and are deprived [like Adam] of the glory of God" (Rom 3:23). At the same time, Paul—like Ignatius much later—knows that any attempt at self-definition, which remained merely negative, would give a picture of human history unfaithful to the revelation of the gospel. Hence he adds, "All are justified by God's free grace alone, through that act of redemption in Christ Jesus—whom God publicly displayed as seat of mercy by his blood, effective through faith" (Rom 3:24-25). Paul (and Ignatius also in turn) is keenly sensitive to the truth that there can be no genuine self-definition without the ever-conscious realization that all is gift. "What room then is left for boasting? It is excluded! On what kind of principle—a law of works? No indeed, but by a 'law' of faith. For my conviction is that any human being is justified by faith, quite apart from works of law" (Rom 3:27-28).

Innovative Contribution to the Tradition

Having seen how firmly, in his teaching on prayer, Ignatius stood within the tradition of western spirituality, we wish to recall his originality in providing new directions to the teaching on prayer. In the article already cited, Godfrey O'Donnell makes an important observation. "Ignatius' genius was to have transposed the best of medieval teaching and terminology on contemplation, and to have re-presented it for those whose calling within the Church was to an active apostolic life."[32] Indeed, the author of the *Exercises* never considered prayer—even contem-

---

31   L. J. Murphy, S.J., "To Find God in Peace," *The Way* 22 (1982), 170.
32   Godfrey O'Donnell, "Contemplation," 34.

plative prayer—as other than a means to the ultimate goal: the service of God in the Church. No doubt his love of order (and innate antagonism to disorder) was rooted in his natural endowments. Yet his deep insight into the ordering of means to the end is to be attributed chiefly to that "so great illumination" by the river Cardoner during his sojourn in Manresa. For that was the source of Ignatius' astonishing grasp of the mysteries of the redemption as a coherent whole, that enabled him from the beginning of the Second Week (in fact, even within the First Week) to align the effort of contemplation, with singular simplicity of purpose, with the Cross. He consistently keeps this unity before the mind of the exercitant: from the *labor* and *gloria* ([95]) of the consideration On the King *(Del Rey)*, through the colloquy on the Incarnation ([109]), in the contemplation of the Nativity ([116]), by his admonition in the Third Week to "summon up frequently in memory the labor, fatigue, and sorrows of Christ our Lord, which he endured from the moment he was born up to the mystery of the Passion, in which I find myself at the moment" ([206]).

Pedro Leturia's nice assessment of the effects upon Ignatius of the sublime experience at the Cardoner deserves to be recalled. "The ideal of the King and the Two Standards was not unknown before. But as a result of this constructive transformation it took on a completely new meaning: Henceforth Christ the eternal king was for Ignatius to be a living king actively at work here and now in this world, who had not completely fulfilled the mission given him by his Father, to bring the whole world under his rule; and who therefore is here and now seeking noble and generous companions and friends who desire to prove their loyalty in battle."[33]

Here two remarks by Hugo Rahner are apposite, because—while he does not advert to it—the first applies to an attitude that is typically Johannine, while the second describes a technique which is a salient feature of the Fourth Gospel. "Here, indeed, is something very characteristic of Ignatius: his acute sense of the 'sacramental' structure of the life of Christ. The whole earthly existence of the Word was one long parable of things invisible, and thus the exercitant is made to contemplate the visible life of God . . . in order that he may 'smell and taste the infinite gentleness and sweetness of the divinity' ([124])."[34] The second

---

33 The remark, cited by Hugo Rahner and attributed to Pedro de Leturia (*Ignatius the Theologian,* p. 97), gives the gist of what the distinguished Spanish scholar states in an article, "Genesis de los Ejercicios de San Ignacio y su influjo en la fundacion de la Compañia de Jesús (1521-1540)" in *Estudios Ignacianos, II: Estudios Espirituales* (Roma, 1957), pp. 15-17.

34 H. Rahner, S.J., *Ignatius the Theologian,* tr. Michael Barry (New York, 1968), p. 98.

observation may serve to introduce our reflections on the presentation of "the mysteries" (John would say "signs") by the fourth evangelist. "Ignatius turns the contemplations of the life of Christ, from a loosely-strung set of devout meditations into a genuine dramatic representation, designed to make evident the great contest between Christ and Satan; and the exercitant who, as spectator and fellow-actor, desires to hearken to the summons and become more like Christ, must then carry on this redemptive contest in the interior of his own heart. This *dramatization of the mysteries* [the emphasis is Rahner's] with its highly individual order of presentation, can only be properly appreciated in the light of the Election to which it is leading."[35] It is significant that Raymond Brown uses similiar language when he describes the various steps in the creation of the Fourth Gospel. After noting the particular apostolic traditions which were its basis, he then speaks of a "stage . . . decisively formative for the material that ultimately went into the Gospel. Some of the stories of Jesus' miracles . . . were developed into superb dramas, for example, ch. ix . . . The sayings of Jesus were woven into lengthy discourses of a solemn and poetic character, much like the discourses of Wisdom in the OT."[36] It is to the consideration of this Gospel as an invaluable source for acquiring that art of contemplation, central to the *Spiritual Exercises,* that we must now turn.

"Remembering," Creative Source of Contemplation

Our discussion of the genetic relation of "meditation" to "contemplation" in the Exercises was mainly devoted to the fairly recent discovery by Ignatian scholars that Ignatius of Loyola's teaching on contemplative prayer is indeed traditional, if also innovative. The reader may have missed any substantive treatment of what is called in the *Exercises,* "application of the senses," which (as James Walsh has shrewdly remarked) "appears, on different levels of awareness or consciousness, at both the beginning and end of the contemplative process, which structures (and is structured by) each day of the Ignatian Exercises, whether in the second, third, or fourth weeks."[37] Silence about the Ignatian directions for the use of the imaginative senses (*vista imaginativa,* [91]; *la vista de la imaginación,* [65]) or "spiritual" senses may well appear strange in a book which deals with the Fourth Gospel. Père Mollat claims

---

35   Ibid., p. 103.
36   R. E. Brown, *John I–XII,* pp. xxxv.
37   James Walsh, S.J., "Application of the Senses," *The Way: Supplement* no. 27 (1976), 61.

that "the use of sense-language to express communion with God in Christ is one of the salient traits of Johannine spirituality."[38]

By way of parenthesis I should like to take note of James Walsh's view that the use of the senses in the meditation on hell ([65-71]) differs from the application of the senses in the other Weeks of the Exercises. "The application of the senses to the state of spirit-existence called hell is different in kind. We seek the truth of damnation by applying the interior senses to descriptions—scriptural, patristic, 'theological'—of hell. This is an admixture of 'sensible' and metaphorical descriptions, which Ignatius believes will give an approximation to the truth and reality of hell."[39]

Before taking up the use of sense-experiences by the fourth evangelist to depict Jesus' mission as "interpreter" of "the truth" about "the God no one has ever seen" (1:18), or to decribe the responses by the disciples or the adversaries of Jesus to his "word," it is necessary to point out the very distinctive meaning which John assigns to the verb, "remember."

Already in Israel's sacred literature her God was characterized as the One Who remembers. This "means that a new situation is created and effective help is extended to man in his need . . . Conversely, a basic element in Old Testament piety is that man remembers the past acts of God."[40] Each of the Synoptic Gospel-writers notes how, even in Jesus' lifetime, his remembered word brought tears of repentance to Peter (Mk 14:72; Mt 26:75; Lk 22:61). It is interesting that John, in his narrative of Peter's denials, does not mention Peter's return to grace in the Passion story. Instead he has chosen to dramatize it as an event of the risen Lord's confrontation of Peter after Easter (21:15-19). For this evangelist such efficacious "remembering" is a paschal gift of the glorified Jesus through the "other Paraclete" (14:16). Of the first three evangelists it is Luke who approximates closest to the Johannine conception of remembering. He depicts the two angels at the empty tomb as admonishing the bewildered women: "Remember what he told you while still in Galilee" (Lk 24:6). When the risen Jesus appears to "the Eleven and their companions" (v. 33), he "opened their minds to comprehend the Scriptures" (v. 45).

Like Mark, John is concerned to explain how it happened that

---

38 D. Mollat, S.J., "Jean l'Évangéliste," *Dictionnaire de Spiritualité,* Vol. 8, col. 217.
39 Father Walsh wrote this in a letter to the author 6 September, 1982.
40 Otto Michel, *"Mimnēskomai,"* G. Kittel, *Theological Dictionary of the New Testament,* tr. G. W. Bromiley, Vol. 4, p. 675.

throughout the earthly life of their Lord, none of his most intimate disciples grasped the mystery that surrounded him. Mark had elucidated this enigma by his celebrated literary-theological construction, the so-called "messianic secret." John achieves the same result by giving an unprecedented sense to "remembering." In his Gospel the word designates the Christian reflection issuing from the new insights of Easter faith into the hitherto uncomprehended words and actions of the earthly Jesus, as well as the equally new grasp of the relationship of "the Scriptures" to the Lord, which Luke had already noted.

In order to draw attention to this important notion, the fourth evangelist makes Jesus' symbolic act of cleansing the sacred enclosure in Jerusalem the solemn inauguration of his public ministry (2:13-22). In his narrative "remembering" is twice mentioned. A first comment on this prophetic charade alludes to Psalm 69. "His disciples were to recall it was written, 'Zeal for your house will devour me' " (2:17). However, that such a supernatural insight into the significance of Jesus' dramatic gambit did not strike his disciples until much later may be gathered from John's subsequent gloss on the enigmatic declaration of Jesus, "Destroy this sanctuary, and within three days I will raise it up" (2:19). He comments: "He however had meant his body as the sanctuary. So when he was raised from death, his disciples remembered that he had said this, and they believed the Scripture and the word Jesus had uttered" (vv. 21-22). This privileged act of reminiscence leads to faith in the Old Testament as God's prior disclosure of His will for Jesus, and this same faith reveals the meaning of Jesus' hitherto mystifying declaration. His glorified humanity was to become the new sign of God's presence to His people, replacing the ancient sign, the unique place of worship in Jerusalem. As Otto Michel notes, "Recollection of the word of Jesus is part of the Easter message, and the resurrection gives new might to this word."[41]

The second occurrence of "remembering" is found with John's presentation of another important symbolic action of Jesus, his final entry into the holy city, which—together with the episode where God-fearing pagans desire "to see Jesus" (12:21)—signals the close of the public ministry in this Gospel (12:12-19). This literary device, with its repetition of the key word "remember," suggests to the alert reader that all that has been related in the intervening section since the "cleansing" of the temple-precincts, derives its value from the evangelical traditions, initial fruit of this Christian reminiscence.

41   Ibid., p. 677.

John's story of this most meaningful, last coming of Jesus into the city and its temple, is in fact, by comparison with the Marcan narrative (Mk 11:1-11), singularly jejune. It is however studded with snippets of citations from the prophets. And once more it is the gloss on the event which is significant. "All this his disciples did not understand at first. But when Jesus had been glorified, then they remembered that they had done these things to him which had been written concerning him" (12:16). The sense of Jesus' actions during his earthly life, like the real meaning of his words, was only dimly perceived by those who witnessed them. "Sayings and events were not understood prior to the resurrection."[42]

This becomes evident from the discourse after the Last Supper, when the Johannine Jesus points to the Holy Spirit as artificer of this new element in Christian faith. "I have spoken these things to you while abiding among you; but the Paraclete, the Holy Spirit, Whom the Father will send in my name, *He* will teach you everything and make you remember all I have told you" (14:25-26). Later in this lengthy set of instructions to his own, Jesus will repeat the promise in other terms. "I still have much to tell you, but you cannot bear it now" (16:13). The evangelist now adds to his notion of remembering, what one might call an "ethical" element. Not only can the disciples at this juncture not understand Jesus' meaning: they are in fact *unable* to live out perseveringly what his earthly life was meant to signify in their conduct as Christians. Jesus continues, "But when *He,* the Spirit of truth will come, He will lead you along the way by the complete truth. For He will not speak on His own, but whatever He will hear He will utter—He will unveil the meaning of future events to you. He in fact will glorify me, because He will take what is mine and unveil its meaning to you" (16:13-14). Michel makes an appropriate comment on this third Johannine instance of "remembering." "What is at issue is neither the quickening of a past tradition nor the keeping in memory of religious truths, but a specific understanding of the word of God as this emerges, especially at a later time. To remind the congregation is to bear witness to the Gospel, to remind oneself is to place oneself under the word of Jesus. Here, too, the whole man is embraced . . . in no circumstances should we misinterpret this biblical 'remembering' along historicising or intellectualistic lines. It includes total dedication to God, concern for the brethren, and true self-judgment (Hb 13:3). It carries with it the thinking in terms of salvation

---

42   Ibid., p. 677.

history and the community, which the whole of Scripture demands."[43]
As any reader familiar with the *Exercises* will have noted, this Johannine
"remembering" is very similar to the practice of "discernment" which
Ignatius advocates for the effective contemplation of the mysteries during the Second and following Weeks.

Role of Remembered Sense-experience in John

Now I venture to suggest that it is only in the context of this "remembering" that our evangelist's "use of sense-language to express the
communion with God in Christ" can rightly be considered "one of the
salient features of Johannine spirituality" (Mollat). Consultation of a
Greek concordance to the Gospels will readily reveal that references to
seeing, hearing, touch, taste, smell, are as frequent in the first three
Gospels as in John. Indeed, it must be admitted that Synoptic usage is at
times quite as effective as that found in the Fourth Gospel, and "the
abundance of verbs for seeing," which Mollat considers "a notorious
fact" in Johannine vocabulary is paralleled in each instance by John's
colleagues.[44] In fact, Raymond Brown has called in question the view,
put forth by Mollat and others, that the variety of terms expressing sight
"correspond to various degrees of seeing (mere visual perception, attentive scrutiny, contemplation, profound penetration of the object of
vision, communion with it)."[45] In my own opinion what may with justification be asserted is that, regardless of which verb for seeing John
employs, the context discloses a number of carefully graduated meanings
from mere human (even superficial) regard to a depth of perception only
possible with genuine faith.

With these reservations and especially in the context of Johannine
"remembering," Pére Mollat's judgment about the values inherent in
sense-experience in the eyes of the fourth evangelist is a valid one, when
he asserts, "This is in the logic of the Incarnation. The Word became seeable, audible, present, palpable. It is by the route of the senses that the
revelation came to men, that divine life has been communicated to them,
and it is by the same route that they accept and welcome it."[46] Actually,
the entire Gospel of John should be regarded as the classical example of
what James Walsh, in a singularly happy phrase, has termed "the particular recall of gospel presence, whose traditional name is *memoria*

---

43   Ibid., p. 678.
44   Mollat, *Dictionnaire de Spiritualité*, 8, col. 217.
45   Ibid., col. 217: see Raymond E. Brown, *John I–XII*, pp. 501-503.
46   Ibid., col. 217.

Christi," that is, keeping our Lord in mind.[47]

One has only to inspect the prologue to the little treatise called the first epistle of John to appreciate this. Its author, like the fourth evangelist himself, belongs to a fourth or later Christian generation. Indeed, it is highly plausible to assume that he writes his tract in order to defend his colleague's Gospel from suspicion of heterodoxy, because of its misuse by Gnostic interpreters. Thus what this apologist expressed in very powerful sense-language is to be taken as an attempt to communicate the privileged experience of one who never knew Jesus during his earthly life, but only through the "spiritual senses," as later spiritual writing would term them. His personal encounter with Jesus glorified he depicts graphically in terms of the senses, whereas—like that of the fourth evangelist—it sprang from his reception, as an inspired author, of the evangelical traditions preserved in the Johannine community.

"What *was* from the beginning, what we have heard, what we have seen with our very eyes, what we held and our own hands touched, concerns the Word who is life.—Now that life was manifested; so we have seen it and bear testimony, and we are announcing to you that eternal life that was with the Father and was made manifest to us.—What we have seen and we have heard we are announcing to you, in order that for your part you may possess fellowship with us. Now this fellowship of ours is with the Father and His Son Jesus Christ. And we are writing to you in order that the joy of us all may be complete" (1 Jn 1:1-4).

This author's strikingly sensorial delineation of how through faith he was brought to know the risen Lord is satisfactorily explicable, once it is understood as a further instance of that Spirit-guided "remembering" on the part of the first disciples, by which in John's Gospel they eventually came to grasp with the eyes of faith the real significance of their former encounters, at the level of the human senses, with the Jesus of history.

The Senses in the Service of the Gospel

On a mere enumeration of references to the five senses, John—as has been already remarked—is not seen to differ notably from other Gospel-writers: Like them, he employs verbs of seeing and hearing with considerable frequency, verbs denoting touch, less so, while taste and smell rarely appear in his picture of Jesus, the disciples, or others. In fact, John rarely portrays Jesus as teaching by parables—which in other Gospels suggest Jesus' openness to nature, his deep sensitivity to what he

---

47   James Walsh, "Application of the Senses," p. 61.

sees, hears, feels in the world about him. By contrast with his predecessors, however, John would seem to display greater awareness of the difficulty, indeed, impossibility—both for Jesus and for his contemporaries—of communicating or accepting "the truth" concerning the unseen God merely by means of our human sense-faculties. 'What is begotten from flesh remains flesh" (3:6). Our evangelist's report on the failure of Jesus' public ministry is consistent with this view: "Although he performed so many signs in their presence, they did not believe in him" (12:37).

Three features of the Fourth Gospel however stand out in any comparison with the books of Mark, Matthew, and Luke. Firstly, John alone knows of Jesus' pre-existence as the personal Word of God (1:1-2), and consequently as the perfect expression of the hidden deity of the One he will make known to men as his Father. Indeed, even before he joined the human family, the Word, himself God, "illuminates every human being" (1:9); and this, by virtue of that "glory," which (as Jesus will announce in his great prayer to the Father) "I possessed with You before ever the world existed" (17:5). Secondly, it is John who expressly indicates his consciousness of the paradox involved in the truth, "The Word became flesh" (1:14). "Flesh" in his view stands for what is creaturely, earthbound, powerless (6:63) in the face of God's might, His Spirit. Still, it is, in the divine plan, through the perfectly human existence of the Word as Jesus, who is the unique "Way" to God (14:6), that the Father can be seen (12:45) and His voice can be heard (12:49), because he, "God an Only Son" became interpreter uniquely of the unseen Father. And if occasionally Jesus permitted his disciples a glimpse of his "glory" during the public ministry (2:11), after his return home to God the community through a credal formula can proclaim, "We have beheld his glory" (1:14). John is acutely aware that what occurred on the level of sense-experience—the historical level—between Jesus and his followers can be used as a kind of symbol, yielding an insight into the mystery of God, and for this reason, the historical is of paramount importance to all believers. In the third place, John is the Gospel-writer who has most clearly shown how *the way* of narrating Jesus' human experience can serve the growth of the Christian's relationship to Jesus. The various scenes in his Gospel are presented as so many avenues by which the believer can "deepen his faith in Jesus" (20:31). In particular, John has depicted the post-resurrection appearances of Jesus to his own as recognition-scenes. Mary Magdalene comes to know Jesus as "the Lord" (20:18), when he calls her by her name (v. 16). Yet in the same scene the evangelist issues a warning to his reader that adhering to the dear, dead past *as past*—even that of Jesus—is unavailing to faith. When Mary clings impulsively to the risen One in a loving gesture, she is abruptly told, "Stop touching me!" (v. 17). The human senses of sight and touch must somehow be "born anew from above" (3:3), otherwise a person "cannot see the Kingdom of God." At the same time, the evangelist insists that these same senses are not destroyed when empowered by the gifts of faith. In some mysterious manner they have a role to play in the bestowal of this new faith by the risen One, as may be gathered from John's narrative of the meeting of ten disciples with Jesus on the first Easter evening. After dispelling their fears and anxiety with his greeting, "Peace to you!", we are told, "On saying this, he showed them his hands and his side; and so the disciples rejoiced at seeing *the Lord*" (v.20). John is very conscious that the resurrection has not destroyed the experience of the Passion, but by transfiguring it has made it the principal avenue of approach to the unprecedented relation with Jesus, which founds faith. Our evangelist is aware that, in his new "life lived unto God" (Rom 6:10), those human, personal, experiences that went to make up his "life in the flesh," have provided the believer with so many precious ways of relating to himself, who otherwise now exists beyond the reach even of human imagination. This truth is dramatized in the story of Thomas, who persists in disbelief until he can see and *touch* the Lord. Yet, despite Jesus' gracious invitation to him to do so, Thomas is nowhere said to touch the risen One, but makes his very solemn profession of faith, "My Lord and my God" (20,28) simply by seeing and hearing the Crucified.

These traits of the fourth evangelist indicate the important role he assigns to the senses in the development of faith in his own contemporaries, and indeed in future generations. This latter concern is explicitly attested when he pictures Jesus as praying at the Last Supper not only for these disciples, who saw and heard and touched him during his earthly life, but also "for those who through their *word* [the Christian gospel] will believe in me" (17:20). And it is upon these believers, who have had no immediate sense-experience of Jesus, that John has him pronounce a final beatitude in his Gospel, "Happy those who have come to believe without seeing" (20:29). The evangelist knows himself to be among this class, and hence it is with complete reliance upon the "remembered" sense-experience of Jesus' original followers (which he depicts by the help of his own imagination) that John composes his Gospel with that serene confidence, mentioned earlier, that what he writes will be an efficacious instrument in leading to belief or deepening it.

To appreciate the effective use John makes in his descriptions of hearing and seeing and touching (and to a lesser extent the other senses) it may be useful to recall here a comment by Reginald H. Fuller concerning the Lucan version of Peter's confession of faith (Lk 9,20). "The doctrine of the incarnation is not the presupposition and premise of our understanding of Christ, but the conclusion of our encounter with him . . . We hear first what he says and see what he does, and then, as we encounter the presence of God in him who is truly man, we confess with Peter, 'You are the Christ of God'."[48]

Consistent with his image of Jesus as the pre-existent Word of God, John attaches particular importance to hearing "the word of Jesus" (2:22; 4:50) as the foundational element in genuine faith. Jesus discloses his mysterious identity to the woman by the well in Samaria by saying, "I am—the One speaking to you" (4:26). And in the sequel, the Samaritan villagers declare, "We have heard for ourselves and we know that he is in truth the Savior of the world" (2:42). The Johannine Jesus asserts, "The person hearing my words and believing in the One Who sent me possesses eternal life" (5:24), while he warns the Jews, "The person who belongs to God can hear God's words. This is why you cannot hear—because you are not God's" (8:47). Jesus reveals himself as "the Son of Man" to the blind man with the words, "You have in fact been seeing him, and the one speaking to you is he" (9:37). To hear and recognize the voice of the good Shepherd is the criterion for distinguishing the true believer (10:2, 16, 27) from the incredulous. "You do not believe, because you do not belong among my sheep" (10:26). "Everyone who belongs to the truth hears my voice" (18:37), for "the word you are hearing is not mine, but that of the Father Who sent me" (14:24b). John knows such "hearing" transcends the human auditory faculty. It is perhaps for this reason that Jesus is said to "hear" in the ordinary sense but twice (9:35; 11:4,6); in him it yields in significance to hearing the Father. "He testifies to what he has seen and heard" (3:32); "I can do nothing of myself: I judge according to what I hear" (5:30); "What I have heard in His [God's] presence, *that* I declare to the world" (8:26); "But now you seek to kill me—a human being who spoke the truth I heard from God" (8:40). To his disciples, Jesus explains, "I have called you beloved friends, because everything I have heard from my Father I have made known to you" (5:15), and to his adversaries, "Why is it you do not understand my way of speaking?—because you cannot hear my word" (8:43).

---

48   Reginald H. Fuller, *Preaching the New Lectionary: the Word of God for the Church Today* (Collegeville, 1976), p. 45.

By contrast with hearing, seeing in the normal sense is ascribed to Jesus some eight times—his "seeing the Father," less frequently. "Not that anyone has seen the Father, except the one from the Father—*he* has seen the Father" (6:46); "What I for my part have seen in the presence of the Father, I declare" (8:38); "the Son can do nothing by himself except something he sees the Father do" (5:19); "We testify to what we have seen" (3:11).

"Seeing" which implies some spiritual insight appears fairly often in this Gospel. "We have seen his glory" (1:14c); "I saw the Spirit descend like a dove" (1:32). "Greater things than this you will see: you will see the angels of God ascending and descending upon the Son of Man" (1:50-51). "Everyone seeing the Son and believing in him may possess eternal life" (6:40). "What if you see the Son of Man ascending where he was before?" (6:62). "If you believe, you will see the glory of God" (11:40). "The one who has seen me has seen the Father" (14:7).

"Seeing" (and this is also a usage peculiar to John) can also connote an experience intermediate between natural sight and spiritual vision. It appears to indicate the process by which the person who remains open to the influence of Jesus can be led to a more profound "seeing." At a turning-point in her dialogue with Jesus, the woman of Samaria confesses, "Sir, I see you are a prophet" (4:19); and, when at the instance of the woman, the villagers advance towards Jesus, he remarks to the disciples, "Lift up your eyes, and see that the countryside is ripe for the harvest" (4:35). God-fearing Greeks on pilgrimage at Passover express a half-conscious desire for faith in their request to Philip, "Sir, we wish to see Jesus" (12:21). Thus John does not discount the historical event of "seeing;" he recognizes its value for the journey into belief in Jesus.

For this reason Jesus becomes a focal point of "seeing" in this Gospel with an almost endless variety of meanings. John his first witness sees him as "the lamb of God who bears away the sin of the world" (1:29); his disciples are to see him as Jacob's ladder (1:51); the evangelist boldly likens him on the cross to "the serpent Moses raised up in the desert" (3:31) and to "the light of mankind" (1:3; 8:12); Abraham "saw" his day "and exulted" (8:56), while Isaiah "saw his glory" (12:41). Such concentration provides a plausible reason for John's omission of the Synoptic narrative of Jesus' transfiguration.

In addition to hearing and seeing, the sense of touch is somewhat prominent in John's picture of Jesus, who with a whip he had hastily fashioned "drove all from the sacred enclosure and upset the specie and tables of the money changers" (2:15), "took the loaves . . . and distributed them to the people" (6:11), "made a paste . . . anointed [the blind man] upon the eyes'' (9:6), ''washed the feet of the disciples, and wiped them with the towel'' (13:5), ''dipped the morsel and gave it to Judas'' (13:26), ''carried his own cross'' (19:17). By contrast with Mark, John rarely describes Jesus as being touched, apart from the Passion narrative: Mary of Bethany ''anointed Jesus' feet and wiped them with her hair'' (11:2), and the beloved disciple ''reclined on Jesus' breast'' (13:25). As we have noted, Mary Magdalene is ordered by the risen Lord, ''Stop touching me!'' (20:17), while Thomas is never said to have touched him.

The sensation of smell is adverted to only twice by John: Martha warns Jesus that Lazarus ''already stinks'' (11:39b), and as Mary anointed Jesus, ''the house became filled with the odor of the perfume'' (12:3b). Yet underlying these brief notices, one feels that a deeper meaning is being insinuated, as it is apparently in John's picture of the lavish burial preparations. He notes that Joseph and Nicodemus ''took Jesus' body and wrapped it in linen strips with the spices'' (19:40). Similarly the sensation of taste occurs but twice: the steward at the marriage-feast in Cana ''tasted'' the ''fine wine'' (2:9-10); Jesus before dying ''took the sour wine'' (19:30). Here again one catches a hint of a more ''spiritual'' sense.

Ignatian Application of the Senses

This exercise is first presented as a final way of repeating the contemplations of the Second Week ([121-126]); hence it is, as such, simply a variant form of contemplation, where in fact seeing and hearing are to be employed to become present to and involved with Jesus—*conocimiento interno del Señor* ([104]), by deepening of love for him in view of the apostolic aim of ''following him.'' Here however there is greater concentration upon all five senses: *traer* or *pasar de los cinco sentidos de la imaginación*, that is, to ''exercise'' the imaginative senses, by ''meditating and contemplating'' ([123]) or ''reflecting upon oneself'' ([123]). In dealing with the sense of smell and of taste ([124]) Ignatius approximates what has just been observed in John, by suggesting that one ''smell and taste the infinite gentleness and sweetness of the divinity, of the soul and its virtues, and of all, depending on the person one contemplates'' ([124]). A gloss by José Calveras explains the obscure ''of all'' *(de todo)* as ''of all it [the soul] receives from above.'' Hugo Rahner suggests that in making this remark the author of the *Exercises* had in mind the preparation of the exercitant for the Election, ''in which, according to the degree of consolation or desolation experienced, he will try to conform his life as closely as possible to that of the King who devoted himself to the exclusive service of his Father."[49] James Walsh also relates this Ignatian exercise to the consideration *Del Rey*. "The exercise on the Kingdom . . . is the essential preface to every Ignatian contemplation, in which the imaginative presence of the ideal leader soon becomes the imaginative presence of Jesus, the One sent by the Father, to 'present' and 're-present' the Father to all men; and, in so far as I am graced to see and to hear, this presence and its total environment will become mine. I shall feel the touch of his hands on my feet, and I shall desire and have part with him."[50]

In fact, Walsh has rendered incalculable service in showing how intimately the use of the senses in the Exercises, as instruments of prayer, is bound up with the deepening of the contemplative process. "It will begin with this vivid evocation of the exterior sense, the first and most immediate human mode of being present to the other. It will then move to the imaginative presence, which . . . effects a more total presence to Christ . . . Finally, under the action of the Spirit, in that mutual and repeated call and response of contemplative presence, where the word is truly heard . . . one is moved, and God himself moves, into 'the inward place' of unitive presence. For Ignatius . . . this is apostolic presence."[51]

The source of this original contribution is the insight that Ignatius, having set the "three ways of praying" into the context of the Fourth Week of the *Exercises* ([4]), in which the prayer of union is assumed to be normally practiced, proposes two distinct manners of praying with the help of "the five bodily senses" ([247]). The second of these is "to imitate Christ our Lord in the use of his senses" ([248]), and Ignatius indicates its goal, by referring back ([239]) to an Addition of the Second Week, as the "desire better to know the eternal Word incarnate in order the better to serve and follow him" ([130]). By the term "imitate," as James Walsh astutely observes, Ignatius intends the exercitant to "share his [Jesus'] experience of understanding himself . . . which is equally his experience of praising and glorifying the divine Majesty."[52]

Now while our evangelists rarely give their readers a glimpse into the process whereby Jesus became humanly conscious of himself and of his mission through his reactions to other human beings or to circumstances, they occasionally do so. Thus Mark depicts Jesus in the face of the

---

49   H. Rahner, *Ignatius the Theologian,* p. 114; for the explanation of *de todo,* see José Calveras, *Ejercicios espirituales y Directorio,* p. 104, note *a.*
50   J. Walsh, "Application of the Senses," p. 67-68.
51   Ibid., p. 67.
52   Ibid., p. 65.

scribes' outrage at his declaration to a paralytic, "Your sins are forgiven," as being "at once aware within himself (*en pneumati autou* means "his consciousness") of their criticism" (Mk 2:8). The Marcan Jesus reacts similarly when certain Pharisees were "putting him to the test" by "seeking a heavenly sign from him:" and there Jesus is pictured as responding to such effrontery "with a sigh from the depths of his heart"—*tō pneumati autou* (Mk 8:11-12). This evangelist shows how Jesus' experience of rejection by his own townsfolk at Nazareth made him aware that his own gifts of thaumaturgy, granted him for the promotion among men of the Kingdom of God (Mk 3:27), remained always under the fiat of his Father: "so he *could not* work any act of divine power there" (Mk 6:5). By being confronted with the villagers' obstinate disbelief, Jesus is seen to learn the lesson that there could be no question of trivializing the display of his miraculous powers: Mark describes his reflection by saying "and he kept wondering because of their unfaith" (Mk 6:5).

The fourth evangelist has, with consummate artistry, contributed a single, most dramatic example of "Christ our Lord in the use of his senses," in narrating his encounter with Mary, sister of the dead Lazarus. "Now when Jesus saw her wailing and the Jews who accompanied her wailing, he groaned from anger deep inside him, and shuddered at what he felt within himself, as he asked, 'Where have you laid him?'—They tell him, 'Master, come and see.' Jesus began to weep. Whereupon the Jews kept saying, 'How dearly he must have loved him' " (11:33-36). John implies that this surmise is superficial, and the real cause of Jesus' reactions lies deeper. He now realizes the awful consequences of death, which he himself will shortly experience. The horror is emphasized by Martha's objection to the opening of the tomb, "Master, he already stinks—he is four days dead!" (v. 39).

Thus Mark and John are aware of the value of "the application of the senses" for assisting their readers "to know better the eternal Word incarnate," by involving them in the intensely human sense-experience of our Lord.

We shall be helped to a greater appreciation of John's concern to bring his reader to grasp the mystery latent in the actions and words of Jesus, the Word of God, by recalling here the important role assigned in his Gospel to the symbolic and the miraculous—the "signs."

Symbolism in the Actions of Jesus

Each evangelist presents certain actions by Jesus for their symbolic value. Mark narrates four of these: the healing of Bartimaeus (Mk

10:46-52), Jesus' entry into Jerusalem (11:1-11), the cursing of a fig tree (11:12-14, 20-25), the expulsion of traffickers from the temple-precincts (11:15-19). Matthew sees symbolism of a threatening kind, when Jesus "summoning a small child made him stand in the midst" of those disciples who have asked, "Who then is greatest in the Kingdom of heaven?" (Mt 18:1-2). Luke intends his lengthy account of Jesus' last journey up to Jerusalem to symbolize his "assumption" (Lk 9:51—19:27). All these writers were aware of the symbolic acts performed by the prophets of Israel.

John in his turn has exploited the symbolic significance of Jesus' actions—yet more thoroughly than his colleagues. We shall have occasion to note this propensity in examining the Johannine report of Jesus' cleansing of the temple-area (2:13-22), in his initial refusal to participate in the pilgrimage-feast of *Sukkōth* and his subsequent presence incognito in Jerusalem (7:8-10), in his final entry into Jerusalem (12:12-16), and his termination of his public ministry when "he went away and hid himself" from the faithless crowd (12:36b), and—most dramatically—in his washing the feet of his own disciples (13:4-15). The Johannine Passion-story makes telling use of the symbolic in the actions of others as well as those of Jesus himself. It appears in the dramatic confrontation by Jesus of his captors in the garden (18:4-9), in Pilate's presentation of the flogged and thorn-crowned Jesus to the Jews (19:4-6), in Jesus' carrying his own cross (19:17), in his consigning of his mother to the beloved disciple (19:25-27), in his "handing over the Spirit" with his dying breath (19:30), in the flow of blood and water from his dead body (19:34), and in the sumptuous burial-rites performed by Nicodemus and Joseph (19:38-41).

Symbolic Statements of the Johannine Jesus

One of the salient traits of the Fourth Gospel is the presence in it of several profound, often lengthy discourses by Jesus, in which he attempts to disclose his real identity as the Son of God. By contrast, the Synoptic Jesus rarely speaks of himself or of the mystery surrounding his person, but proclaims the Kingdom of God and teaches in parables. John never depicts Jesus as announcing the Kingdom. As George MacRae remarks, "The most striking feature of the discourses of Jesus in the Fourth Gospel is that he talks mostly about himself. This is not an irreverent observation but a reflection of the Christocentrism we have already detected elsewhere. Jesus speaks about himself because he is the Son, the revelation of the Father in the world of men. He comes to confront men with the challenge of a word from God that is personal to him and to them. That is why his confrontation is not a miraculous action but a revealing word, and that is why true faith is a response to this word, not merely to signs."[53]

Before we inspect the Christology this evangelist has created by recounting certain "signs," we must recall the importance of the symbolic for his "Christocentrism." John appears to have borrowed religious language from the Greek version of the Old Testament to draw his reader's attention to Jesus' unique relationship to God and to the meaning of his mission to mankind. In the first place, there is his adoption of the sacral usage in the Greek scriptures of 'I am' *(ego eimi)*, where it appears as a surrogate for the divine name (Ex 3:14). "Unless you come to believe that I AM, you will surely die in your sins" (8:24); 'When you have lifted up the Son of Man, then you will know that I AM' (8:28); 'Before Abraham was, I AM'' (8:58). To these instances one may probably add Jesus' reassuring assertion to the frightened disciples as they see him walk upon the lake of Tiberias "I AM: stop being frightened!" (6:20), and also his reply to those come to arrest him in the garden, "I AM" (18:5)—which causes his enemies to fall to the ground. Jesus predicts his betrayal at the last meal with his disciples with the remark, "I am telling you this now before it occurs, in order that when it does happen, you may believe that I AM" (13:19).

The Septuagintal rendering of certain divine utterances found in the second Isaiah appears to have provided John with a paradigm after which to coin another series of Jesus' sayings, in which he describes his relationship with men and women for whom he has come from God to bring the challenge of a new revelation. "I am I AM, the One Who blots out transgressions" (Is 43:25); "I am I AM, the one Who comforts you" (Is 51:12). "My people shall know My name: on that day they shall know that I AM, the One Who speaks" (Is 52:6). The Johannine Jesus employs similar formulae to announce his solidarity with and love for mankind. "I am the bread of life" (6:35), or "the bread come down out of heaven" (v. 41), or "the living bread" (v. 51); "I am the light of the world" (8:12; 9:5); "I am the sheep-gate" (10:7, 9); "I am the ideal shepherd" (10:11, 14); "I am the resurrection and the life" (14:6); "I am the genuine vine" (15:1, 5). Two further instances, as Raymond Brown observes, might be added: "I am the one who testifies on my own behalf" (8:18); "I am from above" (8:23). Such expressions are also found in the Egyptian cult of the goddess Isis and in that of the Gnostic "redeemer-revealer." This is no indication that John was once a gnostic.

---

53   G. W. MacRae, *Faith in the Word,* pp. 41-42.

As George MacRae says, "It only means that he drew upon contemporary revelation literature in order to present Jesus as a heavenly revealer who could speak to the Hellenistic world at large."[54]

This latter group of sayings may be considered to have a relevance to the Ignatian manner of contemplating by the Application of the Senses, once it is realized that, in the context of the Fourth Gospel, they have been created by John as distillations of certain "remembered" sense-experiences in Jesus' company by his original followers. Several in fact reflect the simple day-to-day life in Palestine—bread, sheep-gate, shepherd, sunlight, vine, while others recall participation in Jewish liturgical worship (light, truth); others come from witnessing Jesus' triumphs over disability, disease, death (life, resurrection). Once one appreciates these striking statements as creations of the evangelist, it becomes easier to see that his aim anticipates the Ignatian purpose in praying with the five senses—that his reader might "desire to know better the eternal Word incarnate, in order the better to serve and follow him" ([104]).

Finally, a word must be said about the distinctive usage by the Johannine Jesus of the terms "work" and "works." By the first, Jesus indicates his entire earthly career including his death: "My food is to do the will of the One Who sent me and to carry His work to completion" (4:34); "This is God's work—that you may come to believe in the one He has sent" (6:29). In his great prayer, Jesus tells the Father, "I have glorified You upon earth by carrying to completion the work You gave me to do" (17:4). By "works" (in the plural) Jesus in this Gospel (and he alone with one exception employs the word) designates his actions—miraculous or not—*and* his teaching as the Father's attestation to his claim to be sent from God (5:36; 10:25). Indeed, Jesus never claims these "works" as his own, and when his unbelieving brothers refer to them as "your works, which you do" (7:3), he corrects them sharply by an allusion to *kairos* (God's good time): "My time [that lies under divine determination] is not yet present" (v.6). Later on Jesus declares to the Jews "Many fair works have I shown you from the Father" (10:32), as earlier he had announced, "The Father loves the Son and shows him all He Himself does, and greater works than these will He show him—that you may be filled with wonder" (5:20). To the disciples at the last meal he shared with them, he says, "The words I am speaking to you I am not saying on my own. Rather, the Father abiding in me is doing His works" (14:10). Schnackenburg's conclusion is apposite, "Thus the 'works' are part of the notion

---

54   Ibid., pp. 45-46.

of 'mission,' in the profound Johannine meaning of the sending of the Son by the Father. And one can also see why the works are meant to arouse faith, or, if confronted with disbelief which opposes the testimony of the works, can disclose the sin of disbelief."[55] To this I should like to add that this whole conception John has erected into a dominant theme in his book, which I have elsewhere called that of "the poverty of the Son:" what Jesus does, says, *is,* is actually the action, speech, being of the Father Who is God.

The "Signs" Wrought by the Johannine Jesus

Joseph de Guibert, has remarked that "Ignatius himself remained a man of the Middle Ages."[56] In the light of this observation, it is surprising that the Saint only rarely suggests Jesus' miracles as subject of his contemplations. In fact, within the text of the *Exercises* for the Second Week ([161]) he selects but two: Matthew's account of Jesus' walking on the sea ([280]), John's raising of Lazarus ([285]). And even among "the mysteries of the life of Christ our Lord" only three more are mentioned: the Johannine story of the first Cana miracle ([287]) with the Matthean calming of the storm ([278]), and feeding of five thousand men ([283]). Yet it is curious that, in the points he sets down for the contemplation of the two narratives from the Fourth Gospel, Ignatius does not include the term "sign," which the evangelist employs in a sense distinctive and peculiar to himself among New Testament authors.

The synoptic Gospel-writers designate the miracles of Jesus as "acts of power" *(dynameis),* which usher into history the Kingdom of God. This word does not occur in the Fourth Gospel. The Johannine Jesus himself refers to his healing of the cripple by the pool as "a single work" (7:21). The evangelist invariably uses "sign" for those major miracles of Jesus—major at least in his eyes, since he has chosen to narrate them in detail. John is not unaware of a meaning which "sign" bears in the earlier Gospels, a spectacular marvel calculated to convince the sceptical (Mk 8:11-13), the demand for which, like the Marcan Jesus, our Lord rejects in this Gospel (2:18; 6:30). Moreover, John refers in a general way to a number of Jesus' "signs" (2:23; 6:2; 12:37) which failed to have the desired effect (notably in the saying at 4:48). This sense of the word, which is not that favored by the evangelist, may have been found in some source he employed.

55 Schnackenburg, *John,* I, 519.
56 Joseph de Guibert, S.J., *The Jesuits: Their Spiritual Doctrine and Practice, A Historical Study,* tr. William J. Young, S.J. (Chicago, 1964), p. 166.

What then is the special, Johannine meaning of "sign"? It usually connotes a miraculous action by Jesus, which falls under the scrutiny of the senses indeed, but which can only disclose its intended references to Jesus for those who are open to his gracious influence, like the disciples. For such the "sign" can elicit faith, or at least inchoative belief in him (2:11). Yet this conception of a miracle as "sign" differs from that suggested by the term "work," in which (as has been seen) the notion of God's *testimony* to Jesus was dominant. The "sign" is a manifestation of Jesus' glory (2:11). Even when it is performed "that the works of God be manifested" (9:3) or "for the sake of the glory of God," its immediate purpose is "that the Son of God may be glorified through it" (11:4). Thus the meaning of a miracle as "sign" bears upon the person of Jesus himself, and this, as he is meant to be seen during the public ministry. Accordingly, it is uniquely Jesus who performs "signs"— "John did not perform a single sign" (10:41). And it is to be noted that Jesus nowhere promises, as is the case with "the works I am doing," that his followers will perform "greater than these" (14:12). Schnackenburg remarks, "It might be said that the 'works' are more markedly 'Messianic,' while the 'signs' are completely oriented to Christology, though the two can never be completely disjoined in John."[57]

The fact that the evangelist himself (with one exception) denotes Jesus' miracles as "signs" points to their importance, as John interprets them, for his Christology. Once indeed, at 6:26, the evangelist puts the words on the lips of Jesus himself in the course of a solemn utterance— doubtless to indicate its crucial function in his image of Jesus and to point out how easily the "sign" can be misunderstood. "Amen, amen I tell you: you are seeking me *not* because you saw signs, but because you ate the loaves and had your fill!" The centrality of the "sign" in Johannine Christology, as Karl Rengstorf has noted, comes from "the fact that Jesus brings a new view of God. Its distinctiveness is that God as Father may be known only in Jesus as Son."[58] In order to explain John's omission of exorcisms and the cure of lepers, it is sometimes suggested that the Johannine "signs" resemble the Exodus traditions, as interpreted in the book of Wisdom, regarding the miracles God worked through Moses. However, while John records the early, incomplete Jewish-Christian view of Jesus as the prophet like Moses (1:45), he makes it abundantly clear that Jesus transcends Jewish messianic expectations

---

57   Schnackenburg, *John,* I, 520.
58   Karl H. Rengstorf, *"Sēmeion,"* G. Kittel, *Theological Dictionary of the New Testament,* Vol. 7, p. 249.

(10:24-30), and can only be called "Messiah" in the Christian sense of "the Son of God" (20:31).

While more will be said later in our reflections upon texts in which individual "signs" are described by the evangelist, we wish to conclude the discussion for the moment by picking out three features of this Christology through "signs" which are relevant to the giving or making of the Spiritual Exercises. Firstly, by confining Jesus' performance of "signs" to his early ministry—the post-resurrection appearances are probably not regarded as such by the evangelist, despite 20:30-31—John indicates "an intrinsic connection between the incarnation and the revelation of Jesus Christ in 'signs' which it introduces and renders possible . . . in spite of their symbolic character they have a solidly 'material' aspect, involving very definite corporeal realities and firmly anchored in time and space" (Schnackenburg).[59] Their facticity and the attestation to them by historical testimony are quite as important to John as is their Christological significance. In his Prologue, he affirms with equal solemnity the divine character of the pre-existent Word and the fact that "he became flesh, and pitched his tent among us" (1:14).

Those familiar with the Ignatian writing ("the story of a pilgrim," the few pages of the precious Spiritual Diary, and the text of the *Exercises*) need no reminder that it is the mystery of the Incarnation, revealed to Ignatius with overwhelming clarity at the Cardoner, which thereafter functioned in his spirituality as the central, co-ordinating principle of all the divine mysteries. As he put it so simply and touchingly in his spiritual diary, "Devotion to Jesus does not diminish devotion to the most blessed Trinity—and the converse of this is also true."[60]

Now a somewhat similar insight lies behind John's contemplation of the miracles of Jesus' earthly ministry as "signs." He was thus enabled to make his narratives converge upon the person of the Word become flesh, and so unify in a truly remarkable way the image of Jesus he seeks to present in his Gospel. As Schnackenburg observes, "Jesus himself, it is true, is not designated as 'sign' in John, but this is the meaning of his person, as disclosed in the 'sign' of the healing of the blind man."[61]

The mention of this dramatic scene in the Fourth Gospel can serve to introduce a second striking parallel between this Christology of "signs"

---

59. Schnackenburg, *John*, I, 524-525.
60. Ignatius' *Spiritual Diary*, [138]. It is his entry for Sunday, March 9, 1544. See *Obras completas*, 4 ed., p. 379.
61. Schnackenburg, *John*, I, 523.

and the *Exercises*—the Election, to which all the contemplations of the second and subsequent weeks are orientated. In chapter nine of his Gospel John gives point to the drama in which Jesus is portrayed as "light for the world" (9:5) through the solemn utterance, "For judgment am I come into this world—in order that those who cannot see may see, while those who can see may become blind!" (9:39). A dominant theorem in Johannine Christology is that the entry of the Word into our human family has precipitated for all an unavoidable decision, for or against Jesus. No one can adopt a detached view of the One come as "light of the world." "Now this is the judgment: the light has come into the world and human beings have loved the darkness rather than the light—for their actions were wicked" (3:19). This same delineation of Jesus as judge may be glimpsed in the warning to the cripple he rescued from a thirty-eight year old disability, "Look, you have been restored to health: stop sinning any longer, lest something worse befall you" (5:14). It is this Christological perspective that has created the celebrated Johannine "realized eschatology." The "signs" Jesus performs disclose that he is, already in his earthly existence, source of eschatological salvation (4:42), by portraying him as restorer of life—to a ruler's son (4:50-53), a disabled man (5:5-8), to Lazarus (11:38-44). Karl Rengstorf observes "that on the basis of his 'signs' Jesus is depicted as the One in whom the fate of all men is decided according to the will of God, not at some point in the future but here and now, i.e., when there is confrontation with him."[62] Evidence of this is found in John's repeated animadversions that Jesus is the cause of *schisma* (a split or division) between two groups of people (7:43; 9:16; 10:19).

A third characteristic of the "signs"-narratives is the almost laconic brevity displayed by the evangelist in his telling of them. "For all their importance, Jesus' signs occupy only a relatively small portion of the Gospel of John. The major part of the text is taken up with Jesus' discourses."[63] Accordingly these Johannine stories are admirable illustrations of the wisdom of Ignatius' advice that the director "run through only the chief points by way of a brief summation" (Annotation 2). With noteworthy restraint John restricts his accounts of Jesus' "signs" to what the *Exercises* denominate as *el fundamento verdadero de la historia* (the genuine grounds of the history)—that is, to those elements in the miracle-story which point to the person of Jesus. It is usually in the sequel that, by means of a discourse, the evangelist guides his reader in

---

62. Karl H. Rengstorf, *"Sēmeion,"* pp. 249-250.
63. MacRae, *Faith in the Word,"* p. 41.

contemplating the mystery of the One come from God as revealer of "the truth."

Specialists in Ignatian studies have for some time pointed to the similarities in configuration between Paul's experience of God in Christ and that of Ignatius of Loyola. Accordingly, the parallelism between Pauline and Ignatian mysticism has become familiar to many. Only relatively recently however have the resonances of the *Spiritual Exercises* with the Fourth Gospel caught the attention of certain Jesuit New Testament scholars. It is in the hope of throwing some additional light upon the striking affinity obtained between these two great spiritualities that the present study has been attempted.

Chapter 2

THE JOHANNINE PROLOGUE (1:1-18)

T owards the beginning of the *Spiritual Exercises* Ignatius sets down a statement ([23]) which he intends the director to "talk over" *(platicar)* with the retreatant (Annotation 19), whose assiduous consideration of this tersely worded paragraph, the Principle and Foundation—in part designed as a preliminary to entering the thirty days—is to help him test his own eligibility for undertaking such a significant project. This laconic foundational assertion might be (historically, has been) misread as a kind of philosophical thesis. In reality it is a highly concentrated theological, or better, Christological preview of the entire course of exercises. Hugo Rahner observes that it "contains all that dynamic which emerges explicitly only during the Second Week."[1] Thus it is of paramount importance that the exercitant be brought to appreciate its character as a kind of prologue, which gives a hint of the Election ([169-179]), the meditation on Two Standards ([136-147]), the consideration *Del Rey* ([91-98]), and is designed to find its fullest expression ultimately in the Contemplation for Attaining Love ([230-237]). Indeed, this tripartite reflection upon one's personal salvation, one's impartiality toward created things, and one's single-hearted "desire and choice" regarding "what is more conducive to the purpose for which we are created" anticipates the consideration of "three ways of humility" ([165-168]).

The Christological orientation of the text becomes evident once one realizes that by the phrase "God our Lord" (or, "God our creator and Lord") Ignatius consistently means the risen Christ. For from that "so great illumination" at Manresa the saint had learned that the divine "summons can only be heard in the incarnate Christ."[2]

Moreover, the exercitant's response to the divine graciousness in creating—described as praise, reverence, and service—is meant to function as starting-point for each exercise of the retreat. This is clear from

1 H. Rahner, *Ignatius the Theologian*, p. 66.
2 Ibid., p. 62.

the direction concerning one's immediate preparation for prayer, *invariable* throughout the entire thirty days. I am bid "consider how God our Lord looks upon me," and then "make an act of profound *reverence*" ([75]). At once "I will beg God our Lord for the grace that all my intentions, actions, and operations may be directed solely to the *praise* and *service* of his divine Majesty" ([46]). François Courel comments: "The purpose of this page is not so much to propose a meditation on creation as to aid the retreatant to place himself in the attitude of spiritual impartiality, which is a form of total readiness before God."[3]

Once it is rightly grasped, the Principle and Foundation is seen as a sketch of the descent of all creatures and their final assumption to God in and by Christ. It echoes the ancient credal formula cited by Paul: "But for us there is but one God, the Father, from whom everything [comes] and to whom we [return]; and one Lord, Jesus Christ, through whom everything [comes] and through whom we [return to the Father]" (1 Cor 8:6). Read in this light, the close affinity of the Ignatian statement to the Johannine Prologue becomes evident.

One final observation: Ignatius' reticence about speaking here of divine love as source of the procession of all creation from him and of its return to him has been adversely criticized. "It has, I believe, been made a reproach to the Exercises, and even to Ignatian spirituality in general, that the love of God is not mentioned here." The same author astutely observes that God's love "is simply shown at work, in the things he does for [his creatures] and the gifts he bestows on them. These are things that issue from love; but the word itself would be premature, until more is known about the relationship in act."[4] We shall shortly note the somewhat muted reference to divine love in John's Prologue. In this connection, the suggestion by John Harriott should be operative in any explanation on the part of the director of this densely packed foreword to the Exercises. "The Principle and Foundation . . . needs to be presented in terms of attraction, not imposition. We need to make the point that we do not praise, reverence, and serve because God in some draconian way insists on it, but because if we catch the faintest glimpse of God we cannot help ourselves."[5]

For our reflection on the Prologue it seems reasonable to assume

3 François Courel, S.J., *Exercices Spirituels* (Paris, 1960), p. 28.
4 R. A. F. MacKenzie, "Biblical Theology and the Spiritual Exercises," in *Contemporary Thought and the Spiritual Exercises,* p. 70.
5 John Harriott, S.J., "The Mood of the Principle and Foundation," *The Way: Supplement* no. 16 (1972), 26.

(with Raymond Brown) that the evangelist has prefixed to his book an early hymn, already current in the Johannine community to which he belonged, which he adapted as a kind of introduction to his work by interspersing certain glosses (in prose) among its four original strophes. If indeed these initial verses were added after the completion of the Gospel itself, there is a certain parallel with the revision of the Principle and Foundation by Ignatius during the Paris period and its eventual re-alignment to its present position.

Rudolf Bultmann has characterized the Prologue as "an introduction—in the sense of being an *overture*, leading the reader out of the commonplace into a new and strange world of sounds and figures, and singling out particular motifs from the action that is now to be unfolded. He cannot yet fully understand them, but because they are half comprehensible, half mysterious, they arouse the tension and awaken the *question* which is essential if he is to understand what is going to be said."[6] Among such motifs he enumerates life and light (with its antithesis, darkness), glory, truth, and others. These will only be appreciated at their true value in the course of the Gospel—as was seen to be the case with the Principle and Foundation.

Strophe 1: Preexistence of the Word
1   At the beginning the Word [already] was,
      and the Word was present before God—
      God he was, the Word!
2   He was present at the beginning before God.

The initial phrase of this ode in honor of "Jesus Christ" (v. 17) echoes the opening of the book of Genesis, where however it signified the fundamental divine design for the human race rather than merely the beginning of history. Here, "at the beginning" serves to draw attention to the preexistence of the Word of God—a truth apparently unknown to the three earlier evangelists. Moreover, while affirming the traditional faith of Israel in a God, Who though unseeable is One Who has spoken and Who speaks, the author expresses his Christian belief that the Word of God stands in a personal relation to "the God," as New Testament writers frequently call the Father. That "the Word was present before God" implies some sort of distinction within the Godhead—a distinction the evangelist clarifies later by designating him "God an only Son" (v. 18). For the moment it is enough to reflect on the affirmation, "God he

6   Rudolf Bultmann, *The Gospel of John*, p. 13.

was, the Word!"

It is to be remarked that John in the course of his Gospel will remind his reader that Jesus is "one" with the Father (10:30; 14:1), so that "seeing" him with faith is to "see the Father" (12:45; 14:9). Yet nowhere else will he refer to Jesus as the Word of God. And indeed the Johannine Jesus, over and over again, will insist that the word he utters is not his own, but "that of the Father Who sent me" (14:24; 7:16; 12:49; 14:10). It may be said that our evangelist felt no further need to attribute this Christological title, the Word of God, to Jesus in his book, since, as George MacRae remarks, "It is acted out in the portrayal of Jesus as the revealer of the Father who confronts men with the revealing word and demands a response of faith. Jesus is the Word in the sense that his revealing word is about himself as sent from the Father."[7] There can be little doubt but that this characterization as the Word of God is the dominant feature of John's image of Jesus.

Strophe 2: The Word, Creator of Life, as Light

3   All through him came into being,
     and apart from him no single thing came to be.
4   What came to be found life in him—
     and that life was the light of mankind.
5   Indeed this light is [still] shining through the darkness,
     for the darkness has never mastered it.

The anonymous poet now describes the inauguration of the Word's relationship to mankind by his agency in creating "all" without any exception—doubtless inspired by the first creation-account in the book of Genesis (see Gen 1:3-30) where God is represented as naming all things as He brings them into existence. It will be recalled however that the priestly editor's purpose was to preface his work not with a cosmogony, but rather with a deeply moving summons to faith in the universal goodness of the creation that proceeded uniquely from the hand of the one God of Israel. And it is to be understood as the learned theologian's recital of the first of many beneficent acts, the *mirabilia Dei,* that Israel's God was to work in her favor. Several features of this strophe indicate the originality of its Christian author and deserve attention.

Firstly, a peculiarity of style is seen in the use of the neuter to denote human beings—a usage the evangelist will adopt throughout his Gospel (3:35; 6:39; 10:29). Thus here "All" *(panta)* and "no single thing" ap-

---

7   George W. MacRae, *Faith in the Word,* p. 48.

pear to refer primarily to men and women. The words of Jesus will later echo the second part of this statement, "Apart from me you can do nothing" (15:5). This curious penchant for using the neuter for persons becomes evident from the next line, "what came to be found life in Him." And here a second distinctive feature occurs: "life" consistently signifies the believer's participation in the very life of God Himself, communicated through the Word (10:10b). To signify what is called natural life John will speak of "life in this world" (12:25). In the third place mention is made of two important motifs, life and light, which will feature prominently in John's image of Jesus. He will be depicted as source of life by certain "signs" he performs (4:46-53; 5:1-9; 6:1-15; 11:38-44) and through his symbolic statements about himself, "I am the gate" (10:9-10), "I am the ideal shepherd" (10:11-15), "I am the resurrection and the life" (11:25), "I am the way, that is, the truth and the life" (14:6), "I am the genuine vine" (15:1-5). Jesus will reveal himself as "the light of the world" at the feast of *Sukkōth* (8:12) and through the cure of the man born blind (9:1-7). Fourthly, by the statement "and that life was the light of mankind" the author of the hymn characterizes the saving activity of Jesus as a revelation of his own identity and thereby of the "God no one has ever seen." Finally, we are given a hint of Jesus' ultimate victory over the world (16:33b): "this light [still] shines on through the darkness." We also catch a glimpse of the struggle of Jesus with unfaith and the judgment which ensues upon it: "the darkness has never mastered it." To be noted is the *double entendre,* so dear to the evangelist, conveyed by the word "master"—to understand and also to overcome.

Comment by the Evangelist: John the Witness

6 A human being appeared, having been sent by God—his name, John. 7 This man came for testimony, to bear witness about the light, that all might come to believe by him. 8 He was not himself the light, but [came] to testify about the light. 9 *He* was the genuine light that upon coming into the world enlightens every human being.

The evangelist now inserts a contrast between John and Jesus. Like Jesus himself this man is described as "having been sent by God." His sole function however is to bear witness, and in this Gospel his role as "the Baptist," so prominent in the Synoptics, is played down—his baptism of Jesus is all but ignored (1:31-34). Thus it is made clear from the start that John "was not himself the light," and later he will be compared to "a lamp" (5:33-36a). "The genuine light" is the Word of God, who even before the Incarnation "upon coming into the world" (through creation) "enlightens every human being." In this Gospel Jesus will be seen to "have come into this world for judgment" (9:39), thus precipitating what the *Spiritual Exercises* denominate as "election." As John will make abundantly manifest, the only attitude for the true disciple of Jesus is to remain ever open to the possibility of a religious experience of the risen Lord that lies beyond the bounds of all human expectation. This same insight by the author of the *Exercises* explains the dominant position accorded to "indifference" or "impartiality" in the Principle and Foundation, to which Stanislas Lyonnet has adverted. "What counts for St Ignatius is indeed this attitude of impartiality to which he devotes five-sixths of his text."[8]

Strophe 3: The Word in History

10   He was present in the world—
     the world was made through him:
     still the world did not know him.
11   To his own realm he came:
     yet his own folk did not accept him.
12   But such as did accept him
     he empowered to become children of God . . .

The poet now reflects upon the presence of the Word, its creator, to the world. In this strophe it may well be that the thought moves to a consideration of the Word of God as divine Wisdom, identified in the Old Testament as Torah. It is also possible, as Raymond Brown suggests, that the stanza commemorates Jesus' public ministry, where in fact John will present Jesus as divine Wisdom incarnate—notably in the first part of the discourse on the Bread of Life (6:26-47). Whichever sense is to be preferred, the thought now moves to history and some historical manifestation of the Word. This entry is at first pronounced a failure: "the world did not know him." The biblical sense of "know" connotes a personal involvement which arises from the experience of God's Word. Its force is illustrated by Jesus' plaintive question, "Such a long while have I been in your company, yet you do not know me, Philip?" (14:9).

The hymnist next describes this coming of the Word in some detail: it was "to his own realm," the Holy Land (even though Jesus' true home is with the Father), and to "his own folk," God's people. And these "did not accept him"—not all, however! "Such as did accept him he empowered to become children of God." While Paul speaks of Christians as

8   Stanislas Lyonnet, S.J., "A Scriptural Presentation on the Principle and Foundation," *Ignis* 6 (1973), 25.

"sons of God" (Gal 3:26) by adoption, or as "sons and daughters" (2 Cor 6:18), the fourth evangelist restricts the use of "Son of God" for Jesus alone. He now explains in his own words the sense of "children of God."

Comment by the Evangelist: Divine Generation of Believers
13   [that is] those who believe in his name, who were begotten not from some blood-line, neither from human impulse nor from any man's desire, but from God!

John is at pains to attribute to God alone the Christian's becoming a child of God, and so excludes any influence of racial descent ('bloods' in the Greek), or sexual drive. In his dialogue with Nicodemus about the mysterious birth "from above," Jesus asserts categorically, "What has been begotten of flesh remains flesh, while what has been begotten of Spirit is spirit" (3:6). In the light of this, one may say that the present verse is the nearest the Prologue ever comes to any allusion to the Holy Spirit.

Strophe 4 (part 1): The Word, Member of the Human Family
14   So the Word became flesh,
      and pitched his tent among us.
      And we have beheld his glory,
      glory befitting an only Son [coming] from the Father,
      full of graciousness and truth . . .

The paradoxical character of the statement, "The Word became flesh," all too familiar to us from the recitation of the Angelus, should not be missed. The first strophe dwelt upon the pre-existence of the Word, and his personal relationship with God, while being himself "God," and the verb "was" (indicating the Word's divine, eternal existence) stood in sharp contrast with the "came into being" of all that was created in the second strophe. Now however it is said that the Word himself "became," and even that he "became flesh." The term "flesh" (flesh and blood) in the Bible indicates the human being in all his contingency, creatureliness, earthbound character, implying—in contrast with the Spirit representing the dynamism of God's infinite power—our human powerlessness. In fact, John will quote Jesus as saying, "The Spirit is the life-giver: the flesh is useless" (6:63a). How then can Jesus speak of his flesh as the "living bread": "Now the bread I will give is my flesh on behalf of the life of the world" (6:51b)? Indeed, the resolution of this enigma will occupy John throughout the rest of his Gospel.

"He pitched his tent among us" recalls the desert-experience of

Israel, when her God dwelt under canvas as a divine camper in her midst, and so serves to introduce the covenant-theme, which is shortly to be discreetly suggested by the author. For the evangelist this motif of the dwelling of "God an only Son" as a human being among men is of great significance: Throughout his book John will emphasize the truth that the invisible Father and His will for mankind is disclosed only in the completely human life of Jesus of Nazareth.[9]

"We have beheld his glory" articulates the response of faith by the Johannine community to the earthly existence of Jesus. Upon these Christians of a later generation, who have "come to believe even though they did not see," that is, without personal knowledge of Jesus during his mortal life, the Johannine Jesus will pronounce a final beatitude in this Gospel (20:29b). "Glory"—which already in the Old Testament was a technical term for the manifestation in power to His people by Israel's God—becomes a prominent keyword in John's Gospel. It may be said that Jesus *is* the glory of God, Whom he makes visible, credible, lovable —especially by the supreme act of laying down his life out of love for his friends (15:13). Indeed it may also be said that John's creative redaction of the evangelical traditions which he has received appears most impressively in his highly original presentation of the Passion as the glory of Jesus. In his view it is precisely at the moment of his death that Jesus is "glorified" (7:39b) upon the cross, and John chooses his words carefully to describe this final moment, the last of Jesus' earthly life: "and bowing his head he handed over the Spirit" (19:30). The Crucified has become unique source of the Spirit, who is "the life-giver" (6:63a).

For the present however the hymnist describes this "glory" as the salient feature of the Word, that of "an only Son coming from the Father." As the evangelist will point out to the reader at the conclusion of his narrative of the first "sign" at Cana, it is this "glory" evinced by Jesus that brings his disciples—at least inchoatively—to new faith: "he manifested his glory and his disciples began to believe in him" (2:11b).

The "only Son coming from the Father" appears "full of graciousness and truth." The phrase is the poet's rendering of the pair of Hebrew words *(hesed, 'emeth)* which characterize the covenant-God of Israel.

---

9   George MacRae makes the perceptive observation *(Invitation to John,* pp. 33-34): "The splendor of the prologue to the Gospel must never be lost in exegetical details. It inaugurates the message of the Gospel on a level unparalleled in the gospel tradition. In the human, the limited experience of humans, the evangelist sees the divine presence, and perhaps this is his major insight into the story of Jesus. The unfolding of the story will tell."

Raymond Brown has turned them by "enduring love"—a faithful, if somewhat free translation. Actually the first Greek word *(charis)*, adopted by Paul into Christian theological language as "grace," means basically gracefulness, graciousness. The second term *(alētheia,* or "truth") is employed by John to denote the entire message Jesus brings to men from the Father. The combination of the two indicates the new covenant which results from the Incarnation.

Comment by the Evangelist: The Preexistence of the Word
15   John continues to testify about him, and he cries out, "This is he of whom I said, 'The one coming after me ranks before me, because he existed before me!' "

The theme of Jesus' preexistence as the Son of God is seen to be of great importance to the evangelist (8:58; 17:5), who here dramatically presents John's testimony (like the community's profession of faith) as still resounding for the believer. Actually John the witness will make this statement in one of the early scenes of the Gospel (1:30). Bishop J. A. T. Robinson suggests that such an assertion by John might be historically plausible if the precursor of Jesus had regarded him as Elijah.[10]

Strophe 4 (part 2): Our Sharing in the Word
16   Yes, of his fulness
    we have all received a share—
    indeed, grace instead of grace.

The original hymn concludes at this point with the balance of the community's confession, acknowledging the participation by all believers in the new covenant graciously bestowed by God in place of the Mosaic covenant, as the evangelist will now make clear.

Comment by the Evangelist: The New Covenant
17   Now the Law was a gift through Moses: this graciousness, this truth have become reality through Jesus Christ.   18   No one has ever seen God. God an only Son, who [now] reposes on the Father's heart—*he* it is who revealed Him!

The fourth evangelist does not adopt Paul's polemical attitude towards the Mosaic dispensation, but acknowledges that "it was given" by God Himself. One of the most striking qualities of the Father in this Gospel is His characterization as a "giving" God. He is thus described

---

10   J. A. T. Robinson, "Elijah, John, and Jesus: an Essay in Detection," *New Testament Studies* 4 (1957-58), 263-281.

some thirty-six times. Ignatius of Loyola was deeply penetrated with this same truth; his principal aim in the first week of the Exercises is to bring the retreatant to a profound sense that "all is gift;" and he will, in the crowning exercise[11] of the entire retreat—the Contemplation for Attaining Love, which by its four points recapitulates all the graces received in the four Weeks—seek to guide the exercitant to the love of friendship with this divine Giver.

"No one has ever seen God." This statement of itself appears to preclude the possibility for any human being of encountering God in this life; yet, as has already been remarked, it articulates a theme which will return through this Gospel (5:37b; 6:46). John however has a final word to say, and one that deserves the closest attention. "God an only Son, who [now] reposes on the Father's heart—*he* it is who revealed Him!" In the first place the evangelist implies that the Word, who first through his creative activity inaugurated a profound relationship with our world, who subsequently as divine Wisdom, Torah, entered a special relationship with "his own folk," and who finally became a member of the human family, has now returned to God his Father, and to that intimacy that belongs uniquely to him—"that glory I possessed before the world existed with You" (17:5). The reader is invited to contemplate Jesus as inaugurator of the return of all creatures to God along that path he himself has traced out. Jesus is "the way" (14:6) into the Kingdom of God, which for this Gospel-writer always remains "above."

In the second place, the phrase "God an only Son" is to be noted: we have adopted this translation because it represents the best attested reading of the Greek text—*monogenēs Theos*. Earlier, John's unique use of the term *monogenēs* to designate Jesus was compared with the Ignatian "God our creator and Lord" as title for the risen Christ. In this Gospel the term points ahead to the statement "God so loved the world as to give [over to death] His only Son" (3:16). For John as for Ignatius of Loyola the glorified Lord remains ever "the crucified majesty of God." In his Gospel it is by "being lifted up" on the cross that Jesus, like the bronze serpent in the desert—that daring Johannine comparison! (3:14),—becomes "a sign of salvation" (Wis 16:5-7). Through "being lifted up," Jesus will disclose to the believer his divine identity: "When you have lifted up the Son of Man, then you will know that I AM!" (8:28). By being lifted up to glory as the Crucified, Jesus will exercise that

---

11. Ignatius lists as the third reason for a state of desolation, "to give us true information and knowledge that we may feel deeply . . . that all is gift and grace of God our Lord" *(don y gracia de Dios nuestro Señor)*, ([322]).

mysterious attraction, which Ignatius felt so keenly: "And I, if I be lifted up from the earth, will draw all to myself" (12:32).

Finally, we are now able to perceive a certain resonance between this last verse of the Prologue and the closing line of the Principle and Foundation. There, after stressing the paramount necessity of indifference to all creatures, the author of the *Spiritual Exercises* appears to take a daring leap in logic. "And as a consequence, moreover, only desiring and choosing what may better lead us towards the purpose for which we have been created." The balance and equilibrium advocated so strongly with regard to all creatures is now replaced by a personal preference for the "better" *(magis)*. The hidden term which produced this surprising conclusion will appear in the subsequent Weeks of the Exercises. Hugo Rahner points out that "this summons by God . . . can be heard at all only in the incarnate Christ . . . because the incarnate Word alone is that perfect man in whom and through whom we are enabled to revere, praise, and serve the creator and Lord."[12] Hence it will become evident to the exercitant that "when he uttered the 'more' of the Foundation he was really . . . saying 'yes' to the crucified Christ." The ordering of his life according to the norms of the gospel "means conformity with the crucified Lord of all things."[13] One need not read anything into the Johannine text in order to appreciate how it is echoed in the "more" of Ignatius of Loyola.

12. H. Rahner, *Ignatius the Theologian*, pp. 62-63.
13. Ibid., p. 66.

Chapter 3

THE WORD OF THE CRUCIFIED REVEALS
THE CHRISTIAN SENSE OF SIN

R aymond Brown has suggested by a fascinating study of *The Community of the Beloved Disciple* that the fourth evangelist has set his story of Jesus' earthly history into the context of the spiritual odyssey of that Christian church, of which he himself was a member.[1] It was a journey marked at its inception by "a relatively low Christology," that is, one in which the first glimmerings of its new faith in Jesus were expressed in terms borrowed from the Old Testament or other Jewish writings—prophet, messiah, "Son of God" (the adoptionist sense), which did not articulate his divine character. The community came gradually to profess a "higher Christology," in terms of preexistence and the confession of Jesus' unique relation to God his Father by such names as Savior, Lord, and God. The Johannine community moreover underwent traumatic, embittering experiences from hostility, hatred, persecution at the hands of "the Jews," of certain "baptists" who clung tenaciously to the memory of John, and possibly even of some Jewish Christians, who resented the group's anti-temple attitudes, its early reception of Samaritan and pagan converts.

Our evangelist's preoccupation with ongoing history is paralleled by the concern of Ignatius of Loyola to guide Christians of his own day (and those of subsequent generations) to a profoundly personal encounter with God in Christ, patterned upon his own *itinerarium in Deum*. David Fleming remarks of the saint that he "spent some twenty years constructing the book of the *Exercises* in order that it might embody a certain movement . . . a 'conversion experience'."[2] This concentration by Ignatius upon the dynamic element in the spiritual life is attested by his solici-

---

1 R. E. Brown, S.S., *The Community of the Beloved Disciple* (New York, Ramsey, Toronto, 1979).

2 David L. Fleming, S.J., ed., *Notes on the Spiritual Exercises of St. Ignatius Loyola* (St. Louis, 1981), "The Ignatian Spiritual Exercises: Understanding a Dynamic," p. 2.

tude, expressed in the Rules for Discernment ([313-327] and [328-336]), that the retreatant experience reactions at varying levels of consciousness, and learn to evaluate such movements within himself. For it should be noted that when one speaks of a "conversion experience," the accent falls upon one's turning to Christ with ever deepening love and confidence. What has perhaps not been sufficiently adverted to by many commentators on the First Week is the notable absence in the Ignatian text of any prayer for pardon of one's sins. The presupposition, in the case of the person judged eligible to make the full course of the Exercises, is that such a one has already been accorded forgiveness for all his sins. He is one who "desires to make all possible progress," and can "employ his natural endowments with greater freedom to seek with loving attention what he so much desires" (Annotation 20). Thus Ignatius took it for granted that the suitable candidate be cognizant that his very desire to enter upon the Exercises is a graced response to God, who in Christ is already present in his life, that he has already been "drawn by the Father" (6:44) towards His crucified Son, who alone brings the definitive revelation of sin in the history of mankind ([45-53]), in one's own past sinful life ([55-61]). When he engages in the meditation on hell, the retreatant is to pour out his grateful thanks to the risen Lord "that up to this very moment he has shown himself so loving and merciful towards me" ([71]). This profound sense of loving gratitude is calculated to give rise to "the cry of wonder" ([60]) in the presence of Christ "that up to this very instant he has granted me life" ([61]). It is as a reconciled sinner that one's heart is to overflow with deep feelings of gratitude and praise for Christ's compassion ([61, 71]), that has been and continues to be showered upon him. He is to remind himself, like Paul, that "it is because we have been accorded mercy, that we do not lose heart" (2 Cor 4:1).

William Peters has drawn attention to a misunderstanding of the First Week, which has unfortunately been prevalent. "There is a real danger, when one considers the books of meditations, and the commentaries of the past, that the retreat-director and the retreatant may overlook the important part played by Christ during the First Week. There has been a strong tendency in the past to limit the exercises of this week to a consideration . . . of sin and punishment, of death and judgment . . . The crucified Christ at the end of the first meditation was felt to be something of an anachronism."[3]

---

3 William Peters, "The Kingdom: the Text of the Exercise," *The Way: Supplement no. 18* (1973), 14-15.

Another *caveat* which may also help towards a correct attitude to the exercises of the First Week was issued emphatically by Winoc De Broucker. "It is erroneous to present the first week as a return upon the past or an anticipation of the last things, unless at the same time it is also pointed out that it is upon the present moment that the past weighs heavily, that the last things are imminently present, that it is only divine grace preserving one in life which holds them at a distance."[4] Ignatius himself is seen to have held that the meditations under discussion cannot achieve their desired result, if they do not become *contemplations* through repetition ([64]) of "God's intervention in one's existence, a halt called by Him in the flow of one's daily life." In fact, I venture to suggest that Ignatius' intention is close to the Johannine conception of "the judgment," as will presently become evident.

What then is to be said of the ominous first prelude proposed for the initial meditations ([47, 55])? While this admittedly macabre picture of the human condition undoubtedly reflects those traumatic experiences which Ignatius underwent in the early months at Manresa, attention to its symbolic character will help one assess the author's intent.

According to the Ignatian text, the exercitant is "to see with the eyes of the imagination and to consider my soul to be imprisoned in this body, subject to dissolution [by sickness and death], and the entire composite like an exile in this vale of tears among brute beasts." This curious juxtaposition of seemingly antithetic symbols has given rise to misunderstandings ever since the Jesuit humanist, André des Freux—in Ignatius' own lifetime—undertook to turn the text into elegant Latin for papal approval. In a discerning study of this prelude, Walter Ong has thrown considerable light on its symbolic force. "The connection of the *Spiritual Exercises* with the world of symbolism is due to their concern with the self, which is a major preoccupation of the mind's unconscious and conscious symbolic activity."[5] With the ambivalence inherent in the symbolic, the body here at once represents both the incommunicable self-awareness of the human person and the impassable line of demarcation between the self and other persons. Body as symbol is thus seen simultaneously as prison and protection, as well as exile. "The very organ through which the self becomes aware of the exterior, stands in the way . . . despite its intimate connection with the self . . . so that everything

---

4 Winoc De Broucker, S.J., "La première semaine des Exercices," *Christus* 6 (1959), 30.
5 Walter J. Ong, S.J., "St. Ignatius' Prison-Cage and the Existentialist Situation," *Theological Studies* 15 (1954), 34-51.

which comes *into* the soul . . . is invested with exteriority." At the same time, the body also provides refuge from "brute beasts"—symbolic of the complete absence of interiority, self-possession, and so of "the effective depersonalization of everything outside the tiny interior point of personal awareness." "Brute beasts" represent in addition "the passions . . . present as a kind of living threat . . . Their presence shows why this prison is both stronghold and cage, partaking of the ambivalent situation of the human consciousness, where . . . estrangement from others and . . . self-containment are complementary." Ong feels that this recourse to the symbolic indicates Ignatius' preoccupation with the world of religious realities. "Concern with God is in one way or another tied up with concern about this isolation of the ego. For God alone shares the interior of my self-consciousness, knows intimately what it feels like to be *me*." Once the retreatant is brought to appreciate the symbolic function of this seemingly bizarre prelude, he can be greatly helped toward the onerous task of self-definition—the profound realization of the self as caught in the toils of inescapable alienation and isolation, were it not for the intimate presence of the Word incarnate, transcending such barriers with the life-giving offer of forgiveness through the cross.

Accordingly, to assist the exercitant's reflections during the First Week of the Exercises, I suggest three passages from the earlier sections of the Fourth Gospel: the dialogue between Jesus and Nicodemus, and two pericopes, interjected somewhat awkwardly into the ensuing narrative, which in the opinion of Rudolf Schnackenburg represents summaries of the preaching of the Johannine community.

1. Divine Wisdom Incarnate Confronts Pharisee Wisdom (2:23—3:10)

Introduction

23   While Jesus was in Jerusalem at Passover among the festival throng, many began to believe in his name upon seeing the signs he was performing.   24   As for himself however, Jesus did not entrust himself to them, thanks to the knowledge of all mankind.   25   Indeed he had no need for anyone to provide testimony about human nature, since he himself was well aware what was in human beings.

The mystery of rebirth

3,1   Now there was a man from the Pharisee party, Nicodemus by name, a person of influence among the Jews.   2   This man came to Jesus at night, and said to him, "Rabbi, we know you have come from God as teacher—nobody can perform such signs as you are working, unless God be with him."   3   In reply Jesus said to him, "Amen, amen I tell you: unless a person be begotten over again [from above], he cannot see the Kingdom of God." 4 Nicodemus says to him, "How can any human being be begotten when he is adult? Surely he cannot enter his mother's womb a second time and be begotten?" 5 Jesus replied, "Amen, amen I tell you: unless a person be begotten by water and Spirit, he cannot enter the Kingdom of God. 6 What has been begotten of flesh remains flesh, while what has been begotten of Spirit is spirit. 7 Do not marvel at my saying to you, 'It is necessary that all of you be begotten from above.' 8 The wind blows where it likes: you may recognize the sound of it, but you do not know where it comes from, or where it is going. That is how it is with everyone who has been begotten by the Spirit." 9 In response Nicodemus said to him, "How can these things come about?" 10 By way of reply Jesus said to him, "You are the teacher in Israel—yet are not aware of such things!"

Despite the universally accepted chapter-division in our Bibles (credited to Stephen Langton, the archbishop of Canterbury who brought King John to sign the Magna Carta), the final verses of chapter 2 are actually the introduction to the Nicodemus-narrative, as George MacRae has suggested. In effect they acquaint the reader with a theme that occupies the evangelist's attention, particularly in the first four chapters of his Gospel: the crucial distinction between inadequate faith based on miracles and genuine faith grounded upon the word of Jesus. Many of the participants "among the festival throng" at the first Passover in John's narrative evinced such imperfect belief in the person of Jesus ("in his name"). What was missing, as Jesus will later make clear, was the divine initiative, without which belief in Jesus is counterfeit. "No one can come to me except the Father Who sent me draw him" (6:44). "To believe in his name" requires—since faith is essentially an interpersonal relationship with our Lord—that the Father and Jesus himself inaugurate it. In this instance he rejects this spurious faith, founded merely upon curiosity about the marvellous. And the evangelist's use of the imperfect tense here *(ouk episteuen),* as George MacRae has proposed, amounts to saying "Jesus did not let himself be believed in"[6]—thus underscoring his refusal to admit such misguided enthusiasts to intimacy with himself. In explanation, John appeals to Jesus' divine insight into "what was in human beings," the powerlessness of mortal man to attain "eternal life," unless "empowered" by the Word incarnate to become one of the children of God (1:12).

John now introduces Nicodemus, whose Greek name had already become an Aramaic loan-word, being current in a noble Jewish family of

---

6 G. W. MacRae, *Faith in the Word,* p. 37.

the period, as a distinguished doctor of the Law and member of the Sanhedrin. Schnackenburg finds it plausible that the Talmud makes an obscure reference to this man's having later become a Christian, and remarks that "There is no reason to doubt the historicity of the nocturnal scene."[7] In my opinion it is quite possible that John insinuates that Nicodemus eventually became a disciple by introducing him into the scene of Jesus' burial (19:39-40), and by noting his courageous intervention at an emergency meeting of the Sanhedrin (7:50-52). The basic issue for the evangelist here is a question often raised in the time of Jesus by sincere Jews (see Mk 10:17; Lk 10:25): what is necessary for salvation?

Our interest in this narrative, in the context of the First Week, arises from Nicodemus' struggle and—despite his extraordinary openness to Jesus—his continuing bafflement before the revelation Jesus brings to bear upon the issue. The detail, he "came to him at night," if taken as a symbol of the obscurity and ambivalence of Nicodemus' attitude towards Jesus, might help the retreatant, as he wrestles with the mystery of sin, to identify with this erudite Pharisee and the ambiguous position in which he remains trapped. He comes to Jesus of his own accord, professes to recognize that God is with him, yet at the end of the dialogue he will ask, "How can these things come about?" Nicodemus is presented as one who reasons logically, yet logic is not enough. What he lacks is faith in Jesus, and so his dialectical expertise becomes an obstacle to this precious relationship.

If one's meditation upon the enigma of sin is to be salutary, it is crucial to begin with an act of faith that God in Christ is already present in one's heart, desirous to unveil the mystery. Père De Broucker remarks that "The first sign of God's approach is the entering into oneself; it is even impossible to distinguish the moment when God comes to man, from that in which man comes to himself. The disclosure of the religious sense of sin is not simply a prelude to an encounter with God; it is already its initial effect. It is a necessity that, from the start, God be there and that He speak."[8]

Jesus' opening gambit in the conversation appears to ignore Nicodemus' sincere, respectful acceptance of him. In reality, Jesus introduces —however abruptly—the answer to the real question that he has intuited in the heart of his interlocutor: "What must I do to be saved?" His initial assertion is ambiguous: the *double entendre*—only possible in Greek! —is untranslatable. "Unless a person be begotten over again"—Jesus

---

7   Schnackenburg, *John,* I, pp. 356-365.
8   De Broucker, "La première semaine," 24.

means "by God" (1:13), "from above,"—he cannot *"see,"* that is, experience, "the Kingdom of God." The learned doctor mistakes the revelation for a challenge to debate: he remains at the natural level, that of "the flesh." Thus Jesus is obliged to clarify his statement: "Unless a person be begotten by water and Spirit, he cannot enter the Kingdom of God." While the Christian reader may see a reference to the sacrament of baptism here, that meaning is at most secondary. Water in this Gospel is a symbol of the Spirit (4:14; 7:37-39). Acquaintance with "the Scriptures" should have made Jesus' remark comprehensible to Nicodemus: the outpouring of the Spirit (Is 32:15; Joel 2:28-29) had been announced as the definitive sign of "the last days." Ezekiel came close to the idea of a new birth through God's dynamic operation. "I will sprinkle clean water on you . . . A new heart I will give you, and a new spirit . . . I will remove the heart of stone from your flesh and give you a heart of flesh" (Ez 36:25-26), heart being a symbol of the true self.

Jesus tries to enlighten the Pharisee by reminding him of the dichotomy between "flesh" and "Spirit"—a chasm unbridgeable by any natural effort. He makes use of the mysterious nature of the wind as a parable that illustrates, without explaining, the mystery of being "begotten" as a child of God. "The wind blows where it likes: you may recognize the sound of it, but you do not know where it comes from or where it is going."

De Broucker remarks that "There is no supernatural repentance which is not a regeneration; and the sinner's confusion, at the sight of the evil that is his, is the first step out of such evil."[9] It belongs then to that being "begotten from above," which in the Fourth Gospel corresponds to the Pauline "new creation" (Gal 6:15; 2 Cor 5:17). As the process of birth requires a certain amount of time, so the exercises of the First Week must be accorded a span of time, and effort. This may explain why Ignatius outlines five exercises for the first day only: he assumes that the retreatant will comply with the suggestion that "he labor to acquire what he is seeking in the first week as if he hoped to discover no further good in the second" (Annotation 11). Our evangelist will refer later to the painful, troublesome effort that inevitably accompanies this new birth of the believer. "When a woman is giving birth, she experiences sorrow because her hour has arrived: but when she gives birth to a child, she no longer recalls her tribulation on account of her joy that a human being has been born into the world" (16:21).

9   Ibid., 33.

That Ignatius assumes that a certain joy should normally accompany the exercises of the First Week is evident in his expectation that, in the course of the repetitions, meditation will evolve into contemplation, with which consolation is always associated ([64]). This is clear also from the insistence placed upon a deepening sense of gratitude to our Lord ([61, 71]), as also from the characterization of the Crucified as a "friend" of the exercitant from the very beginning of the retreat ([54]). Such thankfulness reaches a crescendo with the "cry of wonder with ever growing love" ([60]), as one calls to mind the manifold ways in which the entire creation has remained faithfully at the service of one who is a sinner—"sky, sun, moon, stars, elements," no less than earth's "fruits, birds, fish, animals!" The passage is a kind of anticipation of the concluding Contemplation to Attain Love. As evidence that the aim of the First Week reaches beyond the mere renunciation of sin and sinfulness, Joseph Hitter adduces the early introduction of the threefold colloquy ([63, 64])—"Ignatius' own practice whenever he considered that he was seeking an extraordinary grace."[10]

To the Ignatian "cry of wonder" there corresponds, in John's narrative of the meeting between divine Wisdom incarnate and the noble representative of the wisdom of Israel, Nicodemus' astonished exclamation, "How can these things come about!" With the passage of time, this attitude will issue (as we have suggested the evangelist insinuates) in Nicodemus' becoming a disciple of Jesus.

2. The Son's Appearance in History Precipitates Judgment (3:13-21)

In a helpful study of what is to be chiefly sought from the exercises on human sinfulness and the healing love of God, William A. Barry asserts emphatically that the retreatant be guided into "an experience in the present, not just a memory. He experiences himself as alienated, desolate *now*, as needy *now* . . . if he stays with his feelings of desolation and turns to the Lord for help . . . then he does experience the 'good news' . . . like a baptism, like a conversion, a new birth . . ."[11] Likewise Winoc De Broucker, already cited in the same vein, returns to lay stress upon the here-and-now character of this sense of one's sinfulness. "The day of judgment, which the retreat permits us to live, leads us to the present instance. The most unimaginative exercitant is in no wise disadvantaged: death, hell, are not 'mystery-plays' to be acted out on a stage,

10 Joseph Hitter, S.J., "The First Week and the Love of God," *The Way: Supplement* no. 34 (1978), 31.
11 William A. Barry, S.J., "The Experiences of the First and Second Weeks of the *Spiritual Exercises*," *Notes on the Spiritual Exercises*, p. 97.

but the very 'mystery' of our being, here and now present in our reality as sinners.''[12]

While the fourth evangelist does not totally ignore the traditional view of the divine judgment as a future event (5:28-29), he presents it by preference as an ongoing, contemporaneous happening.

> 3:13   No one has ascended into heaven except the One who descended from heaven—the Son of Man.   14   Now just as Moses lifted up the serpent in the desert, so it is necessary that the Son of Man be lifted up,   15 in order that every believer may, in [union with] him, possess eternal life.
>
> 16 For God so loved the world as to give His only Son, in order that everyone believing in him may not perish, but may possess eternal life. 17   Now God did not send the Son into the world that he might judge the world, but that the world might be saved through him.   18   The person believing in him is not being judged: but the one refusing to believe has already been judged, because he has not believed in the name of the only Son of God.
>
> 19 This then is the judgment: the light came into the world, yet human beings loved darkness more than the light because their conduct was wicked. 20   For everyone living a life that is worthless hates the light and refuses to come to the light, lest his activity be exposed.   21   Whereas the person who lives the truth comes to the light, in order that what he does may be manifested as having been performed with the help of God.

In the context of the Fourth Gospel this first abstract of the proclamation by the Johannine community appears as an answer to the puzzled question of Nicodemus, ''How can these things come about?'' The evangelist's answer is to point to the divine revelation in the gospel graciously given on the initiative of God Himself through the life, death, and exaltation of His Son. By the First Week of the Exercises the retreatant is brought to feel deeply his ignorance of himself as a member of the sinful human family. Indeed it might be said that in the mind of Paul, whose letter to the Roman church contains the Christian revelation of original sin (Rom 5:12-21), the sin, which Adam in some mysterious way passed on to all his descendants by his disobedience, was in fact a culpable loss of self-identity. The human family, infected by the first parent's rejection of God's gift to him of a filial relationship, did not know who it was meant to be—adoptive sons and daughters of God Himself. The God-given remedy for such sinful ''ignorance'' was that ''God sent His own Son in the likeness of sinful flesh and . . . condemned sin in that flesh''

12   De Broucker, ''La première semaine,'' 31.

(Rom 8:3). In the Pauline view, it was by his obedient acquiescence to the divine initiative that Christ "was handed over [by God] for our sins and raised [by Him] for our justifying" (Rom 4:23). In Pauline Christology, Christ appears as the first redeemed human being, "the last Adam" become "life-giving Spirit" (1 Cor 15:45). Through faith and baptism the believers "are all sons of God" (Gal 3:25-26). Yet Paul appears to have sensed that the needful recovery from the universal loss of self-identity is a project that may well consume the lifetime of the man of faith, whose adoption by the Father—until his resurrection to glory (Rom 8:23)—is at present only inchoative. Awareness of one's divine adoption can be developed only through the power of the Spirit, and one privileged moment for such an experience occurs in the liturgical recital of "the prayer that Jesus taught us." Paul says, "The proof that you are sons is that God sent forth the Spirit of His Son into our hearts, crying *Abba,* dear Father!—so that each of you is no longer slave, but son, and if son, then heir through God" (Gal 4:6-7). The appearance in this text (see also Rom 8:15) of the bilingual (Aramaic/Greek) formula suggests that what Paul here alludes to is a liturgical (possibly Eucharistic) formulation of the dominical prayer. Ignatius' striking devotion to this prayer is attested by the fact that he makes it the climax and conclusion of every single exercise. One might say, without too great exaggeration, that the overriding aim of the Spiritual Exercises is to teach the exercitant to recite the Our Father with ever deepening awareness of his adoptive sonship.

In our reflections upon the two summaries of the Johannine kerygma, as an exercise of the First Week, it is to be observed that each begins with the announcement of God's initiative in revealing Himself through the death and exaltation of Jesus—"the heavenly realities" (v. 12) in which one is to believe.

The unique revealer of God's saving design is "the Son of Man." This designation, borrowed (in all probability) by the historical Jesus from the book of Daniel, is used by John in a notably different sense from that exhibited in the Synoptic Gospels. For our evangelist, it indicates the exalted Jesus, sent by the Father into our world, and now returned home to God. John wishes to impress upon the reader that it is through the cross as the glory of Jesus that God has disclosed His final offer of salvation, and he now makes use of a bold symbol to present this truth, one that is unique in Christian inspired literature, the bronze serpent Moses had caused to be made and erected on a pole (Num 21:9). The evangelist may have been influenced by the comment of the author of the Wisdom of Solomon. "When the dire venom of beasts came upon them, and they were dying from the bite of the crooked serpents . . . they had a sign of salvation to remind them of the precept of Your Law: for he who turned towards it was saved—not by what he saw, but by You, the Savior of all!'' (Wis 16:5-7).

Actually, this statement "The Son of Man must be lifted up" is a reformulation of the first of the traditional three predictions of Jesus' death and resurrection recorded in each Gospel (Mk 8:31; Mt 16:21; Lk 9:22). The "must" indicates the will of God and His initiative in Jesus' saving death. John's interpretation of the cross as "glory" appears in the term "be lifted up," the initial step in Jesus' exaltation.

The divine purpose is that "every believer" may "possess eternal life," come to share the life of God Himself. But for this there are two prerequisites: to believe and to be united with the Crucified. It is remarkable that in a Gospel that discusses belief in its various stages the word "faith" nowhere appears. Instead John prefers the verb "to believe"—and most often uses the expression, "to believe into" Jesus or God. While contemporary English does not tolerate this turn of phrase, its Greek rendering implies the dynamic act of God in drawing men into this profoundly personal relationship with the risen Jesus—the essence of Christian faith.

The source of this saving act on the part of God is love. Later, John will point out that Jesus' death in obedience to his Father's "command" is the reason "why the Father loves me" (10:17), and it is, at the same time, proof of Jesus' love for the Father (14:31). The astounding disclosure here is that "God so loved the world as to give His only Son"—over to death, and this for "the world," the human race, which frequently in this Gospel appears in collusion with "darkness." The truth that "whilst we were still sinners, Christ died for us . . . when we were God's enemies, we were reconciled to Him through the death of His Son" (Rom 5:8-10) was always a source of wonder for Paul, an astounding revelation of divine love that in the First Week of the Exercises is calculated to seize the heart at its very depths. John's expression may well be a literary allusion to the terrible story (Gen 22) of "the sacrifice of Abraham, our patriarch," appropriately called in Jewish tradition "the binding of Isaac."

The remainder of this summary of the Johannine gospel is concerned with a nuanced discussion of a central theme in John's book: "the judgment." It may cause some surprise to learn that the terms for "repentance" (noun or verb), which figure so prominently in the Synoptics and in the Lucan *précis* of the primitive preaching in Acts (Acts 2:38; 3:19; 17:30), never occur in this Gospel. Instead John speaks of "judgment," both in the sense of saving judgment by God (as in the Old Testament) and in the sense of condemnation. An example of this second meaning is provided by the statement, "God did not send the Son into the world that he might judge the world, but that the world might be saved through him." Thus in John's view, the primordial intent of God, to effect the salvation of the human race, is made evident by being given place of privilege.

This "spiritual Gospel," as Clement of Alexandria aptly called it, exhibits a striking predilection for juridicial or forensic language—testimony, witness, judgment, Paraclete—in order to pin down with stark realism certain symbols or abstractions—truth, falsehood, light, darkness—that might otherwise evanesce in some sort of Gnostic mythology. And it will be recalled that John's image of Jesus is formed around his insight that he is the Word of God—*Logos* (structure in its radical sense—from *legein,* originally "to set, place").

The use of judgment in both a positive and negative sense permits a significant distinction to be expressed by the present and perfect tenses. "The person believing in him is not being judged:" to believe wards off condemnation. On the other hand, "the one refusing to believe has already been judged"—unfaith stands under a condemnation that is self-inflicted. What is expressed here is the kerygmatic summons to a decision for faith "in the name of the only Son of God." We are close to the notion of the Ignatian "Election," a response of love to Christ present in the mysteries of his earthly life.

It is this presence in our world of the divine Word become flesh that has caused what is called the "realized" character of Johannine eschatology: the fact that "the light came into the world, yet human beings loved darkness more than the light because their conduct was wicked." The reality of evil in history is personified as "darkness" that operates to bring many to choose to remain under a judgment of condemnation. What explains such obduracy, despite God's efforts to save all mankind, is that "their conduct was wicked." Ultimately, John knows, the mystery of evil is inexplicable: "sin is a surd," as Bernard Lonergan has observed. Ignatius of Loyola finds its origin in "disorder," to which it in turn also leads. This is close to the thought expressed in the next verse: "Everyone living a life that is worthless hates the light and refuses to come to the light, lest his activity be exposed." The word "hates" is to be given its full value. John's conviction is that no one can take a cool, detached attitude to Jesus—one either falls in love with him through "believing in his name," or one "hates" him. The evangelist sees the lines in history as sharply drawn, as Ignatius does also in Two Standards ([136-147]).

To conclude this first summary of the Christian proclamation, John turns to the brighter side of the cosmic picture. "The person who lives the truth," that is, acts in accordance with the challenging message brought by Jesus from the unseen God, his Father, "comes to the light" —not indeed by his own natural resources—but as will be said later, because "drawn" by the Father's "gift" of faith (6:37, 43, 65). Yet for all that, such endowment does not eliminate man's free choice (6:67-69). In the end, however, the believer knows that this happy outcome is to be credited entirely to God. And it is the saving judgment which discloses to the eyes of faith that "what he does" has "been performed with the help of God." For our evangelist, history is always of supreme importance in the context of man's salvation.

3. The Trinitarian Character of the Confrontation by Jesus (3:31-36)

This second version of the Johannine community's proclamation is similar to the first in its general movement: the divine saving event descends from God to mankind. It differs from the other summary by its concentration upon Jesus' relation as heavenly envoy to the Father and the Spirit; and thus gives special urgency to the summons to belief in Jesus as the Son of God. The passage is of special interest to us because of the dominantly trinitarian stamp of Ignatian spirituality. Hugo Rahner characterizes Ignatian Christology as a movement from above *(de arriba)* to below, "by way of the divine Majesty put to death on the cross . . . The royal throne of the Father is confronted by 'the face and circumference of the earth' ([102, 103]), and below this again . . . the hell into which men must 'descend' ([102]), though they are able to rise again from it in the Mediator to the glory of the Father, because the Word—as the radiant source—had himself 'come down from above' ([237]), and is thus 'at the feet of the most holy Trinity,' where he 'implores the Trinity for forgiveness.' In Christ, then, the 'above' of the Father has become permanently fused into the elements and atoms of the world 'below'."[13]

> 31   The One who comes from above stands above all men, while he whose origin is from the earth remains earth-bound, and his speech is earthly. The One coming from heaven [remains above all men]—   32   he attests what he has seen and heard, yet nobody accepts his testimony.   33   The person who does accept his testimony has set his seal that God is true [to His

---

13   H. Rahner, *Ignatius the Theologian*, p. 17.

word]. 34 Indeed, the One God sent utters God's words—he does not give the Spirit stintingly. 35 The Father loves the Son and has given all into his power.

36 The person believing in the Son possesses eternal life. But the one disobeying the Son will not see life! On the contrary, God's wrath abides upon him.

Hugo Rahner suggests, quite plausibly, that the Ignatian keyword *de arriba* "may perhaps have been an echo of the *anōthen* (from above) in John."[14] It is beyond doubt one of the primary characteristics of the Johannine Jesus, who "stands above all men," and thus—even as the Word become flesh—is accorded place of privilege in this Gospel by contrast with the entire human family, "whose origin is from the earth." For this reason Jesus, as "only Son," is unique revealer of the "God no one has ever seen" (1:18). Through his earthly life he brings "the truth," the challenging message of God's last offer of salvation, because "he attests what he has seen and heard." John employs the two human senses of sight and hearing, the primary sources of communication, to portray the immediacy of the heavenly experience of the preexistent Word of God.

The response of those to whom Jesus has been sent by the Father is first expressed as negative, then abruptly as a positive acceptance by some. Such is the characteristic way our evangelist expresses himself (12:37, 42). The community of faith "does accept his testimony," and its acceptance of Jesus involves confident trust that "God is with him" (3:2; 9:16) and an affirmation that "God is true to His word." John uses the metaphor of the authentication of a document, where Paul (2 Cor 1:20) borrows the liturgical "Amen" of the community's participation at public worship to express the same reaction.

The imperative demand by Jesus to be heard and accepted is now underscored by a theme that will recur in this Gospel. The message is not his own: all that he utters is nothing less than "God's words" (12:49; 14:10). Indeed, Jesus' word is so much his own that he *is* the Word, yet that word is uttered by God speaking within Jesus. I have already called this theme "the poverty of the Son:" everything Jesus speaks is actually the Father speaking, just as all he does in reality remains "the works of the Father." Accordingly, he can say, "The Father and I are one" (10:30), yet "The Father is greater than I" (14:28). The gift of the Spirit by the Father through the glorified Jesus is the ultimate source of this as-

---

14   Ibid., p. 3.

tounding revelation.

The identity of the One "who does not give the Spirit stintingly" has been the subject of a centuries-old debate among commentators: is the Father meant here, or is it the Son? I suggest that John means to signify both. Indeed the next line, "the Father loves the Son," almost appears to imply what the Spirit communicated to the Son is divine love. What is certain is that the Father's love is source of His gift of universal dominion over "all" to Jesus—another theme that will recur (13:3; 17:2). And Jesus will state later, "What the Father has given me is greater than all" (10:29). As with Ignatius long after him, the fourth evangelist presents a spirituality that is thoroughly trinitarian. Throughout his book he returns time and again to the conviction that God's relationship with the world of men is a tri-personal one (7:37-39; 16:7-15; 19:30; 20:22).

The summary concludes with a promise and a warning: the fulfilment of either one or other depends upon one's acceptance through faith of Jesus' message, or its rejection. "The person believing in the Son possesses eternal life:" the presence of the glorified Son of God to such a one makes "eternal life" already a present possession. It is upon the dark side of God's loving commerce with mankind that John now dwells. To refuse to accept Jesus is presented as a crucially moral issue, and it means "disobeying the Son," to refuse to "set one's seal that God is true to His word." This constitutes "the sin of the world" (1:29). The tragic result of man's disbelief is a fearful one: "God's wrath abides upon him"—the antithesis of that mutual "abiding" of Father and Son in the heart of the believer (14:23). This is the single instance in the entire Gospel where there is mention of "God's wrath." Another member of the "school of John," the seer of Patmos, speaks of "the wrath of the Lamb" (Apoc 6:16), and especially that of God (Apoc 11:18; 14:10; 16:9; 19:15).

The response to this starkly worded appeal is presented in the colloquy of the first exercise of the First Week by three questions: "What have I done for Christ?"—"What am I doing for Christ?"—"What should I do for Christ?" The essentially relational quality of such queries indicates how far from mere introspection is the Ignatian purpose through the meditations concerning sin. The implied promissory character of the response by the exercitant is what is sought through an intense experience of the crucified "creator and Lord." To Ignatius' way of thinking, no believer can resist the dynamic attraction of the Crucified—which is what the Johannine Jesus had promised. "And for my part, if I am lifted up from the earth, I will draw all human beings to myself" (12:32).

It is moreover well worth noting that the answer to the question,

"What have I done for Christ?" is not expected to be a merely negative response: the phrase "for Christ" implies that there has indeed been much that is good in the course of my life, as there is actually also at present by the fact that I am being led to make the Spiritual Exercises. Thus a comprehensive reply, that is sincere, must range over my "graced history" as well as my "sin-history." The confrontation with the risen Lord, who remains for Ignatius, as for our evangelist (20:20), "the crucified Majesty of God," is designed to form the basis for the colloquy in the very first exercise ([53]), being calculated to bring home to the exercitant the continued, loving presence of Christ in his or her life. And this becomes increasingly evident in the second exercise, in which, after I recall "the indictment of sins" (Joseph Rickaby), I am brought to ask in the third point, "What can I *by myself* actually be?" ([58]). It becomes increasingly clear from the fourth and fifth points that the only adequate answer is that I have never been left to my own devices. I have been constantly pursued by God's "wisdom . . . omnipotence . . . justice,"—above all—His "goodness" ([59]). And all this evokes "a cry of wonder" ([60]), as I ponder the consoling truth that the entire creation has "preserved me in life," while angels and saints "have been interceding and praying for me." The further marvel is that the entire irrational creation has remained steadfast in supporting me.

Even the macabre meditation on hell, where perhaps Ignatius most clearly indicates how medieval he always remained, is not allowed to terminate without a deeply felt act of thanks to Christ, "because he did not permit me to fall into any of these categories" (of the lost) but "has until now always treated me with such great love *(piedad)* and compassion" ([71]). In the article by Joseph Hitter, already cited, it is stated that "the purpose of this exercise is ultimately directed to the hope for extraordinary degrees of love. It would be foolish to ignore the fact that Ignatius lived during that era now known as the *fièvre satanique* . . . nor do we yet understand fully the subtleties of this special 'application of the senses'."[15]

While some reference to the singular graces anticipated during the First Week has been made earlier in this chapter, it seems useful to emphasize them here, if only to appreciate Ignatius' concern with the exercitant mentioned in Annotation 18. To such a person, even though he be "untutored or illiterate," "of limited understanding and little natural capability," nonetheless "it is only right to give [certain exercises] in line

15   J. Hitter, "The First Week and the Love of God," p. 31.

with his desire to dispose himself for them, in order that he may the better help himself and profit by them.'' This type of retreatant is to be given the exercises of the First Week, in the event that "he desires to receive instruction and to reach a certain degree of peace of soul.''

The distinguished historian of Jesuit spirituality, Joseph de Guibert, has pointed out that "This provision was made for those who, without being capable of that outstanding service which was the end of the complete *Exercises,* could nevertheless be led to a life that was solidly and vigorously Christian.''[16] In his turn Hugo Rahner observes, "While it is true that Ignatius was very keen to keep the things of the First Week separate from those of the Second (11), it is nonetheless important to bear in mind the basic structure of the *Exercises* as a whole, which, although perhaps obscure at first, is always there to see . . . Hence even for those who are being put through the First Week (18) only . . . it is taken for granted that their efforts should culminate in Christ through the reception of the sacrament.''[17] He later calls the following of such exercises permitted in Annotation 18 "an independent piece of spiritual formation.''[18]

By way of concluding this discussion of the high value Ignatius attached to the exercises of the First Week because of his own experiences in prayer at Loyola and in the early months at Manresa, it may not be out of place to recall what has already been stated earlier in a different context about the development of "meditation" into "contemplation." An impressive set of texts in fact indicates that he expected the exercitant to attain, in addition to a lively "abhorrence" of sins and the disorder caused by it, a remarkable degree of contemplative prayer—and this already in the First Week. The point is the more worthy of attention since many Jesuit directors came in the course of centuries to regard "meditation" as the normal, indeed the only, way of praying.

In the general description of the content and movement involved in the full course of the Exercises, we find assigned as the program of the First Week, "the consideration and *contemplation* of sins" (Annotation 4). In three of the Additions "for making the Exercises better" ([73]), which he considered of paramount importance (Annotation 6), it is question of the possibility of contemplative prayer from the beginning of the retreat. "When I awaken, without giving place to any irrelevant thoughts, I must advert at once to what I am going to *contemplate* in the

---

16   J. de Guibert, *The Jesuits: Their Spiritual Doctrine and Practice,* p. 533.
17   H. Rahner, *Ignatius the Theologian,* p. 61.
18   Ibid., p. 93.

first exercise at midnight, inducing in myself confusion for my many sins" ([74]). As immediate preparation for prayer, "I shall stand for the space of an Our Father a step or two from the place where I am to *contemplate* or meditate" ([75]). "I am to enter upon the *contemplation,* now kneeling, now prostrate on the ground . . . always intent on seeking what I desire" ([76]).

Within the text of the First Week itself, it becomes clear that the Saint counts on the exercitant's early arrival at contemplative prayer. He designates the third exercise a "repetition," which is "to repeat the first and second exercises by singling out and dwelling on those points where I felt deeper consolation or desolation, or greater spiritual feeling *(sentimiento)*" ([62]). Father Peters' remark, cited earlier in this book, is certainly in line with Ignatius' own view, when he states that "Contemplation is essentially and closely linked with consolation, for consolation is any interior movement in the soul by which it is inflamed with love or stirred by sorrow or joy, in greater faith, hope, and charity (316). The link is so close that as soon as there is true consolation, meditation turns into contemplation, even though the subject matter remains the same."[19] Consequently, it is clear from the directions given for the third exercise that its author assumed the presence of contemplative prayer even in the first two exercises of the First Week; and this explains his references to "contemplation" in the Additions. In fact, William Peters observes that "the third exercise has been described in terms which are typical of contemplative prayer: to dwell on consolation, desolation, spiritual relish."[20]

The fourth exercise appears, from its descriptive definition ("to resume the third exercise" [64]), in the Saint's mind to be somewhat new. This comes from its character as a further refinement of the previous repetition: "to run through or return assiduously to the recollection of those matters *contemplated* in the previous exercises." From all this there can be little doubt of the very positive nature of the First Week in the view of St. Ignatius.

---

19 W. Peters, *The Spiritual Exercises of St. Ignatius,* p. 38.
20 Ibid., p. 64.

Chapter 4

THE CHALLENGE OF THE CONTEMPORARY CHRIST:
A "CONSIDERATION"

B efore introducing the exercitant into the work proper to the Second
Week, the contemplation of Jesus' earthly life, Ignatius suggests an
"exercise" ([99]), entitled *Del Rey,* "About the King" ([91-98]), which is
not yet a contemplation but rather an induction into contemplation. This
is seen from the subtitle, "The call of the temporal king helps to contemplate the life of the eternal King." Popularly known as the Kingdom (a
term not found in the Ignatian text), the exercise will be seen, on a careful reading, to bear principally, upon the challenging word of the risen
Jesus summoning to the following of himself. Indeed, it is noteworthy
that, like the fourth evangelist, the author of the *Exercises* does not present Jesus' message as a proclamation of the Kingdom of God, a phrase
prominent in the Synoptic Gospels, nor does he ever propose, as material
for prayer, the parables of the Kingdom. He does not speak, as do Paul
(1 Cor 15:24; Col 1:13; see Eph 5:5), Matthew (Mt 16:28; 20:21), and
John (18:36), of a Kingdom that is Christ's. Ignatius' concern is with the
person of our Lord.

Accordingly, this foreword to the Second Week of the *Exercises*
starts where Mark (Mk 1:16-20) and John (1:35-51) begin their narratives
of Jesus' public ministry, with the call to the gospel, to the following of
Jesus. The retreatant is to "beg a grace of our Lord, in order that I may
not be deaf to his call, but ready and diligent in carrying out his most
holy will" ([91]).

Because of the tendency of some modern Jesuit commentators to
minimize the importance of this exercise, some explanation of its nature
and thrust seem relevant here. Williams Peters, as a consequence of his
somewhat singular view that the Election is not the central focus of the
Exercises, has taken the stand that *Del Rey* is intended to be understood
as "low-keyed."[1] Peter Hebblethwaite claims to "see a striking

---

1   W. Peters, S.J., "The Kingdom: the Text of the Exercise," *The Way: Supplement* no.
18 (1973), 11.

contrast" between the Ignatian vision of the world here and that exposed in the Contemplation for Attaining Love.[2] John Ashton, in his turn, finds the conception of Jesus as king in contradiction with the attitudes of the historical Jesus and of the evangelical traditions.[3] And there are others, who (in the words of James Walsh) have "tended to make heavy weather of the 'curial' and military vocabulary and imagery of the exercise on the Kingdom, and yet at the same time to tolerate similar cultural limitations in that on the Two Standards, on the ground, that this exercise is firmly rooted in scripture and thus continues to make a valid and universal appeal."[4]

In the first place, the military, even bellicose terminology, to which objection has occasionally been made nowadays, is firmly grounded in the traditions of western (as of eastern) spirituality. One has only to look at the *Regula Monachorum* of St. Benedict, which admittedly exercised great influence on Ignatius of Loyola. Christine Mohrmann, the distinguished specialist in the Latin of the sixth century, asserts that the Benedictine concept, *servire* "is closely related in the writing of St. Benedict with that of *militia, militare* (soldiering, making war). It is well known that the imaged phrase *militia Christi* takes up a piece of primitive Christian terminology, adopted by monasticism." The reason for this she ascribes to the belief that "the ascetic fights with the armor of prayer and asceticism against the devil and the demons." This traditional vocabulary long employed in eastern monasticism was mediated to St. Benedict through the writings of St. Augustine. Dr. Mohrmann points out, "It is interesting to note that this *militare* in the sense of service is found in the language of the Roman liturgy, notably in the Leonine Sacramentary, where—as with St. Benedict—it is synonymous with service."[5]

Secondly, the New Testament authors employ military metaphors to describe as an ongoing war the struggle of the risen Christ against the forces of evil (1 Cor 15:25-26; 2 Thes 1:7-8; 2:8; Apoc 16:14; 17:14; 19:11-16). Paul pictures his struggle against error as a battle (2 Cor 10:3-6), and the anonymous deutero-Pauline author designates Timothy as "soldier of Christ" (2 Tm 2:3). The life of the Christian in this world

2   Peter Hebblethwaite, "The Kingdom and the world," *The Way: Supplement* no. 18 (1973), 66-67.
3   John Ashton, "The Kingdom: the scriptural background," *The Way: Supplement* no. 18 (1973), 29-32.
4   James Walsh, S.J., "The Christ of the Kingdom and the Company," *The Way: Supplement* no. 24 (1975), 83.
5   Christine Mohrmann, "La langue de saint Benoît," in *Sancti Benedicti Regula Monachorum: Textus critico-practicus sec. cod. Sangall. 914, editio altera emendata* (Maredsous, 1955), pp. 28-31.

is depicted as warfare (1 Thes 5:8; Eph 6:11-13; 1 Pt 5:8-9), as the Lucan Jesus does at the Last Supper (Lk 22:36). The Johannine Jesus announces his victory over the world (16:33b).

Finally, the Ignatian text ([95]) should be read carefully, where the summons of "Christ our Lord, the eternal king" is set forth: "before whom [stands] *the entire world,* to which—and to each one personally— he calls in these words, 'It is my decision to conquer *the entire world* and all my enemies, and thus enter my Father's glory'." Ignatius makes it clear that the call to join the risen Lord in his enterprise of redemption within the Church is issued to all human beings without exception. More- over, his distinction between the two categories of people who respond has often been obscured in translation: The first accept from natural motives, "judgment and reason" ([96]), while those sought by Ignatius "rather desire to act from love and signalize themselves by total service of the eternal King and Lord of all" ([97]). It is these only who, out of love for Christ, "will even go against their own life-in-the-flesh and their natural and this-worldly love" (as James Walsh has turned it). Once the thrust of the statement is accurately grasped, the comment by Hugo Rahner becomes apposite. "Thus to ask whether the meditation is 'apos- tolic' or 'ascetical' in its conclusion is to miss the point. The immediate purpose is not the formation of an apostolic vocation, but the realization that the Kingdom can ultimately be established by people who offer themselves unreservedly to Christ the King . . . carnal and worldly love are only the immediate objects to be fought against; the real battle is against the enemy of human nature, and the victory was, and always will be, possible only through the cross."[6]

It remains, by way of foreword, to distinguish this exercise from "meditation" (it is described ([91]) as an aid to "contemplation"), and also, by reason of its structuring, from "contemplation" itself (it has no "history" as its point of departure, nor does it terminate in colloquy). James Walsh, in a letter, has suggested that *Del Rey* can rightly be desig- nated as akin to the Bernardine *consideratio,* in which the mind is ab- sorbed in the search for truth *(intentio animi vestigantis verum).* Hence, "consideration" is simply a prior step towards "contemplation," which St. Bernard defines as "a true and certain insight of the mind concerning any reality, or a grasp of the truth that is free of all doubt" *(verus certus- que intuitus animi de quacumque re, sive apprehensio veri non dubia).*[7]

---

6   H. Rahner, *Ignatius the Theologian,* pp. 110-111.
7   *S. Bernardi, De Consideratione, caput II, 5. Considerationis a contemplatione distinctio.*

Ignatius himself uses the terms *consideración* ([95]) and *considerar* ([94, 96]).

The fourth evangelist, as if to aid such a "consideration," has placed a grid over the traditions he received regarding John "the witness" and those relating to Jesus' summons of his first disciples, by innovatively arranging them as significant events of the first four days of his story. He will bring his week to a climax with a wedding at Cana in Galilee. The first two days seemingly center upon John and his self-identification: in reality however, through this first witness to be cited in the Gospel, the evangelist is actually sketching for his reader the lineaments of the earliest Jewish-Christian response to Jesus.

Day One: John's Testimony Before an Official Inquiry (1:19-28)

19   Now this is the testimony of John, when the Jews sent priests and levites from Jerusalem to interrogate him by asking "Who are you?"   20   In fact he confessed without ambivalence, as he made this confession, "I am not the Messiah."   21   So they asked him, "Well then are you Elijah?" He says, "I am not."—"Are you the Prophet?", and he answered, "No."   22   So they said to him, "Who are you?—in order that we may report your answer to those who sent us. What do you say about yourself?"   23   He declared, "I am 'a voice in the desert of one that cries "Level out the road of the Lord",' as the prophet Isaiah proclaimed."   24   Now those sent were of the Pharisee sect,   25   and they said to him by way of inquiry, "So why are you baptizing, if you are not the Messiah, nor Elijah, nor the Prophet?"   26   In reply John told them, "As for myself, I baptize with water: in your midst stands one whom you, for your part, do not know   27   —the one who comes after me; the thongs of whose sandals I am not worthy to loose."   28   This occurred at Bethany beyond Jordan, where John was baptizing.

In his reconstruction of the progress of the Johannine community, from a quite rudimentary belief in Jesus to a remarkably well-developed Christology, Raymond Brown has made the point—convincingly in my judgment—that this evolution may be traced in the pages of the Fourth Gospel. The evangelist, after the Prologue affixed to his book upon its completion, begins with a view of Christ similar to that found in the Synoptic tradition, one consonant with Jewish monotheistic belief. This view of Jesus, designated as a relatively "low Christology," has been preserved in John's first chapter. This indicates a common origin between the evangelistic traditions of this writer's community and those of the primitive church of Jerusalem. However, "the easy access to christological titles at the beginning of the Johannine ministry is the indication that Jesus regards these titles as inadequate and promises a greater insight

—they will eventually see that it is in him that heaven and earth meet" (1:50-51).[8]

As was observed earlier, the program laid down in the *Spiritual Exercises* reflects the spiritual journey of Ignatius himself. I venture to suggest that the somewhat lacunary presentation and heavily medieval character of the exercises of the First Week mirror the rather fumbling first efforts of the inexperienced author in his progress towards the contemplative life. James Walsh has hinted that the fifth exercise on hell is not to be confused with the later Application of the Senses in the weeks that follow. "It would be foolish to ignore the fact that Ignatius lived during that era now known as the *fièvre satanique,* so that some of his language appears exaggerated or even ludicrous to a modern ear . . . nor do we yet understand fully the subtleties of this special 'application of the senses.' "[9] To the values Ignatius evidently saw in these early experiences of grace in his own spiritual journey correspond, in the mind of our evangelist, those initial steps of the first disciples of Jesus, after his resurrection, towards fully evolved Christian faith. Accordingly, our interest in reflecting upon these first two days in the Johannine narrative will be taken up with this record of these primitive manifestations of faith in Jesus, which in John's book are to evolve into faith in him as the pre-existent Son of God, a Messiah who transcends, in consequence, the limitations of Old Testament messianism. Brown suggests that "John uses the concept of the Paraclete to justify the audacity of the Johannine proclamation. If there are insights in the Fourth Gospel that go beyond the ministry, Jesus foretold this and sent the Paraclete . . . to guide the community precisely in this direction (16:12-13). Yet the Paraclete is portrayed not as speaking anything new but as simply interpreting what came from Jesus (16:13-15; 14:26)."[10] In an analogous way Ignatius insists upon the paramount importance of the practice—at varying levels of spiritual development—of the discernment of spirits.

In this first vignette, in which John is depicted as a witness before official Judaism, our evangelist shows his awareness of earlier traditions regarding John "the baptizer" (see Mk 1:2-8), but he also evinces his independence in reinterpreting them. This is accomplished most notably by subordinating John to Jesus, so that he has "no significance apart from him."[11] John does not proclaim "a baptism of repentance leading to re-

8   R. E. Brown, *The Community of the Beloved Disciple,* p. 26.
9   Cited from the article, already cited in fn. 10 of ch. 3, by Joseph Hitter, which was largely revised by James Walsh, *The Way: Supplement* no. 34, p. 34.
10 R. E. Brown, *The Community of the Beloved Disciple,* pp. 28-29.
11 Schnackenburg, *John,* I, 283.

mission of sins" (Mk 1:4). He does not so much appear in these opening scenes as a precursor of Jesus. Rather, he works for Jesus, and with him. By refusing the title of Messiah, John indirectly points to Jesus. In the Marcan Prologue, John was depicted as Elijah (Mk 1:6): here he denies any such characterization as one of the eschatological figures prominent in the speculation of late Judaism, which identified the messenger God announced He would send "to prepare the way before me" (Mal 3:1) with Elijah (Mal 3:23). As will be seen shortly (v. 30), John appears to believe that Jesus is the expected Elijah-figure. Finally, John rejects the suggestion that he is "the Prophet," probably the one described by the deuteronomist as predicted by Moses, speaking in the name of God Himself. "I will raise up for them a prophet like yourself from among their brothers, and will put My words in his mouth—he is to declare to them all I command him. If anyone will not listen to My words that he speaks in My name, I Myself will hold him accountable for this" (Deut 18:18-19). It has recently been suggested that Samaritan converts had brought into the Johannine community their idea of a non-Davidic Messiah, the *Taheb* (he who comes back, who restores). And Brown, with some hesitation remarks that "sometimes the *Taheb* was seen as a Moses-returned figure. It was thought that Moses had seen God and then came down to reveal to the people what God had said. If Jesus was interpreted against this background, then Johannine preaching would have drawn from such Moses material but corrected it: it was not Moses but Jesus who had seen God and then come down to earth to speak of what he has heard above (3:13, 41; 5:20; 6:46; 7:16)."[12]

John finally identifies himself positively by applying to himself the Isaian passage by which the Synoptic evangelist had described him. "I am 'the voice in the desert of one that cries, "Level the road of the Lord" ' (Is 40:3)." This declaration stresses John's awareness that his entire significance lies in his relation to Jesus. This includes even his "baptizing with water," which he asserts somewhat cryptically is orientated to Jesus as the "hidden Messiah," a conception current in contemporary Judaism (the motif recurs at 7:27-29). Our evangelist regards such a characterization with considerable interest, for it serves a theme he will return to frequently, by his implied invitation to the reader to ask himself, "Where is the risen Jesus now for me?"

This first day of John's witnessing to Jesus closes with a reference to him as "the one who comes" (Mal 3:1)—a further hint that John looks

---

12   R. E. Brown, *The Community of the Beloved Disciple*, pp. 44-45.

on Jesus as a new Elijah. In contrast with such an exalted figure, John declares himself to be less than a slave, whose task it was to "loose the thongs" of his master's sandals, and wash his feet. The evangelist's concern to involve his reader with Jesus, even before his appearance in his Gospel, through the witnessing of John, it is to be noted, is echoed in the Ignatian "consideration" *Del Rey,* where likewise "the mind is absorbed in the search for truth."

Day Two: John's Witness to the "New Israel" (1:29-34)

Raymond Brown has astutely observed that while in the earlier evangelical traditions, reflected in Paul and the Synoptics, God was considered to make a "new covenant" through Jesus with the Jewish people, the fourth evangelist emphasizes his belief that it is the "new Israel," those who come to believe in Jesus—regardless of their racial origin—that has replaced the old. "The real Israel consists of those who receive the revelation of Jesus (1:13, 47), and so Jesus is the 'king of Israel' (1:49; 12:13) . . . Nicodemus may be a ruler of *the Jews* (3:1); but because he does not understand that begetting from above has replaced begetting of the flesh, he cannot be a teacher of *Israel* (3:11)."[13] Accordingly, the second day of testimony by John is directed towards this new Israel, and so becomes more explicit in its witness to Jesus.

> 29   Next day he saw Jesus coming towards him and announced, "There is the Lamb of God, the one who bears away the sin of the world!   30   He it is of whom I stated, 'A man comes after me, who ranks ahead of me, since he existed before me.'   31   Now I did not know him, but the reason I came baptizing with water is that he may be manifested to Israel."   32   Then John testified by saying, "I have beheld the Spirit descending like a dove out of the sky, and it kept abiding upon him.   33   For my part, I did not know him, but the One who sent me to baptize with water, He it was Who said to me, 'The one on whom you will see the Spirit descending and abiding upon him—he it is who baptizes with a holy Spirit'."   34   And so I have seen and I have testified, 'This is God's chosen One!'"

In this second vignette, while Jesus himself is pictured as saying nothing, John gives an attestation that can be comprehended only by those who entered into a personal relationship with him—the "new Israel." The first title attributed to Jesus is "the Lamb of God." The evangelist has probably drawn this from two Old Testament passages: the prescriptions regarding the eating of the Passover lamb (Ex 12:43-47), to

13   Ibid., p. 48.

which our author will later allude (19:14, 36) and those which celebrate the Servant of God (Is 53:7; Ps 34:19-20; see Jer 11:19). A perceptive suggestion of my colleague, R. A. F. MacKenzie, deserves mention: He pointed out that in the story of Abraham's intended sacrifice of Isaac there is a prophecy made by that patriarch which in the sequel is not fulfilled. When the child Isaac asks his father, "Where is the lamb for the whole-burnt offering?", Abraham answers, "God himself will provide a lamb as whole burnt offering, my son" (Gen 22:7-8). After the climax of the story, it is a ram, not a lamb, that is discovered caught in a thicket (v. 13). Our Gospel-writer, who alludes to this gruesome story (3:16; 19:17), apparently found Abraham's prophecy fulfilled in Jesus' atoning death.

The evangelist now credits John with an attestation to the pre-existence of Jesus, which that witness has already asserted in the Prologue (1:15). "He it is of whom I stated, 'A man comes after me, who ranks ahead of me, since he existed before me'." Raymond Brown cites with approval the suggestion of Bishop J. A. T. Robinson that this surprising statement of John may not implausibly be considered historical, if John believed Jesus to be the returning Elijah-figure.[14] The significance of Johannine water-baptism is now represented as ordered to Jesus' manifestation "to Israel"—that is, those who put their faith in Jesus.

However, the baptism of Jesus by John, regarded as a scandal by some in the early Church (Mt 3:14-15; see Lk 3:20-21 who sidesteps the issue) is passed over in silence. Only the descent of the Spirit upon Jesus is mentioned, since it is by virtue of the permanent abiding of the Spirit upon him that Jesus will "baptize with a holy Spirit"—an event presented in this Gospel as an immediate consequence of the death of Jesus (19:30; see also 20:22). John's testimony reaches its climax in his declaration, "This is God's chosen One"—a reading preferable to the more commonly attested "Son of God." Since the sacred author passed over the announcement of the heavenly Voice, "You are My Son, My beloved, in whom I take My delight" (Mk 1:11), an allusion to the first Servant song (Is 42:1 ff), the honor of conferring this significant title upon Jesus is given to John the witness.

Day Three: John Directs His Own Disciples to Jesus (1:35-42)

From the adherence of certain "baptists" to his own community,

---

14   In *John I–XII*, p. 64, R. E. Brown cites with the approval the view of Bishop J. A. T. Robinson that John the Baptist thought he was preparing for Elijah: see J. A. T. Robinson, "Elijah, John, and Jesus: an Essay in Detection," *New Testament Studies* 4 (1957-58), 263-281.

our evangelist has been alerted to a tradition not found in the Synoptics, that some of the prominent disciples of Jesus had originally followed John. In fact, it is hinted later in the Gospel that Jesus began his ministry as a disciple of John and imitated him by practicing water-baptism. John's loyal followers are depicted as reporting to him, "Look, rabbi, that man who was of your company across the Jordan, to whom you bore witness, is himself baptizing, and everybody is flocking to him!" (3:26). This interesting piece of early tradition is found only in this Gospel.

> 35   Next day John was again at hand with two of his disciples.   36   And gazing at Jesus walking past, he says, "See the Lamb of God!"   37   So his two disciples paid heed to him as he spoke, and they followed Jesus.   38 But Jesus turning round and beholding them following says to them, "What are you looking for?" So they said to him, "Rabbi (which translated means Teacher), where do you abide?"   39   He says to them, "Come, and you will see!" Thus they came and saw where he abode, and they abode with him that day—it was about the tenth hour.   40   Andrew, Simon Peter's brother, was one of the disciples who had heeded John and had followed him.   41   Straightaway this man seeks out his own brother Simon and tells him, "We have discovered the Messiah" (which translated means The Anointed).   42   He led him to Jesus. Gazing at him, Jesus said, "You are Simon, John's son: you will be called Cephas" (which translates as Peter).

This story opens by celebrating John's selfless direction of some of his own followers to Jesus, "the Lamb of God." The principal interest for the writer in this narrative is the presentation of the first beginnings of faith in Jesus. He describes the two disciples as following Jesus at the suggestion of their master and probably also as attracted by some mysterious quality in Jesus himself. His first question to them is intended to make them reflect upon their as yet unexamined motives: "What are you looking for?" The Johannine Jesus takes people as he finds them (see 4:7 ff), gently leading them to a more personal relationship with himself. This first moment in the genesis of a vocation to the gospel Ignatius considered of paramount importance: hence his insistence, in the fragmentary *Directory* he composed concerning the various "times" for making the "Election" ([175-187]), upon the singular importance of "the second time." He asserts, "As regards the three ways of making election, if God does not move in the first manner ([175]), the second way should be insisted on, to recognize one's vocation by the experience of consolation and desolation, that is, by continuing with the meditations on Christ our Lord to pay attention when one finds oneself in consolation to the direction in which God is moving one, and similarly in desolation'' ([377]). Hugo Rahner comments: ''During the exercises of the Election the exercitant should not direct his attention simply to the movement of spirits going on within him, but rather to God's love which both precedes and accompanies all movements of the soul—and he will do this by continuing to contemplate the mysteries of the life of Christ. This means that his attention must not be directed to what would seem superficially to be the sole means of leading him to the right decision.''[15]

The second moment in the call to the gospel is reflected in Jesus' response to the question ''Where do you abide?'' He issues an imperative invitation and makes a promise: ''Come, and you will see!'' The command to come indicates the initiative of Jesus in the beginning of every genuine vocation (see 2:23-25), which implies his own willingness to enter the personal relation with a believer, which is the quintessence of faith for this evangelist. The promise is for now left unspecified: It will be clarified by the saying of Jesus, which the writer keeps for the end of his series of encounters with Jesus (v. 51). What is to be noted here is that it is question of a *word of Jesus,* which, John will insist particularly in chapters two through four, is uniquely the solid foundation of genuine faith—whether or not the believer is led by ''signs'' to believe in Jesus.

A third moment is the immediate response of these two disciples to the call by Jesus: ''they came and saw where he abode, and they abode with him that day.'' As will become evident in the second great section of this Gospel (chs. 13-20), to ''abide'' is freighted with meaning (see 14:10, 17; 15:4-10), as is also ''abiding'' *(monē)* at 14:2, 23. John notices the time of day (''about the tenth hour'': four o'clock in the afternoon), which may imply that the disciples stayed with Jesus through most of the night.

A final, fourth moment is of considerable consequence in a Christian vocation—its ''missionary'' aspect, so to say: ''Straightaway this man [Andrew] seeks out his own brother Simon and tells him, 'We have discovered the Messiah'—and he led him to Jesus.''

Day Four: Following Jesus (1:43-51)

The first vocation-story in the Marcan Gospel (1:16-20) featured two pairs of brothers, Peter and Andrew, James and John, where the lacunary nature of the account together with its careful parallel-structure indicates that Mark got it from the evangelical traditions, created and preserved by his predecessors in the faith. Our author may well have been

---

15 H. Rahner, *Ignatius the Theologian,* p. 146.

influenced by the traditional two pairs, as he speaks of Andrew and an unnamed disciple (to which he adds the call of Peter), then of Philip and Nathanael. The mystery of the anonymous disciple has exercised commentators for many centuries, many of whom consider him to be John, son of Zebedee. Raymond Brown, like Rudolf Schnackenburg, has finally adopted the view that the evidence for such an identification is lacking. Brown however feels that the unknown man is in fact the beloved Disciple, who appears, under that name only at 13:23. If asked why such a one is not characterized here as "the disciple Jesus loved," the distinguished American Johannine scholar answers that at the initial summons by Jesus this disciple had not advanced as yet to such a unique position. It is only in the intimate context of Jesus' final supper with his faithful followers—a context in which love (both of Jesus and his disciples) is prominent—that this man, obviously the principal hero for our evangelist, is given such a title of privilege.[16]

43 Next day he [Jesus] decided to leave for Galilee, and he met Philip. And Jesus says to him "Follow me!" 44 Now Philip was from Bethsaida, city of Andrew and Peter. 45 Philip seeks out Nathanael, and says to him, "We have discovered the one about whom Moses wrote in the Law, as well as the prophets: Jesus, son of Joseph of Nazareth!" 46 However Nathanael said to him, "Can there be anything good from Nazareth?" Philip says to him, "Come and see!" 47 Jesus saw Nathanael coming toward him, so he remarks of him, "Here comes a true Israelite, in whom deceit is non-existent." 48 Nathanael says to him, "From where do you know me?" In reply Jesus told him, "Before Philip called to you, while you were under the fig tree, I saw you." 49 Nathanael responded, "Rabbi, you are the Son of God, you are the King of Israel!" 50 Jesus rejoined, "You believe because I told you, 'I saw you under the fig tree.'—You will see greater things than this!" 51 And he goes on to tell him, "Amen, amen I tell you all: you will see an opening in the sky, and the angels of God ascending and descending upon the Son of Man!"

The first to be called as followers by Jesus responded to him in Judaean territory and were former disciples of John. Jesus "now decided to leave for Galilee," and it is there he calls Philip and Nathanael. Our evangelist seemingly departs from the Marcan notice that it was "After John had been handed over, Jesus came into Galilee proclaiming the gospel from God" (Mk 1:14). That evangelist's observation is however

16 R. E. Brown, *The Community of the Beloved Disciple,* p. 33: "I am inclined to change my mind (as R. Schnackenburg has also done) from . . . identifying the Beloved Disciple as . . . John son of Zebedee."

to be understood as a theological remark, as the passive of a Pauline term for the divine agency indicates—"handed over," that is, by God.

In Galilee, Jesus calls Philip, who is fairly prominent in John's narrative (6:5, 7; 12:21-22; 14:8-9). Philip shows the genuineness of his vocation by recruiting Nathanael (about whom the Synoptics are silent). Indeed, despite the importance of his confession here, this disciple only reappears in the epilogue (21:2). Philip testifies to Jesus as the Mosaic prophet (Deut 18:18), and possibly also the Isaian Servant. His riposte to his friend's cynicism echoes the invitation of Jesus, "Come and see!" Jesus is pictured as displaying his knowledge of men—in fact, a supernatural insight. He praises Nathanael as "a true Israelite" (for John this means he qualifies as a true Christian). Jacob, later "Israel," was full of guile and deceit (Gen 27:35-36), which possibly explains Jesus' cryptic remark. Nathanael is captivated by this evidence of Jesus' supernatural insight. Schnackenburg sees Nathanael as one of "that circle of questing men, well-schooled in Scripture, who awaited the Messiah."[17] If this view be correct, this latest disciple exemplifies the Bernardine/Ignatian *consideration,* the preparatory step to contemplation. It will be observed that in reply to Nathanael's response to Jesus, "You are the Son of God: you are the King of Israel," our Lord promises this sincere believer the precious gift of contemplation: "You will see greater things than this!"

The climactic confession by Nathanael (in the eyes of our evangelist) requires explanation. In the context of the Old Testament, "Son of God" was used to designate Israelite kings as sons by adoption of the unique King of Israel, almighty God Himself. It "is probably meant to express closeness to God, union with God, and perhaps even origin from God."[18] The last title in the entire series "King of Israel" is one dear to our evangelist, who appends it to the acclamation of the crowds (from Ps 118:25-26) at Jesus' final entry into Jerusalem, and erects it into the major theme of his Passion-narrative (18:33-37; 19:2-3, 14-15, 19-22), at the end of which Jesus receives a royal burial (19:39-42).

As the conclusion to this significant exchange between Nathanael and Jesus, the sacred writer inserts a saying by Jesus, which originally had existed independently in the tradition. It is introduced by "Amen," a Hebrew word affirming the unquestionable truth of what follows, which has been denominated by Joachim Jeremias as an *ipsissima vox Jesu,* a usage peculiar to Jesus himself in his ministry. Only this Gospel-writer employs it in the doubled form. "Amen, amen I tell you all: you

---

17   Schnackenburg, *John,* I, 318.
18   Ibid., p. 318.

will see an opening in the sky, and the angels of God ascending and descending upon the Son of Man!'' It is an allusion in the characteristically Johannine manner to the patriarch Jacob's celebrated dream at Bethel (Gen 28:10-22). Father Brown makes the apposite comment, ''The vision means that Jesus as Son of Man has become the locus of divine glory, the point of contact between heaven and earth.''[19]

It will have been noted that Jesus here addresses the promise to the group of disciples with him, that it constitutes for the evangelist an appropriate introduction to his narrative of the ''signs'' which follow, and that it is significant as the first Son of Man saying (in a sequence of twelve) in this Gospel. As the Johannine usage differs from that of the first three Gospels, a word must be said of the meaning it holds for our author. At a first approach, ''the Son of Man'' sayings in the Fourth Gospel appear to contrast sharply with those in the Synoptic Gospels. There these sayings fall into three categories: those that look to the future glory of Jesus and his role as judge (Mk 8:38; 14:62; Mt 25:31-32), those which speak of his Passion and resurrection (Mk 8:31), and those describing his earthly life and ministry (Mk 2:10, 28; Lk 12:58).

As Schnackenburg observes, the Johannine ''Son of Man'' logia are linked most closely with the first group of sayings in the Synoptic tradition (5:27).[20] Still, our evangelist has reproduced in his own terminology the traditional triple prophecy by Jesus of his death and resurrection (3:14; 8:28; 12:32, 34). John of course has articulated the references to Jesus' sufferings and death in terms of his highly innovative conception of these as a ''lifting up, exaltation.'' Yet, if it be granted that the Synoptic examples of this second series derive their inspiration from the fourth Servant song (Is 52:13–53:12), then the opening verse of the Isaian canticle may be judged to have inspired this peculiar Johannine interpretation of the Passion. ''Remember, my Servant shall prosper, he shall be lifted up, exalted to the heights'' (LXX, *hypsōthēsetai kai doxasthēsetai*). ''Here the two dominant Johannine concepts occur together with the same meaning'' (Schnackenburg).[21] As regards the third group of sayings, describing the earthly Jesus as ''Son of Man,'' there would seem to be no direct relationship to those found in the Fourth Gospel, the one exception being the verse we have been considering (1:51), in which Jesus is presented, while upon earth, as ''the place'' of the manifestation of the

19   R. E. Brown, *John I–XII*, p. 91.
20   Schnackenburg, *John,* I, 535.
21   Ibid., p. 536.

unseen God, "the gate of heaven" (Gen 28:17). This initial saying, so full of mystery and promise, constitutes then an appropriate introduction to the Johannine Christology, where a most creative intrepretation of "the Son of Man" sayings stands in relation to those in the earlier Gospels as a further development of that tradition.

How may this "consideration" of this set of "calls" by the Johannine Jesus help towards the practice of contemplation? Firstly, John—like Ignatius later—concentrates attention upon the person of Jesus in all four scenes and, through a series of titles conferred on him, has provided a first sketch of the mission and ultimate destiny of our Lord. Secondly, the imperative invitation, "Come!", "Follow me," in the mouth of the Johannine Jesus, attested as "Messiah," "the Prophet," "the Lamb of God who bears away the sin of the world," the suffering Servant of God who is to be "lifted up," is echoed by Ignatius' "eternal King," who summons the exercitant "to join me in this enterprise . . . to labor with me." And the promise "You will see" (1:39) made to the first two disciples is seen to re-appear in the pledge that "by following me in suffering one may follow me in glory" ([95]). Thirdly, our evangelist's conviction, that the hallmark of the genuine disciple is a continual readiness for ever new and undreamed of experiences of the risen Jesus, is reflected in Ignatius' repeated injunction that, throughout his contemplation of Jesus' earthly history as interpreted in the Gospel-text (*el fundamento verdadero de la historia* [2]), the unvarying prayer of the exercitant be a request for that gracious gift from God of that "profoundly personal knowledge *(conocimiento interno)* of the Lord, who for me has become a human being, that I may the more deeply love and follow him" ([104]). Finally, the evangelist's concern for the historical element contained in the earlier evangelical traditions concerning what Jesus said and did—not simply despite, but because of, his creative use of them—is to be treasured as a significant object of contemplation. John's belief in the values inherent in the history of Jesus of Nazareth as the locus of revelation issues from his assertion that "the Word became flesh" (1:14). Thus the mystery of the incarnate Son of God is to be seen with the eyes of faith as the dominant truth activating one's contemplation of that history. For only through Jesus, "the Way," (14:6) can the believer be "shown the Father" (14:9). Indeed, it is John's conviction that only by believing in Jesus can the scandal of the Incarnation be surmounted. He has, by his narrative of the confrontation between Philip and Nathanael, drawn attention to this view of his. Before the last-called disciple is led to believe in Jesus, he reacts with small-town snobbery to Philip's confession that "Jesus, son of Joseph from Nazareth" is the one long ago announced by Moses and the prophets: "Can there be anything good from Nazareth?" Once graced with the gift of faith in Jesus, however, Nathanael acknowledges him through titles which form the climax of an entire series of confessions.

Chapter 5

CANA I (2:1-11):
INITIAL REVELATION OF THE INCARNATE WORD

The Second Week opens with an arresting vision of the loving concern manifested by the triune God in decreeing the ultimate offer of salvation to the human race: "how the three divine Persons regard the whole surface or sphere of the entire world, teeming with humanity; how seeing that everyone was going down to hell, they decide in their eternity that the second Person should become a human being in order to save the human race" ([102]).[1] Hugo Rahner makes an observation on the Ignatian manner of contemplating the life of our Lord which deserves particular notice. "Ignatius' principal concern could be summed up as bringing to mind the life of Christ, with particular reference to the cross."[2] This is nothing else than the ancient and traditional practice, familiar in eastern and western spirituality—*memoria Christi* (keeping our Lord in mind). What is of paramount interest here however is the constant orientation to the cross. "Thus for Ignatius the life of Christ was more than merely an edifying example, in the sense understood by the *devotio moderna*—it was the basic theological principle behind all Christian spiritual life—ultimately nothing more nor less than the conforming of one's entire being through grace with the crucified and risen Lord of glory."[3] We shall presently perceive that this same reference to

1 John Helyar's text reads, "how the three divine Persons regard the whole (flat) surface *(planitiem)* of the world." He makes the interesting remark in the second prelude, "I said above 'to see the great flat surface of the world' for this reason that I might more easily consider and imagine so many and such various people upon the surface of the world—not that the earth is flat, but round, as scholars show." This piece of scientific information, confirmed by the discovery of America a year after the birth of Ignatius, appears to have escaped his attention in an early draft of the Exercises. The so-called "autograph" is revised to read "the great capacity and sphere of the world" ([103]), while the *Vulgata* by André des Freux has simply "terrae universae ambitus" (the extent of the entire earth). This is evidence for the correctness of view of Fr. Candido de Dalmases that the Helyar manuscript is "the most ancient text of all that have thus far survived" (S. Ignatii . . . Exercitia Spiritualia, Vol. 100 in MHSJ [Rome, 1969], pp. 418-454; on the Incarnation, see pp. 428-439).
2 H. Rahner, *Ignatius the Theologian,* p. 99.
3 Ibid., p. 99.

the "glory" of Jesus (which for John is achieved when Jesus mounts the cross in order to "hand over the Spirit" (19:30) as he breathes his last) is characteristic of the *"historia"* as it is narrated in the Fourth Gospel.

The Ignatian manner of contemplation is a simple, yet most traditional one. Except perhaps for this first exercise, the Incarnation ([101-109]), which appears to reflect that "unprecedented illumination" at the river Cardoner when the saint received the privileged gift of infused contemplation, the point of departure is always the sacred text of the relevant Gospel passage, the reading (aloud) of which was known as *lectio divina.* This is described in the Exercises as "making the history present" to oneself *(traer la historia).* As William Peters has astutely perceived, this "history" does not concern the past, but is very much a reality of the present.[4] And indeed this effort under grace to become present to Jesus in a particular mystery is to be achieved through the imaginative senses: "To see the persons" ([106]), the initial, human way of relating to another; "to hear what the persons say" ([107]), a second natural way of getting to know someone; "to observe what the persons are doing" ([108]), another's actions (like his speech) "give him away," and so provide a basis for the personal relationship that is sought.

As I hazarded the suggestion above that the shape which this first contemplation takes probably stems from a reminiscence of the great mystical experience at the Cardoner, it may be well to support that view with testimonies drawn from Ignatius' contemporaries (he himself as is well known was extremely reticent about what happened). Juan Alonso de Poianco, long-time secretary to Ignatius when general of the Society, asserts in 1574, some time after the Saint's death, that this experience gave him "a remarkable enlightenment about the mystery of the most Holy Trinity, the creation of the world, and other mysteries of the faith."[5] Jerome Nadal, the intimate confidant of Loyola, declares, "There he received a unique comprehension of the persons of the Trinity . . . Even more, he received not only a clear intelligence, but an interior vision of how God created the world, of how the Word became flesh."[6]

The Ignatian contemplation always includes a "colloquy," that is a prayerful, reverent conversation, for which one is to prepare "by thinking out what I ought to say to the three divine Persons, or to the eternal

4   W. Peters, *The Spiritual Exercises of St. Ignatius,* p. 27.
5   Cited by Pedro Arrupe, "The Trinitarian Inspiration of the Ignatian Charism," *Acta Romana* 18 (1981), 121, who refers to Polanco's *De Vita Patris Ignatii* 16, in *Fontes Narrativi,* II, 152.
6   Arrupe, "The Trinitarian Inspiration," 122.

Word incarnate, or to his mother, our Lady, begging—according to the degree to which I am moved in my affectivity *(según que en sí sentiere)*—better to follow and imitate our Lord, *thus become man anew,* and then saying the Our Father" ([109]). The emphasis upon the concluding phrase is my own, to draw attention to what is characteristically Ignatian: it is through the heart and in the heart that God speaks to each individual. Accordingly, it is through the motions in my own affectivity that the mystery happens to me, that I am brought to be present to Jesus. A very ancient Christian document by an anonymous writer speaks of the risen Christ as "the One who appears as new, is discovered to be from of old, is daily born anew in the hearts of believers."[7]

In his exposition of the contemplation on the birth of Jesus ([110-116]), Ignatius reminds the exercitant of the importance of referring each mystery being contemplated to the cross. One is "to see and consider what they are doing [Mary and Joseph], that is how the journey goes, how they toil, in order that the Lord may be born in great poverty, and that after so many painful labors—hunger, thirst, heat and cold, affronts and outrages, he be brought to die upon a cross: and all this for me!" ([116]). In fact, this profound awareness of the unity of all the mysteries of our Lord's earthly life—a result, it would seem, of the *eximia illustratio* at the Cardoner—reappears in a note concerned with the contemplation of the Passion, which strongly urges that "I rouse myself to grief, compassion, anguish, making present by frequent recall the labors, fatigue, and sorrows of Christ our Lord, which he endured from the moment he was born up to the mystery of the Passion in which I am at present engaged" ([206b]).

This very Christian sense of the unity of the paschal mystery evinced in the *Exercises* is of course discernible in the writers who composed the New Testament, but nowhere is it so conspicuous as in the Christological contributions of the two greatest theologians, or rather mystics, Paul and John the evangelist. To speak, as we do, of the Incarnation, is to confess in somewhat static fashion what Paul and John with profound insight regarded as a dynamic process, as a coming-to-be-human of the Son of God throughout his entire earthly career.

For his part Paul insists with astonishing realism upon the consequences for God's Son of joining the sinful, rebellious family of the first Adam. "Him who knew no sin God made into Sin, in order that in union with him we might become God's Justice" (2 Cor 5:21). The nicety of

---

7 *Epistle to Diognetus,* 11,4.

Pauline language is to be noticed: the Apostle takes refuge in hyperbole in order to express the stark truth of the Incarnation. As we, who hope to obtain a share in it, cannot literally "become God's Justice," which remains inalienably God's, so the Son of God can be said to have been "made into Sin"—a personification in Paul—while not a sinner. Paul appears to assert that inasmuch as God the Son became a member of the human race, which without him was made up of "God-haters" (Rom 1:30), he was in a real if most mysterious way alienated from the Father. Paul daringly calls the Crucified "a curse." To his "bewitched Galatians," he declares, "Christ ransomed us from the curse of the Law by becoming for our sakes a curse (since Scripture states, 'Cursed is everyone who hangs upon a gallows'), in order that Abraham's blessing may be extended to the Gentiles, in order that we [Jews] may obtain the promised Spirit through faith" (Gal 3:13-14). And a little further he remarks, "When time reached its fulfillment, God sent forth his Son, born of woman, born under Law, in order that he might ransom those under Law, in order that we might receive the [divine] adoptive sonship" (Gal 4:4-5). Paul enunciates this startling truth in more measured tones when writing to the church of Rome. "What was an impossibility for the Law by reason of its vulnerability from the flesh, God achieved by sending His own Son in the likeness of sinful flesh and as a sin-offering. He passed condemnation on sin in that flesh, in order that the just demands of the Law might find fulfilment in us, who do not conduct ourselves according to the flesh but according to the Spirit" (Rom 8:3-4).

Now what is to be observed in each of these Pauline texts, in addition to what I termed a kind of "alienation" from God, is another reality, which Professor M. D. Hooker has happily called "interchange in Christ."[8] Through the Incarnation, which for Paul reaches to include Jesus' saving death and resurrection, Christ's being "made into Sin" effects our sharing in "God's Justice;" his becoming "a curse" results in the pagan's sharing "Abraham's blessing," the Jews' reception of "the promised Spirit;" his being "born of woman" in subjection to "law," results in "ransom" for the Jews and "adoptive sonship;" and indeed God's "sending His own Son in the likeness of sinful flesh" has contrived not only the divine condemnation of "sin in the flesh" of the incarnate Son, but "the fulfilment in us" of "the just demands of the Law." I venture to suggest that, if I rightly grasp Paul's insight into the

8   M. D. Hooker, "Interchange in Christ," *Journal of Theological Studies,* n.s. 22 (1971), 349-361.

meaning of the Incarnation, it is this. The solidarity with the children of the disobedient Adam, which the Son of God initially attempted, was vitiated by the presence of sinfulness in the human race. It was by his obedience to the Father by "being handed over to death for our sins and by being raised for our justifying" (Rom 4:25)—both, be it noted, caused by the action of his Father—that Christ finally became completely human, by uniting us through faith to himself as "the last Adam" (1 Cor 15:45). In short, the Incarnation reached its apogee in the risen and exalted Lord at his "becoming life-giving Spirit" (1 Cor 15:45).

A similarly dynamic view of the Incarnation as process has presided over the structuring of the Fourth Gospel. The initial notice given in the Prologue was laconically brief, and (as already noted) paradoxical: "the Word became flesh, and he pitched his tent among us" (1:14a, b). Yet in the same verse the community's confession of faith, "We have beheld his glory" (14c), has led the reader to expect a further development of this central mystery. John accomplishes this through the two principal divisions of his Gospel. The first twelve chapters present the incarnate Son as coming from the Father, while the balance of the book describes Jesus' return home to God through his death and exaltation—this latter being begun at his "lifting up" on the cross. One might say quite simply that the Word became flesh as Jesus attempts to enter the human family as the One sent by the Father with a message, "the Truth" about the "God no one has ever seen," which he can only disclose fully by successfully revealing who he himself is, the Son come as a member of the human family. Yet throughout his public career, although Jesus strives by words or revelation and by "signs" to achieve this, John pronounces his efforts an almost total failure (12:37-43). It is only by laying down his life "for his friends" (15:13), the supreme act of love, that Jesus succeeds finally upon the cross in communicating the Spirit, Who is "the life-giver" (6:63), Who, in Jesus' words "will take what is mine, and reveal its meaning to you" and thus "lead you along your way by the complete truth" (16:11).

This somewhat lengthy digression has perhaps been useful as it may assist our understanding of John's story of Jesus' first public appearance, which is also "the first of his signs that Jesus performed." As a consequence, we can understand the narrative we are to contemplate as the author's summons to the reader to witness the inaugural disclosure by Jesus of the mystery of the Incarnation.

1   On the third day a marriage took place at Cana in Galilee, and the mother of Jesus was there.   2   Jesus too was invited to the wedding with

his disciples. 3 When the wine gave out, the mother of Jesus remarks to him, "They have no wine left." 4 Jesus says to her, "Lady, what has that to do with you or me?—My hour has not yet come." 5 His mother speaks to the waiters, "Do whatsoever he tells you."

6 Now six stone water-jars stood there, in connection with Jewish purification-rites, capable of holding up to two or three measures apiece. 7 Jesus tells them, "Fill up the jars with water;" so they filled them to the brim. 8 He then says to them, "Now draw some off and bring it to the steward." So they brought it.

9 Now when the steward had tasted the water which had become wine, yet did not know where it came from (still the waiters who had drawn off the water knew), the steward calls out to the bridegroom, 10 and observes to him, "Everyone sets out his choice wine at the beginning; and then, when people are drunk, that which is inferior. You, on the contrary, have kept your choice wine until now!"

11 This was the first of his signs that Jesus performed at Cana in Galilee: he manifested his glory, and his disciples believed in him.

This story, in which a wealth of symbolism is perceptible, proceeds by a series of exchanges—between Jesus and his mother, Jesus and the waiters, the steward and the bridegroom. The evangelist's gloss on the narrative is designed to point the reader's attention to the incident as the first time the Word become flesh permitted his glory be seen by those who have, already at their initial encounter with Jesus (1:34-49), expressed belief in him within the limits of their Jewish faith.

Jesus and His Mother (2:1-5)

The introductory phrase "on the third day" is probably intended to refer back to the four preceding days, thus indicating this episode as the conclusion of a week. But John's use here of the traditional indicator of the resurrection (1 Cor 15:4; Mt 16:21; 17:23; 27:64; Lk 9:22; 13:32; 24:7, 21, 46; Acts 10:40) is of greater significance. As George MacRae points out, "In this light perhaps we should translate the opening words literally 'on the third day' and allow the inevitable connotation of the resurrection to stand. In this Gospel it is precisely the death and resurrection of Jesus which is the ultimate manifestation of Jesus' divine glory, and that is somehow to be seen as anticipated in the miracle of changing water to wine at Cana."[9]

Mary, "the mother of Jesus," makes but two appearances in this Gospel, here and at Calvary (19:25-27), where she replaces those who (in

9 G. W. MacRae, *Invitation to John,* pp. 47-48.

the Synoptic Passion narratives) jeer at the Crucified. Her importance in the eyes of our evangelist lies in the fact that she symbolizes the ideal disciple of Jesus. Her remark to her son on this occasion is a discreet, confident request for a remedy to an embassassing situation. Jesus' riposte is full of mystery: while he clearly distances himself from her influence, as the formal "Woman" (here rendered "Lady") implies, no discourtesy appears to be intended by his observation "What has that to do with you or me?"

Jesus' next observation, "My hour is not yet come," is best taken as an allusion by the evangelist to Jesus' Passion and resurrection, which John consistently denominates as "his hour" (7:30; 8:20; 12:23; 13:1; 17:1). In this Gospel the phrase indicates the definitive manifestation of Jesus' "glory"—his final disclosure of his own identity at the moment of his death—the Word become flesh as source of the life-giving Spirit (19:30). Accordingly, here the sacred writer presents this first "sign" by Jesus as an anticipation of this ultimate self-identification by the Son of God. His mother's order to the waiters, "Do whatsoever he tells you," is probably intended to inform the reader that she understands her son's apparent refusal as an implicit consent. This remark however, in the context of the opening section of this Gospel, may be seen to have a more significant sense. For throughout chapters 2 to 4 John is preoccupied with instructing his reader that the ultimate basis for genuine faith is *the word of Jesus,* whether or not Jesus intervenes with a "sign."

Jesus and the Waiters (2:6-8)

The presence of the six copious containers "in connection with Jewish purification-rites" seems to symbolize the Johannine theme being developed in these opening chapters of the Gospel of "the replacement of Jewish institutions and religious views" (Raymond Brown) by the presence and activity of Jesus. Brown acknowledges however the secondary character of such symbolism: "the primary focus is, as in all Johannine stories, on Jesus as the one sent by the Father to bring salvation to the world."[10] In the scene Jesus' orders to the waiters are clearly central, and as yet there is no hint of a miracle.

The Steward and the Bridegroom (2:9-10)

The transformation of the water into "choice wine" yields in importance to the puzzlement of the steward, who "did not know where it

10   R. E. Brown, *John I–XII,* pp. 103-104.

came from." Nor, it is to be noted, did the waiters "who knew" enlighten him. Likewise, the other person most concerned with the lack of wine at the festivities—the bridegroom—remains silent in ignorance. The mysterious origin of the wine, bountiful gift of Jesus the guest, becomes a pointer to the mystery of Jesus himself, his heavenly origin with the Father who has sent him. The question, "Whence?" *(pothen)* will run like a thread throughout John's Gospel (1:49; 3:8; 4:11; 6:5; 7:27-28; 8:14; 9:29-30; 19:9), as does also the question "Where?" (1:39; 3:8; 7:11, 35; 8:14, 19; 9:12; 11:57; 13:36; 14:5; 16:5; 20:2, 13, 15). Both themes indicate the importance in the eyes of our evangelist of his under- lying challenge to the reader, as has already been remarked, "Where is the risen Jesus for me now?"

Final Comment by the Evangelist (2:11)

John designates this first miracle by Jesus "the first of his signs," thereby notifying the reader that the primary significance of the miracu- lous in his Gospel lies in its Christological value. In an earlier chapter the salient features of such "signs" were described. Accordingly here it is enough to recall the "sign" is exclusively a work of Jesus (see 10:41), and only during his public ministry. Such "signs", besides exhibiting a sym- bolic meaning, consistently present "a solidly 'material' aspect" (Schnackenburg).[11] This concrete historical character establishes the in- trinsic relationship of "the sign" to the revelation of the mystery of Jesus as the divine Word and Son of God, who "became flesh." It is in large measure by narrating certain carefully selected "signs" that John will lead the believing reader to appreciate how far the term "Messiah" in its Christian sense transcends the original Jewish meaning, just as "Son of God" applied to Jesus surpasses the Old Testament meaning of that title. This is evident from the conclusions of the entire book, where John can declare, "These [signs] have been recorded however in order that you may believe that Jesus is the Messiah, the Son of God, and that by be- lieving you may possess life in his name" (20:31).

One vital question remains to be investigated—the plausibility, from the historical viewpoint, of the evangelist's assertion that Jesus "manifested his glory, and his disciples believed in him." There are in fact a number of reasons for accepting the historicity of the miracle and the reality of the belief in Jesus credited to his followers. While the other miraculous "signs" in the Fourth Gospel parallel those found in the

---

11 Schnackenburg, *John*, I, 525.

Synoptic tradition, this first miracle at Cana appears to be without precedent. However, as Brown remarks, "Is changing water into wine so different from the multiplication of loaves?"[12] In fact, the thaumaturgical element attested in the evangelical traditions is so inextricably interwoven with the teaching of Jesus, that it becomes impossible to accept the latter while rejecting the former.

Indeed, John's claim that this revelation of his "glory" by Jesus caused his Jewish disciples to put faith in him becomes historically comprehensible, once one realizes that, throughout the Old Testament, abundance of wine was regarded as a significant feature of the future messianic age. The prophet Hosea announced, "On that day, says the Lord, I will answer: the earth will respond to the grain and wine and oil" (Hos 2:23-24; see Gen 49:11), while Amos had promised, "And then on that day the mountains shall drip new wine" (Am 9:13-14; see Joel 3:13-18). Accordingly, it is perfectly plausible that these disciples, whom this Gospel portrays as always open to the possibility of unprecedented religious experiences in their following of Jesus, should have seen in this miracle the incipient realization of Israel's messianic hope.

Indeed, Jesus' presence at this wedding-celebration and his bountiful gift of a huge quantity of "choice wine"—some one hundred and twenty gallons!—corresponds to certain characteristics of his which appear in the Synoptics. There he speaks of himself parabolically as "the bridegroom" (Mk 2:19-20). In fact, the earlier evangelical traditions incorporated into the first three Gospels preserved the memory of a reproach made to Jesus as a *bon vivant* by contrast with the ascetical John the Baptist (Mt 11:18-19). Luke in particular records Jesus' not infrequent dining with Pharisees (Lk 11:37; 14:1), no less than "sinners" (Lk 15:2), while several of the peculiarly Lucan parables feature splendid dinners. The fourth evangelist narrates a dinner-party held in Jesus' honor by the grateful family of Bethany (12:1-11). It is significant that one of the Marcan sayings, which contemporary critics judge to be an authentic logion by the Jesus of history *(ipsissima vox Jesu)*,[13] foretells his own vindication by God beyond his death, picturing it as a participation in the messianic banquet. "Amen I tell you: I shall no longer drink of the fruit of the vine, until that day when I drink it new in the Kingdom of God" (Mk 14:25).

---

12   R. E. Brown, *John I–XII*, p. 101.
13   R. H. Fuller, *The Foundations of New Testament Christology* (London and Glasgow, 1965), p. 107: "This saying, unlike the bread and cup words, suffered progressive atrophy in the church's liturgical tradition, and is therefore not open to suspicion as a church formation."

Mention was made earlier in this chapter of the deep awareness displayed by Ignatius of the unity of Jesus' entire earthly career. This keen sensitivity to the unity of the paschal mystery, it was asserted, is especially characteristic of Paul and the fourth evangelist. Indeed, it may be said that in a very real sense each episode in any of our Gospels contains in miniature the good news of salvation. Accordingly, it is justifiable procedure to present the first of Jesus' "signs," the story of the wedding at Cana, as a contemplation of the Incarnation. That in fact in so doing one is faithful to the mind of Ignatius may be gathered from his instructions that in all the contemplations from the Gospel-texts for the Second Week, the third prelude remains the same. It is instructive to recall his insistence upon the invariability of this prayer in the remark he makes regarding this prelude in the contemplation on the nativity. "The third (prelude) will be the same as in the preceding contemplation and identical in form with it" ([113]). William Peters describes this petitionary prayer accurately, when he says "What the exercitant in fact asks is that he may pray well, that he may completely become his own true self in the new reality re-created for him in the first and second preludes . . . When in the second week 'what I desire' is to know the Lord better in order to love Him more intensely and follow Him more faithfully, the exercitant really prays for the grace not to be a mere outsider or spectator . . . this is the same as asking for the grace to be true to his own self, here and now being present at the mystery of the Incarnation, Nativity, Baptism and so forth."[14]

---

14   W. Peters, *The Spiritual Exercises of St. Ignatius,* p. 34.

Chapter 6

JESUS' FIRST SYMBOLIC ACTION IN JERUSALEM
(2:13-22)

T he transitional statement, employed by the evangelist as a divider between his story of the wedding in Cana and that of the symbolic purging of the temple-area in Jerusalem, may catch the interest of the student of the *Exercises,* since it appears to contradict a remark by Ignatius (possibly a borrowing from medieval piety), which is used to introduce the contemplation of Jesus' baptism by John in the Jordan. "After Christ our Lord had bid farewell to his blessed Mother, he went from Nazareth to the river Jordan . . ." ([273]). John states, "After this he descended to Capharnaum with his mother and his brothers [and disciples], though they remained there not many days" (2:12). This inclusion of an item taken from some independent tradition by John assumes that the mother of Jesus accompanied him during his public ministry as he journeyed about Galilee. And in fact this is consonant with what is known of the practice by itinerant rabbis, who were accompanied in their peregrinations by their family. A propos of the contemplation suggested for the fifth day of the Second Week, Hugo Rahner observes, "The departure from Nazareth, which the Bible mentions only in passing (Mk 1:9) . . . becomes of supreme importance for Ignatius in the process of the Election as a whole, since 'The matter of the election will be introduced from the contemplation on Nazareth to the Jordan inclusive;' and this is the place for the consideration ([164]) which culminates in supreme conformity with Christ and his victory over Satan—the third kind of humility."[1] In view of this, it is of interest to recall that the fourth evangelist had already drawn attention to Jesus' awareness that, with the opening of his public life (at Cana), he was determined to devote himself entirely to the service of his Father, free of any influence by his mother. This I have taken to be the fundamental meaning of the otherwise obscure remark, "What has that to do with you or me?—my hour is not yet come" (2:4). Such "freedom for the gospel" Jesus will assert in re-

1   H. Rahner, *Ignatius the Theologian,* p. 105.

jecting the worldly suggestion of his unbelieving brothers that he court publicity in the center of Judaism (7:2-9). In fact, his constant devotion to seeking and carrying out his Father's will becomes a refrain (4:34; 5:30; 6:38-40; see also 9:31).

In view of the Ignatian interest in Jesus' departure from Nazareth, Rudolph Schnackenburg's comment on the Johannine verse is relevant. He considers the phrase, "not many days," to be a hint by the sacred writer that "Jesus is eager to start his mighty work in Jerusalem." And the distinguished German Catholic exegete asserts that "This is more than a merely historical record. It indicates a deliberate purpose on the part of Jesus, which is dictated by the will of the Father. Hence 2:12 is also more than a stage in an itinerary, in the eyes of the evangelist. Jesus is not tied to home or family or friends, but presses on to the self-revelation which is to be made in the city of God."[2]

By way of prolegomenon to the contemplation of Jesus' action in vindicating the sacredness of "the holy place," the precincts of the temple in Jerusalem, it may be helpful to take cognizance of the diverging insights into its prophetic symbolism which all four evangelists, as well as the author of Hebrews (Heb 9:11-14), are at pains to highlight in relating this significant incident. Despite the varying facets of meaning which these inspired writers have intuited in the act of cleansing the area surrounding the central shrine of Judaism, all agree in ranking it with those prophetic "charades," familiar to readers of the Old Testament from the conduct of Israel's prophets. Thus Isaiah under divine orders walked about naked three years as a warning to his people, during the imminent peril to Judah from the might of Sargon II of Assyria (711 B.C.), not to attempt the relief of Ashdod (Is 20:1-6). Jeremiah in his turn, after the Neobabylonians had defeated Egyptian armies at Carchemish (605 B.C.), was by God's command to bury a loin-cloth in a riverbank, until it rotted (Jer 13:1-11), as a prophetic warning to Judah of Nebuchadnezzar's destruction of Jerusalem in 597 B.C. Thus it is plausible that "the Jews," on witnessing this symbolic act by Jesus, from their familiarity with the Scriptures of Israel, might well have recognized the prophetic character of what he was attempting.

It will be recalled that Jeremiah had predicted the destruction of the sanctuary in Jerusalem in his so-called temple discourse, which Mark excerpted in his account of the event we are contemplating. "Do you think that this house, this house that bears My name, is a robbers' cave?

---

2   Schnackenburg, *John,* I, 343.

. . . Go now to My place that stood at Shiloh, where at first I made My name to dwell and note what I did to it because of My people Israel's wickedness . . . Now what I did to Shiloh I will do to this house . . . in which you put your trust, the place I gave to you and your fathers'' (Jer 7:11-14). Mark refers to this prediction to interpret the mimed prophecy which Jesus acts out. As will be seen, John has recourse to other Old Testament passages.

To appreciate our evangelist's originality, it may help to realize that he has (by contrast with Mark and his Synoptic colleagues) combined three items of the evangelical tradition, which—to judge from Mark— originally existed as independent, one of the other. There is the symbolic act of Jesus itself (Mk 11:15-18); the querying, by "the high priests, the scribes, and the elders," regarding the licitness of Jesus' action: "By what authority are you doing this, or who gave you this authority to do this?" (Mk 11:28); and finally the statement alleged at the Sanhedrin trial to have been uttered by Jesus: "I will destroy this sanctuary made with hands and within three days I will build a different one, not made with hands" (Mk 14:58). One might in addition recall that the mockery of passersby at the cross refers back to this prophecy (Mk 15:29), while Mark himself notes its fulfillment as a consequence of Jesus' death (Mk 15:38)—both incidents omitted in John's Passion-account, which also passes over in silence the trial before the Sanhedrin. This sacred writer seems to have judged them to have been included in his account of the cleansing of the temple-precincts.

Before one contemplates John's version of this episode, it may be useful to observe the dramatic manner of its presentation in a sequence of seven moments: (1) Jesus' prophetic action with an authoritative word of command (vv. 13-16); (2) John's gloss on the (post-Easter) "remembering" of Psalm 69 (v. 17); (3) the challenge to Jesus by Jewish unfaith (v. 18); (4) Jesus' enigmatic prediction (v. 19); (5) the Jewish retort (v. 20); (6) a second gloss by the evangelist (v. 21); (7) a fuller description of the apostolic "remembering," with resultant Christian belief in both the Old Testament and the utterance of Jesus. The notable feature of this careful structuring by the writer is the centering of the unit in Jesus' prophecy, intended to draw attention to it as the dominant theme in the entire narrative (see 4 above).

2:13   As the Jewish Passover was near, Jesus went up to Jerusalem. 14   Now in the temple-precincts he found the dealers in cattle, sheep, and doves, with the money-changers sitting at their tables,   15   and making a sort of whip with some cords, he expelled them from the sacred enclosure together with their sheep and cattle, and he spilled out the specie of the money-changers by overturning their tables,   16   while to the dealers in doves he said, "Get these things out of here! Stop turning my Father's house into a market!" [Zech 14:21].

17   His disciples were to recall that it was written, "Zeal for your house will devour me" [Ps 69:10].   18   Whereupon the Jews challenged him, "What sign are you showing us, to account for these things you are doing?"   19   Jesus replied by stating, "Destroy this sanctuary, and within three days I will raise it up!"   20   At this the Jews rejoined, "Forty-six years has this sanctuary been under construction: yet you yourself will raise it up in three days?"   21   He however had meant his body as the sanctuary. 22   Thus when he was raised from death, his disciples remembered that he had said this. So they believed the Scripture and the word Jesus had uttered.

1. Jesus' Symbolic Prophetic Action (2:13-16)

In the brief introduction he gives, John draws attention to the proximity of Passover and to Jesus' attendance at this pilgrimage-feast. While Mark's structuring of his Gospel permitted mention of only a single journey by Jesus to the cultic center of Judaism, Matthew and Luke had alluded in passing to his earlier efforts to win over the Jerusalemites (Mt 23:37; Lk 13:34). Our evangelist repeats his remark, "the Jewish Passover was near") at 6:4 (when Jesus seems not to have observed the feast in the holy city), and at 11:55 (see also 12:1). And in his solemn introduction to the second major section of his Gospel he again mentions this third Passover (13:1). In each instance the Jewish paschal observance provides a context for a revelation concerning the new religious relationship with God Jesus is come to inaugurate. This disclosure of the sacred writer's intention is an important clue to the meaning of this first appearance by Jesus in Jerusalem.

Rather breathlessly John describes the scene that met Jesus' eyes in the sacred enclosure—vv. 14 through 16 are a single sentence in the Greek text. In order to appreciate the symbolic nature of Jesus' subsequent actions, it is necessary to bear in mind that, like Mark before him, John nowhere implies criticism of the various commercial transactions, and it is noteworthy that he makes no mention of an objection by Jesus towards those who were buying or having their money changed (see Mk 11:15), devout Jews who wished to offer sacrifice or pay the temple-tax. These operations were indeed legitimate, as the ancient cult of God in Israel prescribed offerings of animals or birds. Moreover, the presence of "money-changers" was to provide worshippers with the Tyrian half-shekel no longer in currency for two centuries. Jesus' less violent treatment of "the dealers in doves," who made it possible for the poor to offer a less costly sacrifice, has occasioned a sympathetic remark in the Ignatian text (a typical medieval embroidery of the narrative, probably taken from Ludolf the Carthusian): "To the poor vendors of doves he said kindly, 'Take these away: do not make my Father's house an emporium' " ([277]).

The symbolic nature of Jesus' conduct also becomes clear when it is recalled that the expulsion of traffickers, like the misnamed "triumphal entry" of our Lord into the city, is nowhere included in the Gospel-accounts of Jesus' indictment before the Sanhedrin. The most significant feature of this first part of the Johannine narrative however is the author's allusion to the description by Zechariah (in fact, an addition by a later editor, possibly about 200 B.C.) of the triumphal "Day of the Lord," as a kind of eschatological celebration of *Sukkōth,* to honor God as king of Israel. The prophet observes that all military and commercial interests are to be subject to religious authority, and he ends his book abruptly by announcing, "On that day . . . every pot in Jerusalem and in Judah will be holy to the Lord of hosts . . . On that day there shall no longer be any merchant in the house of the Lord of hosts" (Zech 14:20-21). John's formulation of Jesus' words to the "dealers in doves" is reminiscent of this prophetic text: "Stop turning my Father's house into a market!"

2. *"Remembering": First Comment (2:17)*

Mark cited two different scriptural texts to help his reader grasp the meaning he himself had detected in Jesus' action: "My house shall be called a house of prayer for all the nations" (Is 56:7), and he adds an excerpt from Jeremiah: "Yet you have made it 'a robbers' cave' " (Jer 7:11) (Mk 11:17), originally a condemnation of the practice of superstition under Jehoiakim. For Mark the incident was a prediction that the Christian community was meant above all to become "a house of prayer" for all believers, and thus, in line with this intention of Jesus, Mark's own church must undergo a profound moral conversion.

For John however the prophetic-symbolic act of Jesus points ahead to that religion "in spirit and truth" (4:21-24) yet to be ushered in—and only in consequence of Jesus' glorification. Accordingly, the sacred author makes a reference to Jesus' saving death, which is to be caused by his "zeal" for the house of God. To this end he employs a line from a psalm which the early Church read as a prophecy of Jesus' death. To make his point, John changes the verb into the future tense: "Zeal for your house will consume me" (Ps 69:10), and he makes the first reference to the post-Easter "remembering" on the part of the disciples after their reception through the Spirit of Christian faith. To this important Johannine conception we shall return presently. For the moment it is sufficient to be aware that, by his reference to God's creation of the future, spiritual place of worship (from Zechariah) and to the link (through Ps 69) between the death of Jesus and his reformation of religion, the evangelist is preparing his reader to understand the enigmatic saying by Jesus, which he has made the chief focus of his entire narrative.

3. Jesus' Action Challenged by the Jews (2:18)

The riposte of "the Jews" is most commonly translated "What sign . . . can you show as authority for your actions?" (New English Bible), where the term "authority," missing in John, is found at Mark 11:28. In my opinion the archaic King James' version is more accurate: "What sign shewest thou unto us, seeing that thou doest these things?"[3] My own rendering of the sentence leaves open the possibility that John regards Jesus' symbolic act as a "sign," like others in his Gospel. The majority of commentators however consider the miraculous as an essential element in the Johannine sign, with the exception of Dr. C. H. Dodd.[4]

4. The Enigmatic Prophecy by Jesus (2:19)

The question by the Jews leads into what for our evangelist is the focal point of his entire story: "Destroy this sanctuary, and within three days I will raise it up!" Many interpreters have tried unsuccessfully to explain this mysterious statement by Jesus from an erroneous presupposition that he meant the contemporary structure, the Herodian temple in the first half of the assertion, while in the second part he signified his own body. The evangelist's aside to his reader (v. 21), "He however had meant his body," might seem at first glance to lend weight to such a superficial view. However, the real clue has been provided by Xavier Léon-Dufour, who pointed out that the declaration in its entirety is comprehensible only when taken at two distinct levels of meaning: that which those who heard Jesus utter it could have grasped in the context of Old Testament prophecy, and that which would be intelligible only later to a

---

3 Robert W. Funk, *A Greek Grammar of the New Testament* (Chicago, 1961), #456 (2), remarks that here *hoti* (which I have turned as "to account for") is equivalent to "why."

4 C. H. Dodd, *The Interpretation of the Fourth Gospel* (Cambridge, 1963), pp. 303, 384-385.

Christian reader of this Gospel.[5] This satisfactory solution deserves further amplification.

To the ears of the original auditors, Jesus' use of the ironical imperative "Destroy this sanctuary," should have been familiar from the usage typical of Israel's prophets (Is 8:9; Am 4:4), who were accustomed to couch an ominous prediction of the divine punishment to be visited upon their people's wickedness in this menacing manner. And in fact the entire saying might have recalled to their minds the graphic language Malachi had employed to foretell the messianic rebuilding of the temple by the eschatological purification of divine worship. "Take heed! I am sending My messenger to ready the way for Me; and on a sudden the Lord, Whom you seek, will come into the temple, with the messenger of the covenant in whom you take delight . . . But who can endure the day of His coming, and who can stand when He appears? He is like a refiner's fire, like fuller's lye . . . He will cleanse the sons of Levi, and refine them like gold and silver, until they can offer acceptable sacrifice to the Lord" (Mal 3:1-3). And in his reflections upon the life of Jeremiah, who of all the prophets most closely typified Jesus himself, the sage Sirach had declared, "With the exception of David, Hezekiah, and Josiah, they were all evil, those kings of Judah: they deserted the law of the most High, and so the royal line came to an end. Accordingly, He handed over their power to others, their glory to a foreign nation, who burned the chosen city, the city of the sanctuary, leaving its streets deserted, as Jeremiah had prophesied. For they had maltreated him, who from the womb had been consecrated a prophet, to root up, destroy, and demolish, but also to build and to plant" (Sir 49:4-7).

5. Objection of the Jews (2:20)

Raymond Brown observes in his commentary that the rejoinder by "the Jews" in the following verse of John's narrative is an indication that they had understood Jesus to be speaking of the contemporary sanctuary.[6] It will be recalled that Mark had included in his report of Jesus' trial the fact that he was judged, from the testimony of "false witnesses," to have made an earlier claim to be Messiah by his alleged distinction between "this sanctuary made with hands" and "a different one, not made with hands" (Mk 14:58). For in the sequel the high priest immediately demands to know, "Are you the Messiah, the son of the

---

5   Xavier Léon-Dufour, S.J., "Le Signe du Temple selon saint Jean," in *Mélanges Jules Lebreton* I, *Recherches de Science Religieuse* 39 (1951), 155-175.
6   R. E. Brown, *John I-XII,* p. 121.

Blessed?'' (v. 60). These reflections are of considerable help in enabling the exercitant to assess the plausibility of Jesus' saying in John as one actually uttered by the historical Jesus.

6. Jesus Glorified, New Sign of God's Presence (2:21)

Of greater value for our contemplation in the context of the Exercises is the evangelist's manifest intention to direct attention principally upon the person of Jesus and so underscore the deeply Christological sense of this statement. Such indeed, when correctly understood, is the real point of John's comment, ''He however had meant his body as the sanctuary.'' Since its erection under Solomon the inner shrine on the holy mountain in Jerusalem had been the unambiguous sign of God's abiding, protective presence to his people. In the eyes of the fourth evangelist, it is now the exalted Jesus, once lifted up in glory upon the cross, who is the new locus of God's presence, replacing the old sanctuary. As a result, John will not find it necessary to include the Marcan story of the rending of the veil hiding the holy of holies, which for that author symbolized the ''desacralization'' of Israel's shrine as an immediate consequence of the death of Jesus (Mk 15:38). The homilist who composed the so-called epistle to the Hebrews would in turn interpret the meaning of Jesus' entire earthly career by a bold use of imagery derived from the Gospel-account. ''But now Christ has come, high priest of good things already in existence, through the greater and more perfect tent, not made by hands—that is, not pertaining to this creation. He has entered once for all with his own blood . . . into the sanctuary, having secured an everlasting deliverance'' (Heb 9:11-12). And this same preacher has ingeniously employed the incident of the tearing of the sanctuary-veil to summon his wavering flock to participate in the Christian liturgy, by announcing that this event, which followed upon Jesus' death, has provided free access to God himself. ''Since then, my brothers, we have confidence for the entry into the sanctuary by the blood of Jesus, [an entry] he has inaugurated as a recent and living way through the veil, that is, his flesh, and since we have a great high priest set over the house of God, let us approach with a sincere heart in serene confidence of faith . . .'' (Heb. 10:19-22).

As one endeavors through contemplation to impress on oneself the centrality in the Johannine narrative of Jesus' saying, ''Destroy this sanctuary, and within three days I will raise it up,'' it is helpful to bear in mind that this occasion constitutes the first confrontation in this Gospel between Jesus and ''the Jews.'' Consequently, John wishes to set their opposition to Jesus in sharp contrast with the attitude of the disciples, whom he depicts in the preceding verse as seeking an explanation of their master's symbolic act in "the Scriptures." This rationalistic demand for a proof by Jesus of his messianic role may well be articulated in the Jewish question, "What sign are you showing us, to account for these things you are doing?" It would then be equivalent to the query later addressed to Jesus at Capharnaum, "So what sign will you yourself perform, in order that we may see and believe you?" (6:30), and these hostile critics would already be displaying that incredulity for which they become notorious in the course of this Gospel. Yet, even if (as I suspect) John here implies that the cleansing of the temple-precincts is a "sign," his silence here about any manifestation of his "glory" by Jesus (2:11) shows that Jesus is even now passing judgment upon these opponents by the act of cleansing the temple-area. This may be the theological reason for John's setting this narrative at the commencement of Jesus' public life, as Père Léon-Dufour has suggested, in the article already mentioned, where he alludes to a remark by the author of First Peter, "God's own time *(kairos)* has come for initiating the judgment upon the house of God. Now if it commences with us, what will be the fate of those refusing faith in the gospel of God?" (1 Pt 4:17).[7]

In the framework of the *Spiritual Exercises,* this early antithesis between the openness of the disciples to an as-yet unsuspected religious experience in their following of Jesus and the deliberate self-inflicted blindness of "the Jews" may be seen as an anticipation of Two Standards and the process of the Ignatian Election.

7. *"Remembering": Second Comment (2:22)*

The evangelist terminates his dramatic story by providing an initial explanation of what he means by "remembering," that post-Easter reflection of the earliest disciples, with the help of their new-found faith in Jesus. Father Brown remarks that "The evangelist has been kind enough to warn us in vs. 22 (and perhaps 17) that his theological understanding of the scene far exceeds what was understood when the scene took place."[8] Accordingly, it will be helpful to repeat here something of what was said in an earlier chapter about this Johannine name for what Anselm would later describe as *fides quaerens intellectum* (faith seeking understanding).

While John correctly credits those who had known Jesus personally

---

7   Léon-Dufour, "Le Signe du Temple," 167.
8   R. E. Brown, *John I-XII,* p. 121.

during his earthly life with inaugurating the highly significant activity of "remembering," it should be borne in mind that it was also faithfully continued by Paul and by the earliest Gospel-writers. Yet it must be acknowledged that the book John produced for his community remains the supreme example of this "remembering." Moreover, it may without exaggeration be suggested that this characteristically Christian reflection with faith, which has been traditionally known in eastern and western spirituality as *memoria Christi* (keeping our Lord in mind) has ever been an important feature of what is known as "apostolic succession." While the handing on to succeeding generations of believers the *vera imago Jesu* (the genuine image of Jesus) is the chief service of the teaching office of the Church, as Vatican II teaches in *Dei Verbum,* the Constitution on divine revelation [10], still this duty devolves also in a meaningful way upon all believers.[9] The Christian is summoned not only to bear witness to the gospel by the way he or she lives it out, but also to assimilate the message of Jesus presented by the inspired writings in the Bible. In brief, it is not too much to say that each believer should be concerned to create his or her own image of Jesus, by means of the prayerful contemplation of those personal images of our Lord exhibited by each of the four evangelists, as well as that displayed in the Pauline letters. This surely is the intention of Ignatius of Loyola which he expressed so forcefully in Annotation 2. "The person who contemplates the genuine grounds of the history [found in the Gospels], by ranging over it and reflecting upon it *for oneself,* will surely uncover something which clarifies that history and makes it deeply felt, whether by his own reflection, or through the enlightenment of his understanding by the divine power."

Accordingly, John's final statement in this narrative of the cleansing of the temple-area by Jesus deserves one's close consideration. "Thus

---

9   The perceptive comments of Josef (now Cardinal) Ratzinger on this point deserve attention. "The last section of Chapter II describes the relation of the Church to Scripture and tradition as the heritage which has been entrusted to it. It first makes the point that the preservation and active realization of the word is the business of the whole people of God, not merely the hierarchy. The ecclesial nature of the word, on which this idea is based, is therefore not simply a question which concerns the teaching office, but embraces the whole community of the faithful. If one compares the text with . . . *Humani Generis* . . . the progress that has been made is clear . . . For the first time a text of the teaching office expressly points out the subordination of the teaching office to the word, i.e. its function as a servant . . . The explicit emphasis on the ministerial function of the teaching office must be welcomed as warmly as the statement that its primary service is to listen . . . At the same time the contrast between the 'listening' and the 'teaching' Church is thus reduced to its true measure . . .": see *Commentary on the Documents of Vatican II,* Vol. III (Freiburg-im-Br., 1968), gen. ed. H. Vorgrimmler, tr. W. Glen-Doepel, Hilda Graef, et al., pp. 196-197; Ratzinger reflects on no. 10, Ch. 2, *Dei Verbum.*

when he was raised from death, his disciples remembered that he had said this. So they believed the Scripture and the word Jesus had uttered." Such remembering (as has been remarked in an earlier chapter) is not simply historical recall of the past earthly life of Jesus. Rather, it is, under grace, an important element in the loving effort to make present to oneself Jesus' words and actions, in such a way that they speak to one's own contemporary situation, flooding the understanding with wonder at the depths of meaning they contain, firing the heart with love towards the risen Lord, who thus speaks at the very center of one's affectivity.

It will be only in the second half of his Gospel that the evangelist will reveal to his reader the identity of the One, Who while bringing forward no new revelation, speaks through the words and actions of the earthly Jesus, disclosing to the eyes of faith their hidden sense. John and his community will know that, already in his own lifetime here below, Jesus had announced this great good news to his disciples. "I have spoken these things to you, while abiding among you; but the Paraclete, the Holy Spirit, Whom the Father will send in my name, *He* will teach you every-thing and make you remember all that I have told you" (14:25-26). "I still have much to tell you, but you cannot bear it now. But when *He,* the Spirit of truth will come, He will lead you along the way by the complete truth. For He will not speak on His own, but whatever He will hear He will utter—He will unveil the meaning of future events to you. He in fact will glorify me, because He will take what is mine and unveil its meaning to you" (16:12-14). It is this promise by Jesus to send the Spirit to each member of the community, Who alone at the very center of the self can shed light upon the mystery of Jesus, that is to guide the believing Chris-tian in the life-long quest of meaning for his or her own life by contem-plating the words and actions of Jesus. It is in fact this ongoing enterprise which Ignatius took so seriously in trying to articulate what he meant by "Spiritual Exercises." "By the name, Spiritual Exercises, is to be understood every way of examining one's conscience, of meditating, contemplating, of prayer both vocal and mental, and of other spiritual activities to be described later on. For indeed as strolling, walking, run-ning are bodily exercises, so in similar fashion every way of readying and disposing a person to rid the self of all disordered affections, and—once rid of them—to seek and find God's will for the direction of one's life, for the soul's salvation, is named 'Spiritual Exercises' " (Annotation 1).

As he concludes the narrative we have been considering, John points ahead to the source of his own deeper understanding of Jesus' words and actions, which lies in the blessed period after the resurrection, when (although as yet he does not name Him) the Paraclete will be bestowed upon the community of faith by the glorified Jesus (7:39). For the moment, our evangelist contents himself with enunciating two principal results of this presence of the Holy Spirit: The disciples "believed the Scripture," where through their new Christian, Easter faith they found God's will and dynamic action in the life of the Lord announced beforehand; and they "believed the word Jesus had uttered" on this significant occasion during his earthly life. The lesson which John considers of paramount importance and which he is concerned to instil in his reader in these opening chapters of his Gospel, is that the true ground for authentic faith remains always *the word of Jesus*—whether or not its inception and growth be also assisted by "signs."

Chapter 7

JESUS' SUCCESSES AMONG THE SAMARITANS
(4:4-42)

The first evangelist, Mark, nowhere mentions Samaria or its inhabitants when narrating Jesus' public ministry, and the Matthean Jesus in his instructions to the Twelve, before dispatching them on their initial missionary enterprise, expressly excludes any contact with these people, for long enemies of "the house of Israel" (Mt 10:5). The Lucan Gospel begins the account of Jesus' last journey to Jerusalem from Galilee by reporting how his attempt to seek hospitality in a Samaritan village was repulsed (Lk 9:51-56). Luke however displays a certain interest in and sympathy for Samaritans by recording the celebrated parable of the Good Samaritan (Lk 10:30-37), and also the singular gratitude expressed by one of ten lepers he had cured during the journey to Jerusalem—"and he was himself a Samaritan" (Lk 17:11-19). In his second volume, indeed, this evangelist has the risen Jesus include Samaria in his commission to the now Christian apostles (Acts 1:8), and he later describes a highly successful evangelization of that territory by Philip, who is followed by Peter and John (8:4-25)—an event caused by the expulsion from Jerusalem of the anti-temple Hellenists, following the death of Stephen. Luke somewhat later inserts a brief summary of the progress of "the church throughout the whole of Judea and Galilee and Samaria" (Acts 9:31). And he notes a visit by Paul and Barnabas, delegates of Antioch to Jerusalem, to Samaritan Christians (Acts 15:3). These data about the Christianization of certain sections of Samaria provide some background for John's story of Jesus' sojourn in a particular Samaritan town, designated in his narrative as "Sychar" (4, 5), probably Shechem in the opinion of Raymond Brown.

This dramatic account by our evangelist, which will be seen to reflect the presence in his own community of a number of Samaritan converts towards the end of the first century, falls naturally into three episodes. Firstly, the well-loved narrative of Jesus' winning an anonymous woman to faith in himself without any of the "signs" he had previously performed (4:4-30). Secondly, a dialogue between Jesus and his disciples, which develops into an instruction on the future Christian missionary enterprise (4:31-38); finally, a brief account of the reactions of the Samaritan townsfolk to Jesus and his message (4:39-42). Accordingly, our reflections on this series of events will follow this tripartite division.

1. Jesus Reveals His Identity to a Samaritan Woman (4:4-30).

4   Now he [Jesus] had of necessity to travel through Samaria.   5   Thus he comes to a city of Samaria called Sychar, near the terrain Jacob had given his son Joseph.   6   It was there the spring of Jacob was located; so Jesus, thoroughly tired out from his journey, simply sat down at the spring—it was about the sixth hour.

7   A woman from Samaria arrived to draw water. Jesus asks her, "Give me a drink."   8   (For his disciples were absent, having gone off to the city in order to buy food.)   9   Now the Samaritan woman says to him, "How is it that you, Jew as you are, ask a drink of me, who am a Samaritan?" (Jews have no dealings with Samaritans).   10   In reply Jesus said to her, "If you only knew God's gift, and who it is who asks you, 'Give me a drink,' you for your part would have asked him, and he would have given you living water."   11   The woman says to him, "Sir, you haven't even a bucket, and the well is deep! So where can you obtain living water?   12   Surely you are not greater than Jacob, our father, who gave us the well —and himself used to drink from it, as well as his sons and his flocks?"   13   In response Jesus said to her, "Everyone drinking some of this water will become thirsty again.   14   But whoever drinks the water I will give him will never in future thirst. Indeed, the water I will give him will become a spring within him, bubbling up unto eternal life."   15   The woman says to him, "Sir, give this water to me, so that I may not be thirsty, nor have to keep coming here to draw water."

16   He says to her, "Go home, call your man, and come back here!"   17   The woman answered him, "I've no man!" Jesus says to her, "You put it nicely—'I've no man!'   18   Actually you have had five men, yet the man you now have is not your man. There is some truth in what you say."   19   The woman tells him, "Sir, I perceive you are yourself a prophet!—   20   Our fathers have worshipped upon this mountain, yet you people claim the place to worship is in Jerusalem."   21   Jesus tells her, "Trust me, lady, an hour is coming when neither upon this mountain, nor in Jerusalem will [all of] you worship the Father.   22   As for you others, you know nothing of what you worship, whereas we know what we worship—salvation is to come from the Jews.   23   And still, an hour is coming—it is already here!—when true worshippers will adore the Father in Spirit and truth. For actually it is worshippers of this kind the Father is seeking.   24   God is Spirit: thus it is the worshippers in Spirit and truth He wills to adore Him."   25   The woman tells him, "I know Messiah is to come—the one called 'the

Anointed.' Whenever he comes, he will unveil the meaning of everything for us." 26 Jesus informs her, "I am *he*—the One who speaks with you!"
27 Upon this, his disciples returned and were disconcerted that he was talking with a woman. None however said, "What are you seeking?", or "What are you talking about with her?" 28 Thereupon the woman left her bucket and went off to the city, where she keeps telling people, 29 "Come, see a person who told me everything I ever did!—Might he not be the Messiah?" 30 They came forth from the city, and began to make their way to him.

John's main interest in Jesus' short stay of "two days" in Samaria is his revelation of himself as "Messiah" to the woman and as "the Savior of the world" to the villagers, and this, without working any "sign." In line with this, the evangelist provides, in this first section, a carefully nuanced account of the gradual change in the woman's reactions to Jesus. While she repeatedly misunderstands Jesus and the statements he makes, she remains interested and open to his mysterious promises.

The story starts with the remark that Jesus "had of necessity to travel through Samaria,"—a hint that his selection of this route, instead of the alternative one avoiding Samaria, was governed by the will of God *(edei)*. Accordingly, he passed through territory associated with the patriarchs, Jacob and Joseph, where Jacob's well, the deepest in Palestine, is still found. It is fed from a source, hence John refers to it as "the spring of Jacob" or "the well." The description of Jesus draws attention to the reality of the Incarnation: completely human, he was so "thoroughly tired out from his journey" that he "simply sat down at the spring." The detail that it was noon-time ("the sixth hour"), a time when no woman would normally draw water, provides a clue to the characterization of the woman who now "arrives to draw water." She is a pariah in her town, avoiding the customary times, sunrise and after sunset, when other women gathered at the well to obtain water and exchange gossip—of which she was probably a frequent object.

Jesus takes the initiative by violating semitic convention: a man did not speak to any woman, even his wife, in public. He "seeks" to disclose his identity to this person. The term appears later in the disciples' unexpressed question, "What are you seeking?", and in Jesus' announcement of the new kind of worshipper "the Father is seeking." Here John's insistence on the Incarnation is to be noted: it is in Jesus that the Father seeks to reveal Himself.

The woman's first reaction to the simple request, "Give me a drink", appears hostile and critical, reflecting the centuries of bitterness and hatred which poisoned relations between Jews and Samaritans. The latter, a hybrid race descended from a small remainder of members of the northern kingdom, who escaped deportation by the Assyrian invaders (722 B.C.), then intermarried with pagans from Babylonia and Media forcibly transplanted by the conquerer to the former kingdom of Israel. Jewish hostility to Samaritans sprang from attempts to sabotage the rebuilding of Jerusalem after the Babylonian exile in the Persian period, and, in the second century B.C., from collaboration with the Seleucid kings in their wars on the Jews. The Jewish high priest, John Hyrcanus, in 128 B.C. destroyed the Samaritan temple on Mount Gerizim, erected in opposition to the centralized worship in Jerusalem. The Samaritans regarded only the Pentateuch as "the Scriptures;" and the central figure in their messianic expectations was not a Davidic one (associated with the royal city and its temple), but a Moses-like prophet, the *Ta'eb*, "the one who returns" (Deut 18:15-18).

Jesus is not put off by the spirited riposte of the woman, but responds with a counter-offer. "If you only knew God's gift," that is, Jesus himself, as the reader already knows (3:16) . . . "you for your part would have asked him, and he would have given you living water." Water from a spring is, from its movement, designated "living," by contrast with the dead water caught in a cistern, and consequently considered of superior quality. The prophet Jeremiah had cited the reproach of Israel's God: "Two evils have My people perpetrated: they have forsaken Me, source of living waters, and dug for themselves cisterns, broken cisterns, that hold no water!" (Jer 2:13). The "living water" of which Jesus is source is "the truth" he has come to bring to his own. It will also symbolize the Spirit (7:39), eternal life (10:28). The woman's interest is aroused, yet she remains sceptical, "Where can you obtain living water?" The recurrence of the question, "Whence?", which was noted as having occurred to the steward at Cana (2:9), and had been raised in Jesus' parable concerning the Spirit to Nicodemus (3:9), is of considerable moment for John throughout his Gospel, and he continually seeks to make the reader aware that the giver gives himself with his gifts.

In her ignorance the woman provides a delightful example of Johannine irony with her retort, "Surely you are not greater than Jacob, our father?" (see 8:53). However, her continuing interest prompts Jesus to lead her to a desire for his gift, which alone can quench thirst: "Whoever drinks the water I will give him will never in future thirst." It then surpasses the wisdom extolled by the Jewish sage (Sir 24:20), for Jesus himself is divine wisdom incarnate. He thus describes himself later: "I am myself the bread of life: the one who comes to me will never go hungry, and the one believing in me will not be thirsty at any time" (6:35). Further, this mysterious gift by Jesus "will become a spring within him, bubbling up into eternal life:" it is a dynamic and vital reality, which permanently abides within the believer, and permeates his entire being. While guiding the believer towards that "eternal life" which lies in the future beyond history, it is already a present possession. The woman's longing is effectively aroused, only her enthusiasm is misdirected. "Sir, give this water to me, so that I may not be thirsty, nor have to keep coming here to draw water." The dialogue, as with Nicodemus earlier, is at cross-purposes: Jesus will immediately confront her with the anomalous moral situation in which she is living. Yet the vehemence of this lonely woman's desire is reflected by her eagerness to be free of the intolerable burden of her ostracism by other village-women, of which her having "to keep coming here to draw water" is a daily reminder.

"Go home, call your man, and come back here!" Jesus' peremptory demand gives a new turn to the conversation which is in danger of becoming a *pis aller*. The use of "man" for husband or paramour in Greek and Aramaic makes possible a pun, difficult to render in English, perceptible in the woman's retort, "I've no man!" and in Jesus' supernatural insight into the woman's life, "Actually you have had five men, yet the man you now have is not your man." This display by Jesus of such unprecedented knowledge brings the woman to an initial declaration of faith in him: "Sir, I perceive you are yourself a prophet!"

Yet once again she goes off at a tangent: with a real prophet before her, she desires a definitive answer to the question that had long divided Samaritans and Jews—the divinely approved site for the worship of God. But Jesus transcends this debate, now become irrelevant with his own presence. His address to her as "Woman," the term used towards his mother at Cana (2:4), may well indicate John's intention of suggesting a friendlier note (hence my rendering "Lady"). And in the sequel Jesus now discloses the revelation of the new religion which it is his mission to inaugurate (see Mk 2:21-22).

The salient feature of the new religion, as John repeatedly emphasizes, is its character of worshipping God as "the Father." Such adoration celebrates the believers' ever growing consciousness of their new relationship with God, made possible by the incarnate Son of God's disclosure of "the truth" about "the God no one has ever seen," and the dynamic operation of "the Spirit." Paul had already focused the attention of his Galatians upon this truth (Gal 4:4-6), and in his disquisition on Christian prayer to the Roman church had insisted on the deepening experience of "adoptive sonship" through the liturgical recital of the prayer Jesus had taught (see Romans 8:15-17).[1] Here once again we see the persistent Johannine theme of "replacement" by Jesus of the old, outmoded forms of worship.

As he introduces this significant revelation, Jesus is reported as vindicating the truth of the traditional religion of Israel over against the aberrations of Samaritan worship. "As for you others, you know nothing of what you worship, whereas we know what we worship—salvation is to come from the Jews." Paul, a Jew himself like Jesus, had evinced a similar respect for the ancient religion. "What advantage then is there in being a Jew? . . . Great indeed, from every point of view. First of all, to the Jews were entrusted the oracles of God!" (Rom 3:1-2). And later in the same letter the Apostle's enumeration of his people's prerogatives is reminiscent of the present passage. "They are Israelites, and to them belong adoptive sonship, and the glory [of the divine presence], and the covenants and the making of the Law, and the [true] adoration of God, and the promises. Moreover, theirs are the patriarchs, and from them by natural descent sprang the Messiah!" (Rom 9:4-5). Like Paul, John of course and his readers are aware that this old dispensation has now been abrogated through the death and resurrection of Jesus (2:19-22). Yet the evangelist's remark is proof of his esteem for the values found in history.

Jesus describes the new religion in terms that require some explanation: "true worshippers will adore the Father in Spirit and truth." Firstly, these "true worshippers" are such as have accepted Jesus, the Word become flesh, to whom he imparts "power to become God's children" (1:12), those "born of water and Spirit" (3:5), those "scattered children of God," for whom Jesus dies to create into the community of believers (11:52). Secondly, the possibility of such true adoration of God as Father can only arise from the glorification of Jesus (7:39), when he "handed over the Spirit" (19:30), Who is "the life-giver" (6:63). Thirdly, it is the glorified "body" of Jesus, the new sanctuary and sign of God's presence (2:21), through which God "gives the Spirit unstintingly" (3:34). Finally, in the context of John's total teaching regarding this "worship in Spirit and truth" it becomes evident that there is no question of any "religion

---

1 For a fuller discussion of these important Pauline texts, see David M. Stanley, S.J., *Boasting in the Lord: The Phenomenon of Prayer in Saint Paul* (New York/Paramus/Toronto, 1973), pp. 115-130.

of the heart" that is individualistic and anti-ritualist. The place of privilege our evangelist accords to the Incarnation makes such a view erroneous.

The woman replies by a confession of faith in the coming of "Messiah" (probably the Samaritan *ta'eb,* a Moses-like figure), and she adds "the one called [by the Jews] 'the Anointed'." Her next remark is an expression of hope: "Whenever he comes, he will unveil the meaning of everything for us." Jesus himself will employ the same expression later in speaking of the role of the Paraclete: "He will unveil the meaning of future events to you . . . He will take what is mine and unveil its meaning to you" (16:13-14). Despite her failure to realize that Jesus is announcing a new reality that is already present in his person (the woman still looks to the future), still, as Schnackenburg observes, "Her religious yearnings are sincere, she has also perhaps some intimation of the mystery of Jesus, and this provides him with the occasion of revealing himself to her."[2]

Jesus at the climax of the narrative is represented as informing the woman of his own identity, "I am *he*—the One who speaks with you!" The Greek words of this revelation, *egō eimi,* are those found in the Septuagint version of God's reply to Moses' request to tell him His name (Ex 3:14). This formula, to be employed by the Johannine Jesus later in the Gospel (8:24, 28, 58; 13:19; 18:5) to reveal his divinity, may well have that sense here. However, in view of the citation from Deutero-Isaiah used to complete the statement, the absolute use is probably not intended, and can be turned as "I am *he.*" The revelation-formula is an allusion to Isaiah 52:6: "On that day My people will know My name: they will know it is I Who am speaking—here I am!" The excerpt from the prophet which designates Israel's God as a *speaking* God has been deliberately selected by John to remind the reader that genuine faith is founded always upon the word of Jesus.

If the woman's belief in Jesus is presented as authentic, it is still lacunary, as John suggests in the sequel, after the disciples' return interrupts this precious dialogue. What has made the deepest impression on her is Jesus' knowledge of her sinful past. "The woman left her bucket and went off to the city, where she keeps telling people, 'Come, see a person who has told me everything I ever did!—Might he not be the Messiah?' " While the sincerity of her "good news" for the townsfolk is sufficient to overcome their earlier prejudices against this outcast, still John depicts her as yet somewhat hesitant about Jesus' messianic character.

2   Schnackenburg, *John,* I, 441.

Further experience in the presence of Jesus with her compatriots appears necessary to bring her to full faith (v. 42).

2. Conversation of Jesus with His Disciples (4:31-38)

> 31 Meantime the disciples kept urging him, "Master, do eat something!"
> 32 So he informed them, "I have food to eat you do not suspect." 33 As a result the disciples went on saying to one another, "Surely no one has brought him food?" 34 Jesus tells them, "My food is to do the will of Him Who sent me, and to carry through His work to its completion. 35 Don't you yourselves have a saying 'Four more months before the harvest arrives'? Listen: I am telling you! Lift up your eyes and take a look at the fields that are white with harvest! 36 The reaper is getting his reward, and gathering in a yield for eternal life, so that sower and reaper can rejoice together. 37 To this extent the proverb is correct, 'One sows—another reaps,' 38 —that it is I who sent you to reap where you have done no work. Others have done the hard work, while you have come in for the yield from their work."

At first glance this intercalated dialogue would seem quite unrelated to the story of the Samaritan woman. However, the evangelist has taken pains to connect the two sections by re-introducing the disciples as "disconcerted that he was talking with a woman." Their inhibitions prevent their asking the question in their minds: "What are you seeking?"—"What are you talking about with her?" In the story no hint is given that Jesus sends the woman off to the city: she appears to go spontaneously, full of her newfound faith in Jesus, to "evangelize" her neighbors. John evidently feels it necessary to prepare the reader for the astonishing dénouement of his narrative by introducing, as a kind of commentary of what ensues, some information about the real meaning of the Christian mission, exemplified in the subsequent history of Christianity in Samaria.

The discomfiture of the disciples only reveals their ignorance of Jesus and his God-given mission. Consequently, in response to their insistent plea, "Master, do eat something!", he speaks of a mysterious "food" he has, which "you do not suspect." Their misunderstanding of his meaning (as always in Johannine dialectic) brings Jesus to clarify his enigmatic assertion by remarking, "My food is to do the will of Him Who sent me, and to carry through His work to its completion." This is the answer to the unspoken question, "What are you seeking?", for the Father in the person of Jesus has actually come "seeking" the woman, and through her, the Samaritan villagers. In Christianity it is God always who takes the initiative in bringing people to faith, where in other great world-religions man is thought to go in search of God.

Jesus, in his attempt to instruct the disciples about their future mission (which for John can only begin after his own return home to God), begins by recalling a proverb current in their agrarian culture, a reminder to wait patiently until the harvest is ready (see Mk 4:26-29). He breaks off with a sudden exclamation to draw attention to the approach of the Samaritan villagers in their white robes: "Lift up your eyes and take a look at the fields white with harvest!" And in his joy at seeing the successful completion of this work the Father (as sower) had originated, he refers to himself as "the reaper." "The reaper is getting his reward and gathering in a yield for eternal life, so that sower [the Father] and reaper [Jesus] can rejoice together."

It will have been remarked that the Fourth Gospel contains no mission by Jesus of the disciples. During his lifetime only Jesus carries out his Father's "works" (5:36; 9:3; 10:32, 27); in fact, it is "the Father abiding in me [Who] is carrying out His own works" (4:10). It will be only after Jesus' departure from this world that the disciples will take up his "work"—on one proviso: "The one believing in the works that I myself am doing—he too in turn will do: yes! even greater than these will he do, because I am going home to the Father" (14:12).

At this point in the discourse John represents Jesus as looking into the future to behold the missionary efforts of the disciples: he probably thinks of the future success of the gospel among the Samaritans, made possible by his own sojourn among this alienated folk. He announces that where he (and the Father) "sows" at present, they at another time will "reap"—and precisely because "It is I who sent you to reap where you have done no work." It is of some importance to note that in the third part of John's account, it is Jesus alone, not the disciples, who will win over the Samaritans to faith in himself.

3. The Samaritans Accept Jesus with Profound Faith (4:39-42).

The woman with her imperfect faith has succeeded in leading the rest of the village out to Jesus. With that her mission is at an end. Only Jesus can bring them to enunciate a profession of faith which surpasses in depth all the titles thus far conferred upon him.

39   Now many of the Samaritans from that city came to believe in him on the word of the woman—her testimony, "He told me everything I ever did."
40   As a consequence, when these Samaritans came out to him they kept begging him to abide with them; and so he abode there for two days.   41

Thus many more came to believe on account of his word, 42 and they kept telling the woman, "No longer do we believe on your say-so, since we have ourselves heard him, and we now know that he is truly the Savior of the world!"

The evangelist probably wishes to contrast the readiness to believe in Jesus on the part of these Samaritans with the superficial "signs-faith" of the citizens of Jerusalem (2:23-25), and that of the people in Galilee (4:45, 48). The genuinity of their belief overcomes any hesitation they may have had about inviting this Jew into their city. Jesus' stay with them is very brief, "two days" only, but the power of his "word" is strikingly effective. And the human witness the woman has so courageously given yields in importance to "hearing him." And John concludes his account by citing the title they gave Jesus—unique in his Gospel: "He is truly the Savior of the world!"

In the introductory chapter a comment was made regarding the relatively rare use of miracle-stories as the object for contemplation during the second week of the *Spiritual Exercises.* This apparent lack of interest in the thaumaturgical aspect of Jesus' mission, which in the Synoptic Gospels (and notably that by Mark) is found to be inseparably interwoven with his teaching, is cause for wonder in a man so thoroughly medieval as Ignatius of Loyola, especially when he shares with the first evangelist Mark a greater interest in Jesus' activity than in the formal aspects of his teaching. This feature of the *Exercises* is probably explicable by the fact that in his day Ignatius could take for granted the knowledge and acceptance of Christ's *sagrada doctrina* ([145]) and "the love of the true doctrine of Christ our Lord" ([164]). Accordingly there was not the same need to assist the retreatant in assimilating the teaching of Jesus continued by the Church as there sometimes is today. For all that, it remains something of a puzzle that there is no space in the little book of Ignatius devoted to the parables of Jesus, so significant a facet of his pedagogy. A third surprising phenomenon in the *Exercises,* as Stanislas Lyonnet has observed,[3] is the fact that "the devil occupies an extraordinary limited place" in the Ignatian contemplations.[4] The single refer-

---

3   Stanislas Lyonnet, "La Méditation des Deux Étendards et son fondement scripturaire," *Christus* 12 (1956), 436-437.
4   See however Annotations 7, 8, 12, the General Examination of Conscience, [32], the twofold set of Rules For Discernment, [314, 318, 320, 325, 326, 327, 329, 331, 332, 333, 334, 335, 336], the Notes concerning Scruples, [345, 347, 349, 350], and also the Rules for Eating, [217]. In these, reference is made to "the enemy," "our enemy," "the enemy of our human nature" (some 17 times), "the evil spirit" (9 times), "the evil one" (twice), "the adversary" (once).

ence to "the enemy" or "the tempter" (apart from Two Standards) occurs in the Temptation of Christ ([274]). It is indeed curious that even in connection with Judas' betrayal in the Third Week the devil is not mentioned. Louis Puhl's much used translation of the *Exercises* has intercalated the term "Satan"—a designation that appears *nowhere* in the original text—into Two Standards ([140, 142]).

Each of these three salient characteristics of the author of the *Spiritual Exercises,* it may be of interest to note, are also distinctive of the fourth evangelist. John has omitted the exorcism-narratives found in the earlier Gospels, as well as any story of the cure of lepers. In addition to his somewhat radical restriction of accounts of "signs" performed by Jesus, our Gospel-writer has made abundantly clear (2:23-25; 3:2; 4:48) his deep suspicion of that superficial belief in Jesus that arises merely from wonder at the miraculous. Nor does John display any great interest in the preternatural: the name "Satan" appears but once (13:27), "the devil" twice (8:44; 13:2—it refers to Judas at 6:70), while "the prince of this world" is employed but three times (12:31; 14:30; 16:11).

In contemplating these beautifully drawn scenes of Jesus' Samaritan interlude, the exercitant should be impressed with the dramatic conversion of the woman and (through her initiative) the coming to faith in Jesus of her compatriots, which John describes as achieved without the working of any "sign" by Jesus. Nor does the sacred writer allude in any way to the presence of the power of evil among the inhabitants of Samaria, cut off for centuries from fellowship with the Chosen people, and from that "salvation" which "is to come from the Jews."

Chapter 8

CANA II (4:43-54): JESUS LIFE-GIVER
JOHANNINE DISCERNMENT

A s the exercitant turns to contemplate the second "sign" which John
locates at Cana where Jesus "had made water wine" (4:46), it will
be of considerable help to recall the consensus among modern New
Testament scholars that none of our four evangelists was personally involved as an "eyewitness" of Jesus' public ministry. As each of the four
Gospel-writers belonged to the third or fourth Christian generation, not
one of them had known Jesus personally during his life on earth. Whatever be the correct explanation of the relation of Matthew and John to
the Gospels that (only since the second century) bear their names, it is
generally agreed that the two so designated in the list of the Twelve did
not author those books.

One consequence of this judgment is that each of the evangelists is
now regarded as a recipient of the evangelical traditions concerning what
Jesus said and did during his lifetime, which in the earliest Christian
communities had been preserved, interpreted, selected, lived upon. The
Second Vatican Council accepted these conclusions in its Constitution on
Divine Revelation. After noting how the first disciples "interpreted his
words and actions according to the needs of their listeners . . . and
employed various forms of expression suited to their own purpose and
the mentality of their listeners," the decree speaks of the creation of the
Gospels. "This primitive instruction . . . was committed to writing by
the sacred authors in four Gospels for the benefit of the churches, with a
method suited to the peculiar purpose each author set for himself. From
the many things handed down they selected certain data, compiled other
items into a synthesis, still others they explained with a view to the situation of the churches" (*Dei Verbum,* 8-9).

This teaching of the Church has a relevancy for the approach to the
Ignatian contemplation, which, as has been earlier noted, begins with
lectio divina, the attentive reading of the Gospel narrative. One comes to
realize that the evangelist is much more than a gatherer of historical data
about Jesus: he in fact played a significant role in the evolution under-

gone by the living tradition preserved by the Church of the first Christian century. We are particularly indebted to Paul for his frequent appeal to this tradition in his letters. He not only attests to its crucial importance for the spiritual life of the churches (1 Cor 15:1-2; 1 Cor 11: 23-25), but certain statements of his have added immeasurably to our appreciation of its character. The Apostle, like the later evangelists, was not an eye-witness of Jesus' activity on earth. Like them also, however, he—as an inspired writer—underwent a specially privileged experience in receiving the apostolic traditions. "The gospel proclaimed by me is not of human origin; nor did I receive it from any human being, nor was I taught it except through a revelation by Jesus Christ" (Gal 1:11-12). This unnuanced statement by one, who on his own admission had learned from Peter and others about Jesus' life and teaching (Gal 1:18; 2:1-2), deserves close attention. It testifies to his belief that his own reception of the earlier traditions regarding Jesus was not any natural process of data-gathering, but an intense experience of the action of the risen Lord in communicating to him the gospel, which he would later acknowledge to be "God's dynamic force leading to salvation" (Rom 1:16).

Consequently, the normative value of our Gospels for the following of Christ, the express purpose of the Second Week of the *Exercises* ([104 *et passim*]), is seen not to stem from the perceptiveness of "the original eye-witnesses" (Lk 1:2), the accuracy of the memories of the first disciples, or their fidelity in passing along exact information. The authoritative and sacral character of the Gospels (like all other New Testament documents) arose from a personal, profound experience of the active presence of the Holy Spirit which each of these authors enjoyed. The Council in fact reserved the place of honor in Christian spirituality for these four inspired books: "The Gospels have a special pre-eminence, and rightly so, for they are the principal witness to the life and teaching of the incarnate Word, our Savior" (*Dei Verbum*, 8).

In view of all this, a large part of the exercitant's attention in his contemplation should be directed to the various, distinctive ways in which each Gospel-writer has reacted to the traditions he received—and this, without allowing oneself to be distracted by the often irrelevant, mostly unanswerable question, "What really happened?" Instead of asking, "What happened to Jesus?" in a certain situation, a more pertinent concern is "What happened to Mark or John?" through their reception of such traditions about Jesus. This practice of discerning the evangelists' reactions to the Jesus of tradition will be of considerable aid to the retreatant for the "discernment of spirits" in his own heart, which (as will shortly be seen) Ignatius considered of crucial value in orientating one's contemplation to the Election.

John's account of the rescue from death of the young son of an unnamed court official in the employ of the Herod, who was tetrarch of Galilee in Jesus' lifetime, provides an arresting example of his innovative re-interpretation of an episode which also appears in quite different form in the Gospels by Matthew and Luke (see Mt 8:5-13; Lk 7:1-10). In all three stories, it is question of the same miracle: the cure, at some distance from Capharnaum where it happened, of a young man in grave danger of death from some dangerous illness. This is the view adopted by an impressive number of contemporary Catholic exegetes, including Rudolf Schnackenburg,[1] Raymond Brown,[2] George MacRae,[3] John Meier,[4] and Joseph Fitzmyer.[5]

In the context of the *Spiritual Exercises* however, the creative handling by the evangelists of this miracle, preserved in the memory of a previous Christian generation, invites attention not as an item of interest to the history of traditions. Rather each of the three quite distinctive narratives is to be esteemed as the precious starting-point for contemplation, *el fundamento verdadero de la historia* (Annotation 2), the event as presented by the sacred writer. That the Saint has sometimes "harmonized" the varying Gospel accounts points to the fact that he was understandably a man of his own age and culture. The procedure is unjustifiable today, when with the assistance of Form and Redaction criticism we have been brought to see the values inherent in carefully attending to the divergencies, even contradictions, in the varying accounts of a single episode, which frequently evoke a deeper awareness of the very personal portrait of Jesus, which each author is intent on presenting to the reader.

Thus, in the present instance, Matthew's version of the cure of a pagan soldier's "paralyzed boy" (or servant) allows a glimpse of "the majestic, all-powerful Christ. He . . . acts as the mighty yet humble servant of God, gathers together and sustains his community, and shares his power with his community."[6] The Lucan story speaks of the restoration to health of a "deathly ill slave," "highly prized" by his owner, the centurion. It depicts Jesus as "a person who is at once very human,

1 Schnackenburg, *John,* I, 471-475.
2 R. E. Brown, *John I-XII*, pp. 192-195.
3 G. W. MacRae, *Invitation to John*, p. 69.
4 John P. Meier, *Matthew (New Testament Message 3)* (Wilmington, Delaware, 1980), p. 83.
5 Joseph A. Fitzmyer, S.J., *The Gospel According to Luke I-IX* (Garden City, N.Y., 1981), pp. 648-649.
6 J. P. Meier, *Matthew*, p. 80.

dramatic, and at times even romantic''—''probably qualities which reflect the sensibilities of Luke himself,'' whom Dante once called ''the scribe of the gentleness of Christ.''[7]

In turning to contemplate the Johannine account (4:43-54), one observes certain similarities to the event described by Matthew and Luke: it is a question, as already remarked, of the instantaneous cure of a young man critically ill, performed by Jesus without his being present, at the loving behest of one from whom the subsequent magnificent display of complete trust in Jesus might scarcely be expected. At the same time, however, one can see how John, in pursuit of his theme that true faith necessarily reposes on the word of Jesus, manages to set forth for the reader his own distinctive image of Jesus, the Word ''become flesh.'' Jesus is seen as a completely human being: Galilee is ''his homeland,'' even though he has ''come down out of heaven'' (6:41), sent by the Father (7:28-29). While on this particular occasion his reception by his fellow-Galileans is superficial, like their faith in him, he will be afforded protection in Galilee, when the Judeans wish to kill him (7:1). Indeed his Galilean origins will constitute a scandal to many in Jerusalem since ''the Anointed'' comes not from there but Bethlehem (7:41-42), and the Sanhedrin remind Nicodemus that in fact ''the prophet does not arise from Galilee'' (7:52). As Father Schnackenburg observes, ''the factual reality of the event is to be made clear . . . it is precisely in the 'flesh' of his earthly coming that the incarnate Logos reveals the underlying divinity and his significance for man.''[8]

The Johannine Jesus as Source of Life (4:43-54)

43 At the end of the two days, he [Jesus] set forth from there for Galilee. (44 Now Jesus had himself borne testimony that a prophet enjoys no honor in his own homeland.) 45 And so, when he came back to Galilee, the Galileans welcomed him, since—as they had themselves gone up for the feast—they had seen all he had performed among the festival-throng in Jerusalem. 46 He came then once more to Cana of Galilee, where he had made water wine. Now a certain court official was staying there, whose son at Capharnaum was ill. 47 This man on hearing Jesus had come back from Judea to Galilee, went to see him, and began begging that he come down and cure his son, since he was at the point of death. 48 Accordingly Jesus said to him, ''Unless you people see signs and prodigies, you will never believe!'' 49 The royal official says to him, ''Sir, do come down

7 J. A. Fitzmyer, S.J., *The Gospel According to Luke I–IX,* p. 257.
8 Schnackenburg, *John,* I, 476.

before my boy dies!'' 50 Jesus tells him, ''Begin your journey: your son will live.'' The man put his trust in the word Jesus spoke to him, and he started out on his journey. 51 Now already as he was making his way down, his slaves met him with the news that his son was indeed alive. 52 So he inquired as to the [precise] hour when he had taken such a marvelous turn for the better. Thereupon they told him, ''Yesterday at the seventh hour the fever left him.'' 53 As a result, the father realized that it was at that very hour Jesus had told him, ''Your son will live;'' and he himself became a believer, as did his entire household. 54 Such was the second sign Jesus performed upon coming from Judea into Galilee.

The evangelist links this new story with the preceding ''two days,'' when half-pagan Samaritans had given such magnificent testimony of their faith in Jesus. John thus appears to indicate that he will now give an example of superb faith by a Galilean, an ''official'' at the court of ''king'' Herod Antipas, ruler of Galilee. It has been suggested that this may be the writer's motive in changing the man's character from that of a pagan centurion to a Jewish resident of Galilee. And indeed, after the parenthetical remark at v. 44 that has caused commentators no little trouble, John depicts Jesus' fellow-countrymen as giving him an enthusiastic reception. He goes on however to underscore the superficial nature of their acclaim: their ''faith'' is as inauthentic as that of the people in Jerusalem (2:23-25).

The very awkward insertion of John's gloss (taken over from tradition), ''Now Jesus had himself borne testimony that a prophet enjoys no honor in his own homeland,'' seemingly contradicts the assertion immediately following it, ''the Galileans welcomed him.'' It may be taken as deliberate on the evangelist's part: he wishes to stress what a sham that ''welcome'' really was.

John completes his introduction to his narrative by linking it with the first ''sign'' recorded in his Gospel, and so situating the miracle now performed by Jesus at ''Cana of Galilee, where he had made water wine.'' Thus the alert reader will understand this as a promise of a new revelation by Jesus of his ''glory,'' where an anonymous ''court official'' happened to be, while his ''son at Capharnaum was ill.'' This man had got wind of Jesus' return ''from Judea to Galilee,'' and approached him with an urgent plea to ''come down and cure his son, since he was at the point of death.''

Jesus' first recorded reaction is an expression of frustration that arises from his experience of the counterfeit faith in him displayed already by his own compatriots. And it is towards them, not merely to the boy's father, that his impatient remark is directed (as the use of the second person plural in Greek makes clear). "Unless you people see signs and prodigies, you will never believe!" The petitioner however is not put off, but presses his request with heightened pathos: "Sir, do come down before my boy dies!" The renewed plea implies that Jesus should be present to the sick child in order to cure him—perhaps by laying his hands on the sufferer. The element of surprise at a cure worked at a distance is thus being prepared.

Jesus responds by putting the official's faith to a severe test: "Begin your journey" home—and without me! Yet Jesus sends the man off with an amazing promise (to be repeated twice again in the sequel): "Your son will live!" This saying presents Jesus here as the source of life—physical life indeed, yet which functions as a symbol of that "eternal life" to be bestowed on the father and "his entire household" through the new gift of faith in Jesus by the end of the story. Yet even now, John tells us, "the man put his trust in the word Jesus spoke to him, and he started out on his journey." The arresting character of this "second sign" is again hinted at: the cure will be effected by Jesus at considerable distance from the dying child.

The anxious father had not even completed the descent from Cana to Capharnaum, when "his slaves met him with the news that his son was indeed alive." The Greek version is an almost exact repetition of the promise by Jesus—"his child lives!" The astonished father is portrayed as making a minute investigation into the "hour" at which his son "had taken such a marvelous turn for the better." This last phrase in Greek is a picturesque one: it might be rendered in colloquial English as "was doing fine." The verification of "the hour," one o'clock in the afternoon, is considered important by the evangelist. While he judges "signs-faith" to be lacunary, he is aware that such a "sign" is a precious gift of the divine Giver, himself also "the gift of God:" and consequently the beneficiary of such divine bounty is bound by reverence and gratitude to investigate its reality and discern its meaning for himself, as the believing father is here shown to do. As George MacRae remarks, "In this instance, the miracle, carefully attested in verses 51-53, serves to confirm the power of Jesus' word. Jesus manifests himself as the one who gives life. Belief in the signs of this life-giving power is inadequate only if it focuses on the signs alone and not on the revealing person of its author."[9]

John actually points this out by noting that it is the very memory of

9   G. W. MacRae, *Invitation to John*, p. 69.

Jesus' word, "Your son will live," that leads him, together with "his entire household," to true faith. The final comment of the sacred writer, by drawing attention to the fact that this "was the second sign Jesus performed upon coming from Judea into Galilee," appears intended to mark the termination of the initial development of his Gospel. Consequently, it may be judged appropriate to present some reflections on Johannine discernment as provided in the first twelve chapters of the Gospel. An occasion to complete John's teaching on this important topic will present itself when we come to Jesus' farewell discourse at the last meal he shared with his few faithful followers, and review the five promises of "the Paraclete" which the evangelist reserves for that solemn moment.

The Role of Discernment in the Exercises and in the Fourth Gospel

As is well known, Ignatius sets out two series of Rules for the Discernment of spirits: those "more suitable for the First Week" ([313-317]), and those "conducive rather to the Second Week" ([328-336]). A survey of his teaching on discernment however is incomplete unless account be taken also of the Notes on Scruples "and snares of our enemy" ([345-351]), as well as Rules "we must observe as a true criterion within the Church militant" ([353-370]). Finally, discernment of the divine action in one's day-to-day living is seemingly suggested in "A way to make the general examination" ([43]).[10]

A remark by Hugo Rahner supports the view just expressed that the Ignatian doctrine of discernment must take account of the Notes on Scruples and the Rules for thinking with the Church. In the opinion of the late distinguished specialist in Ignatian spirituality, its orientation to the *magis,* towards greater perfection, defines the limits in which the movement of "spirits" occurs: "First, the requirement that all aspiration to greater perfection must be put into effect within the hierarchically organized Church; second, the selection made earlier in the *Exercises* of those whose gifts of nature and grace make them suited for a spiritual conflict of this sort; and finally, the constant emphasis that any Election made by discerning the fluctuations of consolation and desolation must always be formed and guided by the continued prayerful contemplation of the mysteries of Christ's life on earth. Such were the safeguards which Ignatius and his first companions quite unmistakably brought forward in

---

10   George A. Aschenbrenner, S.J., "Consciousness Examen," *Review for Religious* 31 (1972), 14-21.

reply to all accusations of Illuminism."[11]

Before investigating what is asserted, or assumed, or implied in the Fourth Gospel about discernment, a few brief remarks concerning the place of honor assigned it by Ignatius may not be out of place. Firstly, the distinction between the two sets of rules is obviously practical and relative. The first series is directed to the disciplining of one's sensibility, and so "more suitable for the First Week," while the second, "conducive rather to the Second Week," aims at assisting a magnanimous exercitant to avoid being side-tracked, by unmasking the intent of the evil spirit, "who disguises himself as an angel of light" ([332]). As the final rule makes abundantly clear, the second set is meant to provide guidance to the more spiritually advanced person in the crucial transition from contemplation to action ([336]). Secondly, discernment is not restricted to the First and Second Weeks of the Exercises; its practice embraces the experiences of the entire thirty days. François Courel (in a note on the third rule of discernment for the First Week) points out that "The different aspects of consolation embrace the graces of all Four Weeks of the Exercises . . . the end of the Note on physical penances ([87]) had already alluded to the graces of the First, Third, and Second Weeks."[12] In the third place, Ignatius' extraordinary ability in discernment goes back to the mystical experience of the Cardoner. Pedro Arrupe calls it "the greatest transformation," "the supreme lesson," and cites the testimony of both Jerome Nadal and Juan Polanco to the effect that it was at Manresa that Ignatius "learned to discern spirits."[13] "When Ignatius left Loyola," observes Hugo Rahner, "he brought with him the two basic elements, i.e. his presentiment of the struggle of spirits and the contemplation of the life of Christ—though they were still totally disconnected; but later, in the light of mystical grace, they became joined together as the opposite poles between which the *Exercises* oscillate."[14] The important inference from all this is that Ignatian discernment is thoroughly Christological and in no way egocentric. The process of discernment, which culminates in the Election, is carried through by the contemplation of Jesus' earthly history.

Now, as had already been suggested, it is this Christological focus of discernment that is also characteristic of the Fourth Gospel. One might say, in fact, that for the evangelist Jesus, during the public ministry, re-

11   H. Rahner, *Ignati⋅s the Theologian*, pp. 144-145.
12   François Courel, *Exercices Spirituels*, p. 168.
13   Pedro Arrupe, S.J., "The Trinitarian Inspiration of the Ignatian Charism," *Acta Romana S.I.* 18 (1981), 123.
14   H. Rahner, *Ignatius the Theologian*, pp. 57-58.

mains throughout the principal discerner; hence his repeated stress on Jesus' ability to read hearts. This dominant note in his personality is struck at his encounter with the first two disciples, when he asks, "What are you looking for?" (1:38), in his prior knowledge, which so amazes Nathanael and evokes from him a singular confession of faith (1:48-50), in his alertness to divine the plea for help in a delicate hint from his mother (2:3), above all, in the evangelist's comment on his refusal to trust himself to the surface-faith of the crowds at Passover, "As for himself, he knew what was in human nature" (2:25). Jesus is seen to invite his interlocutors to discernment by his enigmatic, often abrupt assertions: his "Unless a person be begotten again" (3:3) to Nicodemus, and to the woman at the well, "If you only knew God's gift" and his mysterious promise of "living water" (4:10), his challenge to "Go home, call your man, and come back here!" (4:16), his climactic word of self-revelation, "I am *he*—the One who speaks with you!" (4:26), his repeated attempts to raise the consciousness of his disciples by refusing to eat, his "I have food to eat you do not suspect" (4:32), his peremptory demand, "Lift up your eyes and take a look at the fields that are white with harvest!" (4:35). His exasperation is voiced towards his own countrymen of Galilee, "Unless you people see signs and prodigies, you will never believe!" (4:48), and he confronts the anxious court official, almost daring him to put complete trust in him, by his "Begin your journey: your son will live" (4:50).

As he continues his narrative of the public life, John repeatedly draws attention to the division which is created by the diverse reactions of those who are confronted with Jesus and his challenge. The entry into history by the incarnate Word as "the light" precipitates "the judgment," which many (in the negative sense of condemnation) pass on themselves already in this life, while those who "live the truth" and "come to the light" enjoy now the possession of eternal life (3:19-21). The evangelist provides concrete instances of this "division" in his narrative of the celebration of *Sukkōth,* the feast of Booths (7:12, 37, 31, 40-43), in the story of the blind man (9:16) and its sequel (10:19).

Thus it can be said that by means of his narratives in the first twelve chapters of the Gospel the evangelist intends to instruct the believing reader in the art of discernment, rather than speak of it in so many words. The later author of First John treats the topic explicitly, in the face of a crisis that has arisen in his Christian community. "Dearly beloved, do not trust every spirit, but test spirits (to discern) whether each be from God, since many false prophets have entered the world.

Here is how you can recognize spirits belonging to God: every spirit that confesses Jesus as Christ come in the flesh is from God, while every spirit that does not confess Jesus is not from God" (1 Jn 4:1-3). For this writer of another Christian generation, belief in the Incarnation has become the chief principle in discernment.

Our evangelist, with his deep respect for history, takes the view that the Incarnation has created the need for discernment, which only becomes possible with the gift of the Paraclete by the exalted Jesus as a result of his "hour." During Jesus' mortal life the disciples, with the aid of their Israelite faith and through "the Scriptures," remain open to Jesus and to the as yet unknown religious experiences which their relationship of trust in him will bring. "The Jews" on the contrary by their refusal to believe in Jesus continue, with increasing contumacy, to persevere in an attitude of disbelief. John draws attention to the ambiguity that attaches to the Incarnation as to every historical event. At Capharnaum the Jews complain at Jesus' statement, "I am the bread come down out of heaven," because they know his parents (6:41-42) and attack his promise of the Eucharistic bread, "How can this fellow give us his flesh to eat?" (6:52). Even some of his own followers declare themselves unable to "swallow" this "tough saying," and thus desert his company (6:60-66). The evangelist dramatizes the paradoxical nature of the foundational element upon which his Gospel is built, "The Word become flesh:" he quotes Jesus as saying, "It is the Spirit that is the Lifegiver: the flesh is useless!" (6:63). John permits himself another paradoxical statement: if Jesus had indeed promised the gift of the Spirit under the symbol of "living water," yet "the Spirit did not yet exist because Jesus was not yet glorified" (7:39). And while he pictures Jesus' struggle to reveal his identity to "the Jews" throughout the course of his ministry, he feels compelled to point out that, with few exceptions, Jesus did not succeed (12:37-43). It will only be by his supreme act of love, through his "laying down his life for his friends" (15:13), that finally he will "hand over the Spirit" (19:30).

I venture to suggest further that one may discover certain principles of discernment which our evangelist has, in the first half of his Gospel, placed here and there on the lips of Jesus. "This is my Father's will that everyone who beholds the Son and believes in him will possess eternal life" (6:40): to "behold the Son" in Jesus of Nazareth is basic for genuine faith. The comment on the allusion to the prophets, "And they shall all be taught of God" (probably Is 54:13; Jer 31:34) is particularly relevant: "Each one who has listened to the Father and learned comes to me'' (6:45). The person who has responded to the mysterious ''drawing'' by the Father (v. 44) and has ''learned'' from the words of Jesus ''the Son''—the objective safeguard against self-delusion—achieves the personal relation with Jesus which for John is true faith. To the Jews, amazed at Jesus' display of wisdom during the feast of *Sukkōth,* he declares, ''My teaching is not mine but His Who sent me. If a person chooses to do His will, he will know if this teaching is from God, or whether I am speaking on my own'' (7:17). And somewhat later he tells this same audience, ''Why is it you do not understand my manner of speaking? It is because you cannot lend a ready ear to my word'' (8:43). Refusal to accept the revelation Jesus brings can only result in spiritual deafness.

Chapter 9

"I AM THE LIVING BREAD COME DOWN OUT OF HEAVEN"
(6:1-71)

W e have already observed how, in the opening chapters of his Gospel, John was concerned to clarify the nature of genuine faith in Jesus as the Word of God incarnate, and it was pointed out how he tailors his accounts, particularly those of the two "signs" he narrates, to ensure that attention be concentrated on the Christological focus, which dominates each episode. When, however, with chapter five, he begins the story of Jesus' public ministry in the proper sense, there is a perceptible change in the pattern of his presentation which calls for closer inspection.

Firstly, while broadly speaking the unity of the development to the end of chapter twelve is achieved through its articulation by means of four (or five) "signs," these are employed simply as the point of departure for some important self-revelation by Jesus through discourse or discussion. Secondly, the accent now falls principally upon the public character of these "signs," hitherto performed within the confines of a narrow circle of friends (as at Cana I), or in favor of an individual (Cana II). This emphasizes in turn the publicity Jesus aims to give his teaching. When, before Annas, Jesus is asked about his teaching, he refuses to discuss it on the grounds that "I have spoken openly before the world. I have taught in synagogue or in temple-precincts, where all the Jews assemble, and in secret I have said nothing" (18:20). Thirdly, "the Jews" now become the unique object of his message—even at Capharnaum (6:42, 51). The "truth" which Jesus is come to bring about the "God no one has ever seen" is meant primarily for the leaders of official Judaism. Fourthly, this precise orientation of his revelation about himself and about his Father Who sent him provides the most plausible explanation for the consistent manner in which the reader's attention is drawn to "a feast of the Jews" (5:1), which almost always is identified, as Passover (6:4), *Sukkōth* or "booth-building" (7:2), *Hanukkah,* "the dedication [of the temple] in Jerusalem" (10:22), and the final Passover of the crucifixion (11:55; 12:1; 13:1; 18:28; 19:14). Fifthly, each of the several "signs" (with the single exception of the walk upon the sea) leads to controversy: the healing of a cripple on Sabbath, the feeding of the crowd, the cure of the blind man, while the raising of Lazarus will become a principal cause of Jesus' own execution. Sixthly, throughout these chapters depicting Jesus' ministry John highlights the incredulity of "the Jews," rarely mentioning the faith of those who come to believe in Jesus. A notable exception is Peter's magnificent confession for the Twelve (6:68-69). As centerpiece of this entire exposition the evangelist has, with a kind of "impressionist" technique, mounted a breathlessly narrated series of vignettes, in chapters seven and eight, by which with ever mounting hostility and hatred, "the Jews" repeatedly seek to kill Jesus while rejecting his message. And finally, it is in this lengthy section that John introduces the significant set of symbolic, self-revealing statements by Jesus, which will be completed by an additional pair in what is called "the Book of Glory" (see 14:6; 15:1). "I am the Bread of life" (ch. 6); "I am the Light of the world" (chs. 8-9); "I am the gate for the sheep", "I am the ideal Shepherd" (ch. 10); "I am the resurrection and the life" (ch. 11).

Accordingly, the astute retreatant will constantly be reminded of the meditation on Two Standards, which will be considered in the following chapter. In fact, much of this Johannine material may well be found helpful for anyone desirous of making the Ignatian Election. At the same time, the exercitant familiar with the *Exercises* will have observed a significant contrast between Ignatius' reticence in proposing Jesus' miracles (and his teaching) for our contemplation, and the use John makes of these "signs" in structuring his account of the public life. While this is an important point of difference between these two great mystics, one must recall that the evangelist has consistently designated the thaumaturgical element in Jesus' work as "signs," chiefly to bring out their intimate relation to the person of Jesus and to the paschal mystery. Ignatius, in his turn, has taken care to place the contemplations of the Second Week of the Exercises under the sign of the cross. In the present contemplation, the feeding of the crowd, it is highly significant that this stupendous miracle is made clear in John's narrative only when the disciples gather up the remainder of the uneaten loaves. That it was in fact an item of importance in the pre-Gospel traditions, which preserved the episode, may be seen from a brief consideration of the Marcan narrative, although the variants in Mark's story would appear to point to a different source from that used by John. Accordingly, we include the Marcan version as a possibly useful point of comparison with that of our evangelist.

Mark's Account of the Feeding in the Desert (Mk 6:34-44)

34   Upon disembarking, he [Jesus] saw a vast crowd, and his heart was moved to compassion for them, since they were "like sheep without a shepherd" [Num 27:17]; and he began to teach them at considerable length. 35   As it was now quite late, his disciples came to him and said, "This place is a desert, and it is already late.   36   Send them away that they may go to the hamlets and villages round about and buy themselves something to eat." 37   But he said to them, "Give them food yourselves." So they said to him, "Are we to go and buy loaves that will cost two hundred denarii that we may give them food?"   38   But he replied, "How many loaves have you?—Go and see!" Now on finding out, they say, "Five, and two fish."   39   Then he ordered them to make the people sit down like picnic parties on the green grass.   40   So they sat down in "hundreds and fifties" [Ex 18:25], neatly arranged like flower beds.   41   Then he took the five loaves and two fish, and looking up to heaven, he blessed and broke the loaves, and gave them to the disciples to pass round to them; and the two fish he divided among all. 42   Now all ate until they were full.   43   Then they took up the left-overs —twelve basketsful, besides what remained of the fish.   44   Those eating the meal numbered five thousand men.

At a first level of interpretation this oldest of the Gospel-accounts of a miraculous meal in a "place [that is] a desert," which in the Marcan Gospel forms the climax of the Galilean ministry, depicts Jesus as the prophet like Moses (Deut 18:15), who renews the wonders of the exodus —regarded in Judaism as a sign of the messianic times. It is significant that Mark makes an allusion to Moses' prayer before the appointment of Joshua to replace him in leading the people into the promised land. "Let the Lord, God of the spirits of all flesh, appoint one as leader over the community . . . that the Lord's community may not be like sheep without a shepherd" (Num 27:16-17). He also recalls the advice Jethro gives Moses, his son-in-law, regarding the need of subsidiarity in sharing his leadership with others. "So Moses selected able men from all Israel and appointed them leaders over the people as captains of units of a thousand, one hundred, fifty or ten" (Ex 18:25). Jesus in the Marcan version of the story (but not, as will be seen, in John's) shares his power with the disciples. This aspect of the narrative looks back through history to "the time of grace of the journey through the desert."[1]

---

1   Schnackenburg, *The Gospel According to St. Mark,* Vol. I, tr. Werner Kruppa (New York, 1971), p. 111.

But as the account proceeds attention is directed (and this is a second level of interpretation) to the future actions of Jesus at his last meal with his own, recognized by the young Church as a symbolic prophecy of the Eucharist they would celebrate only after the resurrection. After invoking the power of his Father by "looking up to heaven," Jesus is described as performing the three actions central to the Eucharist: "he blessed and broke the loaves, and gave them." As Mark has taken care, in his account of the Last Supper, to cite the liturgical formula employed, in all probability, by the church for which he wrote his Gospel (Mk 14:22-24), the original readers cannot have missed the evangelist's point in using the same words for his description of the feeding. They would recognize the risen Lord Jesus in the compassionate Shepherd, bringing his people to "sit down . . . on the green grass" to feed them bountifully. It evokes the beloved picture sketched by the psalmist: "The Lord is my Shepherd—I shall want for nothing. He makes me repose in green pastures . . . he renews life within me" (Ps 23:1-3).

This transcendent dignity of Jesus, which he shares with Israel's God, was already underlined in the tradition which had linked with the feeding the wondrous deed of Jesus in walking upon the sea. And Mark has taken care to connect the two events by his comment upon the disciples' failure to grasp the Christophany they experienced. Of them he remarks, "They were utterly and completely beside themselves; for of course they had not understood about the loaves—their minds remained obtuse" (Mk 6:51-52). Mark's manner of relating this sequel to the feeding is evidently meant as a plea to his community to recognize the presence of the glorified Lord in its celebration of the Eucharistic liturgy. He emphasizes the initiative of Jesus by describing him as "forcing his disciples at once to embark in the boat and precede him on the crossing to Bethsaida" (Mk 6:45). Then, as Jesus "came walking towards them upon the sea," Mark makes the curious statement, "He had it in mind to *pass by* them" (v. 48d)—the term reminiscent of the great theophanies granted in turn to Moses (Ex 33:21-23) and Elijah (1 Kgs 19:11). Indeed, it may well be that in his version of Jesus' words of reassurance to his terrified disciples, Mark has intentionally made use of the divine name, which the Johannine Jesus assumes repeatedly. "Take heart! I AM—stop being afraid" (v. 50). In our reflection upon John's description of these two great miracles with which the Galilean ministry comes to a climax, we shall have occasion to refer to the Marcan interpretation. In fact, one might easily use the first evangelist's narrative in making a repetition of the contemplation.

1. Jesus Feeds the Crowds in Galilee (6:1-15)

1   Sometime after this, Jesus went off across the sea of Galilee, or of Tiberias.   2   Yet a crowd kept following him which was large, because it had seen the signs he was performing upon the sick.   3   Then Jesus went up the mountain, and he sat down there with his disciples.   4   Passover, the Jewish feast, was near.   5   Now Jesus, on raising his eyes and observing that the crowd is coming to him, says to Philip, "Where can we buy loaves, in order that these may eat?"   6 (He made this remark by way of testing him, since he himself knew what he was going to do.)   7   Philip answered him, "Loaves costing two hundred denarii would not be enough for each to have a little."   8   One of the disciples, Simon Peter's brother Andrew, says to him,   9   "There is a lad here who has five loaves of barley-bread and two dried fish.—But what good are these for so many?"   10   Jesus said, "Have the people sit down." There was abundant grass in that place; so the men sat down, some five thousand in number.   11   Jesus then took the loaves and, on giving thanks, distributed them to the people as they sat there. He did the same with the dried fish—as much as they wanted.   12   When they were full, he says to his disciples, "Gather up the pieces left over, lest any of it perish."   13   So they gathered them up, and filled twelve baskets with the pieces left uneaten from the five barley-loaves.   14   Then the people seeing the sign he had performed began to say, "This in truth is the Prophet who is come into the world!"   15   So Jesus, knowing they meant to come and carry him off to proclaim him king, withdrew again up the mountain by himself.

We may pick out some obvious divergencies from Mark's story in this interpretation of the feeding-episode. John begins by drawing attention to the lack of any real faith in the crowd, which "kept following him because it had seen the signs he was performing:" they resemble the people of Jerusalem (2:23-25). Here no mention is made of Jesus' compassion for these people: he neither teaches them (Mk 6:34), nor heals their sick (Mt 14:14), nor is he portrayed as their Shepherd, as in the Marcan cameo. If the locale is not "a desert," on the other hand, "the mountain" is given prominence: Jesus enters God's presence with his disciples. His situation upon the mountain, together with the references to Passover, seems intended to recall Moses, who will figure prominently in the first part of the following discourse. Above all, however, attention is concentrated on Jesus as provider of food: upon catching sight of the crowd, his decision is taken, so that his question to Philip is characterized as "testing him," to emphasize that Jesus "himself knew what he was going to do." Where in the Marcan account, the bread and fish come from the disciples' own store of provisions, here "a lad" is introduced, "who has five barley loaves and two dried fish."

This description which differs notably from the Marcan narrative may indicate that John used an independent source, which drew a parallel with a less impressive miracle in the Elisha cycle of legends (2 Kgs 4:42-44), where that prophet had fed one hundred men with twenty barley-loaves—"And when they had eaten, there was some left over, as the Lord had said" (v. 44). Unlike Mark, John has not made use of a Eucharistic liturgical formula in describing the actions of Jesus, who without "raising his eyes to heaven," or breaking the loaves, simply "took the loaves and, on giving thanks (*eucharistēsas:* see also v. 23), distributed them." To be noted also is that Jesus himself, not the disciples, handed the food round "to the people,"—a typical example of the Christological optic of our evangelist, important to him in view of the Eucharistic section (6:51-58) of the ensuing discourse.

Jesus' command to the disciples, "Gather up the pieces left over" is probably a reflection of the care taken in the early Church of the Eucharistic species, but also the remark, "lest any of it perish," prepares for the subsequent contrast between the bread of the miracle "that perishes" with "the food abiding unto eternal life, which the Son of Man will give you" (v. 27). Like Mark before him, John only provides evidence of the miracle with his note about the "twelve baskets" that were filled with "the pieces left uneaten." Yet, characteristically enough, he does not emphasize it, as Mark did by noting at this point the number fed. He has instead included that figure with his description of "the abundant grass in that place" (v. 19b).

The most striking contrast with the Marcan story however is the explicit mention of the reaction of the people, which he forms into a bipartite choral ending. The first exclamation might appear on the surface to be a real act of faith in "the Prophet" like Moses. However John invokes again Jesus' supernatural reading of hearts; he well knew "they meant to come and carry him off to proclaim him king." It will be remembered that John had earlier omitted mention of Jesus' baptism and his subsequent sojourn in the desert, recorded by all three Synoptic writers. He also passed over the "testing" by Satan (Mk 1:13), and hence also the triple expansion of that experience according to a scheme recalling Israel's experiences in the desert (Mt 4:1-11; Lk 4:1-13). However, as Raymond Brown once observed, the fourth evangelist has managed to include these three "temptations;" here, that of seeking worldly power. The temptation to provide food miraculously seems to be reflected in the crowd's uncomprehending demand at Capharnaum, "Sir, give us this bread always!" (6:34), while the insidious suggestion that Jesus seek publicity is proffered by his unbelieving brothers (7:3-5).

The story of the feeding concludes with Jesus' escape from the deluded, if grateful, crowd, and leaving his disciples to fend for themselves—unlike the Marcan Jesus—he once again enters the presence of his Father to seek support in prayer by "withdrawing again up the mountain by himself."

2. Jesus Walks Upon the Sea (6:16-21)

16 But when it got late in the evening, his disciples went down to the sea,
17 and getting into the boat, started out across the sea towards Capharnaum. Now darkness had already fallen—Jesus had not yet joined them.
18 Moreoever, the sea became turbulent, when a mighty wind began to blow up. 19 Now when they had been driven some twenty-five or thirty stadia, they see Jesus walking upon the sea and drawing near the boat: and they took fright. 20 But he says to them, "I AM! stop being frightened!"
21 Accordingly they wanted to take him into the boat; yet at once the boat touched land towards which they were trying to make.

The most notable feature of John's description is the surprising abruptness with which it concludes: once the disciples realize that Jesus is present the writer's design has been accomplished. The disciples are represented as embarking on their own intiative, not—as in Mark—on that of Jesus. Jesus' absence is symbolically recalled by the remark, "Darkness had already fallen." With the gale-like force of the sudden squall which came up, the boat was apparently driven some three or four miles off course, when "they see Jesus walking upon the sea and drawing near the boat." To the disciples, in the grip of fear from this demonstration of the numinous, Jesus utters—for the first time in this Gospel—the divine name, "I AM," communicated to Moses by God when He had refused to give that patriarch his unutterably sacred name. Instead God had declared, "Here is what you are to tell the Israelites, 'I AM sent me to you' " (Ex 3:14). Throughout his book, John will have Jesus identify himself by this divine name (8:24, 28, 58; 13:19; 18:5, 6, 8). George MacRae points out that probably the scene as here described is meant to recall the psalmist's picture of the divine presence to creation. "Your way was through the sea—Your path through the deep waters, yet Your footsteps were not seen" (Ps 77:19). In his comments on the use to which John has put the traditional data, Father MacRae observes that "this miracle is a sign in the full Johannine sense," and he suggests that this experience of the disciples contrasts with that of the crowd. While at the end of Jesus' discourse only Peter and the Twelve profess faith in Jesus, "You are the holy One of God!" (v. 69), whereas they failed to grasp the Christophany conveyed by the walk upon the sea, the crowd, so enthusiastic about being fed, reject his elaborate attempt to reveal himself by their interventions, and even a large group of his disciples abandon him (v. 66).[2]

3. The Discourse on the Bread of Life and the Sequel (6:22-71)

Properly speaking, this is a series of dialogues between Jesus and a changing set of interlocutors: the crowd that had been fed miraculously now present in the synagogue at Capharnaum (6:22-59), then a group of disgruntled disciples (6:60-66), and finally 'the Twelve," who appear only this single time (see 20:24) in the Fourth Gospel (6:66-71). The "discourse" falls naturally into two sections (after an introduction, vv. 22-24): Jesus as the incarnation of God's wisdom is himself "the Bread of life" (vv. 25-48); then, after the transitional verses 49-50, it becomes a question of the Eucharistic bread (vv. 51-59). John presents the consequences of Jesus' disclosure of himself in two stages in such a way as to remind one of the Ignatian teaching on the Election.

A. Jesus, Bringer of Divine Revelation (6:22-50)

Jesus is first presented as the embodiment of God's wisdom, who is to be accepted with faith by the will of his Father, if he is to bestow eternal life on the believer in the present era and bring him to share in the eschatological resurrection. Jesus is then God's emissary: to him the Father "draws" all who "listen" to Him, that they may "learn" from the teaching of Jesus. This development revolves around a Scriptural citation, freely cited by John, probably Psalm 78, which commemorates the wonders of Israel's exodus from Egypt. George MacRae is undoubtedly right, however, in suggesting that "The background of the discourse is the story, first told in Exodus 16, of the manna sent by God to feed the Israelites in the desert."[3]

> 22 Next day, the crowd, still standing on the other side of the sea—they saw there was no other but one boat there, and that Jesus had not got into the boat with his disciples, but his disciples had gone off by themselves.
> 23 However other boats came out from Tiberias to near the place where

---

2   G. W. MacRae, *Invitation to John,* pp. 84-85.
3   Ibid., 89.

they had eaten the bread [when the Lord gave thanks]— 24 So when the crowd saw that Jesus was not there, nor even his disciples, they themselves got into these boats and came across to Capharnaum seeking Jesus.

These awkward verses, with their overabundance of detail, form a somewhat breathless transition to the discourse itself. It may well be that the reference back to "the place where they had eaten the bread" is intended to alert the reader to the Eucharistic part of Jesus' teaching—particularly if the clause "when the Lord gave thanks" was actually part of the original text.

25 And on finding him on that side of the sea, they asked him, "Rabbi, when did you get here?" 26 Jesus answered them by saying, "Amen, amen I tell you: you seek me not because you saw signs, but because you ate your fill of the loaves. 27 Do not work for food that is perishable, but rather for the food that abides unto eternal life, which the Son of Man will give you—it is he on whom the Father has set His seal—and *He* is God!" 28 Thereupon they said to him, "What must we do to work the works of God?" 29 Jesus replied by saying to them, "This is God's work: you must believe in the One He sent!" 30 So they said to him, "Now what sign are you yourself going to perform so that we see it and can trust you?— What work will you do? 31 Our Fathers ate manna in the desert. As Scripture puts it, 'Bread from heaven he gave them to eat' " [Ps 78:24]. 32 Accordingly, Jesus said to them, "Amen, amen I tell you: it was not Moses who gave you bread out of heaven. No! rather it is my Father Who is giving you the real bread out of heaven. 33 For God's bread is the One who comes down out of heaven and is giving life to the world." 34 So they said to him, "Sir, give us this bread always."

35 Jesus said to them, "I am the bread of life; the person coming to me will never hunger—the one believing in me will never at any time thirst. 36 But as I told you, you have seen me, yet you do not believe. 37 All that the Father gives me will come to me, and the person coming to me I will never drive out, 38 because I have come down out of heaven, not to do my own will, but the will of the One Who sent me. 39 Now this is the will of Him Who sent me: I should lose nothing of what He has given me, but I am to raise it up at the last day. 40 For this is my Father's will: that everyone who sees the Son and believes in him may possess eternal life, and I, for my part, will raise him up at the last day."

41 Threat the Jews began to grumble about him because he said, "I am the Bread come down out of heaven." 42 And they kept asking, "Is not this fellow Joseph's son, Jesus, whose father and mother we know? How then can he claim, 'I have come down out of heaven'?" 43 Jesus told them in reply, "Stop grumbling among yourselves! 44 No one can come to me unless the Father—the One Who sent me—draw him; then I on my

part will raise him up at the last day. 45 It stands written in the prophets, 'And they shall all be taught by God' [Is 54:13]. Everyone who has listened to the Father and learned comes to me. 46 —Not that anyone has seen the Father, except the One from the Father, *he* has seen the Father! 47 Amen, amen I tell you; the one who believes possesses eternal life. 48 I am the Bread of life! 49 Your fathers ate manna in the desert, yet they died. 50 This is the Bread which comes down out of heaven: a person may eat it, and will never die!''

The crowd that had enjoyed a meal the previous day finally discovers Jesus at the synagogue in Capharnaum (v. 59), and at once begins the dialogue with an irrelevant question, "When did you come here?" This Jesus appears to ignore. It is, of course, the same question, in slightly different form, that John prompts his reader to ask himself throughout this Gospel, "Where is the glorified Jesus now for me?" For the moment, however, Jesus confronts the crowd with its lack of faith: it had contented itself with the satisfaction of hunger, and did not see the "sign" in the food, which, though miraculous, "is perishable" (see v. 12).

Jesus now announces an unprecedented kind of food, which transcends the crowd's experience, "food that abides unto eternal life, which the Son of Man will give you." The evangelist apparently points ahead to the Eucharist that will be given only after Jesus' "lifting up" as "the Son of Man." And he now identifies himself as the one "on whom the Father has set His seal" of approval, the Father, he says emphatically, Who "is God."

The crowd however does not pay attention to this revelation; as Jews, its members are concerned about "works," regarded as a kind of *quid pro quo* by which they may gain a reward. Jesus counters such calculating attitudes by pointing to the reality of "God's work" in the creation of faith in hearts receptive of His gracious gift. The crowd now betrays its lack of openness by a demand for a "sign" to convince it—"so that we . . . can trust you," and points to the great "sign" performed by Moses, "manna in the desert," backing up the demand with a loosely cited passage from the psalmist.

Jesus gives a word-for-word interpretation of the passage, "Bread from heaven he gave them to eat." The text means "not Moses" but "my Father"; "gave" refers not to any past gift, but to the present "gift of God" (4:10), which is himself—"the real bread out of heaven," bearer of the "truth" concerning the "God no one has ever seen." Moreover, the revelation is not a theological insight, but a gift of "life to the world." The uncomprehending crowd voices a desire for this mysterious bread, apparently like that of the Samaritan woman (4:10). Unlike her longing however, this request remains at a superficial level.

Jesus nonetheless now identifies himself as "the Bread of life." It will have been noted that, in his creative explanation of the psalm, he passed over in silence the word "eat," of which no mention will be made until verse 50. Should the crowd, who heard "the Scriptures" constantly in the synagogue, not have grasped Jesus' meaning against that background? The deuteronomic historian had taught that "God fed you with manna which you did not understand, nor did your fathers understand: that He might make you realize that a person does not live by bread solely, but lives by every word that issues from the mouth of the Lord" (Deut 8:3). And the sages of Israel repeatedly pictured divine wisdom as dispensing bread and drink to the believer. "Come, eat of my bread" (Prov 9:5). Sirach says of wisdom, "She will nourish him with the bread of understanding, and give him the water of learning to drink" (Sir 24:21; see Wis 16:26). Israel's prophets had spoken of God's word of revelation in similar vein (Am 8:11-13; Is 55:1-10; 65:11-13).

Jesus, proclaimed in the Prologue as the personal Word and "only Son," fulfills these prophetic promises given to Israel, and is in consequence "the real bread out of heaven." To accept him however is possible only through faith, as the remainder of this section of his discourse will now make clear to the reader. The crowd, John well knows, lacks this crucial grace of believing Jesus.

Thus the Johannine Jesus refers back to his previous judgment on the crowd, "You seek me not because you saw signs, but because you ate your fill of the loaves" (v. 26). "As I told you, you have seen me, yet you do not believe." He first insists that such belief in himself is a pure gift. John's curious penchant for employing the neuter to designate human beings was earlier mentioned. "All that the Father gives me will come to me, and the person coming to me I will never drive out." The will of his Father, as Jesus previously told his disciples (4:34), is "my food," his very life. And by His gift of "all," the Father's will is expressed to Jesus, as he now says repeatedly. John's conception of faith contains a "contemplative" element, absent from the Pauline notion with its accent upon "justification," a term appearing in a single passage of this Gospel—and with a different meaning (16:8, 10). Faith is the insight of one "who sees the Son" in Jesus; and he, in obedience to the Father's will, enables such a one to "possess eternal life" even now, and "at the last day" share in Jesus' own resurrection.

Once again John draws attention to the scandal of the Incarnation, which proved a stumbling block to "the Jews" in Jerusalem (2:19-20; see 5:17-18). "The Jews" reject categorically Jesus' disclosure of his identity on the grounds that they know him and his parents. "Is not this fellow Joseph's son, Jesus, whose father and mother we know?" The evangelist is intent on bringing the reader to remain open to every (even as yet inconceivable) experience of the unseen Jesus. Like their Israelite ancestors in the desert, the Jews "murmur" or "grumble" (Ex 16:2, 7-9, 12).

With great patience Jesus tries one final time to bring them to accept the mystery of God's action through himself. He insists upon the Father's initiative in bringing men and women to belief in himself. "No one can come to me unless the Father—the One Who sent me—draws him." He reminds them that this had been the teaching of the prophets by a freely cited text from Deutero-Isaiah: "All your sons will be taught by the Lord" (Is 54:13; see also Jer 31:34). He goes on to point out that the interior word which God utters to the heart is to be correctly discerned only through the teaching of the emissary of the Father, who alone has "seen the Father." This is the sense of the difficult verses, "Everyone who has listened to the Father, and learned, comes to me.— Not that anyone has seen the Father, except the One from the Father." Jesus terminates this first part of the dialogue-discourse by repeating the symbolic statement, whose meaning he has endeavored to explain. "I am the Bread of life." And he also recalls the promise of eternal life which, as the revealer of the unseen God, it is his task to make. "Your fathers ate manna in the desert, yet they died. This is the bread which comes down out of heaven—a person may eat it, and will never die!" For the first time Jesus speaks of eating—a sign that a transition is being made to the Eucharistic part of the discourse.

B. Jesus' Gift of the Eucharist (6:51-59)

The theme of the Eucharist, which was only hinted at in the first development, now comes to the fore in the remainder of the discourse, which also ceases to be a dialogue. Raymond Brown remarks, "Even though the verses in 51-58 are remarkably like those of 35-50, a new vocabulary runs through them: 'eat,' 'feed,' 'drink,' 'flesh,' 'blood'."[4] The same author also points out that, while in the verses prior to this, it is faith that brings eternal life, now life is promised through the eating and

---

4   R. E. Brown, *John I-XII,* p. 284.

drinking of the flesh and blood of the glorified Son of Man.

> 51   "I am the living Bread that came down out of heaven. If anyone eat this Bread he will live forever. But in fact the Bread I will give—it is my flesh for the life of the world!"   52   The Jews began to dispute violently among themselves. "How can this man," they asked, "give us his flesh to eat?"   53   Jesus accordingly told them, "Amen, amen I tell you: unless you eat the flesh of the Son of Man and drink his blood, you have no life in you.   54 The person feeding on my flesh and drinking my blood has eternal life, and I myself will raise him up at the last day.   55   For my flesh is real food, and my blood is real drink.   56   The person feeding on my flesh and drinking my blood abides in me, even as I abide in him.   57   As the living Father sent me and I have life because of the Father, so the one feeding on me will in his turn have life because of me.   58   This is the Bread come down out of heaven—not such as the fathers ate, and still died. The person feeding on this Bread will live forever."   59   He asserted this in a synagogue-instruction at Capharnaum.

The key word which forms the unifying factor in John's presentation is the term bread (or loaf), already used in two distinct senses: the bread of the "sign," material and "perishable" (v. 27), the bread (manna) of which the psalmist spoke (v. 31), Jesus as revealer and emissary of the Father (v. 35). Now the evangelist employs the word to signify the Eucharist, gift of love from the exalted Son of Man, once he has "laid down his life for his friends" (15:13).

John effects the transition by recapitulating verses 48 and 50: "I am the living Bread that came down out of heaven. If anyone eat this Bread he will live forever." More significantly, however, in the second part of the next verse he points to the event by which the Eucharist was created, Jesus' death, which John will present as his "lifting up" on the cross, his royal throne, from which he "hands over the Spirit" (19:30). The emphatic adversative (here rendered "But in fact") draws attention to this all-important event. Moreover, John, it would appear, has expressed it by means of a liturgical formula resembling the Pauline words over the bread (1 Cor 11:24), which Luke in turn has made more explicit, "This is my Body that will be given for your sake" (Lk 22:19). "The Bread I will give . . . is my flesh for the life of the world." The appearance here of "flesh" in place of "body" is a more exact rendition of the eucharistic words of Jesus at the Last Supper, since Aramaic (like the Hebrew of the Old Testament) did not have the word "body." In fact, "flesh," which always connotes a *living* person in the Bible, is more appropriate for the Eucharist than "body" which can also denote a corpse.

141

The words cause the Jews "to dispute violently among themselves." Schnackenburg is the first commentator to point to "the typological background" from which John has taken the word "dispute," or argue. "During the wandering in the wilderness not only 'murmuring' (see on 41), but also 'arguing' is reported among the people with Moses (Ex 17:2; Num 20:3) and against the Lord (Num 20:13)."[5] This observation is a reminder of the significance, as background for the entire discourse, of Israel's experiences in the desert.

The Johannine Jesus, far from rescinding his intolerable claim, expresses it with even greater realism in words that cannot be interpreted as metaphor. Using his characteristic, solemn formula, Jesus insists, "Unless you eat the flesh of the Son of Man and drink his blood, you have no life in you." Two significant features of the statement deserve comment. Firstly, it is "the flesh of the *Son of Man*" and "his blood." In the Fourth Gospel, this title indicates Jesus as the One who comes from the Father and returns to Him—that is, the exalted Lord. Our evangelist seems more concerned than his predecessors to point out that the Eucharist is the sacrament of the risen Jesus, and it is seemingly for this reason that he has replaced the Marcan liturgical formulae of "institution" (Mk 14:22-23) with a prophetic, symbolic act by Jesus, the footwashing (13:1-17). Secondly, Father Raymond Brown[6] has observed that the metaphorical use of the phrase, "eat someone's flesh," in biblical usage connotes an act of hostility. The psalmist speaks of "evildoers" who "assail me to eat up my flesh" (Ps 27:2; see Zech 11:9). The drinking of blood in the literal sense was categorically prohibited by the Torah (Lev 3:17); in a transferred sense, it indicated brutal slaughter in battle. Jeremiah prophesies, "The sword shall devour and be sated, and drink its fill of their blood" (Jer 46:10b).

In verses 54-57 Jesus now points out two meaningful results of the reception of his Eucharistic "flesh." Firstly, he promises the possession, already in this present existence, of "eternal life" (realized eschatology), which transmuted to the traditional, semitic point of view (futurist eschatology) comprehends the ultimate perfecting of the human person by the glorious resurrection "at the last day." In the second place, he insists unambiguously on the personal nature of this communion with himself as the risen Lord, which is crucial if any hint of magic is to be avoided. This loving exchange by which the believer "abides in me, even as I abide in him" constitutes a theme that will be fully orchestrated in

5   Schnackenburg, *John,* II, 60.
6   R. E. Brown, *John I-XII,* p. 284.

Jesus' farewell discourse to the disciples after his revelation of the coming of the Paraclete (14:16 ff). In view of this growth into so interpersonal a union, Jesus here emphasizes that, "My flesh is real food, and my blood is real drink"—they "really are what food and drink should be."[7]

Before he ends his instruction, the Johannine Jesus recalls the primordial event that created the possibility of "abiding in me," and insinuates that this Eucharistic communion is intended to lead ultimately to an experience of God Himself. "As the living Father sent me and I have life because of the Father, so the one feeding on me will, in his turn, have life because of me." Earlier in the discourse which followed the cure of the cripple by the pool in Jerusalem, Jesus had asserted, "Just as the Father possesses life of Himself, so too He has granted the Son to possess life in himself" (5:26). All that Jesus has and is comes to him from the Father and is meant to lead those with faith back to the Father.

"This is the Bread come down out of heaven—not such as the fathers ate, and still died. The person feeding on this Bread will live forever." Father Schnackenburg finds this final statement to contain "the essence of the eucharistic doctrine and of the whole discourse." His comment deserves to be cited. "It is that 'this'—here referring back to the Son who gives life—is the bread come down from heaven. The statement looks back to the definitions of 33 and 50, and says that everything which could be expected from the true and perfect heavenly bread, the real overcoming of death, life for eternity, is fulfilled in the eucharistic bread . . . While the primary allusion is to the Eucharist, there is also a reference back to the metaphor; the eating of the eucharistic bread is the final acting out of the eating mentioned in the text of 31."[8]

C. The Mystery of Jesus' "Election" of the Faithful Disciples (6:60-71)

The evangelist's introduction of (later Christian) doctrine concerning the Eucharist now results in the desertion of Jesus by certain of his followers, a crisis which the Church has had to face often enough in the course of her history. As George MacRae has reminded us, "In other places . . . the Gospel [of John] addresses the situation of its own time, near the end of the first century . . . It is not easy to decide whether the issue . . . is the eucharistic practice of the church or its christological faith. Perhaps both are at issue, for if one does not understand that the human Jesus is really the divine Son who has come down from the

7   C. K. Barrett, *The Gospel According to St. John,* p. 299.
8   Schnackenburg, *John,* II, 64-65.

Father, then the Eucharist too has become meaningless."[9]

> 60   As a result many of the hearers among his disciples said, "Such talk is hard to swallow! who can listen to it?"   61   Jesus, however, aware within himself that his disciples are grumbling over this, said to them, "Does this cause you to lose faith?   62   Then what if you behold the Son of Man mounting to where he formerly existed?   63   The Spirit is the life-giver: flesh is useless. The words I have spoken to you are Spirit and they are life.   64   Still some there are among you who do not believe." (For Jesus knew from the beginning which were the non-believers and who it was who would betray him.)   65   So he went on to say, "This is why I told you that no one is able to come to me, except it be given to him from the Father."   66   At this, many of his disciples fell away and no longer went about with him as disciples.   67   Accordingly Jesus said to the Twelve, "Do you also intend to go off?"   68   Simon Peter answered him, "Lord, to whom shall we go? You possess words belonging to eternal life.   69   And we for our part have come to believe and we know you are the holy One of God!"   70   Jesus made this reply to them, "Did I not freely choose the twelve of you? And yet one of you is an informer!"   71   (He was speaking of Judas, son of Simon Iscariot: for he was the man who was going to betray him—one among the Twelve.)

Awareness of John's telescoping of distinct historical levels, the period of those followers who knew Jesus in his lifetime with the later era of the Johannine community, is of paramount importance if one is to grasp the meaning of this desertion by certain of his disciples. In the early part of the discussion Jesus portrayed himself as the human embodiment of divine wisdom: "I am the Bread of life—come down out of heaven" (6:33, 35, 41, 47, 50). And it is seemingly this disclosure that certain disciples had heard without accepting it. This explains the bitterly ironic pun about bread that "is hard to swallow." And in fact these disgruntled followers are described here as "grumbling" as "the Jews" had done, "because he said, 'I am the Bread come down from heaven' " (v. 41).

Characteristically the Johannine Jesus, far from retreating from his position, takes the offensive by asking whether his words have shaken their faith in him (the sense of the Greek "scandalize"). And he recalls his statement, which the Jews had found offensive, about his "coming down out of heaven," by referring to his future glorification as glorified "Son of Man mounting to where he formerly existed." He goes on to contrast "flesh" (impotent, earth-bound human nature) with "the

9   G. W. MacRae, *Invitation to John,* pp. 95-96.

Spirit," as he had done with Nicodemus (3:6-8). Once again it is question of the scandal of the Incarnation, which the words of the earthly Jesus had caused, *not* of the Eucharistic "flesh" of the glorified Son of Man, which will result from his "mounting to where he formerly existed."

Jesus' next statement only becomes intelligible when the force of the perfect tense is taken into account. "The words I *have spoken* to you,"—not "which I am speaking"—in the context of this Gospel refer to the "remembered" words and actions (2:22; 12:16), which after his return to God and sending of the spirit, "the life-giver," will have the power to bestow "life" upon the believer. As late as the Last Supper his disciples will be represented as grasping nothing of the life-giving words of Jesus (13:36–14:22). Indeed, Jesus immediately makes it clear that he is now aware that "some there are among you who do not believe." And the evangelist underscores the mystery of the "election" of those other, *true* followers. In the first place he adds a gloss to these words of Jesus: "For Jesus knew from the beginning which were the non-believers and who it was who would betray him." Then he has Jesus himself refer back to his earlier assertion concerning the necessity of being drawn to Jesus by the Father (v. 44). To "be able to come to me" remains an utterly free and gracious gift "from the Father." Ignatius of Loyola was very sensitive to this truth, as the consideration concerning the Election in the Exercises clearly indicates. "That love which is moving me and makes me 'choose' a certain course descends from above *(de arriba)* from God's love" ([184]). The Saint employs the term "Election" in its biblical sense (Deut 7:7-8; Is 43:1-7) of God's untrammeled free choice of his creatures. In fact, a favorite formula of Ignatius may be seen to appear as a constant theme in his letters. "I beg God our Lord that he may deign in his generosity and goodness to grant us a superabundance of grace, in order that we may fully experience his most holy will and carry it out entirely."

The evangelist now presents a classical example of such an "Election" by Jesus, as he asks the Twelve (mentioned in this Gospel for the first time): "Do you also intend to go off?"—the Greek form of the question expects "no" as answer. Peter's response in question-form is not intended to express uncertainty about where to turn: despite the evangelist's obvious bias in favor of "the disciple whom Jesus loved" (13:23-26; 20:3, 8), he here pays tribute to Peter's eminence within the Twelve, presenting his profession of faith and loyalty to Jesus in solemn form. "You possess words leading to eternal life. And we, for our part, have come to believe and we know you are the holy One of God!" Such is Peter's whole-hearted response to Jesus' "election" of himself, as Jesus' immediate question indicates. "Did I not freely choose the twelve of you?" Still, there is a dark side to this mystery of Jesus' unerring choice, which John's community has doubtless pondered with anguish. "And yet one of you is an informer!" The Greek word for devil *(diabolos)* means slanderer, accuser. It is part of the irony of history that the historical existence of the Twelve in Jesus' lifetime, questioned by some scholars, is attested by the perfidy of Judas. "He was speaking of Judas, son of Simon Iscariot: for he was the man who was going to betray him—one of the Twelve." It seems plausible that Judas' patronymic means "man from Kerioth;" if so, Judas was the single Judean amongst the intimate, Galilean disciples.

Chapter 10

CURE OF A BLIND MAN PROVOKES A
DEFINITIVE TAKING OF SIDES (9:1-41)

I n the initial chapter of this study reference was made to Two Standards ([136-148]), where its early, intimate association with the spiritual experiences of Ignatius was indicated as the fruit of his reading during the convalescence at Loyola and—much more profoundly—as the
result of the "so great illumination" at Manresa, which caused his aban-
donment of a hermit-like existence at the first stirrings of an apostolic
vocation. That this exercise, together with its sequel, the meditation on
Three Classes ([149-156]), was considered quintessential to the making of
the Exercises by the earliest companions of Ignatius during the Paris
period (before 15 November, 1536) now seems demonstrable. This is the
view adopted by the two Ignatian scholars José Calveras and Candido de
Dalmases, who edited an early manuscript of the Exercises which they
regard as "the most ancient of all that have survived."[1] This meticulous-
ly transcribed document was copied out in Paris no later than 1535, so
the two Spanish experts insist, by the young Englishman, priest and
humanist, John Helyar, who had earlier done degrees at Oxford under
the celebrated Juan Luis Vives.

It is moreover the view of these two eminent specialists that Helyar,
having fled to Paris in the spring of 1535, where he pursued exegetical
and patristic studies before going on to Louvain at the beginning of 1536,
made the Exercises in the French capital—probably under the direction
of Pierre Favre. (It will be recalled that Ignatius himself had quitted Paris
for his own homeland in April of 1535.) It is also suggested that Father
Helyar took this step after learning of the martyrdoms in England of
Thomas More and John Fisher (in June and July, 1535). An examination
of this ancient text, copied with such painstaking diligence by the erudite
young scholar, appears to indicate that at this time the Second and

---

1   S. *Ignatii de Loyola Exercitia Spiritualia* (nova editio), José Calveras and Cándido de
    Dalmases, in Monumenta Historica Societatis Iesu, Vol. 100 (Romae, 1969), pp.
    418-454.

Fourth weeks had not yet evolved to their full efflorescence exhibited by the definitive edition of the *Exercises;* nor in fact is there mention of the Contemplation to Attain the Love of God ([230-237]).

If these deductions from the data are accurate, the Helyar manu-script—contrary to the view of Joseph de Guibert[2]—actually antedates Ignatius' final work of revision which continued into the 1540s. Accord-ingly, this precious witness becomes significant for its attestation to the evolution of Ignatius' thought. What is of interest to us however at the moment is the evidence it provides to the high esteem in which Two Stan-dards was held by the first Jesuit directors of the Exercises. For from the version known to this young English humanist, Two Standards together with Three Classes at that time followed directly upon the consideration of the Call of the King, the Incarnation, and the Nativity. These, without any further contemplations of the earthly life of Jesus, were considered sufficient preparation for the Election of which Helyar gives notice in the immediate sequel.

In the final text of the *Exercises,* the purpose of Two Standards—to which most of the fourth day of the Second Week is devoted([148])—is announced in The Consideration of Different States of Life prior to the discussion of the Election itself. "As some introduction to this, we shall see, in the next exercise, the aim of Christ our Lord, and by contrast, that of the enemy of human nature, and how we ought to prepare ourselves to come to perfection in whatever state or way of life God our Lord may give us to choose" ([135]). The petitionary prayer which opens this im-portant meditation/contemplation bids the exercitant pray to escape the delusion of imagining himself or herself arrayed in the battle of life under Jesus' banner, when in reality one is an unwitting pawn of "the evil chieftain." It is accordingly proposed that the prayer "will be to ask for a knowledge of the deceits of the evil *caudillo,* as well as help to be on my guard against them; and also for a knowledge of the genuine life which the sovereign and true commander discloses, and the grace to imi-tate him" ([139]). Thus this dramatic presentation of a theology of his-tory is not an apocalyptic picture of past or future, but it is intended to give an insight into contemporary spiritual reality.

Moreover, as Stanislas Lyonnet has shrewdly perceived, this is in fact the first time in the *Exercises*—apart from a cursory reference to the fall of the angels ([50])—that "Lucifer" is allotted an extended role. (It will have been noted that nowhere in the Second Week is any of the exor-

2   J. de Guibert, *The Jesuits: Their Spiritual Doctrine and Practice,* pp. 115-116.

cisms narrated in the Gospels assigned for contemplation, and indeed none of these stories find a place in the Fourth Gospel.) Lyonnet draws the conclusion that "The presence of this new personage should, in the first place, remind the retreatant, about to engage upon the Election, that he is now to become the stake in a struggle between Satan and Jesus Christ."[3]

Yet, for all that she or he may acknowledge the very important truth of faith embedded in the Ignatian portrayal of the contrasting tactics employed in every age by the risen Christ against Satan, the modern Christian may be put off by the medieval character of this somewhat flamboyant picture presented in Two Standards. Accordingly, one may find more helpful a reflection on the dramatic story of the cure of a man blind from birth and the struggle he undergoes in remaining loyal to his almost unknown benefactor.

In his meditation, Ignatius—as is characteristic of him—is concerned to lead the exercitant to a deep awareness of *movement.* In fact he displays his conviction that there are two opposed and progressive sets of experience in the spiritual life, to which the believer in any age is continually exposed. The stratagems devised by Satan begin by instilling an exaggerated hankering after security ("riches"), which in turn evolves into covetousness for self-affirmation and self-seeking ("the empty honors of the world"), and this ultimately culminates in what Louis Puhl somewhat quaintly translates as "overweening pride," which actually entails contempt, even hatred for God himself ([142]). Christ's strategy of liberation represents the very reverse of this ([146]): beginning from a sincere sense of one's need of God ("spiritual poverty"), it progresses to a desire for contumely and affronts for Christ, to arrive finally at "humility," which is the true love of friendship *(amor amicitiae)* for God.

The introductory remarks set down in Helyar's text—probably a suggestion by his director—runs as follows. "The one [standard] is that of Christ, the supreme commander and our Lord, who does not offer anything pleasing and joyful here below, only constant warfare—whatever is harsh, rough, and bitter (except for the inner joy of a good conscience). Still, for the future life, he promises all that is most delightful—joy, peace, eternal happiness, those things that 'never has ear heard,' and so on (Is 64:2-3; 1 Cor 2:9). The other [standard] belongs to Satan, principal enemy of our human nature, who here deceitfully holds out all that is agreeable and gives gratification, yet soon leads to eternal exile. 'The

3   S. Lyonnet, S.J., "La méditation des Deux Étendards et son fondement scripturaire," *Christus* 12 (1956), 439.

wages of sin is death' (Rom 6:23)."[4]

To return to the Fourth Gospel, it may be said that our evangelist, possibly more than any of his colleagues, has kept the clearly defined lines of battle between "the light" and "the darkness" before the minds of his reader ever since the Prologue (1:5, 11). A prominent theme which (as already noted) he consistently exploits is the truth that no human being can take a detached view of Jesus. One is reminded of this in the refusal of evil-doers "to come to the light" and their love of "the darkness" (3:19-20), the very antithesis of that coming to "the light" by all who "live the truth" (3:21). Our evangelist moreover indicates the ongoing nature of this struggle in his own day, as he recounts the defection of certain disciples of Jesus after his disclosure of his own identity as "the Bread of life" and his promise of the Eucharist (6:60-66). Throughout the two chapters which follow on this event, John concentrates attention upon Jesus' unavailing efforts to disclose the mystery surrounding himself to "the Jews," representative of official Judaism. As was earlier noted, our evangelist has set in almost breathless sequence some eleven vignettes (7:1-8:59), by which he shows the increasing hostility and murderous intent of Jesus' adversaries on the occasion of the celebration of the great Israelite pilgrimage-feast of "booths" or "tabernacles." Against the backdrop of this most joyous of Jewish festivals, with its ritual of intercession for rain in the coming year (a liturgy borrowed from a primitive pagan rain-making ceremonial), Jesus proclaims that he himself is the unique source of "living water"—a symbol for John of Jesus' future gift of the Spirit (7:37-39) once he is glorified. On another occasion, probably during the nightly illumination of the sacred enclosure during the seven or eight days of this thanksgiving feast, Jesus announces to the Pharisees, "I am the light of the world . .. the person following me will not walk about in the darkness, but will possess the light of life" (8:12). This characterization of himself Jesus now acts out in the cure of an anonymous blind man. With his flair for drama, which we already saw illustrated in his narrative of Jesus' cleansing of the sacred enclosure, John has arranged this story in seven scenes. Here we follow a suggestion by George MacRae, who observes that, "The underlying literary principle is derived from classical drama—the so-called law of stage duality, by which a scene is identified as two characters or groups of characters in dialogue on the stage."[5]

---

4   See *S. Ignatii de Loyola, Exercitia Spiritualia,* Vol. 100 in MHSJ, p. 441.
5   G. W. MacRae, *Invitation to John,* p. 124.

Scene One: Jesus with the Disciples (9:1-7)

1 Now as he [Jesus] was passing by, he saw a poor human being, blind from birth, 2 and his disciples asked him, "Rabbi, who was it who sinned—this fellow or his parents, that he should be born blind?" 3 Jesus replied, "Neither this man nor his parents sinned—it was to let the works of God be manifested through him. 4 For our part, we must perform the works of Him Who sent me, while day lasts. Night is coming when no one can work. 5 As long as I am in the world, I am light for the world." 6 On saying this, he spat on the ground and made some mud with his spittle, and smeared the mud upon his eyes. 7 Then he said to him, "Go, wash them in the pool of Siloam" (which means the One who is sent). So he went, and washed, and came back seeing.

That Jesus had cured a number of cases of blindness is evident from the Synoptic tradition (Mk 8:22-26; 10:46-52; see Mt 11:5; Lk 7:21). John alone however describes the healing of a man "blind from birth." From the beginning this writer points to the event as caused by Jesus' desire to reveal his true identity by employing the technical term, "pass by." In two notable scenes in the Old Testament this expression signals a theophany. When God refuses Moses' request to see His "glory," He promises, "I will make all my goodness *pass by* you . . . My face you cannot see . . . when my glory *passes by,* I will put you in a crevice of the rock and cover you with my hand until I have *passed by*" (Ex 33:18-23). The term appears also in the description of Elijah's great mystical experience on Mount Horeb, when "the Lord was *passing by*" (1 Kgs 19:9-18).

In this opening scene of his drama John directs attention to the dialogue between Jesus and his disciples, who shared the misconception, current in that day, that sickness or disease was a divine punishment for sin. This notion that God would punish the children for their fathers' sins was incorporated into a version of the decalogue (see Ex 20:5), and it was only during the period of the Babylonian exile that the two great prophets, Jeremiah and Ezekiel, who announced the new covenant, would insist upon personal responsibility for wrong-doing (Jer 31:29-30; Ez 18:2-4). Jesus makes this prophetic doctrine his own, and in correcting the disciples' point of view, he points to the true purpose behind this pitiful affliction, "It was to let the works of God be manifested in him."

Surprisingly, Jesus now employs the first person plural (attested by the best manuscripts, although many copyists changed it to singular). "For our part we must perform the works of Him Who sent me." Like the Christ of Two Standards, who "selects so many persons as apostles, disciples, and sends them throughout the entire world, spreading his sacred teaching'' ([145]), Jesus here—for the only time in this Gospel—associates his disciples with his own God-given mission, which he characterizes in terms of the struggle between "light" and "darkness" implied in the Prologue (1:5), appealing to the disciples to recognize and obey the divine imperative ("must") under which their future mission, like his own, stands. "Night is coming when no one can work" hints at the imminent termination of Jesus' ministry, but by its general formulation extends its application to include his followers, who are to carry out God's work despite opposition, hardship, even persecution. This is forcibly clarified by the urgent summons with which Jesus closes his public ministry. "It is yet but a short while that the light is present to you. Travel about while you have the light, lest darkness overtake you. Indeed the traveler in darkness does not know where he is going. While you have the light, believe in the light in order that you may become sons of light!" (12:35-36). This summons of the Johannine Jesus is echoed in the message of the Christ of Two Standards.

On the present occasion Jesus' final words announce the significance of what he is about to do: the curing of the blind man is a symbol of the gift of faith in himself which Jesus will bestow. "As long as I am in the world, I am light for the world." Jesus' actions will be his response to his Father's will; as such they are a lesson intended for his disciples on the Christian mission.

Curiously enough, as the evangelist narrates his story, the man born blind has been ignored up to this point, nor is he given an opportunity to ask for deliverance from his disability. Jesus is represented as taking the initiative without consulting the poor man: "He spat on the ground and made some mud with his spittle, and smeared the mud upon his eyes." Only now does Jesus address the blind man, "Go, wash them in the pool of Siloam." The good king Hezekiah had had a tunnel constructed to divert the water from the spring of Gihon into this pool (2 Chr 32:30), the existence of which is now attested by the copper scroll from Qumran. The evangelist interprets the name as a reference to Jesus, "The One who is sent."

In his customary manner John relates the miracle tersely, but dramatically: "So he went, and washed, and came back seeing." This stupendous miracle—like the rescue from death of the royal official's little son (4:51)—occurs at a distance. That it was attributed to Jesus however will be made clear in the later remark by some of the Jewish friends of Mary and Martha, "Could not this man who opened the eyes of the blind man have kept this man from death?" (11:37).

Scene Two: The Blind Man with His Neighbors (9:8-12)

8   So his neighbors and those formerly accustomed to see him begging kept saying, "Isn't this the one who used to sit and beg?"   9   Some were claiming, "It is he;" others insisted, "Not at all, but only someone who looks like him:" the man himself declared, "I'm the one alright!"   10   So they went on to ask him, "How does it happen that your eyes have been opened?"   11   The man replied, "The man they call Jesus made some mud, and smeared my eyes, and told me, 'Go to Siloam and wash them;' so I did go, and I washed, and I can see!"   12   Then they asked him, "Where is that man?" He says, "I don't know."

It should be observed that Jesus now disappears from the story to re-enter it only in the two final scenes. In his absence, which is more apparent than real, the man once blind is seemingly left on his own to struggle against the powers of evil arrayed against him and to suffer for his association with his benefactor. Through this painful process the man's progressive advance towards faith in him who declared himself "light for the world" is carefully enucleated. Indeed, it may not be reading too much into the text to suggest that there are hints of his assimilation to the character of the absent Jesus. For like Jesus the formerly blind beggar provokes the taking of sides for or against him. It is not difficult to see in his evolution to full faith the three steps marked out in the Ignatian meditation from poverty through contumely to genuine humility.

In the present scene, the man's appearance among "his neighbors and those who were formerly accustomed to see him begging" at once causes a division of opinion as to his identity; and the issue is settled by the declaration of the man himself—here translated colloquially as "I'm the one alright!" It may not be accidental that in the Greek text this reply takes the form "I am" *(egō eimi)*, which in the mouth of Jesus has already signified his divine name (8:24, 28, 58; see Ex 3:14). The *miraculé* recounts the story of his cure in the same laconic style the evangelist had employed. "The man they call Jesus made some mud, and smeared my eyes, and told me 'Go to Siloam and wash them;' so I did go, and I washed, and I can see!" The mention of Siloam recalls the feast of *Sukkōth,* the backdrop used for the controversies in the two preceding chapters. It was from this pool that water was carried to the altar of holocausts that stood outside the sanctuary, where it was poured out by the priest. This ceremonial occasioned the momentous announcement by Jesus "on the final, great day of the festival" that he was source of the life-giving Spirit. "If anyone is thirsty, he must come to me—I mean, the person believing in me. As Scripture [Prov 18:4] says, 'Streams of living water will flow from his heart' " (7:37-38). A gloss by the evangelist alerts the reader to the real sense of Jesus' words: "He was speaking here of the Spirit, which those believing in him were to receive; for the Spirit did not yet exist because Jesus was not yet glorified" (7:39). As elsewhere in the Bible, the Spirit is said "not yet to exist" to indicate that He had not yet begun His activity as gift of the exalted Jesus.

To the query as to the whereabouts of "the man Jesus"—"Where is that man?" (the question already pointed out as central to John's Gospel)—the man replies with complete candor, "I don't know." This admission suggests the absence as yet of real faith, as it will later after the resurrection in the Magdalene's disconsolate announcement, "I don't know where they have laid him" (20:3, 13). Yet for all that he is ignorant, the man testifies unhesitatingly to the reality of the miracle, which has caused a certain scepticism among those who knew him to have been blind. In contrast with that attitude the man evinces genuine openness to Jesus by his testimony to a happening that appears highly questionable in the eyes of his acquaintances.

Scene Three: A First Inquiry by the Pharisees (9:13-17)

> 13 They take the man who had been blind to the Pharisees. 14 (Now it was Sabbath that day when Jesus had made mud and opened his eyes. 15 Consequently, the Pharisees in their turn began to cross-examine him about how he was able to see.) He told them, "He put mud on my eyes, and I washed them, and I can see." 16 This led some of the Pharisees to declare, "This fellow is no man of God—he does not keep Sabbath!" Yet others kept objecting, "How can any sinful human being perform such signs?" Thus there was sharp division among them. 17 So once more they interrogate the blind man, "Here you! what do you say about him, since it was your eyes he opened?" So he said, "He is a prophet."

In their uncertainty and doubt, the simple friends of the man once blind bring him to the official interpreters of Torah, here designated as "the Pharisees," who by the evangelist's time were the only remaining party among "the Jews"—thus the two terms have become synonymous. Only at this point does John inform the reader "it was Sabbath," when the miracle was wrought. Under cross-examination the man once more tells his story without wasting any words, "He put mud on my eyes, and I washed them, and I can see."

Raymond Brown points out that "kneading" was classed as one of thirty-nine actions which Pharisaic legalism denounced as violations of Sabbath-rest, and he notes that in later Jewish interpretation "it was not

permitted to anoint an eye on the Sabbath."⁶ Hence "some of the Pharisees" now show they are already caught in the first of "the snares" set by
"the enemy of human nature." Their casuistic expertise constitutes their
vaunted security *(codicia de requezas)*, from which position of strength
they at once pronounce sentence. "This fellow is no man of God—he
does not keep Sabbath!" Others of their number informed of other
miracles by Jesus—perhaps that of the cure of the cripple on an earlier
Jewish feast-day (5:1-9)—state their rebuttal, "How can any sinful
human being perform such signs?" So, like Jesus himself the blind man
creates a "sharp division among them." In fact, it would appear to be a
sign of their intense frustration that they stoop somewhat contemptu-
ously to appeal to this ignorant fellow as arbiter in their dispute—one of
"that crowd that knows nothing of the Law" and whom they had already
declared "to be damned" (7:48). "Here you! what do you say about
him, since it was your eyes he opened?" At this point these legalists are
apparently willing to concede the reality of the cure, which they will later
deny. In his simplicity the former blind man gives evidence of his growing faith in Jesus, "He is a prophet." The only prophets, apart from
Moses, to whom miracles are attributed in the Old Testament, were Elijah as well as Elisha. John has already presented Jesus as the Moses-like
prophet, and so this avowal in the mouth of such an unlettered witness
probably indicates his nascent belief that the God of Israel has acted
through Jesus. What is essential for the development of such faith, as Ignatius points out, is further experience of "contumely and contempt"
([146]), which the protagonist in the drama is shortly to suffer.

Scene Four: Jewish Examination of the Man's Parents (9:18-23)

18   Now the Jews refused to believe he had actually been blind and now
could see, until they summoned the parents of the one who had been given
sight,   19   and cross-questioned them, "This fellow is your son—who,
you claim, was born blind? So how can he now see?"   20   To this his
parents responded "We know this is our son and he was born blind.   21
But as to how he can now see—we don't know. Ask him—he is of an age; he
will speak for himself."   22   (His parents made this deposition because
they were frightened of the Jews, since the Jews had already decided that if
anyone should publicly confess him as Messiah, such a one would be expelled
from the synagogue.   23   So that is why his parents declared, "He is of an
age—interrogate him.")

---

6   R. E. Brown, *John I-XII*, p. 313.

It may cause some surprise that according to the scheme followed here in constructing the drama this scene, in which the man's terrified parents are subjected to inquisition by "the Jews," stands at the very center. This alignment however indicates its importance to the author. The significance for John of this development appears also from the gloss which he appends to it. While he has earlier referred to "fear of the Jews" (7:13; see also 12:42; 19:38; 20:19), he introduces the reason for this paralyzing fear—public confession of faith in Jesus was punishable by expulsion from the synagogue, a measure that entailed serious personal and social consequences. Such ostracization meant the end of employment, of buying and selling in a Jewish environment. Under Rabbi Gamaliel II a curse on "heretics" *(minim)* was inserted into the Eighteen Benedictions recited by all devout Jews, and this harsh measure enforcing "apartheid" introduced about 90 AD was directed against "the Nazarenes." It had undoubtedly inflicted severe hardships upon the Johannine community, and moreover it evidently brought certain Jews with genuine belief in Jesus to hesitate to make public acknowledgement of this allegiance. These people are a major concern of the evangelist, who at several points in his Gospel may be seen to appeal to them (8:30-31; 12:42). Nicodemus, twice characterized as coming to Jesus "by night" (3:3, 11; 19:19-39), and Joseph from Arimathea (19:38) seem to be representative of this unhappy group. And in fact the close disciples of Jesus on the evening of the resurrection (20:19) are in the same predicament—if one recalls Jesus' prediction after the Last Supper that the Jews "will expel you from the synagogue" (16:2). In the context of Two Standards, these religious leaders from their position of strength ("riches") as honored guardians of a legalistic interpretation of Torah are being led to ambition "the empty honors of the world," directing to their own glorification what should be attributed to God alone.

Before such an awesome tribunal, the timorous parents admit the man is their son, that he was in fact born blind, but venture no opinion about the one who healed him, and how he effected the miraculous transformation from blindness.

Scene Five: A Second Interrogation of the Blind Man (9:24-34)

24 So a second time they summoned the man who had been blind, and told him, "Give glory to God! For our part we know this man is a sinner."
25 At this the other replied, "If he is a sinner, I don't know. One thing I *do* know—before, I was blind; now I can see." 26 So they interrogated him, "What did he do to you? how did he open your eyes?" 27 He

answered them, "I already told you, yet you wouldn't listen! Why do you wish to hear it over again?—Don't tell me you yourselves want to become his disciples!"   28   Then they heaped abuse on him with the retort, "*You* may be that fellow's disciple. As for us, we are disciples of Moses.   29   In fact, we know God spoke to Moses. As for this fellow, we don't even know where he is from."   30   The man made them this answer, "Now that's really remarkable! Here you don't know where he is from, yet he opened my eyes.   31   We all know God doesn't listen to sinners, but He does listen to anyone who is God-fearing and is doing His will.   32   Time out of mind nobody ever heard of a person, who opened the eyes of one born blind.   33   If this man weren't from God, he couldn't have done anything."   34   They made him this response, "You were born and bred in sin! Yet you are trying to teach us!" And they threw him out.

All this time Jesus has remained absent, while the stalwart witness to Jesus has been pitting his wits against the religious establishment. Like the woman by the well in Samaria, this man is limned sympathetically as a real personality, who successfully counters the objections of his inquisitors with candor and humility. He confesses what he does not know, but clings tenaciously to the genuineness of his cure; and thus forces the antagonistic judges to return tediously to their initial question as to how the cure was effected. The conventional formula by which they put him under oath, "Give glory to God!", is cited with irony by the evangelist: the witness is truly to glorify God by his loyal, quick-witted defense of his benefactor. The repetitiousness of their cross-examination is shown up as devoid of meaning by contrast with the common-sense and humor of the witness whose testimony they are bent on suppressing. He courageously replies, "I already told you, yet you wouldn't listen! Why do you wish to hear it over again?—Don't tell me you yourselves want to become his disciples!"

The exchange between the witness to Jesus and his relentless questioners now reaches a climax. In their frustration and fury the Jews are brought under the influence of "the darkness" to the final stage of "overbearing pride" ([142]). Their conceited arrogance and disdain for this unschooled beggar is shown by the emphatic "we" (vv. 24, 28, 29) and their self-assured "We know" (vv. 24, 29). José Calveras traces the progress of those guilty of "overbearing pride" in his note to Two Standards: "By considering themselves much superior to other men, with a right to intervene and impose their will completely, [they become] rebels against all human authority and even contemptuous of God Himself."[7]

7   José Calveras, *Ejercicios espirituales y Directorio,* edición reducida (Barcelona, 1958), p. 111.

When these despotic defenders of their own legalistic view of the Law are baulked in their plan to make the man contradict himself in a new account of his cure, "they heaped abuse on him" and take refuge in their boast that "*we* are disciples of Moses". In their anger they make a bad blunder of confessing their ignorance of Jesus and his origins. "As for this fellow, we don't even know where he is from." Their contempt for Jesus leads them into making the damaging admission that they have failed to recognize Jesus' divine origin, and so are culpably ignorant that in him God is making His ultimate offer of salvation. They show too that they are closed to the truth that Moses, whose disciples they claim to be, actually wrote of Jesus (5:46) as reported by the Deuteronomist, "The Lord your God will raise up a prophet like myself from among your own brothers: to him you must listen" (Deut 18:15).

The former blind man by contrast evinces a growing belief in Jesus "who is God-fearing and doing His will." He shows a more and more profound insight into the meaning of the unique miracle. "Time out of mind nobody ever heard of a person, who opened the eyes of one born blind. If this man weren't from God, he couldn't have done anything." For his courageous confession the man now suffers vilification and even violence. Those conducting the hearing first attack him verbally, "You were born and bred in sin!" (They are seen to adopt the view about sin dismissed earlier by Jesus.) "Yet you are trying to teach *us*!" Instead of refuting the lucid reasoning of their opponent, they take refuge in pride of place. "And they threw him out." The physical expulsion of the man from what should have been a court of justice symbolizes the much-feared ostracism, inflicted in John's time, upon recalcitrant "Nazarenes" with all its religious, social, and economic consequences.

Scene Six: Jesus Bestows the Gift of Faith in Himself (9:35-38)

> 35 Jesus heard they had thrown him out, so when he found him, he said, "Do you believe in the Son of Man?" 36 The other asked, "And who is he, sir, so I may believe in him?" 37 Jesus informed him, "You have in fact been seeing him, and the one speaking to you is he." [38 He said simply, "I do believe, Lord,"—and he fell on his knees in worship before him.]

Throughout the severe trials the man undergoes at the hands of his Jewish inquisitors, Jesus has seemingly left him to his own devices. The former blind man's constancy and fortitude may be taken to exemplify the advice given by Ignatius to the exercitant who experiences "desolation." The instruction to the director (Annotation 7) that he display gentleness and kindliness towards such a one appears to imply that he not attempt to bring his retreatant out of such a state prematurely. Such misguided protectiveness might seriously impede growth in spiritual maturity. Rather the director is to "instil drive and stamina to go forward, both by unmasking the trickery of the enemy of human nature, and by making him ready himself by acquiring the [right] dispositions towards the consolation that will come" ([7]).

The Rules for Discernment, which spell out in detail the strategy to be adopted against the power of evil "in times of desolation" are admirably exemplified in the conduct of the chief actor in the drama. He recalls repeatedly the joy and gratitude at being given his sight ("consolation"), and thus remains steadfast in the trials he experiences ([318]). He presents a paradigm of the person whom "the Lord has, as a test, left to his natural powers to resist the different disturbances and temptations of the enemy" ([320]): the man relies on his own quick-wittedness and sense of humor, and "works hard to keep up his endurance" ([321]). His situation becomes the classic instance of the second and third reasons why Christ permits an experience of "desolation." It may be that "He wishes to test our worth and to see how far we advance in his service and praise without the 'rewards' of consolation and great favors;" or it may be that "He wishes to make us learn with real knowledge by interior feelings that He does not depend upon us to impart or maintain an ever-deepening devotion . . . but that all is a gracious gift of God our Lord" ([322]).

The evangelist seeks to inform the reader at the beginning of the scene that Jesus has not abandoned the man whose blindness he had cured —despite his lengthy absence from the drama. John has deliberately set in contrast the actions of the man's biased inquisitors, who "had thrown him out" bodily from the courtroom, with the solicitude of Jesus who had earlier promised that "The person who comes to me I shall never throw out" (6:37). On hearing of the man's pitiful plight, Jesus began a search for him, and "when he found him, said, "Do you believe in the Son of Man?" The abruptness of the question without any apparent preparation matches the bluntness of Jesus' display of initiative in curing the blindness without even permitting the man to ask him to do it. John may well have thought such disconcerting directness of speech characteristic of Jesus' challenging word (see 3:3; 4:16; 6:26).

The form which Jesus' question assumes may strike the reader as peculiar, until he reckons with the particular sense in which John has applied the title, "the Son of Man," to Jesus. It is to be understood in the context of Jesus' coming from and returning home to the Father; hence it is, in this Gospel, the exalted Jesus who is properly "Son of Man" and it is precisely in that capacity that "the Father has given him authority to pass judgment" (5:27). John here is, in part, fashioning the setting for the final scene in his drama where Jesus is to assume the role of judge of the unfaith of the Pharisees. In fact, however, this query of Jesus leads to what John considers a central issue in his entire Gospel, "And who is he, sir, that I may believe in him?" As "Son of Man," Jesus will shortly announce to the people of Jerusalem that he will soon show forth the attractiveness of the Crucified: "As for myself, when I am lifted up from the earth, I will draw all to myself" (12:32). The response of the incredulous crowd on that occasion stands in sharp contrast to the former blind man's openness to Jesus. "We have heard from the Law that the Messiah abides forever; so how can you say, 'The Son of Man must be lifted up?'—Who is this Son of Man?" (12:34).

Accordingly, one is meant to see that the strange form of Jesus' question is an invitation to this man, to whom he has given sight, to accept him as "the light of the world," who already promised that "the one following me . . . will have the light of life" (8:12). This becomes evident in the answer Jesus now gives: "You have in fact been seeing him"—a present experience that began with the man's cure—"and the one speaking to you is he"—for John acceptance of Jesus' word is essential to genuine faith, which the man is represented as receiving.

The concluding verse, placed within brackets, is missing in certain very early and important witnesses to the text, and it exhibits some non-Johannine features. The most notable of these is that it displays the single instance in this Gospel where worship—paid to God at 4:20-24 (see also 12:20)—is accorded to Jesus. This, with the liturgical gesture of "falling to one's knees," has led Father Brown in his commentary to suggest that "Perhaps we have here an addition stemming from the association of John ix with the baptismal liturgy and catechesis."[8] For all that may well be true, the verse forms a fitting conclusion to this important scene.

Scene Seven: Judgment Passed on the Would-be Judges (9:39-41)

39 Thereupon Jesus announced, "To pass a sentence of judgment am I come into this world, in order that those who cannot see may see, while those who can see may become blind!"   40   Some of the Pharisees in his company heard this, so they asked him, "It is not we surely who are also blind!"

8   R. E. Brown, *John I–XII*, p. 375.

41   Jesus told them, "If only you *were* blind, you would not be guilty of sin. But as it is, you claim 'We can see'—your sin remains."

The evangelist's penchant for the use of forensic terms was remarked on earlier. Indeed, it might be said that the entire Gospel is presented as a courtroom drama: John the witness is first to take the stand to give testimony to Jesus (1:19-27); later he reminds his protesting disciples of the witness he had given to Jesus (3:27-30). Our author devotes two sections of this presentation of Jesus' disputes with "the Jews" to this same theme (5:31-47; 8:13-19), and the proclamation by Jesus which terminates the first great section of the book contains Jesus' own testimony (12:44-50). As John closes his account of Jesus' public ministry, Jesus announces the coming of "the hour for the Son of Man to be glorified" (12:13), which coincides with "the judgment of this world" and the defeat of "the prince of this world" (12:31). It is however the Paraclete (a term for the defense-lawyer in hellenistic legal language) Who throws light upon the condemnation of the world for those who believe in Jesus (16:7-11). Throughout this long development the evangelist with characteristic irony makes abundantly clear that "the Jews," Jesus' would-be judges are themselves judged, and found guilty of "the sin of the world," the refusal to put faith in Jesus.

Here the Johannine Jesus announces that he has "come into this world [to pass] a sentence *(krima)* of judgment;" indeed his very entry into our human family is *ipso facto* a judgment, which legal term (as has already been stated) connotes the same reality as the biblical word, "Election," in the *Spiritual Exercises*. Elsewhere in this Gospel, Jesus asserts that "God did not send His Son into the world in order to judge the world" (3:17), and "I judge no one" (8:15), since in reality the man or woman who obdurately rejects Jesus "is already judged by his or her own freely chosen decision" (3:18b). Thus our evangelist has stated, more clearly perhaps than other New Testament authors, that while the *saving* judgment is to be attributed wholly to the initiative and action of God through Jesus, the judgment that issues in condemnation is to be laid solely at the door of human incredulity. With his penchant for *double entendre* John here plays upon the twofold meaning of sight and blindness. Jesus has given sight to one "who cannot see," while this very act has now caused "those who can see" to "become blind." And the Pharisees are quick to seize this implication: "It is not we surely who also are blind!" The inherent ambiguity of this objection sums up the action of the whole drama, which has traced out the progressive growth of the former blind man from the "poverty" of sightlessness to an increasingly intimate knowledge of Jesus—first with his Jewish faith, "I don't know" (v. 12), "He is a prophet" (v. 17). In his deposition at the second hearing by the Jews (vv. 27-28) the man's relationship to Jesus has become that of "disciple," a word freighted with meaning in this Gospel: he declares equivalently, "This man" is "from God" (v. 33). During his reunion with Jesus the man who had been born blind transcends the traditional faith of Israel and confesses a new belief in Jesus as "the Son of Man," calling him "Lord," and falling down "in worship before him" (vv. 35-38).

The case of the Jews or Pharisees is correspondingly marked by a deterioration which stands in stark contrast: conscious of their "riches" as guardians and interpreters of the Law of Moses, they begin by declaring "This fellow is no man of God—he does not keep Sabbath!" (v. 16). Their overbearing arrogance in brow-beating the frightened parents discloses an unbridled lust for "empty honor by the world." The qualities for which men reverence them they ascribe to themselves, instead of to the divine goodness. This smug self-reliance mingled with contempt for others, as we noted, is underscored by John in his emphasis upon "we" and "*we* know." Their anger at being baulked by the simple fellow's defense of Jesus as one who "is God-fearing and doing His will" brings these learned legalists first to seek evidence (from the parents) to deny the cure, and now to reject the hand of God in it. They denigrate the man as "born and bred in sin" and resort to violence when they cannot refute his testimony. Their final state of "overbearing pride" brings Jesus to pronounce an ominous "sentence of judgment" upon them. "If only you *were* blind"—ignorance through no fault of their own—"you would not be guilty of sin. But as it is, you claim 'We can see'—your sin remains." The word rendered here "remains" is ironically that consistently used by John to describe the permanent relationship of faith and love ("abide") between Jesus and the disciples.

This theme of sin in fact (which in Two Standards is attributed to "the enemy of human nature") runs like a thread throughout John's drama. George MacRae has remarked that "The issue of sin . . . introduced as a red-herring issue by the disciples . . . returns in the last scene . . . where 'sin' is understood in the Johannine sense of unbelief . . . Note also how the issue of sin is ironically raised both about Jesus (v. 24) and the man born blind (v. 34)."[9]

---

9   G. W. MacRae, *Invitation to John,* p. 125.

Chapter 11

RAISING OF LAZARUS, LAST AND GREATEST
OF JESUS' "SIGNS" (11:1-44)

T he meditations of the First Week, made in the presence of the Crucified (and hence calculated to become "contemplations"([64])),
were clearly intended as an introduction to the Second Week. Here likewise the contemplations are orientated to the cross from the first day
([116]), since the Election is central to the prayerful work of the exercitant. Now, in the view of the best commentators, Ignatius' preference
was for "the second time" when the Election is the result of "suitable
clarity and knowledge through experience of consolations and desola-
tions and through experience of discerning divergent spirits" ([176]). Accordingly, when with the fourth day the retreatant is introduced to "the
consideration of different states of life" ([135]), he or she receives the
following exhortation. "Let us begin, simultaneously with the contemplation of his [Jesus'] life, to probe prayerfully in what state of life he
wishes us to serve his divine Majesty." And because Ignatius is keenly
sensitive that the selection of one's particular vocation depends primarily
upon the divine initiative, he proposes Two Standards in order to see
"how we ought to dispose ourselves to attain perfection in whatever state
of life God our Lord will grant us to choose." For the same reason the
Saint never presumes to fix a particular moment when the Election is to
occur. Indeed in his suggestions for adapting the length of time spent on
the Second Week, he assumes it will happen at different times in each individual case ([162]).

Ignatius does however make a noteworthy suggestion that "prior to
entering upon the elections . . . it will be of great benefit to consider with
attention the following three kinds of humility, coming back to this consideration from time to time throughout the entire day" ([164]). By
"humility," as François Courel remarks, Ignatius means a combination
of obedience and that "love which requires a resemblance to him one
loves."[1] It may come as a surprise that it is during the Second Week and

1   F. Courel, *Exercices Spirituels*, p. 91.

before the contemplation of the Passion that one is bid "petition that our Lord may wish to choose him for this third humility, which is greater and better, in order better to imitate and serve him" ([168]).

The Ignatian anticipation of the Third Week is also paralleled in the Fourth Gospel in several ways (as will be discussed later), but perhaps nowhere is it more striking than in the narrative of the raising from death of Lazarus, the last of the "signs" of Jesus' public life, in which attention is directed to the future death and resurrection of our Lord himself. It remains something of a mystery, it must be confessed, why Ignatius assigned this contemplation to the second last day of the Second Week, immediately preceding the contemplation of Jesus' final entrance into Jerusalem. What is more puzzling is the fact that in the text of the *Exercises* the connection which the evangelist has noted between this miracle and the plot to kill Jesus is ignored (11:46-53).

In our presentation of the story the threefold division adopted by Ignatius will be followed: the request by Martha and Mary; Jesus' interviews with the two sisters; and the raising of Lazarus ([285]).

1. The Message to Jesus by the Two Sisters (11:1-16)

1   There was a certain man, Lazarus from Bethany, of the village of Mary and her sister, Martha, who fell ill.   2   (Mary was the woman who anointed the Lord with perfumed ointment, and wiped his feet with her hair; it was her brother Lazarus who was ill.)   3   So the sisters sent him [Jesus] a message by word of mouth, "Master, he whom you hold in affection is ill."   4   Upon hearing it, Jesus said, "This sickness is not meant to end in death, but it is for the sake of God's glory, in order that the Son of God may be glorified through it."   5   Now Jesus loved Martha and her sister, and Lazarus.   6   Accordingly, when he heard he was ill, he then continued to abide two more days in the place where he was.   7   Only then did he say to the disciples, "Let us go back to Judea again."   8   The disciples say to him, "Rabbi, just now the Jews were seeking to stone you! Yet you are going back there again?"   9   Jesus replied, "Are there not twelve hours in the day? If one walks about in daytime, he does not stumble, because he sees the light of this world.   10   But if one walks about at night, he stumbles, because the light is not in him."   11   He made this remark, and later he added, "Our dear friend Lazarus has fallen asleep: yet I am making this journey in order to waken him."   12   So his disciples said, "If he has fallen asleep, his life will be saved."   13   (Jesus had however been speaking of his death, while they thought "He means natural sleep.")   14   At this point Jesus told them straight out, "Lazarus has died.   15   Yet I rejoice on your account—so that you may believe, I mean—because I was not there. However, let us go to him."   16   So Thomas (the name means

Twin) said to his fellow-disciples, "Let us also go, in order that we may die in company with him."

In the verses immediately preceding this simply told, yet powerful story, Jesus is pictured as taking refuge "across the Jordan in the place where John was baptizing in the beginning" (10:40), a town also named Bethany (1:28) that still retained many memories of this primordial witness to Jesus (v. 41). Regarded by many commentators as the original termination of the narrative of Jesus' public life, these verses (10:40-42) appear to function as a kind of introduction to the narrative of the last of the "signs" (see 10:41). Raymond Brown's view, that the late insertion of the tale of Lazarus caused the displacement of the narrative of Jesus' symbolic-prophetic action in cleansing the sacred enclosure in the holy place, is quite a plausible one.[2] While such questions may appear irrelevant to the retreatant who contemplates this last and greatest of all the "signs" of Jesus, still he or she may be helped towards "composing oneself" by reflecting on the loving care taken by the final editor(s) of this beautiful Gospel to preserve this moving narrative, which is meant to serve as a transition to the death and resurrection of Jesus.

While Lazarus fell ill in one Bethany, just under two miles from Jerusalem itself, Jesus "was abiding" in the other Bethany "across the Jordan" (10:40), and it was here he received the discreet plea for help from the two sisters, Mary and Martha, reminiscent of the request of "the mother of Jesus" at Cana (2:3), with its appeal to his affection to cure their seriously sick brother. Jesus' first reaction reminds one of his remark when correcting the disciples' view of the piteous condition of the man born blind (9:3), and (besides removing any impression that Jesus' delay sprang from his indifference to the plight of the family he dearly loved) it provides the reader with a first clue to Jesus' intention. "This sickness is not meant to end in death"—even though Lazarus is actually to die—, "but it is for the sake of God's glory, in order that the Son of God may be glorified through it." Jesus' entire mission is to reveal "the God no one has ever seen" (1:18), indicated here as "God's glory," according to Johannine terminology. Yet, as has been seen already, Jesus can only accomplish his mission through the disclosure of his own identity as "the Son of God," that glorification which is to come only when he "is lifted up" on the cross. It is for this reason that the author or editor will single out the restoration to life of Lazarus as the immediate cause of Jesus' death (11:46-53). Moreover, as Father Schnackenburg observes,

2   R. E. Brown, *The Gospel According to John I–XII*, p. 118.

"The 'Son of God' is not just calling this dead man into life, but because it is a sign, announcing his own resurrection."[3]

"Now Jesus loved Martha and her sister, and Lazarus." This story is notable within the whole first twelve chapters of the Gospel as the single place where Jesus' love for any of his followers is mentioned (see 13:1). Where the sisters' request sent to Jesus by word of mouth spoke of his affectionate love for Lazarus *(phileis)*, here John uses the customary Christian term *(ēgapa)* connoting supernatural love. Jesus will shortly call Lazarus "our dear friend" (v. 11), and when later Jesus weeps in the presence of the Jews, they exclaim, "How dearly he must have loved him!" (v. 36). Such consistent and unusual references to Jesus' love play a significant role in this presentation of this great "sign," which points ahead to the meaning of Jesus' death as the "laying down his life for his friends" (15:13). Here this love for the family of Bethany is underscored by Jesus' abiding "two more days" in Bethany across the Jordan: Jesus wishes to demonstrate that love not by a cure of the sick man, but by raising him again to life.

The disciples' objection to Jesus' return to the dangerous situation, "just now the Jews were seeking to stone you," is countered by Jesus' reassuring reference to the sun (as at 9:4), a symbol for the divinely allotted time for the carrying out of his mission, and thus a period when his safety, until his "hour" arrives, is not in jeopardy. Jesus' next remark, that a person "stumbles, because the light is not in him," reflects the Semitic notion (see Mt 6:23) that it is the light within a person which makes seeing possible. It is only by virtue of the mutual abiding of the believer in Jesus and of Jesus in the believer (14:23), that the disciple is saved from "stumbling" in his faith. Jesus will make this clear by his command, "Abide in my love" (15:9). The present saying of Jesus, so freighted with symbolic meaning, reminds the reader that Jesus was announced in the Prologue as "the life that is the light of mankind" (1:4).

Jesus' ambiguous remark that Lazarus "has fallen asleep" and that he himself is going "in order to awaken him" leads the disciples into a typical Johannine misunderstanding. John here uses the verb, to fall asleep, in its Christian usage (1 Thes 4:13; 1 Cor 15:20; Mt 27:52), from which comes our word "cemetery" (= "dormitory"), expressive of faith in the future resurrection. Jesus removes any ambivalence here by stating, "Lazarus has died," and he adds, "I rejoice on your account— so that you may believe." Throughout his public ministry Jesus has

---

3   Schnackenburg, *John,* II, 323.

shown concern for the strengthening of his followers' faith in himself which was initiated at the wedding in Cana (2:11)—shortly to be shaken by his own Passion and death. The loyal declaration by Thomas, who makes his first appearance now in this Gospel, provides an example for the Christian reader—despite his ignorance of promise hidden in Jesus' words—who wrestles in darkness to keep faith with his Lord. The phrase "die in company with him"—from the preposition *(meta)* that is used —means more than mere accompaniment *(syn)*. It denotes an experience in the company of Jesus that is influenced by him. The experience of Christian death is part of that "new creation" which Jesus' dying will inaugurate.

2. Jesus Interviews the Two Sisters (11:17-37)

17   On his arrival, Jesus found that he [Lazarus] had already been four days in the tomb.   18   (Now Bethany was near Jerusalem, just under fifteen stadia distant.   19   So many of the Jews had come out to Martha and Mary to condole with them over their brother.)   20   Now when Martha heard Jesus was coming, she came to meet him, while Mary remained in the house.   21   Martha accordingly said to Jesus, "Master, had you been here my brother would never have died.   22   Still even now I know that whatever you ask God, God will give you."   23   Jesus assures her, "Your brother will rise again."   24   Martha says to him, "I know he will rise at the resurrection on the last day."   25   Jesus told her, "I am the resurrection and the life: the person believing in me, even though he die, will live on;   26   and no one who is alive and believes in me will ever die. Do you believe this?"   27   She says to him, "Yes, Master: I firmly believe that you are the Messiah, the Son of God, the One who is coming into the world."

28   Saying this she went off and called Mary her sister aside whispering, "The Teacher is here asking for you."   29   Now she on hearing this got up in haste and came to him.   30   (Jesus had not yet entered the village, but was still at the spot where Martha had met him.)   31   Accordingly, the Jews who were keeping her company in the house and consoling her, on seeing Mary suddenly get up and go out, followed her, thinking "She is off to the tomb in order to wail there."   32   Now when Mary came to where Jesus was, seeing him she fell at his feet, exclaiming, "Master, had you been here my brother would never have died!"   33   Now when Jesus saw her wailing and the Jews who accompanied her wailing, he groaned from anger deep inside him, and shuddered at what he felt within himself,   34   as he asked, "Where have you laid him?"—They tell him, "Master, come and see."   35   Jesus began to weep.   36   Whereupon the Jews kept saying, "How dearly he must have loved him."   37   Some of them however remarked, "Could not this man who opened the eyes of the blind man have

done something to keep this man from dying?"

This second scene in the drama opens with the very important information that Lazarus "had already been four days in the tomb"—irrefutable evidence of his death. Contemporary Jewish opinion held that during the first three days after burial (which occurred on the day of death), the life-principle kept returning to the tomb. It was only on the fourth day that, with the inception of decay, the "soul" went off to Sheol. This view indicates the supreme importance of "the third day" in Christian credal formulae: Jesus was raised from death by God before corruption occurred. Martha and Mary were known in the tradition behind Luke's Gospel (Lk 10:38-42), where—as here—Martha is the more important figure. The name Lazarus occurs in the Lucan parable of the rich man (Lk 16:19-31), and it will be recalled that this same evangelist has preserved the story (Lk 7:11-17) of the resuscitation of a "young man," who —like the Johannine Jesus—is "an only son" *(monogenēs huios)*. It will be noted that 'the Jews" in the narrative are simply inhabitants of Jerusalem, more sympathetic to Jesus and the sisters, than "the Jews" who in this Gospel represent the religious establishment opposed to our Lord.

Now it is the active Martha who goes out to welcome Jesus, "while Mary remained in the house." Her first remark to the "Master"—the Greek term *(Kyrios)* in later Christian faith for the risen One—is not meant as a rebuke, but a regret that the reputed healer did not come in time. Yet Martha voices a hope which is not without ambiguity, "Still even now I know that whatever you ask God, God will give you." Jesus' immediate response is no less ambiguous, "Your brother will rise again." This permits Martha to articulate the Pharisaic belief in bodily resurrection, which by the time this Gospel was composed was common to most Jews. "I know he will rise at the resurrection on the last day." This somewhat vague faith in a far distant resurrection is, in the context of this Gospel with its "realized eschatology," insufficient, and Jesus seeks to develop Martha's belief in himself. "I am the resurrection and the life." This fifth of the seven "I am" sayings is further elucidated by John by the explanation, "the person believing in me, even though he die, will live on, and no one who is alive and believes in me will ever die." George MacRae's comment is appropriate: "Jesus is the resurrection, an image central to a future eschatological perspective . . . whoever believes in him, even after death will come to life. And he is the (eternal) life . . . whoever believes in him and possesses eternal life will never die in a definitive sense. The point may be to assert that whatever are the eschatological perspectives of the Christian, Jesus is the basis of them."[4] And Rudolf Schnackenburg observes, "Jesus is bearing witness to himself as the one who has been given and fully possesses (5:26) the power which belongs to God alone to 'give life' (cf. 5:21)."[5]

Martha, in response, voices an impressive belief in the person of Jesus—one, however, like those confessions of disciples at the beginning of John's book, which is to be construed as articulating a "low Christology:" thus "Messiah" is the answer to Jewish expectations; "the Son of God" expresses the tradition of royal messianism, while "the one who is coming into the world" indicates the expected Moses-like prophet. It will be only after the risen Jesus' gift of the Spirit, bringing "life" and Christian faith, that the terms will acquire their full meaning under the evangelist's pen (20:31).

At Martha's news of Jesus' presence, Mary responds with alacrity and comes to meet Jesus, accompanied by the sympathetic Jews, who conjecture wrongly, "She is off to the tomb in order to wail there." Such an outburst of grief, according to the conventions of the era, would be no more than an expression of hopelessness in face of death. By contrast with Martha, the more emotional Mary "fell at his feet," but she simply echoes the sentiments of her sister, which in the sequel induces some of the Jews to remark reproachfully, "Could not this man who opened the eyes of the blind man have done something to keep this man from dying?" Thus in the story Martha's role appears in part as the link between Jesus and the Jews. Much more significantly, Mary with her "wailing" Jewish sympathizers occasions an outburst of anger on the part of Jesus, and thus leads into the dénouement of the entire story.

Mindful of the Ignatian admonition to adhere to "the genuine grounds of the history" ([2]), we feel it necesary to point out the inadequacy of most English renderings of verbs expressing emotions in this passage. Mary and her Jewish friends are represented as "wailing" *(klaiein)*, while it is Jesus alone who "weeps" *(dakryein)*. His reaction to such keening and lamenting is described as one of deep anger *(embrimasthai)*, scarcely conveyed by such phrases as "sighed heavily" or "was deeply moved." I venture to suggest that John is attempting to describe the violence of the emotion of anger Jesus experienced within himself, as well as the outward expression of that anger: hence I have rendered the Greek *enebrimēsato tō pneumati* by "groaned from anger deep inside

---

4   G. W. MacRae, *Invitation to John*, p. 141.
5   Schnackenburg, *John*, II, 330.

him''. The second verb *(etaraxen heauton)* also connotes violent emotion related to fear (see 12:27; 13:21) on the part of Jesus, or of his disciples (14:1, 27); here I have turned it as "shuddered at what he felt within himself." Why did Jesus become angry at the wailing of Mary and the Jews? Probably for the same reason he had expressed anger at people "wailing and keening loudly" before Jairus' house, when he demanded, "Why make such a din with your wailing?" (Mk 5:38-39). As on that occasion so here Jesus' anger surges up against the devil—"a murderer from the beginning" (8:44)—manifested in the death of Lazarus, as also in the unfaith of those wailing. The fear he expresses by his shuddering springs from his awareness of the proximity of his own death. This is all part of that "labor" and "suffering" the risen Christ had promised in the consideration *Del Rey,* prelude to this Second Week of the Exercises ([95]).

Jesus evinces another emotion, as he inquires, "Where have you laid him?"—he "began to weep." Why does Jesus weep? The evangelist notices the sympathetic reaction of some of the Jews only to dismiss it as superficial. Not indeed that the Johannine Jesus is incapable of concern and sympathy with human needs (as at the wedding feast), with men's hunger (as at the feeding across the lake), with the bodily disabled (by the pool of Bethesda), with the terrible affliction of one born blind: mere sentimentality however is not part of his character. Schnackenburg has accurately explained Jesus' weeping. "On the sad journey to the tomb Jesus too is moved by the darkness of the inevitability of death. The evangelist does not gloss over the horror of death, but believes that it is conquered in faith . . . The scale of Jesus' act can only be recognised if the bitterness of physical death is not minimised."[6]

3. Jesus Confronts Death with Confidence in his Father (11:38-44)

38   So Jesus once again groaning with the anger within himself goes over to the tomb. (It was a chamber-tomb, and a stone was set against it.)   39   Jesus says, "Take away the stone!" Martha, sister of the dead man, says to him, "Master, he already stinks—he is four days dead!"   40   Jesus says to her, "Did I not tell you, if you believe, you will see the glory of God?"   41   Thereupon they took away the stone. Then Jesus raised his eyes upwards and said, "Father, I thank You because You have granted my prayer!   42   For myself, I knew You always hear me, but I said this for the sake of the people standing round, in order that they might believe You sent me."

---

6   Ibid., 337.

43   And on saying this, he called out with a mighty voice, "Lazarus, come out here!"   44   The dead man came out, swathed feet and hands with linen bands, his face wrapped round with a cloth. Jesus says to them, "Loose him, and let him go free!"

Again a wave of anger sweeps over Jesus, not implausibly at the faithless remark of some Jewish bystanders, "Could not this man who opened the eyes of the blind man have done something to keep this man from dying?" He is angered at such an affront to his Father. He had earlier declared, "The Son can do nothing by himself except what he sees the Father doing" (5:19); "The works I do in the name of my Father—it is these that testify about me" (10:25). And later to Philip during his last meal on earth he will assert, "The utterances I make to you I do not speak by myself: rather the Father abiding in me is doing His works" (14:10).

A later editor has described the tomb so as to have it resemble that of Jesus—with "a stone set against it" (20:1). Martha's objection to Jesus' command, "Take away the stone!" creates a dramatic delay in the action, while her realistic remark, "he already stinks" heightens the horror of death. Jesus does not simply repeat now what he had said earlier to Martha, "I am the resurrection and the life." His cited promise, "If you believe, you will see the glory of God," is nearer to his remarks to the disciples about Lazarus' illness, "It is for the sake of God's glory, in order that the Son of God may be glorified through it;" and "I rejoice on your account—so that you may believe." At the tomb Jesus' reply transcends his present action of bringing Lazarus back to life; or rather, it presents that act as a theophany (John regards it as "a sign")—a manifestation of God's life-restoring might through His empowering Jesus to raise the dead man.

"Father, I thank you!"—this is (surprisingly) the first time in this Gospel that Jesus is presented as praying to God (see 12:28). It is strange that, once his great prayer is completed (17:1-26), the Johannine Jesus never prays throughout the Passion-narrative in this Gospel. The prayer of thanks uttered here by Jesus presupposes a prior petition, or (and this is more likely) it indicates the complete oneness of Jesus with his Father. It may appear curious that Jesus insists that his prayer is "for the sake of the people standing round;" it seems more an exhibition before an audience than communion with God. In reality, however, the entire life of Jesus, the Word of God become flesh, is prayer in its purest form, for the word Jesus utters even in prayer, like his teaching "is not mine but that of Him Who sent me" (7:16). This probably explains why John never speaks of Jesus as at prayer during the Passion, which he regards as his return home to the Father.

The stupendous miracle occurs at "the mighty voice" of Jesus, the Word of God; and Lazarus *obeys*: he "came out." Our evangelist has not missed the ethical character of the resurrection, of which Paul was so much aware. This explains the invariable Pauline habit of speaking of Jesus not as rising from death (1 Thes 4:14 cites an earlier credal formula), but as "having been raised by the glory of the Father" (Rom 6:4). The Apostle views his resurrection as the ultimate act of obedience by Jesus as the Son. And Paul is ultimately led to adopt the same view of the glorious resurrection of all believers, since "the One Who has worked things out for us in just this way is God—the One who has given us the Spirit as His pledge" (2 Cor 5:5).[7]

The evangelist has seen this greatest of Jesus' "signs" as the immediate cause of the plot on his life by the Sanhedrin (11:46-53). Yet, as was noted earlier, it is puzzling that Ignatius has overlooked this connection in the *Exercises*—the more so, since he included verse 45 in his Scripture reference, "Thus many of the Jews who had come out to Mary and had witnessed what he had done, found faith in him." How explain John's perception of this connection between the raising of Lazarus and the death of Jesus—a view seemingly at odds with the view of the Synoptic writers? Rudolf Schnackenburg's explanation is plausible, when he remarks that for John this "sign" became "the high point of the underlying development, Jesus the resurrection and the life. Moreover the subject invited dramatic treatment: the supreme revelation of Jesus as the life-giver is balanced by the determination of unbelief to destroy him."[8] I may point out that Schnackenburg views the miraculous event as having actually occurred, while giving due consideration to the development of the story in the history of tradition. The difficulty often urged against the historical character of this "sign"—its omission in all the Synoptic Gospels—is explicable in view of the fact that the earliest evangelical traditions preserved, for the most part, only those miracles wrought in Galilee. What led historically to the death of Jesus at the hands of the Romans by the machinations of Jewish religious leaders was beyond any doubt his teaching and his miracles, inseparable from that teaching. The evangelical traditions retained the memory of the high esteem in which the common people held Jesus to the very eve of his death. Thus Mark, in

---

7 A fuller explanation of this aspect of the resurrection is found in my article "The Glory about to be Revealed," *The Way* 22 (1982), 273-286; see especially 279-283.

8 Schnackenburg, *John*, II, 345.

reporting the plot by Jewish religious leaders, mentions them as "conspiring as to how they might seize him by some trick and kill him. For, it was asserted repeatedly, 'Not in the presence of the festival throng, lest a riot break out among the people!' " (Mk 14:1, 2). With his inimitable flair for dramatization, the fourth evangelist has singled out this last and mightiest of Jesus' "signs" as the immediate cause of his death.

While indeed undue concern about "what really happened" can be a serious distraction from one's contemplation, still inasmuch as Christianity, like the religion of Israel, stands amongst other great world religions as an historical, not a mythical religion, the basic historical character of a miracle like the raising of Lazarus is to be regarded as convincingly attested by the fourth evangelist. This is not to say that every story in our Gospels is (or can be proven) historical: some, like the Transfiguration, lie beyond the competence of historiography, while others, including several in the Passion-narratives—the darkness that descended on the earth, the rending of the veil in the sanctuary—may be judged to be of a symbolic, not factual nature. In the contemplation of Jesus' earthly life, however, the object of one's attention, as the Vatican Council II pointed out, is not historical truth, but rather "that truth which God has put upon the sacred page for the sake of our salvation."[9]

One final observation may be relevant here. It should be borne in mind that John regarded the raising of Lazarus from death as a "sign" (12:18)—an indication that he realized how very different it was from the unique event of Jesus' resurrection to which it pointed. For the resuscitation by Jesus of this dead man before a crowd of witnesses, like the raising of Jairus' little daughter (Mk 5:35-42) or the widow's son at Naim (Lk 7:1-17), restored these beneficiaries of our Lord's thaumaturgical powers to life when they had already died; but they were brought back to this present, earthly, limited existence. Moreover, they did not escape—despite the grace of such an extraordinary favor—the inevitable necessity of facing death once more, and finally.

Jesus by contrast, as Paul asserts, has been raised by God to an utterly new, unprecedented mode of existence. "You know that Christ raised from death can no longer die: death has no more power over him. The death he died was a death once for all to sin: the life he now leads is one lived unto God" (Rom 6:9-10). It is grossly inaccurate to say that Jesus "has been brought back to life" by his resurrection, which would

---

9   See *Dei Verbum,* the Constitution on Divine Revelation, no. 11.

be to think of his resurrection after the manner of Lazarus' raising from death. One can only adequately state this central truth of our faith by saying that Jesus has gone forward into Life, into which he has taken his entire humanness and all his earthly history. We shall have occasion to return to these considerations in the reflections on the Fourth Week of the Exercises.

Chapter 12

LAST DAY OF PUBLIC MINISTRY:
JESUS' FINAL ENTRY INTO JERUSALEM (12:12-36)

F or the twelfth and last day of the Second Week Ignatius proposes for contemplation "Palm Sunday" ([116]) from the text of Matthew, which recounts Jesus' last entry into the holy city and the cleansing of the sacred precincts of the temple (Mt 21:1-17). This latter demonstration of his authority was contemplated earlier where it occurs in the Fourth Gospel at the beginning of the public ministry. Here we shall make a contemplation of what John considers to have made up the final day of Jesus' activity of evangelizing the city to which his mission, in the Fourth Gospel, is consistently directed: Jesus' last approach to Jerusalem, with its immediate sequel, his meeting with "the Greeks," by which term John designates certain God-fearing pagans from the Hellenistic world. These profess faith in the one God of Israel, but have not as yet assumed the burdens of the Mosaic Law by accepting circumcision. In the Johannine narrative, Jesus' attempts to disclose his identity to the people of Jerusalem are then terminated by a discussion with the crowd about the identity of "the Son of Man" and a last exhortation to put faith in "the light": "Jesus finished saying this, and going off he hid himself from them" (12:36b).

The evangelist Mark, first of Gospel-writers, had set the pattern for his two colleagues by prefixing to his story of the Passion Jesus' lengthy discourse on the significance of Christian hope in the second coming for the daily living of the gospel (Mk 13:1-37), and this procedure was followed somewhat closely by Matthew (Mt 24:1-26:1). Luke, who had presented Jesus' instructions to the disciples about "the day of the Son of Man" as a warning not to adopt the attitudes of the Pharisees (Lk 17:20-37), has Jesus predict the destruction of the city and its temple somewhat later (Lk 21:5-28), concluding with a warning to watchfulness in view of the coming Kingdom of God (Lk 21:29-36). Then this evangelist ends his account of the public life on a very divergent note from that on which John ended, by suggesting a certain eagerness of "the people" *(laos)* for his teaching. "By day he was teaching in the temple area, while by night going out of the city he was spending the night on the mountain, called 'of Olives.' And the entire people rose at early morning to come and listen to him in the sacred precincts" (Lk 21:37-38). In the *Spiritual Exercises,* another Lucan summary, distinctly different in tone, had been proposed as the contemplation for the entire tenth day. This pair of verses, following immediately on Luke's account of the entry into Jerusalem, and the cleansing of the temple-enclosure, functions as an introduction to the series of controversies with various religious leaders. "Now he was teaching daily in the temple area, while the high priests and scribes with the leaders of the people *(laos)* kept seeking to destroy him. Still they did not discover a way to bring it off, as the entire people *(laos)* was hanging on his words" (Lk 19:47-48). The Greek term *laos* indicates the people of God.

It is instructive to weigh the divergencies discoverable between the four evangelists as each brings his very personal presentation of Jesus' public ministry to a conclusion. For in this way we may gain some insight into the quite independent manner in which Ignatius constructed his own "Gospel"—at least as regards the Second Week. In his discussion of the sequence set down in the *Exercises* for the last three days of the Second Week, William Peters speaks of "a very significant deviation from the chronological order."[1] In my judgment, it is of some moment to realize that there is no such thing as a "chronological order" (except in the most general terms) followed by any Gospel-writer. Whether or not Ignatius himself entertained such an anachronistic notion is, of course, impossible to surmise, but he achieved (perhaps without knowing it) precisely what Mark, Matthew, Luke, and John had accomplished by creating his own alignment of the evangelical materials.

What guided Mark, the original Gospel-writer, in the creation of his book? There were chiefly two realities that presided over the way he laid out his Gospel: his own image of Jesus (the Teacher with authority) and the needs and concerns, as he saw them, which exercised the particular community for which he wrote. Chief of these was undoubtedly the imminent persecution confronting this church, as well as a dangerous overemphasis on the miracles of Jesus—this would lead to confusing him with those Hellenistic wonder-workers, the tales of whose incredible feats abounded in that day. While Matthew and Luke, who wrote in the generation after Mark's book had won a name for itself among the early

---

1   W. Peters, *The Spiritual Exercises of St. Ignatius,* p. 112.

Christian communities, were guided to a notable degree by the structure of the Marcan Gospel, each produced a book that is recognizably different. For each had his own image of Jesus, and each addressed a church with problems of its own. Both of these successors of Mark had, moreover, command of certain traditions concerning Jesus' work and teaching unavailable to Mark. John in his turn composed the Fourth Gospel out of a very different set of experiences from his fore-runners. The syncretistic character of his community, composed of former "baptists," Samaritans, anti-temple Hellenists, appears to have been looked on with suspicion by the other Jewish-Christian groups directed by the Twelve; and years of bitter antagonism directed at this church by the Jews posed a peculiar set of problems for its membership.

Hugo Rahner remarks of Ignatius that, while he allowed for a certain amount of adaptation in his own ordering of the Second Week, "there can be no doubt that the mysteries which appear in a very definite order . . . were considered by Ignatius to be of vital importance for the Election."[2] This observation by the late German specialist in Ignatian studies may be taken to describe the concerns of the constituency for which Ignatius wrote the *Exercises,* described in Annotations 4, 19, 20. As for the saint's image of Jesus, which largely influenced his choice and arrangement of passages for contemplation from the Gospels, we find it clearly limned in the consideration About the King and in Two Standards —an image, it will be recalled that was the fruit of that "so great illumination" by the river Cardoner at Manresa. The Ignatian vision of "our creator and Lord" centers upon the risen Jesus dynamically present to this world's history, at work within the Church, and seeking the collaboration of those who "desire to act from love, and signalize themselves by total service of the eternal King and Lord of all" ([96]). Since it was exercitants of such calibre that Ignatius envisaged as suitable candidates for the Exercises of thirty days, it becomes evident why, from the early contemplations of the Infancy narratives, he pointed them continuously towards the cross of Christ. Such high expectations also explain why, from the sixth to the twelfth day of the Second Week, he proposed but a single mystery for daily contemplation, since he had every right to assume that the contemplation of Two Standards would, with the divine grace, bring to the retreatant a flood of consolation and a new pitch of contemplative prayer, as she or he is drawn irresistibly toward the Election. Ignatius with his deep sense of reverence *(acatamiento)* did not in-

2   H. Rahner, *Ignatius the Theologian*, pp. 103-104.

deed presume to specify the moment at which "God our Lord will grant us to choose," any more than he sought to determine in "which state of life he wishes us to serve his divine majesty" ([176]). He had however supreme confidence that through his own "Gospel," so carefully selected, the one capable of making the entire Exercises would "seek and find the will of God" (Annotation 1), because "the creator and Lord in person would communicate himself to such a devout person, embrace such a one with his love and praise, and lead that person towards the way in which he might be better capable of serving him for the future" (Annotation 15).

Before we turn to our own reflections upon John's presentation of the last day of Jesus' public ministry, it may be in order to ask why, for this last day of the Second Week, Ignatius chose the text of Matthew for the concluding contemplation, which he calls "Palm Sunday"—only in the Fourth Gospel are palm branches mentioned, and the day probably implied is a Sunday (see 12:1). Moreover, Matthew, unlike John, does not set his account of Jesus' entry into Jerusalem at the conclusion of the narrative of the public life. Matthew also deviates from the Marcan sequence of episodes by his inclusion of the cleansing of the sacred precincts as an event following the entry on the same day. As Ignatius, while including this act by Jesus in his scriptural references, omits any mention of it in his "points" ([287]), we too may here set it aside. Following Mark, whose lengthy introduction he abbreviates, Matthew gives Jesus the post-resurrection title, "the Lord" (Mt 21:3). He presents Jesus, with the help of one of his formula-citations (in which Is 62:1 appears in combination with Zech 9:9), as manifesting his royal dignity to be acclaimed by the crowd as "the Son of David"—a favorite Matthean title (Mt 1:1). And, with what may well be a reference back to the reaction of Herod "and all Jerusalem with him" (Mt 2:3), he pictures "all the city" as "rocked"—as if by an earthquake (*eseisthē*, Mt. 21:10) at the awe-inspiring entry of "the prophet Jesus from Galilee" (v. 11). One can only surmise that this dramatic presentation would appeal more to the Ignatius who composed the consideration On the King as prolegomenon to this Second Week, than the subdued, laconic description of John, in which only three of the eight verses in the passage describe the actual entry (and these include two citations from Scripture).

1. Jesus' Entry into Jerusalem (12:12-19)

> 12 Next day the great crowd that had arrived for the festival, on hearing "Jesus is coming into Jerusalem,"   13   took branches from palm trees

and went out to meet him. Now they kept shouting, " 'Hosanna! blessings on the one coming in the Lord's name' [Ps 118:25-26]—the king of Israel!" 14 As for Jesus, finding the colt of an ass, he sat upon it, in accordance with Scripture, 15 "Cease your fear, daughter of Zion!" [Zeph 3:14-16]. "See your king is coming seated upon the foal of an ass" [Zech 9:9]. 16 All this his disciples did not understand at first. But when Jesus had been glorified, then they remembered that they had done those things to him, which had been written concerning him. 17 Thus the crowd that had been in his company when he summoned Lazarus from the tomb and raised him from death, kept bearing witness to him. 18 This was the reason the crowd had come out to meet him—they heard he had performed this sign. 19 Accordingly, the Pharisees said to one another, "Look here! you are getting nowhere—the world has run after him!"

John pictures this important event in the evangelical tradition as occurring "the next day" after the anointing of Jesus by Mary of Bethany during a supper "six days before Passover" (12:1); thus it would seem to have occurred on the "first day of the week," the Sunday before Jesus' resurrection. The "great crowd" would appear to be those pilgrims up from the countryside for Passover, who "were seeking Jesus and asking one another as they stood in the temple precincts, 'What do you people think? Will he really come up for the festival?' Actually, the high priests and Pharisees had issued orders that "if anyone knew where he was, he should turn informer so they could arrest him" (11:54-55). The somewhat confusing editorial reference to "the great crowd" in the paragraph preceding our passage apparently points to those "of the Jews," who had gone out to Bethany while he was dining with Lazarus and his sisters to catch a glimpse of Lazarus, already an object of public interest (vv. 9-11).

When word got about that "Jesus is coming into Jerusalem," the pilgrims "went out to meet him carrying palm-branches" (a Coptic loan-word in Greek) which "they took from palm trees"—a somewhat tautological combination. The detail about palm-fronds, as remarked, is missing in the Synoptic accounts: it was a symbol of victory and played some part in the ceremonies of *Sukkōth,* the feast of Tabernacles, which traditionally was the most joyous of the three great pilgrimage-festivals. The snippit from Psalm 118 cited here by the evangelist also figured in the liturgy of *Sukkōth;* the cry for help, *hōšīyāh nā '* (Hosanna = "save, we pray"), formed part of the prayers for rain at Tabernacles.[3] The late Jean Cardinal Daniélou, S.J., once suggested the interesting but undemons-

---

3   R. E. Brown, *John I–XII*, p. 457.

trable thesis that Jesus actually entered the city on that feast, rather than at Passover.[4] More to the point is the relation of the citation from Zechariah (9:9) to "the King, the Lord of hosts" (Zech 14:16), whose appearance on the Mount of Olives (Zech 14:4) was predicted for the eschatological Day of the Lord—as Raymond Brown observes in the reference given above.

John describes the initiative taken by Jesus almost laconically—by contrast with the elaborate Marcan picture (Mk 11:1-7). Still he does point to Jesus as the one "finding the colt of an ass," noting that "he sat upon it, in accordance with Scripture." The donkey was the dignified mount of ancient Jewish royalty; hence Jesus' action indicates his intention to manifest himself to Jerusalem as her king. Yet it is important to observe *the kind of kingship* the evangelist points to by his omission of the word "triumphant" in the quotation from Zechariah here. George MacRae remarks that while this event "is often called the 'triumphal entry' . . . that description may be misleading . . . we could call this episode a triumphal entry only in an ironic sense."[5]

In addition, it may be observed that while all four evangelists refer to the text of Psalm 118 (in the context of this royal progress by Jesus the "Hosanna" becomes the equivalent of *vivat,* "Long live the king!"), the benediction originally indicated a blessing pronounced by the priests upon all pilgrims as they ascended for the feast. If one asks, "What really happened on this occasion?", no satisfactory answer is forthcoming. That the entry did not happen as our Gospels describe it may be inferred from the fact that what may seem a grandiose demonstration by the people never became an issue at either the Jewish or the Roman trials in the Passion-narrative.

John's chief concern, seemingly, is to justify these scriptural quotations by recalling to his reader that "remembering" which occurred as the result of the gift of Christian faith. As was pointed out earlier, this significant experience was referred to as John began his account of Jesus' Jerusalem ministry with the cleansing of the temple-area (2:17, 22). He concludes his description of this solemn ingress by Jesus into the city by noting the reaction of those people who were present at the raising from death of Lazarus, and who now "kept bearing witness to him." To this testimony he attributes the enthusiasm expressed by "the crowd [that] had come out to meet him." In sharp contrast stands the despairing con-

---

4   Jean Daniélou, S.J., "Les Quatre-temps de Septembre et la fête des Tabernacles", *La Maison Dieu* 46 (1956), 114-136.
5   G. W. MacRae, *Invitation to John*, p. 149.

fusion exhibited by Jesus' enemies, the Pharisees, "Look here! you are getting nowhere—the world has run after him!" Again the characteristic irony of the evangelist can be detected: these opponents unwittingly anticipate the thought underlying Jesus' third prediction of his Passion, when he will announce, "As for me, when I am lifted up from earth, I will draw all people to myself" (12:32).

2. Jesus and Some God-fearing Greeks (12:20-28)

20   Now there were some Greeks among those who had come on pilgrimage to worship at the feast.   21   So these men approached Philip (the man from Bethsaida in Galilee), and kept making this request, "Sir, we desire to see Jesus."   22   Philip comes and tells Andrew. Andrew and Philip come and tell Jesus.

23   Jesus, for his part, replies to them in these words, "The hour has come for the Son of Man to be glorified!   24   Amen, amen I tell you: unless a grain of wheat die when sown in the earth, it remains by itself in isolation; but if it dies, it produces a rich harvest.   25   Anyone who loves his life is destroying it: the person who hates his life in this world will guard it for eternal life.   26   If anyone is to serve me, the Father will do him honor.   27   Now my heart is deeply troubled—[I do not know] what I am to say!   28   Father, save me throughout this hour. Yes, this is the reason I have come to this hour—Father, glorify your name!" At this, a voice came out of the sky, "I have glorified it, and I will glorify it again!"

The revulsion displayed by the Pharisees at the acclaim of the people during Jesus' entry into Jerusalem is now seen to perform another function. It provides John with an opportunity to include a delegation of God-fearing pagans, who manifest a wish to come to Jesus. George MacRae notes that "their presence here actually has a good deal more significance . . . On the level of the Gospel—as opposed to the history of Jesus—the evangelist is inserting gentiles, who in his time make up the bulk of the Christian communities, into the Gospel at the crucial moment when 'the hour has come'."[6] Thus the scene is a composition by the evangelist on the basis of several sayings by Jesus contained in the earlier evangelical traditions. That these Greeks in their wish "to see Jesus" address themselves to Philip, one of the two disciples in the Gospel who bear (like Andrew) Greek names, lends an air of verisimilitude to the conversation, since Philip, who hails from Galilean Bethsaida (again like Andrew, 1:44), would have spoken some Greek. Thus that Philip "comes

6   Ibid., p. 153.

and tells Andrew" is plausible, especially since these two were associated together earlier (6:8).

Jesus' reaction to this news about the approach of well-intentioned pagans (who appear in the sequel to be entirely ignored) is of great moment in a Gospel where the reader has been told repeatedly that Jesus' "hour was not yet come" (7:30; 8:20; see 2:4). Accordingly John would seem to interpret the Greeks' request "to see Jesus" as implying an inchoate movement towards real faith. And the dramatic announcement which now comes from the lips of Jesus is one of the most significant in the entire Gospel. "The hour has come for the Son of Man to be glorified!" "The hour" becomes a symbol for the entire series of saving actions, which taken as a unity result in salvation for all believers. "The hour" comprises the sufferings and death, resurrection of Jesus, and his return home to the Father, which culminates in his sending of the Spirit of truth, the Paraclete. For it is through this same sequence that Jesus becomes "glorified," that is, reveals his own identity as the one who "lays down his life for his beloved friends" (15:13), "hands over the Spirit" (19:30) in the moment of dying, thus disclosing himself as source of eternal life through his gift of the Spirit, "the life-giver" (6:63). "The Greeks," having played the brief, but important role assigned to them by the evangelist, now disappear—we are never told whether their politely voiced "desire to see Jesus" is fulfilled, or not. The ensuing instruction of Jesus is reserved exclusively for his disciples, and contains echoes of the teaching of the Marcan Jesus on discipleship. "If anyone desires to come to me, he must say 'No' to self, take his own cross on his shoulder, and follow me. For whoever desires to save his life will destroy it: whoever destroys his life for my sake and for the gospel will save it" (Mk 8:34-35). Like the Marcan Jesus also, the Johannine Jesus begins with a brief parable of growth: "Unless a grain of wheat die when sown in the earth, it remains by itself in isolation; but if it dies, it produces a rich harvest." While there is no parable in our Gospels that corresponds to this strikingly brief one, there is a statement by Paul that resembles it. Like other echoes of Jesus' parables in the Pauline letters,[7] it may be that Paul took over a parable preserved in the evangelical traditions he had learned. The Apostle uses it to refute a difficulty raised by some adversary against the resurrection to glory of the faithful. "Now someone will ask, 'How do dead men rise? with what sort of body will they come

---

7   David M. Stanley, S.J., "Pauline Allusions to the Sayings of Jesus," *Catholic Biblical Quarterly* 23 (1961), 26-39.

back?' You fool! what you sow does not come to life except it die. Yet as for what you sow, you do not sow the body that will evolve, but a naked seed—say, of wheat or of some other grains. It is God Who gives it a body as He decides—indeed to each seed its own body" (1 Cor 15:35-38).

This little parable, so pregnant with meaning, Jesus here applies first to himself—his parables were not intended to express eternal truths, but to comment in some way on his own mission in the world. It might be considered John's reformulation of the traditional predictions of the Passion and resurrection. The Johannine Jesus however goes on to apply its insight—through death one comes to life—to discipleship and to the later apostolic mission. Laying under tribute certain logia of Jesus preserved in the common evangelical tradition, John applies them sharply to the follower of Jesus. "Anyone who loves his life is destroying it:" the refusal of the crucial summons to "exodus" was illustrated dramatically in the ancient book which bears that name. No sooner did Moses lead the Hebrews into freedom in the desert, than they became fearful of such unwonted freedom, and demanded to return to the bondage of Egypt. The message of Jesus which lies at the heart of the gospel is the paradox that only when one "says 'No' to self" can one find the true self. John translates this into "hating one's life *in this world*," since in his Gospel "life" consistently means the sharing in the life of God Himself. Such an "outgoing" disciple, Jesus promises, "will guard" himself "for eternal life." Our evangelist, in whose view only God and Jesus can "save," has changed the traditional expression to "guard."

The most distinctive feature of John's rephrasing of the traditional sayings of Jesus however is that following him is essentially service. "If anyone is to serve me, the Father will do him honor." One recognizes at once an echo of this notion in the consideration, On the King, preliminary to the Second Week, where the summons of the risen Christ warns that "whoever may wish to come with me is to labor with me, that by following me in suffering he may also follow me in glory" ([95]). In the suggested response to this call, the volunteer expresses the wish and desire "on the sole condition it be for your greater service and praise, to imitate you in bearing every affront and contempt" ([98]). Rudolf Schnackenburg comments on this Johannine verse, "Nowhere as clearly as in this passage has John used the original idea of following. Following Jesus in death in order to share also in his victory and his perfection sets the Christian message apart from all myth."[8]

---

8   Schnackenburg, *John*, II, 386.

Jesus concludes his call to discipleship with its promise by a cry of anguish: "Now my heart is deeply troubled *(tetaraktai)*." The "now" recalls "the hour" (v. 23), and its arrival heralded by the coming of God-fearing pagans, seeking to believe in Jesus. Yet there is a dark side to this reality, which also presages the tragic rejection by Jesus' own people of his loving offer of salvation. Paul had voiced his grief over this same issue in his letter to the Roman church (Rom 9:1-5). The sadness of this "now" will re-echo through Jesus' discourse to his own after their last meal together: in the context of Judas' departure to betray his Master (13:31); in the words addressed to the remaining disciples, "So you also feel grief now" (16:22). In the present circumstances the Johannine Jesus appears to hesitate, as he betakes himself to prayer, about the tenor of his plea to the Father. Still the prayer he now utters is a real, *not* a hypothetical prayer—as most translations present it: "Father, save me from this hour?"

I venture to suggest that the interpretation of this difficult verse recording Jesus' request proposed by Xavier Léon-Dufour, is much more plausible, "Father, save me throughout this hour!"[9] Jesus has been depicted already as fully aware of the arrival of his "hour." That he should be tempted to reject it is unthinkable in this Gospel especially, where his sufferings and death are his "glory." The phrase I have rendered "throughout this hour" is expressed in Greek as "out of this hour" *(ek tēs hōras)*. It should be noted that the identical Greek expression is used by another writer of the Johannine school, the seer of Patmos. "Because you have preserved the word of my endurance, I in turn will preserve you *throughout the hour* of testing" (Apoc 3:10). In the Fourth Gospel, salvation is—without exception—given a positive content: nowhere is there mention of what men and women are "saved" *from.*

Jesus then is asking the Father here to bring salvation to him "out of this hour," not to deliver him from the hour itself which in God's design is to be source of eternal life for all believers. Indeed, it is Jesus' unwavering trust in the Father and his unquestioning faith in the divine "command I have received from my Father"—to "lay down my life in order to take it up again" (10:17-18), that has brought Jesus unhesitatingly "to this hour."

---

9   Xavier Léon-Dufour, "Père, fais-moi passer sain et sauf à travers cette heure" *Neues Testament und Geschichte: Historisches Geschehen und Deutung im Neuen Testament: Oscar Cullmann zum 70 Geburtstag,* eds. H. Baltensweiler und Bo Reicke (Tübingen, 1972), pp. 157-165.

John now articulates the prayer of Jesus with the help of his characteristic word "glorify." The request will be expanded at some length in the great prayer inserted immediately before the Passion-narrative (17:1-5). It appears to be a Johannine variant on the first petition of the dominical prayer, "Hallowed be Thy name!"—may You make Your name (Father) the source of holiness in us: Consecrate us to Yourself as "our Father" by making us aware of our adoptive sonship. The idea will be found later in the great prayer. "Holy Father, protect with Your name those whom you have given me, in order that they may be one, even as we are. When I was with them, I protected them with Your name which You gave me, and I have guarded them . . ." (17:11b-12). And as Jesus offers himself and his life to the Father, he declares, "I consecrate myself for their sake" (17:19a).

In my judgment there can be little doubt that our evangelist is here presenting his version of the traumatic experience by Jesus which Mark and his colleagues pictured as occurring during the terrible struggle in Gethsemane, antecedent to Jesus' capture by his enemies, when he won the victory through prolonged and fervent prayer (Mk 14:33-42). While the earlier Gospel-writers clearly *imply* that Jesus received an answer to his prayer to the Father, the hymn cited by the early Christian homilist, author of Hebrews, describes how Jesus "in the days of his flesh offered as sacrifice pleas from need and supplications to Him Who had power to save him from death's thrall, with a mighty cry and tears. And God heard his prayer" (Heb 5:7).

John adopts the same point of view—notable indeed in his Gospel as the first and only time the Father is heard to speak (as it will be recalled that our evangelist omitted both the theophany which occurred at Jesus' baptism and the majestic scene of the Transfiguration, the two occasions in the Synoptics when the voice of God was heard). "At this, a voice came out of the sky, 'I have glorified it, and I will glorify it again!' " During the period of Jesus' life on earth the Father had revealed His presence within him (10:38) through the words and "signs" by which "Jesus manifested his glory" (2:11). The definitive revelation of the "God no one has ever seen" lies still in the future, when during his "hour" Jesus will disclose his identity as source of life by "handing over the Spirit" (19:30). All this however is the "work" of God acting in Jesus, since as "the Son" he "can do nothing on his own" (5:19).

3. Jesus' Final Warning to the Crowd (12:29-36)

29 Consequently, the crowd standing round, upon hearing this, was saying

it had thundered: others kept insisting, "Some angel has spoken to him." 30 Jesus rejoined, "It was on your account, not mine, that the voice came. 31 The judgment of this world is now. It is now the prince of this world will be driven out. 32 Yet, as for me, when I am lifted up from earth, I will draw all people to myself." 33 (He said this to indicate what sort of death he was destined to die.) 34 As a result, the crowd continued with this objection, "We have heard from the Law the Messiah abides forever—so how can you assert it is God's will *(dei)* that the Son of Man be lifted up? —Who is this 'Son of Man'?" 35 Accordingly, Jesus told them, "Yet but a short while light is with you: walk while you have light, for fear darkness overtake you. One who walks in darkness does not know where he is going. 36 While you have the light, believe in the light, that you may become sons of light!" Jesus finished saying this, and going off he hid himself from them.

"The crowd" now appears to replace the disciples as audience for Jesus' ultimate warning. As was pointed out earlier the various references to a "crowd" in this chapter (12:9, 12, 17, 18) are ambiguous; hence it is difficult to decide the composition of this group here. Their only function is to experience in some vague way the divine response to Jesus' prayer, and to hear—without accepting it—Jesus' final call to faith. These peoples' reaction is depicted as diversified—to indicate they have understood nothing of the theophany. It probably echoes the extravagant language of apocalyptic, although the voice of God is described as thunder in the Old Testament (1 Sam 12:18), especially in the dramatic Psalm 29. Thunder is associated with God's awesome majesty in the book of Revelation (Apoc 5:4; 11:19; 16:18). The angel as divine intermediary of a revelation is found frequently in the Old Testament (Gen 21:17; 1 Kgs 19:5, 7), particularly in apocalyptic (Dan 10:5-21; 12:1-12). John's point here is to underscore the total incomprehension of the crowd: it is only the word of Jesus that can bring understanding through the gift of faith in himself, as the one to whom God has on this occasion borne witness.

Jesus now explains the meaning of God's answer to his prayer in "the hour." "The judgment of this world is now!" By "now" reference is made back to the actuality of "the hour" (v. 23) and "this hour" (v. 27). We saw earlier that "the judgment" was ambivalent in meaning: it spells doom for anyone "living a life that is worthless" and who "hates the light and refuses to come to the light" (3:20); but it means salvation for "the person who lives the truth" and "comes to the light" (3:21).

"The hour" also entails victory over "the prince of this world" who "will be driven out." This is the first time John has so designated "the darkness," the power of evil. At the original ending of his discourse at the Last Supper Jesus will announce, "The prince of this world is coming, yet he has no claim against me" (14:30). Towards the conclusion of his instructions to the disciples (in the expanded discourse) Jesus asserts that the coming of the Paraclete upon the disciples will reveal to them that "the prince of this world has been definitively condemned" (16:11), as a result of Jesus' saving death. This title for the devil as enemy of God and of the human race reminds one of Ignatius' favorite designation, "the enemy of human nature"—an expression associated with St. Onuphrius, "the savage saint," whose life Ignatius had read in the Castilian version of the *Legenda Aurea*.[10]

Jesus completes his discussion of "the hour" by what is the third prediction of his Passion and resurrection (see 3:14-15; 8:28), in which he dwells upon the universal fascination of the Crucified. We have already remarked upon the central position in the *Exercises* occupied by "our creator and Lord" and "the crucified majesty of God." In John's view, what had earlier been acknowledged as the exclusive prerogative of the Father (6:44, 65) will now be exercised by Jesus himself, "when I am lifted up from earth"—at the crucifixion, as the text makes clear.

The objection of the crowd indicates that it has not accepted Jesus and his message, but still clings to "the Law." Its expectation of the Messiah, riddled with its nationalist hopes, had been refuted by Jesus in his discussions with the inhabitants of Jerusalem (7:27-29, 41-42). For John, the designation of Jesus as "the Messiah, the Son of God" (20:31) must be understood to transcend any mere nationalistic aspirations. The first Isaiah had indeed promised that the reign of the royal Messiah was to endure, but its totally new character was ascribed to "the zeal of the Lord of hosts" (Is 9:6). Jesus himself, in speaking "to the Jews who had found faith in him" about the new liberation he would bring, had in fact stated that "the Son abides forever" (8:31-36). In the context of the Gospel this retort by the crowd permits John to remedy his omission of "the Son of Man" from Jesus' prophecy of his death. "How can you assert it is God's will"—the source of the "must" *(dei)* as elsewhere in the New Testament—"that the Son of Man be lifted up?" Moreover, the evangelist is enabled here to introduce the question which is central to the entire Gospel: "Who is this 'Son of man'?" One senses also an echo of the controversy which his "community of the beloved disciple" was carrying on with the synagogue. Rudolf Schnackenburg comments, "Jesus

---

10   See H. Rahner, *The Spirituality of St. Ignatius Loyola*, pp. 30-31; also Pedro de Leturia, *Iñigo de Loyola*, pp. 91-93.

does not discuss the difficulty raised by the crowd, nor does the evangelist see any need to refute the objection for the benefit of his readers . . . They know . . . that their Christ does 'remain for ever'; the Jews bear witness to this against their will (Johannine irony)."[11]

John takes advantage of the crowd's manifestation of disbelief to present Jesus' last appeal to it to turn to himself in faith; and the Johannine Jesus returns to the familiar theme of daylight and darkness (9:4-5; 11:9-10) to disclose once again his identity as "the light of the world" (8:12). Consistent with his habit of teaching in parables, Jesus speaks first of the natural phenomenon and then makes his plea that the crowd believe in him. "While you have the light, believe in the light, that you may become sons of light!" This last expression had been used by Paul in his first extant letter (1 Thes 5:5), and the post-Pauline letter "to the Ephesians" attests to the use of the image in baptismal liturgies (Eph 5:8-14).

George MacRae's comment on these last lines by Jesus which conclude his efforts to reveal himself to the people is a perceptive one. "To the extent that the fragments of discourse in verses 35-36 may be considered an answer to the question 'Who is this Son of Man?', it is a beautiful recapitulation of the light-darkness theme in christological terms. The light and the dark, alternative symbols to the above and the below, the truth and the lie, and other contrasts, align the Son of Man with the world of God appearing in the world of humanity."[12]

"Jesus finished saying this, and going off he hid himself from them." With this comment the evangelist informs his reader that the story of Jesus' public ministry is come to an end. Henceforth, Jesus will instruct only a few faithful followers. This turning-point in the earthly life of Jesus was already commemorated in the Marcan Gospel in his scene of Peter's confession at Caesaraea Philippi (Mk 8:27-33). With his characteristically innovative re-working of the earlier traditions, the fourth evangelist has placed the line of demarcation between Jesus' "speaking openly to the world" (18:20) and his farewell discourse to "his beloved friends." The consideration of the Last Supper, moreover, in the *Spiritual Exercises* belongs to the Third Week ([190-198]).

11   Schnackenburg, *John*, II, 395-396.
12   G. W. MacRae, *Invitation to John*, p. 154.

Chapter 13

THE FAREWELL MEAL (13:1-30)

A notable insight into the character of the author of the *Spiritual Exercises* is provided by the spiritual affinity he has been found to manifest with that other Ignatius, first bishop of Antioch. As is well known, it was out of devotion to this martyr-theologian that Iñigo de Loyola assumed the name Ignatius. Now it is of considerable assistance to our understanding of Ignatian spirituality to realize the impact which the letters of the earlier Ignatius had upon his medieval namesake. The Syrian bishop testified to his conviction that the gospel-traditions constituted a veritable "incarnation" of the Son of God, inasmuch as those traditions, eventually set out in our four Gospels, were a presentation in human words of the risen Lord—his person, message, and saving activities. Thus, Ignatius writes to the community of Philadelphia in Asia Minor of the urgent necessity of "taking refuge in the Scripture as in the flesh of Jesus" (Phil 5:1). A principal reason for seeking sanctuary in the evangelical traditions, Ignatius perceived astutely, lay in the dangers to orthodox faith inherent in Gnosticism, which in his time had infected a certain number of Christians. Originally, this chameleon-like set of esoteric and eccentric beliefs had arisen in paganism, and then had even invaded some sectaries within Judaism itself. Fundamentally, Gnosticism laid claim to possess secret "knowledge" *(gnōsis)*, by which alone salvation came to the initiate. These Christian "spirituals," who despised the material elements of God's creation (including human sexuality) clung to a notion of an ethereal "redeemer," who descended from heaven to collect the "sparks" buried in the evil flesh of humans, to return once more to heaven. As these divine particles were originally parts of himself, the so-styled "redeemer" was in fact portrayed as saving himself. The devotees of such arcane *gnōsis* rejected the central doctrine of Christian revelation that the Son of God had "come in the flesh" (1 Jn 4:2), and that he had—thus showing himself to be truly human—died on the cross to save all mankind. Ignatius of Antioch was well aware of the great need for discernment and vigilance to guard against "the spirit" that had seduced believers like the Gnostics. Such "spiritual" invasions had always to be judged against the humble career of the Word become flesh and, above all, by one's readiness to embrace the cross of Jesus. It was earlier noted that the Johannine term *Logos* originally connotes structure, and hence that "order" of which Ignatius of Loyola was a keen proponent. Hugo Rahner once described Ignatius of Antioch's teaching on discernment as consisting "in two basic propositions: the tendency of the genuine spirit to assimilate men to the man Christ and to obey the visible Church; the visibility of the cross and of the Church therefore must be surety for invisible things."[1]

While anyone familiar with the spirituality of Loyola will have already recognized the striking affinities between this doctrine of the bishop of Antioch and that exposed in the *Spiritual Exercises,* it may be of interest to observe that the medieval Ignatius adopted and adapted a motto of his sub-apostolic eponym, which appears in his letter to the church of Rome, "My love is crucified" (Rom 7: 2). It appears however among the maxims of Ignatius of Loyola (as Hugo Rahner noted) in the form, "Jesus, my love is crucified," and so the saying has undergone an evolution which "gives a different sense to the apothegm."[2] Whereas the Antiochian Ignatius had meant that his love for the world had been nailed to the cross of Jesus, his spiritual legatee emended the aphorism to express his personal image of his Lord as "the crucified Majesty of God."

Consequently, as the exercitant approaches the contemplations of the Third Week, under the direction of the fourth evangelist, it is of some importance to see how much these attitudes of the first and second Ignatius are congenial with those of this sacred writer. "Christological concentration" has already been picked out as a salient feature of the *Spiritual Exercises,* and it is a primary technique of our chosen evangelist. John's insistence on the cosmic parameters of salvation is attested in the confession of faith, "Jesus is the Savior of the world" (4:42). The Johannine version of the words of Eucharistic institution appear on the lips of Jesus, who speaks of "My flesh [given] for the life of the world" (6:51b). A propos of this latter text, Rudolf Schnackenburg makes the following perceptive comment. "It is possible that we have here a received formula of the Eucharist, another form of the words of institution (surviving in Ignatius of Antioch)."[3]

The question whether the Fourth Gospel contains any intended polemic against Gnosticism becomes difficult to answer in the affirma-

---

1 H. Rahner, *The Spirituality of St. Ignatius Loyola*, pp. 61-62.
2 Ibid., p. 122, n. 103.
3 Schnackenburg, *John*, I, 157-158.

tive because "it opens out to the Hellenistic world of syncretism."[4] Indeed, as George MacRae notes, "The Fourth Gospel could lend itself to misunderstanding. It did so early in the history of interpretation, for two of its first known interpreters in the second century were Gnostic heretics, Ptolemaeus and Heracleon, who saw in it a justification of their totally anti-worldly dualist approach."[5] And in fact, as the same writer remarks in discussing the intention of our evangelist, "For John there are many ways to Jesus . . . but Jesus is not bound up in any of them. For faith must lead to the perception of the divine in totally self-giving love and must engender love in the Christian community—or else it is not Christian faith. For the fourth evangelist, one can approach Jesus as a Jew or a Greek, a Samaritan or a Gnostic, but one can have life in him only as a Christian."[6] In answer to the question posed above, we accept the view of Rudolf Schnackenburg that, "There can be little doubt of the anti-Gnostic intention contained in the assertion of the Incarnation (1:14) . . . [which] must be directed against a docetic watering down of primitive Christology in the Church, such as is typical of Gnosticism while taking many forms."[7] The same author acknowledges, after a discussion of "possible anti-Gnostic trends in John," that "The yield is not rich; but if it were only the Christology of the Incarnation which could be shown to have an anti-Gnostic character, the result is of great importance. It means that faith's aptest answer and strongest barrier has been set up by John against the growing menace of Gnosticism, which was to be a mortal danger to the Church of the second century. If, on the other hand, the evangelist perhaps threw open the door to Gnostic questioning, and attracted Christian Gnostic heretics by his language and approach . . . his profession of faith in the *Christus incarnatus* was enough to expose Gnosis and its myth and the error of its way of salvation."[8]

It should by now not be difficult for the reader to see, more clearly than ever, how much the Ignatian "Gospel" resembles the Gospel of John. This is readily perceptible in the high values attaching to the humanness of Jesus in the *Spiritual Exercises*. On this point, I venture to suggest that this concern may well explain their author's otherwise curious down-playing of the miraculous in the life of Jesus. Ignatius moreover is celebrated for that "discerning love" *(discreta caritas),* discernible in his insistence upon correctives, for a valid discernment of

4 Ibid., 135.
5 G. W. MacRae, *Faith in the Word*, p. 9.
6 Ibid., p. 58.
7 Schnackenburg, *John*, I, 170.
8 Ibid., 172.

"the spirits," found only in the challenge offered by the actions and words of the earthly Jesus. In addition, there is the characteristically Ignatian emphasis upon the service of the risen Lord by that reciprocity of love, accepted as well as proffered within the believing community.

Actually this concord of which we speak between John and Ignatius is observable also in the way the latter opens the series of exercises for the Third Week, in which Jesus' Passion is to be contemplated, with the same episode, the Last Supper, with which John introduces the second great movement of his Gospel—the return of God's only Son to the bosom of the Father. It is in fact noteworthy that, where Mark and his colleague Matthew had begun their Passion-narratives with accounts of the plot of the priests (Mk 14:1-2), the anointing at Bethany (vv. 2-9), and the betrayal by Judas (vv. 10-11), John inaugurates his "story of the cross" with a leave-taking meal, wherein however no mention is made of the food to be prepared, and little attention is paid to eating. Instead, our evangelist begins with a highly charged sentence, which in effect points to the main action of Jesus at this final meal, the foot-washing, as a significant prophetic action intended to explain the meaning of his death, the thrust of the 'new command,' and the importance, for the future community of believers, of their post-Easter celebration of the Eucharist. A second important moment in John's portrayal of the Last Supper is the entry upon the scene of a (seemingly) new figure, "the disciple whom Jesus especially loved," whose presence is noted when Jesus announces his own betrayal by one of his own. The third great moment is marked by a (first) discourse by Jesus at the conclusion of the meal (13:31–14:31), which will furnish the theme of the ensuing chapter.

1. Prolegomenon to the Glorification of Jesus (13:1)

As the exercitant enters the Third Week of the Exercises with the help of the Fourth Gospel, it may be helpful to recall how our evangelist has, already in the first part of his Gospel, been preparing the reader for involvement in his innovative version of the Passion-story. And it may assist the appreciation of John's creativity to contrast it with that of the first evangelist, Mark. That writer had readied his intended audience (the church for which he originally wrote) for the contemplation of the Passion in two ways. Firstly, by means of a carefully structured section (Mk 8:31–10:45) marked out by Jesus' triple prediction of his death and resurrection. Two features of this development are to be remarked: The expression of this prophecy was couched, in the first two instances, *not* in the words of the historical Jesus, but through an early Christian formulation (8:31; 9:31), and in the third, by a summary of his own presentation of the Passion. Secondly, Mark next adopts a mode of discourse less characteristic of his usual manner and more in line with that of John, in which four stories about Jesus are recounted for their symbolic value: the miraculous cure of the blind Bar Timaeus (10:46-52), Jesus' entry—for the first and only time in this Gospel—into Jerusalem (11:1-11), his curse upon a barren fig tree (11:12-14, 20-25), out of which a kind of envelope is fashioned to enclose the account of a prophetic action by Jesus, his cleansing of the sacred precincts of the temple (11:15-19).

John readies his reader for the consideration of the Passion—which strictly speaking is contained within chapters eighteen and nineteen—by composing a unique version of Jesus' last meal with his disciples, a series, in two parts, of instructions for the disciples (13:31–14:31, and 15:1–16:33), and a solemn prayer, in which Jesus anticipates his departure from this world (17:1-26).

Our evangelist moreover has moved up into the first great section of his Gospel several episodes which Mark had, in one form or another, included in his Passion narrative. First, in his ordering of the book and possibly also in the significance he attaches to it (by reason of an innovative interpretation), is Jesus' cleansing of the temple-precincts (2:13-22), centered in verse 19, "Destroy this sanctuary and within three days I will raise it up." This procedure enables John to omit any account of false testimony at the hearing by the Sanhedrin (see Mk 14:55-59). Indeed, he skips over that trial, having anticipated its principal issues in the scene of Jesus' confrontation by "the Jews" at *Hanukkah* (10:22-39). Moreover, by telling this story of Jesus' prophetic action as he has done, John can omit the tearing of the curtain in the sanctuary, which for Mark was one of the chief consequences of Jesus' death (Mk 15:38). By his portrayal of the approach to Jesus of some God-fearing "Greeks" come to Jerusalem for Passover (12:20-36),—a scene which, in his Gospel, constitutes the closure of Jesus' public ministry—John can leave out the dramatic Marcan account of our Lord's struggle and prayer in Gethsemane (Mk 14:26-42). That he has deliberately done this can be inferred by several references in his text to this poignant experience, that had been preserved in the evangelical traditions (e.g. 14:31; 16:32; 18:11). Finally, John's singular insight into the raising of Lazarus, as one of the chief causes of the death of Jesus, has made it possible to depict the first two elements of the Marcan Passion-story, the plotting of the religious leaders and the anointing at Bethany (Mk 14:1-9) as the sequel to this greatest of Jesus' miracles (11:45-53; 12:1-8).

13:1   Before the feast of Passover, knowing that his hour was come for him to pass out of this world home to the Father, Jesus—who had loved his own who were in the world—showed his love for them to the last.

This solemn statement, with its emphatic assertion of the supernatural knowledge by Jesus of his divinely ordered destiny, functions as a kind of prologue to the second great movement of this Gospel. The reference here to the Jewish festal cycle, noted earlier as a feature of our evangelist's accounts of Jesus' earthly life, will be seen to provide an important clue to the Eucharistic symbolism of the foot-washing. For the first of Jesus' symbolic actions, the cleansing of the sacred enclosure, was introduced by the observation, "The Passover of the Jews was near" (2:13), and this, as was noted before, constituted a prophetic announcement of an utterly new "worship in Spirit and truth" (4:21-24). On the anniversary of this incident Jesus' feeding of the crowd in the desert, his last and greatest "sign" of the Galilean phase of his public life, was depicted as having messianic and Eucharistic significance, and the evangelist had employed a similar phrase, "The Passover, feast of the Jews was near" (6:4).

Moreover, Jesus is portrayed now as "knowing that his hour was come for him to pass out of this world home to the Father." We have already seen the centrality of this concept of "the hour" within the Fourth Gospel: it is the hour of Jesus' glorification and self-revelation through his "laying down his life for his beloved friends" (15:13). It thus includes Jesus' return "home to the Father" through resurrection and ascension, and most importantly his sending of the Paraclete, who will endow the disciples with a new faith enabling them to live out the teaching of Jesus, which "you cannot bear now" (16:21), since as "the Spirit of truth," he will "take what is mine and unveil its meaning for you" (16:14). It is helpful to recall that Luke presents Jesus' words and actions of Eucharistic institution as occurring "when the hour had come" (Lk 22:14). For that Gospel-writer "the hour" possessed a different significance. It became in his view the moment of Satan's return to destroy Jesus (Lk 22:3). As the Lucan Jesus would tell his captors, "This is your hour and the power of the darkness" (Lk 22:54). Luke saw that it was in that ominous "hour" that Jesus had bequeathed to those faithful men who "persevered with me in my trials"—as his last will and testament—the privilege and responsibility of presiding at the Eucharist and governing the future Christian church (Lk 22:28-30).

The most significant element in this introductory statement by our evangelist is beyond any doubt his testimony to the abiding love of Jesus. Indeed, this is the first time John has explicitly mentioned the love Jesus entertained for his faithful disciples, although he had earlier described the affection Jesus displayed towards Lazarus (11:3), and his sisters Martha and Mary (11:5). It is this animadversion to the love of Jesus which provides a very meaningful clue to the symbolism latent in the foot-washing.

Accordingly, it is of some moment, at this point in our reflections, to recall that John has intentionally reserved for the second part of his Gospel the treatment of the theme of love, particularly Christian love. As has been seen, the earliest chapters of this book indicated how concerned the evangelist was to make clear that genuine faith—whatever might be the influence, in bringing men and women to belief in Jesus, his "signs" could exercise—must be firmly grounded upon the word of Jesus, that "truth" about the unseeable God that constituted his message. Conversely, "the sin of the world," unfaith, was regarded as a deliberate, persistent refusal to open one's mind and heart to Jesus.

It is in consequence not surprising to find that John is reticent in speaking of love in the "Book of Signs." His muted reference to love throughout the Prologue has been commented on. In fact, when love was spoken of in the first twelve chapters, it was a question almost exclusively of the Father's love for Jesus and for humanity, or of Jesus' own love for his Father. "God so loved the world as to give His only Son, in order that everyone believing in him may not perish, but may possess eternal life" (3:16)—the single assertion in the entire book concerning God's love for the world. "The Father loves the Son, and has given all into his power" (3:35)—this, to endow him for his redeeming mission among men and women. In this connection, we also learn how "The Father dearly loves *(philei)* the Son, and shows him everything He Himself is doing; and greater works than these will He show him, in order that you may believe" (5:20). And again, "This is why the Father loves me: because I lay down my life, in order to take it up again" (10:17).

Conversely, the "dark side" of Jesus' coming from God into our world—humanity's refusal to accept Jesus—is sometimes expressed as the antithesis of love. "This is the judgment: the Light came into the world, yet men loved darkness rather than the Light, for their actions were evil" (3:19). "I know you do not have love for God in your hearts!" (5:42). "If God were your father, you would love me; for I have come forth from God, and am returning [to Him]. Now I did not come on my own initiative, but He has sent me" (8:42). "The man who loves his life in this world destroys it" (12:25). "For they loved glory from men rather than the glory from God" (12:43).

2. The Prophetic Symbolism of the Foot-washing (13:2-20)

2 And so at supper—when the devil had already put the thought of betraying him into the mind of Judas, son of Simon Iscariot— 3 Jesus, knowing that the Father had given all into his power, and that he had come forth from God and was returning to God, 4 rises from supper and removes his clothes; then taking a towel he wrapped it round himself. 5 He next pours water into the basin, and began to wash the feet of the disciples, and to wipe them with the towel tied round his waist. 6 So he comes to Simon Peter, who says to him, "Lord, are you going to wash *my* feet?" 7 In reply Jesus told him "What I am doing you cannot know for the present, but you will know by and by." 8 Peter says to him, "You are never going to wash my feet—no never!" Jesus replied, "If I cannot wash you, you cannot share anything with me!" 9 Simon Peter says to him, "Lord, then not only my feet, but hands and head as well!" 10 Jesus says to him, "The one who has taken a bath needs only to wash his feet to be entirely clean. Now as for you—you are already clean, but not every one of you." 11 (For he knew who would betray him: for that reason he added, "Not every one of you is clean.")

12 Now when he had washed their feet, and put on his clothes, and taken his place at table, he said to them, "Do you know what I have done for you? 13 You call me 'Teacher' and 'Lord;' and you are right, for that is what I am! 14 Now if I—the Lord and the Teacher—have washed your feet, then you yourselves in turn should wash one another's feet. 15 For I have set you an example, in order that you will carry out what I have done for you. 16 Amen, amen I tell you: a slave is not superior to his lord, nor a messenger superior to him who sent him. 17 If you come to know these things, you will be happy if you carry them out. 18 I am not speaking of all of you. I know which of you I have freely chosen. Yet, let the text of Scripture be fulfilled, 'The man eating my bread has lifted his heel against me' [Ps 41:9]. 19 From now on I shall tell you things before they occur, in order that when they occur you may believe that I AM! 20 Amen, amen I tell you: the person welcoming anyone I send welcomes me: the one welcoming me welcomes the One Who sent me."

John's account of the foot-washing falls into two quite distinct phases: the description of Jesus' actions and words (vv. 2-11), then a commentary by him which introduces a new interpretation of this symbolic act (vv. 12-20). In the course of our reflections, three levels of meaning will be seen to emerge: that of Jesus' redemptive death, of "the new command" (13:34), and finally a prophecy of the Eucharist, sacrament of the future Church.

The notice, "at supper," is of paramount importance since it draws the reader's attention to an extraordinary aspect of the action by Jesus:

he interrupts a meal already in progress to wash the feet of his disciples, who are the invited guests at this leave-taking meal. One may recall that, in the conventions of that day, the first offer of hospitality by a solicitous host occurred at the guest's entry into the house, when the house-holder summoned a slave to wash the dust of the road from the feet of the one come to dine. The saying, taken from the evangelical tradition regarding the relation of John "the witness" to Jesus, is probably a reference to this custom. The precursor declares, in speaking of "the one who comes after me," that "the thongs of his sandals I am not worthy to loose" (1:27). Such was the work of an attendant slave in preparation for washing a guest's feet. Only when this menial task was finished did the host lead the guest into dinner.

Now it will further be remembered that the Marcan supper-account gives evidence of a similar intrusion into that more detailed description of this meal as a Passover celebration, into which the liturgical formula of Eucharistic institution has been intercalated. As I have remarked elsewhere,[9] "The most significant part of Mark's redactional effort is intended to produce the impression that Jesus actually celebrated Passover with his disciples on the eve of his own death. In point of fact, we do not know the exact year when Jesus died. He was executed on a Friday probably in A.D. 30 or 33; hence we cannot be sure on which day Passover occurred (either the 14 or 15 Nisan)." Once one appreciates the presence of a text, not of Mark's composition, taken from the young Church's public worship, it becomes clear that the evangelist intends to portray (as I noted in the text just referred to) "Jesus' words and actions in the course of this final meal as a crucial link between the ancient Jewish liturgical tradition and the newly evolved Christian cultus which centers in the Eucharist."

To draw the reader's attention to the relation of this symbolic act by Jesus with his imminent death, the sacred writer now mentions the connivance of the evil one in the treachery of Judas—earlier called "a devil" (6:70): "the devil had already put the thought of betraying him into the mind of Judas, son of Simon Iscariot." John sets in greater relief the portrayal of Jesus as the Slave (or Servant) of God (Is 52:13–52:12): "he rises from supper and removes his clothes." The nakedness of Jesus emphasizes the voluntary humiliation and "emptying of himself" (Phil 2:7-8) involved in his saving death, while "knowing the Father had given

---

9   David M. Stanley, *The Call to Discipleship: The Spiritual Exercises with the Gospel of St. Mark*, p. 151.

all into his power." In the course of this self-effacing service, "he comes to Simon Peter," who in this Gospel will rarely be accorded (20:5) the place of pre-eminence he enjoys in the Synoptics until the epilogue (21:15-19). Peter objects energetically with astonished incredulity—"Lord are you going to wash *my* feet?" Jesus' rejoinder is meant to apprise the reader of the utter impossibility of grasping the saving significance of Jesus' death until after his glorification—"What I am doing you cannot know for the present, but you will understand by and by." Confronted with the vehemence of Peter's refusal to accept what will be seen in the sequel (13:34) as an act of the Master's proffered love, Jesus retorts with a threat as amazing to the reader as it is ominous for Peter. "If I cannot wash you, you cannot share anything with me!" Thus one becomes aware that it is question, through Peter's acquiescence in having his feet washed, of his sharing in that "eternal life," which Jesus is come to impart to all. And Peter himself, as his almost greedy response would indicate, seems at least to have understood that definitive separation is involved in his refusal, while remaining ignorant of the sense of the symbolic in this action. The reader may be acquainted with a similar message God had given Aaron. "The Lord said to Aaron, 'You shall have no patrimony in the land of Israel, no holding among them! I am your holding in Israel: I am your patrimony!'" (Num 18:20). And the seer of Patmos closes his book on this intimidating note, "Should anyone delete anything from the words in this book of prophecy, God will take from him his sharing in the tree of life and the holy city" (Apoc 22:19).

It is indeed difficult to assess the meaning of the explanatory remark now made by Jesus, about "the one who has taken a bath." Does it contain a reference to Christian baptism, as it does elsewhere in the New Testament (1 Cor 6:11; Eph 5:26; Tit 3:5; Heb 10:22)? Actually the same Greek word for "wash" *(louein)* is found, in a variant reading of Apocalypse 1:5, to designate Jesus' redemptive death for mankind. Given the great discretion which John displays in alluding to any of the Christian sacraments, we can content ourselves with an interpretation of this problematical verse (the phrase, "only to wash his feet" is frequently considered an intrusion into the original text), which finds it to assert simply that, through their association with Jesus and his instruction, the disciples "are already clean" from all sin, by anticipation of Jesus' "laying down his life" out of love for them (15:13).

While this section of the foot-washing narrative may be taken unquestionably as a commentary on the meaning of Jesus' death as the Deutero-Isaian Servant of God, it is interesting to recall that at least two ancient texts in which Jesus is presented as the Servant were created for use in the public worship of the Palestinian church, the cup-saying cited by Mark, "This is my blood for the covenant, to be poured out on behalf of many" (Mk 14:24), and the pre-Pauline hymn quoted by the Apostle to the Philippian community (Phil 2:6-11). Consequently, it becomes quite probable that this dramatic scene, constructed by John's creative imagination, was intended to replace the liturgical formula of Eucharistic institution which Mark had intruded into his supper-account. And one should be prepared to find certain Eucharistic overtones in a passage that commemorates the redemptive character of Jesus' proximate death.

The second part of John's story contains a further interpretation of the foot-washing, presented in the form of a speech by Jesus. The question introducing this instruction appears strange, in the light of the previous assertion to Peter, "What I am doing you cannot *know* for the present, but you will *know* by and by." For now Jesus asks all his disciples, "Do you *know* what I have done for you?" The reader has been made aware already twice (2:22; 12:16) that these followers of the Master will only be inducted into the mystery latent in the words and actions of the earthly Jesus, when after his exaltation and through his sending of the Paraclete they receive the precious gift of "remembering" (14:26). As a consequence, Jesus' present query becomes intelligible only if taken as addressed by John to his own community as a challenge to reflect upon the multiple meanings underlying Jesus' unconventional action.

Before moving to enucleate the further significance of his little drama, however, the evangelist indicates how Jesus resumes his place at table, so that the meal may continue. He is pictured as dropping his role as the Servant of God to continue his function as host. Thus he is seen to "put on his clothes, and take his place at table," becoming once again their "Teacher" and "Lord." If he is "Teacher" inasmuch as he provides an insight into his action as slave, it is as "the Lord" (a resurrection-title) that he now issues a quite new command, "You yourselves in turn should wash one another's feet." Beneath the exemplary facet of this act, "I have washed your feet," lies a deeper dynamic power that will issue from his "lifting up." The command of iteration is to be grasped as no banal—if menial—service to the community. Since it is to be performed "as a memorial of me" (1 Cor 11:24, 25), so solemn an order can only ultimately be obeyed when, "As often as you eat this bread and drink from the cup, you proclaim the death of the Lord until he come" (1 Cor 11:26).

Still John wishes to elucidate further the thrust of Jesus' symbolic action. Thus he has Jesus declare, "I have set you an example, in order that you will carry out what I have done for you." What the now exalted Lord has done above all is "to lay down his life for his beloved friends" (15:13). This overwhelming act of love, for these dear ones "he loved to the last," the evangelist will shortly express as "a new command" (13:34). We noted earlier John's penchant for employing forensic terminology. Only by comprehending the reality underlying such a juridical expression—"God's love poured forth in our hearts through a Holy Spirit given to us" (Rom 5:5)—can the unprecedented character of this "new command" be rightly gauged by the man of faith. The Christian is called to stand ever in relation to the risen Christ as "a slave" in service to "his Lord" and as "a messenger" of the good news to "the one who sent him." Indeed, as the Servant of God, the Johannine Jesus will announce shortly that "The Father is greater than I" (14:28c), and he never tires of repeating the truth that "It is the Father Who sent me." As Ignatius of Loyola would do after him, the fourth evangelist insists that the vocation of the Christian is the *service* of God in the church.

Jesus now pronounces a beatitude on those who have been gifted with this insight of faith. "If you come to know these things, you will be happy if you carry them out." And what are "these things," which all are to "come to know"? The significance of Jesus' death as the Servant of God out of "love for his beloved friends," obedience to a "new command" to be realized by the reciprocity of love within the community of faith, and finally, the celebration of Jesus' loving action in dying for all as well as the Christian response to that love by mutual loving service, which they are to carry out in prospect at "the Lord's Supper."

It may seem strange to hear, in such a context, the distressing counterpoint of Judas' treachery. With the aid of a psalm, which the rabbis of the age thought to have been written by David with the traitor Ahithophel in mind, John expresses—more poignantly than Mark had done (Mk 14:20)—this damnable violation of trust. I believe the evangelist's selection is significant. He might in fact have chosen Psalm 55:12-14, with its reference to a faithless friend, who had in days gone by shared the joy of the psalmist in the sacred liturgy of Israel. John however has deliberately emended the Septuagintal version "my meals" *(artous mou)* to read "my bread *(mou ton arton)*. "The man eating my bread has lifted up his heel against me." When one remembers the Johannine formula of institution, "The bread I will give is my flesh on behalf of the life of the world" (6:51b), it becomes quite plausible that our evangelist has the Eucharist in mind. When one sees the close parallel between the Eucharistic statement, "The man eating my flesh *(ho trōgōn mou tēn sarka)* . . . possesses eternal life" (6:54) and John's version of Psalm 41:10, "The man eating my bread" *(ho trōgōn mou ton arton)*, it becomes almost certain.

John now introduces a new function for the predictions of Jesus henceforth in this Gospel (14:29; 16:4). These are now expressly related to the Christological orientation of genuine faith. "From now on, I shall tell you things before they occur, in order that when they occur you may believe that I AM!" The unmistakable inclusion of the divine name, "I AM," inaugurates a theme which will return presently when Jesus insists that the disciples' faith in the God of Israel must be enlarged to include divine faith in himself. "You believe in God: you must also believe in me" (14:1b). The concluding saying taken from tradition (see Mt 10:40) provides the basis for belief in the divinity of Jesus: "the person welcoming me welcomes the One Who sent me." Rudolf Schnackenburg comments: "What is expressed in this logion is the article of Jewish law which insists that the one who is sent is equal to the one who sends him."[10] Here then we have the definitive answer to the Jewish objection to Jesus' Eucharistic promise, "How can this fellow give us his flesh to eat?" (6:52). The first half of the saying, with its assertion of the dignity of the disciple ("the person welcoming anyone I send welcomes me"), appears to gainsay Jesus' earlier statement, "a messenger is not superior to him who sent him" (v. 16). For whatever reason (and it is hard to be certain), John may simply wish to cite the traditional saying in its entirety: the disciple of Jesus will notwithstanding share *pro modo suo* in his Lord's dignity and mission.

We are surely indebted to our evangelist for his inspired insight into the meaning of what happened at that last supper. Through his creative insight he has solved a serious difficulty the reader may well have felt in understanding the relation between the words and gestures of the Jewish Jesus before his Jewish disciples on this sad occasion and the post-resurrectional "breaking of the bread" by the first Christian community. By creating the dialogue with Peter, John reminds us that, at this point in his story, the thrust of our Lord's action could not be understood: "What I am doing you cannot know for the present, but you will know by and by." And, as had been remarked, Jesus' other question is meant for John's readers, "Do you know what I have done for you?" The inspired writer's use of a prophetic, symbolic action (instead of quoting, as Mark did, a later Christian liturgical formula) has made it clear that these words and actions by the historical Jesus looked ahead to the time, after

10   Schnackenburg, *John*, III, 27.

his own death and resurrection, when with Christian faith his command to repeat what he himself had done in symbol would be obediently carried out in the celebration of the sacrament of the Eucharist.

When at its thirteenth session the Council of Trent solemnly declared, "All our predecessors—whoever formed part of the true church of Christ . . . confess with utmost candor that our Redeemer instituted this so estimable sacrament at the Last Supper,"[11] it employed the juridical term "instituted" in an obviously analogous and proleptic sense. For, properly speaking, it is laws which are "instituted," coming into force by the will of the legislator at a given point in time. The terminology was useful to the Tridentine fathers, who wished to assert that the origins of the Eucharist lay in the mission of Jesus himself—and specifically in his saving death and resurrection, which brought to birth the Christian church. By its "obedience of faith" (Rom 1:5) the earliest community first celebrated this august sacrament after its Lord's resurrection as its central act of worship.

In the text of the *Exercises* where he sets forth in some detail the first contemplation of the Third Week, Ignatius exhibits that lack of a critical historical sense so characteristic of the medieval mind—as may be seen in his *historia* of the Last Supper ([191]), a conflation for the most part of the Matthean account with that from John. "The first prelude is to make present the history *(traer la historia)*, which is here how Christ our Lord from Bethany sent two disciples to Jerusalem to prepare the supper, and then he himself came to it with the other disciples [Mt 26:17-20]; and how, after having eaten the paschal lamb [see Lk 22:15-18] and finished supper, he washed their feet [Jn 13:4-12], and gave his most sacred body and precious blood to his disciples [Mk 14:22-26], and he made then a sermon [Jn 13:31–14-31], after Judas had gone to sell his Lord [Mt 26:14-15; see Jn 13:30]." The Ignatian description of the same contemplation, repeated among "The Mysteries of Christ our Lord," adds certain legendary details ([289]). "Firstly, he ate the paschal lamb with his twelve apostles [Lk 22:14] to whom he foretold his death: 'Amen I tell you one of you will sell me' [see Mt 26:21 + 15]. Secondly, he washed the disciples' feet, including those of Judas, beginning with St. Peter, who, out of consideration for the majesty of the Lord and his own lowly status, did not wish to consent, but said: 'Lord, are you going to wash *my* feet?' [Jn 13:6]; but St. Peter did not know that thereby he was giving an example of humility, which is why he said, 'I have given you an exam-

11   Denzinger, Bannwart, Umberg, Rahner, *Enchiridion Symbolorum* (Freiburg im. Br. and Barcelona, 1952), no. 874.

ple, in order that you may do as I have done' [Jn 13:15]. Thirdly, he *instituted* the most sacred sacrifice of the Eucharist, as the greatest sign of his love, by saying 'Take and eat' [Mt 26:26b]. Supper over, Judas goes forth to sell Christ our Lord.''

I advert to this here, not to criticize the author of the *Spiritual Exercises*, who cannot be faulted for being a man of his own times, but to indicate the need for adaptation to contemporary questions arising in light of twentieth century biblical scholarship.

What is however of crucial importance for the present day exercitant on entering the Third Week is that he or she take cognizance of three new "points," in addition to the three for the Second Week. By "points" is meant facets of the "mystery" being contemplated—a word used in the Third Week with increased frequency. Thus besides the already familiar seeing the persons, hearing what they are saying, observing what they are doing (all this to be considered as actually happening before the exercitant, who is by now deeply involved in the "mystery"), one is directed "to consider what Christ our Lord *is suffering* in his humanity, or desires to suffer, according to the text contemplated; and now to begin with great energy and effort to bring oneself to grieve and sorrow, and shed tears, and in this manner labor through the other points which follow" ([195]). "The fifth point, to consider how the divinity hides itself, that is, how it could destroy its enemies, yet does not do so, and how it permits the most sacred humanity to suffer so cruelly" ([196]). "The sixth point, to consider how he is suffering all this for my sins, etc. [that is, for me personally], and what I ought to do and suffer [here and now] for him" ([197]). The concentration upon the suffering Jesus and upon one's compassion here and now with him is vital to the retreatant's involvement in the Passion. Where in the Second Week, emphasis was placed upon the following or imitation of Jesus, now there is no question of these aims. Ignatius, like Paul when he cites the ancient hymn to the church of Philippi (2:6-11), is intensely aware that any such "imitation" of the sufferings of the one who is at once God and man, is out of the question. Besides, the purpose of the contemplation in the Second Week was to bring the exercitant to a love "of enlightened self-interest" *(amor concupiscentiae)* for the Jesus of the public life, whereas now he or she is being led to the love "of friendship" *(amor benevolentiae)*, that is, no longer to love Jesus as good for me, but for his own sake. As William A. Peters remarks, "The central point of the Third Week is the great mystery of the close union between the suffering Christ and the exercitant."[12] The

12   W. Peters, *The Spiritual Exercises of St. Ignatius*, p. 134.

presence of the term "consider" *(considerar)* in each of the three new points directs the involvement away from "the person who is exercising himself" ([205]) to communion with Jesus who is enduring the Passion before one's eyes.

Surprisingly, at this point in the *Exercises*, new instructions are given in a Note on the colloquy ([199]). The more intimate verb "converse" *(hablar)*—"as one friend converses with another, or as a slave with his lord" ([43])—now yields place to "talk over motives *(razonar)* and make petition" *(pedir)* (regarding) "certain things I now desire with greater effectiveness." The explanation of such advice, relatively late in the retreat, lies most likely in Ignatius' concern that one is here and now to suffer *with* Christ by effectively sharing, inasmuch as is possible, in the Passion.

3. The Beloved Disciple Enters the Story (13:21-30)

21 On saying this Jesus became deeply troubled, and he testified to his profound agitation of spirit, "Amen, amen I tell you: one of your number will betray me!" 22 The disciples kept looking at one another, at a loss to know of whom he spoke. 23 One of his disciples—the one Jesus especially loved—was reclining at table closest to Jesus. 24 So Simon Peter nodded to him to ask who it might be of whom he spoke. 25 Consequently, leaning back against Jesus' breast he says to him, "Lord, who is it?" 26 Jesus replies, "It is that man for whom I shall dip this bit of bread and hand it to him." Then upon dipping the bread he hands it to Judas, son of Simon Iscariot. 27 And with the bit of bread Satan took possession of that man. So Jesus tells him, "Be quick about what you have to do!" 28 However, not one of those at table knew what he meant by telling him this. 29 Some took it for granted, since Judas kept the common purse, that Jesus was telling him, "Buy what we need in view of the feast," or "Give something to the poor." 30 Then on taking the bit of bread that man at once went out. It was night.

Despite his apparent insistence upon returning again to the sad fact of Judas' disloyalty, John's chief preoccupation in this paragraph is with the introduction of one who, as will be seen from the sequel, commands his love and loyalty even over Peter, who in the Synoptic tradition enjoys unquestioned place of privilege among the Twelve. This disciple, whom "Jesus especially loved," makes surely (one may think) a belated entry into the story. Has not this man, who from now on will occupy the most honored position among all the followers of Jesus, been in the company of the Master from the beginning? How otherwise explain his prominence in "the Book of Glory," where he is mentioned in six passages?

Raymond Brown's somewhat hesitant suggestion that this man was actually the anonymous disciple who, with Andrew, had been the first to follow the suggestion by John their first master (1:35) makes good sense.[13] Father Brown's still more hesitant identification (in the same context) of this unnamed disciple with John, son of Zebedee has been more recently retracted in his reconstruction of the history of the Johannine community.[14] In this later work however he has added to his earlier explanation for the late appearance of the Beloved Disciple ("Perhaps . . . the evangelist wished to introduce him as an antithesis to Judas")[15] by remarking that "The unnamed disciple of chapter 1 was not *yet* the Beloved Disciple because at the beginning . . . he had not yet come to understand Jesus fully." And he adds, "The Beloved Disciple makes his appearance by name only . . . when Jesus 'now showed his love for them [the disciples] to the very end.' This does not mean that this Disciple was not present during the ministry, but that he achieved his *identity* in a Christological context."[16]

The evangelist begins by describing Jesus' reaction at the thought of his treacherous disciple with the same expression he had used upon hearing of the request of certain God-fearing "Greeks" to see him (12:27). "Jesus became deeply troubled," and he adds, "He testified to his profound agitation of spirit, 'Amen, amen I tell you: one of your number will betray me!' " Once again, as when he began his account of the footwashing, our author makes a reference to Jesus' proximate death through the connivance of Judas. This however is intended (as has already been suggested) as an appropriate context for the appearance of "the one Jesus especially loved," here depicted as "reclining at table closest to Jesus." John's somewhat partisan loyalty to this disciple is evident in his placing Peter at once at a disadvantage: He is nowhere near Jesus at table, and so could only nod his plea to his more privileged colleague to find out the traitor's identity. The Beloved Disciple's greater intimacy with the Master is revealed through the familiarity of his spontaneous action, "leaning back against Jesus' breast," as he asks, "Lord, who is it?" Father Brown's comment is apposite: "This first description of the Beloved Disciple is typical in its emphasis on his closeness to Jesus and on his friendship with Peter. He is resting on Jesus' bosom, just as in 1:18 Jesus is described as in the Father's bosom . . . the Disciple is as in-

---

13   R. E. Brown, *John I–XII*, p. 73.
14   R. E. Brown, *The Community of the Beloved Disciple*, p. 33.
15   R. E. Brown, *John XIII–XXI*, p. 577.
16   R. E. Brown, *The Community of the Beloved Disciple*, p. 33.

timate with Jesus as Jesus is with the Father.''[17]

There has been a tendency on the part of some commentators to view the Beloved Disciple as a fictitious person, a symbol of the genuine believer. George MacRae rightly remarks that, "The Gospel itself suggests that this disciple is the authority for the tradition contained in it, if, as is likely, the same person is meant in 19:35. The appendix explicitly states the Johannine church's confidence in his testimony (21:24).''[18] As in the case of the mother of Jesus, the fact that this disciple was an historical personage does not preclude his also being a model for the Christian reader.

The identification of the traitor by Jesus is much more circumstantial in this Gospel than in that of Mark (Mk 14:20) or of Matthew (Mt 26:23), while Luke says nothing of it. However, it is important to note that the Johannine Jesus really does not give away the hideous secret, except perhaps to the Beloved Disciple, who in fact (apart from Jesus himself) retains the center of the stage. Whether Peter, who seems to have taken one of the lowest places at the meal, was given the answer to his inquiring sign by the Beloved Disciple is not indicated in the text. Schnackenburg infers that Peter did find out, and concludes from the fact that neither of these prominent disciples did anything about it, "that the scene lacks all historical credibility."[19] Brown however thinks, "It is less a strain on credulity to think that the evangelist was dealing with a reminiscence enshrined in the tradition that came to him."[20] The editor who composed the epilogue to this Gospel evidently accepted the episode as historical (21:20). I bring up this difference of viewpoint between two of the most distinguished Catholic commentators on the Fourth Gospel simply to remind the reader that the concern about "What really happened?" is a modern tendency and is, moreover, a distraction in the important business of contemplation.

Jesus' gesture—"Upon dipping the bread he hands it to Judas," who like the Beloved Disciple is reclining nearest to him—is one of loving attention characteristic of oriental hospitality. From what has already been said earlier it cannot be the Eucharistic species; nor, according to the evangelist's dating of Passover (see 18:28; 19:42), is there any question of herbs dipped in the red sauce *(haroseth)* taken customarily at the Passover meal. In the mind of our author the importance of the exchange

17   R. E. Brown, *John XIII-XXI*, p. 577.
18   G. W. MacRae, *Invitation to John*, p. 173.
19   Schnackenburg, *John*, III, 30.
20   R. E. Brown, *John XIII-XXI*, p. 574.

is that "with the bit of bread Satan took possession of that man." This provides a satisfactory explanation for the curious feature of the highly Christological scene in the garden before Jesus' arrest, where the traitor's role is minimized "to the point of reducing the betrayal . . . to merely pointing out where the garden was."[21] As will be seen after, in John's eyes it is the ultimate and triumphant confrontation between Jesus as "the light of the world," and Satan, leader of "the darkness," and "prince of this world."

Jesus' cryptic injunction, "Be quick about what you have to do!", and the ensuing misinterpretation on the part of those who overheard it may well be an attempt to make the whole episode more plausible. The observation that "Judas kept the common purse" reminds the reader of the Gospel of the earlier characterization of Judas as "a thief" (12:6). John's heightened denigration of Jesus' unfortunate betrayer—possibly intended to underline, by contrast, the attractive faithfulness of the Beloved Disciple—reaches its climax with the note on which the scene closes. "On taking the bit of bread that man at once went out. It was night." The symbolic force of this final detail should not be misconstrued, as it has been by the comment that "the long night of the Passion has begun." John's innovative re-interpretation of the evangelical traditions depicts the Passion as the "glory" of Jesus. This insight will be highlighted especially in his presentation of the scene on Calvary, from which he has carefully removed any of the tragic or ominous details prominent in the Synoptic narratives. To grasp the sense of John's concluding remark here ("It was night"), it is helpful to remember the ambivalent nature of any symbol, which yields a dual meaning. As Rudolf Schnackenburg observes, "For Judas, 'night' represents the sphere of darkness into which he has fallen and, what is more, of which he has become a definitive part . . . For Jesus, it is the hour that marks the end of his work among men (cf. 9:4) . . . for the evangelist (this brief statement) only serves as a dark foil to set off the words about Jesus' glorification that follow."[22]

---

21   G. W. MacRae, *Invitation to John*, p. 203.
22   Schnackenburg, *John, III*, 32.

Chapter 14

FROM "FOLLOWING JESUS" TO "ABIDING" IN
THE FATHER AND THE SON (13:31–14:31)

E arlier it was pointed out how, with chapter five, John had introduced a new mode of dealing with Jesus' "signs." The narrative of
the cure of the cripple at the Sheep-pool and the feeding of a great crowd
in Galilee were each made simply the introduction to a significant discourse designed to throw light upon certain aspects of the mystery of
Jesus. Now however, after giving his quite distinctive account of Jesus'
last meal with his own, John reverses his procedural method. In the discourse we shall here consider, we are given the evangelist's suggestions to
his reader, who never knew Jesus personally during his life on earth, for
a profitable reading of the Passion-narrative, which will be presented in
chapters eighteen and nineteen. A second discourse (15:1–16:33),
together with the great prayer of Jesus (17:1-26), was probably added by
a subsequent editor. We shall have occasion to refer to the three Paraclete-sayings in this added instruction (15:26-27; 16:7-11, 12-15), when
we fulfil an earlier promise to return to the question of discernment in
this Gospel.

The Problem of Not Knowing the Earthly Jesus

It would appear that a major concern, which arose in the very early
years of the Church, had to do with those believers who had not been
privileged to have known and followed Jesus during his public ministry
and his sufferings. What could replace that personal acquaintance with
the Master which those disciples enjoyed (and which they regarded as
their basic formation), who had seen his actions, heard his words—above
all, had lived in his company?

The continuing significance of this question, at least since the Council of Trent, and even into our own century, may be seen reflected in the
heated debates which attended the preparation of the Constitution on
Divine Revelation during Vatican II. One of the most controverted issues
was a piece of unfinished business regarding the relation of Scripture to

tradition, handed down from the Council of Trent in the sixteenth century. Not a few fathers were exercised over the inadequacy of the Bible as sole medium of the transmission of revelation; and while the conciliar declaration—object of pre-occupation throughout Vatican II until its closing weeks—did not settle the issue completely, still the second chapter of *Dei Verbum* ("The Transmission of Divine Revelation") attests the considerable advance made over the juridical statements of Trent. Where that earlier Council took as the single starting-point of Christian tradition, the *preaching* of Jesus together with that of his first disciples after his resurrection, Vatican II included two additional realities, the (living) examples of the apostles and their "institutions."[1] The intent of this latest Council was to provide a more concrete and inclusive idea of what revelation in fact is. In the words of Joseph (now Cardinal) Ratzinger, the conciliar fathers proposed, "in place of a narrowly doctrinal conception of revelation, as had been expressed in the Tridentine word theology, to open up a comprehensive view . . . found not only in the word that Christ preached, but in the whole living experience of his person . . . what is said and what is unsaid, what the Apostles . . . are not able to express fully in words, but which is found in the whole reality of the Christian existence . . . far transcending the framework of what has been explicitly formulated in words."[2] In the same paragraph the distinguished German theologian also observed the importance of the terminological switch to denote the role of the Spirit—instead of "at the direction of the Holy Spirit" the new text reads "by the suggestion of the Holy Spirit," an allusion to the Johannine discourse we are about to consider (14:26).

Paul's Proposed Solution to the Problem

Paul, whose Christian existence began with his confrontation on the Damascas road by the risen Lord (Phil 3:7-12; 1 Cor 15:8; 2 Cor 4:6; Gal 1:12, 15-16), had never known the earthly Jesus (2 Cor 5:16b). It would appear that some of his Jewish-Christian rivals made this a reproach to discredit his claim to apostleship (1 Cor 9:1-2; 2 Cor 11:4-5; Gal 1:6-12).

---

1 *Dei Verbum*, no. 7: "As a consequence, Christ the Lord . . . laid an injunction on the apostles that they preach the gospel . . . to all, by communicating the divine gifts to them. This was indeed faithfully carried out . . . by the apostles, who handed on by oral proclamation, by their example and by their institutions, that which they had received from the mouth of Christ, from their experience of living with him *(conversatione)*, and from his works, or in fact what they had learned through the suggestion of the Holy Spirit . . ."
2 See *Commentary on the Documents of Vatican II*, Vol. III, p. 182.

The suffering he felt from such detraction made him sensitive to the same lack in his Greek-speaking converts of any personal acquaintance with Jesus; and this would appear to explain his repeated insistence that the members of his foundations *imitate himself* as their immediate exemplar for living out the gospel, and, as a result of their own experience of his way of life, come to imitate the risen Lord (1 Thes 1:6; 2 Thes 3:7-9; Phil 3:17; 1 Cor 4:16). He puts it emphatically to the community in Corinth, "Become imitators of me by reason of the fact that I am [an imitator] of Christ" (1 Cor 11:1). It is striking that such imitation-spirituality appears elsewhere in the New Testament (apart from 3 Jn 11) only in authors influenced by Paul (Eph 5:1; Heb 6:12; 13:7b).

Later on, when his own thought had matured as a result of suffering borne by him in the apostolate, he formed a series of neologisms from verbs which express facets of the paschal mystery, compounded with the preposition *syn* (with), to limn authentic Christian existence. To the Galatians he writes, "I have become (and remain) crucified with Christ" (Gal 2:19), while to the Romans he describes the baptismal experience as a "being buried with him" (Rom 6:4), "having been crucified with" him (v. 6) in the hope "we will be made alive with him" (v. 8). Further on, he speaks of Christians as "heirs of God, co-heirs of Christ, provided we suffer with him, in order that we may be glorified together with him" (8:17).

That the Apostle described the living of the gospel in such terms indicates his esteem for the experiences of those who were the original followers of Jesus, as well as the crucial significance of the specifically Christian experiences which had replaced them. We shall shortly have occasion to observe how, in the *Spiritual Exercises*, instead of praying for the grace to "follow" or "imitate" Jesus as the exercitant contemplates his life during the Second Week, in the Third Week he or she is instructed to ask for compassion with our Lord's sufferings, and (in the Fourth) to be able to rejoice at his joy in the risen life.

Attempts to Bridge the Gap by the Synoptic Evangelists

Mark, the creator of a totally new kind of religious literature—the Gospel, has proposed the gospel-proclamation of the Church as the link with the experience of those who followed Jesus during his ministry in Galilee and Jerusalem. He sets out to compose a work which he entitles "the beginning of the gospel of Jesus Christ, God's Son" (Mk 1:1). "Beginning" is not intended to be taken in any chronological sense, but designated the (now risen) Jesus as *source* of the Christian "good news of victory." The gospel is both *from* Jesus Christ and *about* him, who is "God's Son," and hence has become the medium of that "dynamic power of God," which Paul had already associated with the message of salvation (Rom 1:16). The principal Marcan theme is that the call to discipleship, once issued by the Jesus of the public life, may still be heard (and is in fact to be heeded) in the official announcement by the Church of God's definitive offer of salvation. This evangelist brings his Prologue to a climax with the description of the opening of Jesus' Galilaean ministry. "After John had been handed over, Jesus came into Galilee heralding the gospel from God: 'God's time has found its fulfillment—the Kingdom of God has drawn near. Reform your lives and put faith in the gospel!' " (Mk 1:14-15). In the course of his book Mark employs the term "gospel" four additional times. He has twice introduced it into sayings of Jesus which touch significantly upon the meaning of discipleship. The first deals with the cost: "But whoever will destroy his life for my sake and for the gospel will save it" (Mk 8:35b). The second points to the reward that is promised: "Amen I tell you: there is no one who has left household or brothers or sisters or mother or father or children or property for my sake and for the gospel, but will receive a hundredfold now in this present age . . . with persecutions, and in the age that is coming life eternal" (Mk 10:29-30).

When later he inserts the so-called eschatological discourse into his book between the end of the public ministry and the Passion-narrative, Mark attempts to brake the frenzied excitement disturbing his community by insisting "the end is not yet" (Mk 13:7). He also points to one of the critical signs of delay, "The gospel must first be proclaimed to all nations" (Mk 13:10). Finally, this writer concludes Jesus' defense of the loving gesture of an unnamed woman, who had anointed him with costly perfume: "Amen I tell you: wherever throughout the entire world the gospel will be heralded, what she has done will also be told as a memorial of her" (Mk 14:9).

It is moreover of interest to observe how Mark has employed ancient summaries of the gospel to set off certain moments of great significance for the movement of his entire story. Two such credal formulae from very early tradition are used to articulate the first two predictions by Jesus of his death and resurrection. "The Son of Man must suffer grievously, must be rejected by the elders, the high priests, and the scribes, must be killed, while after three days he must rise" (Mk 8:31). The second prediction is, in the opinion of scholars, the most primitive Christian form of the prophecy, "The Son of Man is being handed over into the power of human beings: they will kill him, yet after three days he will rise" (Mk 9:31). In the final scene of his book, the three terrified women hear the good news of Jesus' resurrection in words borrowed from an archaic Christian creed, "Jesus the Nazarene—the One who has been crucified—has been raised!" (Mk 16:6b).

The evangelist Matthew, whose ecclesial interest is well known, discloses dramatically in the final scene of his Gospel how, as a consequence of Jesus' death and resurrection, the following of the earthly Jesus by the eleven faithful disciples has been transformed: they are commissioned by the risen One to "go make disciples of all nations" (Mt 28:19a). This new Christian discipleship is inaugurated by baptizing and by "teaching them to observe everything I enjoined upon you" (v. 20a). For the first time in this Gospel the disciples are commanded to teach— why? On the very last line of his book Matthew gives the answer: the new, invisible, yet perennial presence of the Lord to his Church. "And remember I am with you all days until the end of the [present] age" (v. 20b). There is no account of the ascension in this Gospel: the glorified Lord abides in the community, where he teaches and makes disciples through the teaching of those who originally followed him. It is noteworthy that, before he speaks to the Eleven, Jesus is portrayed as "drawing near them" (v. 18). Father John Meier, who finds that the only other instance where the verb "draw near" is predicated of Jesus in this Gospel occurs in the story of the Transfiguration (Mt 17:7), perceptively describes this action as "a proleptic parousia."[3] The exalted Jesus, invested with "universal authority in heaven and upon earth," now "draws near," in order to create the unprecedented experience of Christian discipleship, which is meant to supplant the "following" of himself in his earthly career.

Actually, Matthew has been pointing ahead to this scene from the beginning of his book, where in the annunciation to Joseph he cited the Isaian text which provided his "throne-name" for the still unborn "Son of David". "They will call his name Emmanuel, which translated means 'With us is God' " (Mt 1:23). In his instruction to the divided community for which he writes his Gospel, he cites a saying by Jesus not found elsewhere, "Again I tell you: if two of you will agree on earth over any project whatsoever about which they make petition, it will be granted them by my heavenly Father. For where two or three have been assembled under my name, I am there in their midst" (Mt 18:19-20). Indeed, it is a notable feature of this writer's Passion-narrative that stress is laid upon being *with* Jesus: at the Last Supper (Mt 26:18, 20, 23, 29), on

3   John P. Meier, *Matthew*, p. 369.

the way to Gethsemane (v. 36), during his prayer (vv. 38-40), at his arrest (v. 51). For Matthew, the poignancy of Peter's denials lies in his rejection of the fact he was "with Jesus"(vv. 69, 71).

In his turn, Luke lays stress upon the future role of the Twelve (Acts 1:8) as the authoritative witnesses to the teaching and actions of the earthly Jesus. He situates the call of the three best known disciples, Simon, James, and John, within a story of a miraculous catch of fish (Lk 5:1-11). He surrounds the creation of the Twelve with a certain solemnity, representing it as the result of an entire "night spent in prayer to God" (Lk 6:12) by Jesus. In the immediate sequel Jesus is portrayed as addressing four beatitudes to these newly selected followers (vv. 20-23). Accordingly, when in the elegant periodic sentence with which he opens his Gospel Luke appeals to those "eyewitnesses from the beginning, who also became servants of the word" (Lk 1:2), there can be little doubt but that he has the Twelve particularly in view. At the Last Supper the Lucan Jesus speaks to "the apostles" (Lk 22:14) pointedly in terms of their personal experience of his own activity, when he appoints them to preside over the Eucharist and to assume leadership in the future Church. "You are those who have persevered in my company through my trials; and I, for my part, bequeath sovereignty to you, by virtue of the fact my Father has bequeathed it to me. You shall eat and drink at my table in my kingdom and shall sit upon thrones judging the twelve tribes of Israel" (vv. 29-30).

Luke manages to give the impression that these intimate disciples witnessed certain significant scenes during the Passion of Jesus. They were all within sight and earshot of Jesus while he prayed "about a stone's throw" (Lk 22:41) from them. They do not run away (as in Mk 14:50) at Jesus' arrest; in fact "his companions" are ready to offer resistance (Lk 22:49). Indeed, "*all* his friends, as well as the women who had followed him from Galilee, stood at a distance to observe these things" (Lk 23:49), that is, the death of Jesus.

On Easter day the risen Jesus confronts "the Eleven and those with them" (Lk 24:33), and after establishing the reality of his bodily presence by eating, "he opened their minds to understand the Scriptures" (v. 45). Then he gave them their commission, saying "It is you who are the witnesses to it all" (v. 48). It is clear that Luke is concerned to establish continuity between the events of Jesus' public ministry shared by the Twelve and their proclamation of the gospel to win others to belief in Jesus, who had never been privileged to know him during his earthly career.

There is another singular feature of the Lucan Gospel which may well be evidence of his intention to bridge the gap of which we are speaking. Alone of the four evangelists, Luke designates Jesus during his public ministry some eighteen times by the post-resurrection title "the Lord" (see Lk 24:34). At least eight instances occur in episodes derived from a special Lucan source (e.g. 7:13; 10:1; 19:8), while others appear in narratives reworked by Luke (e.g. 7:19; 12:42; 22:6). Hence one may suppose that the evangelist has wished to preserve a traditional method of catechesis aimed at helping those new Christians, who had not known Jesus in his lifetime, to relate to the risen Lord. For he, in his new existence now "lives unto God" (Rom 6:10), and so remains beyond the reach of merely human understanding. To express this more concretely—Luke is equivalently saying to his reader, "Do you wish to know what kind of Lord it is, to whom you are attempting to relate in faith and love?—He is a Lord, who once raised the only son of a widowed mother from death, out of compassion for her plight (Lk 7:11-15), who recognized in the tax-collector Zacchaeus 'a son of Abraham,' and brought 'salvation to his house' (Lk 19:1-10), a Lord, who with a look of compassion at once granted Peter the grace of repentance for having denied 'knowing him' (Lk 22:61)." Such are the ways Luke proposes to bridge the gap of which there is question. We shall have occasion to discuss what Ignatius has substituted for following Jesus during his public life at the end of the present chapter, after studying the Johannine solution to this problem.

While there appears to be no completely satisfactory way of dividing the discourse we are about to consider, the tripartite division suggested here may prove helpful in following the movement of the thought.

1. Jesus' Departure Terminates "Following" Him (13:31-38)

As has been already remarked, John announced the conclusion of Jesus' ministry by noting his abrupt withdrawal from the crowd in Jerusalem (12:36b). He now draws the reader's attention to an important aspect of the coming of "his hour . . . to pass out of this world home to the Father" (13:1). The privileged set of experiences enjoyed by the disciples during Jesus' public life is shortly to be ended by his departure also from them.

> 31 When he [Judas] went out, Jesus declares, "Now has the Son of Man become glorified, and God has become glorified in him. 32 [If God has become glorified in him,] God will also glorify him in Himself: indeed, He will glorify him at once. 33 My little children, I am in your company still for but a short while. You will seek me: yet—as I told the Jews—'Where I am going, you yourselves cannot come;' and I now am saying it also to you.—

34   A new command I am giving you: you must love one another! By virtue of the fact I have loved you, so you in turn are to love one another.   35 Here is how everyone will know you are my disciples: if you preserve love for one another."

36   Simon Peter says to him, "Master, where are you going?" Jesus replied, "Where I am going, you cannot follow me *now*: still, you will follow later on."   37   Peter says to him, "Master, why cannot I follow you now? —I will give up˙my life for your sake!"   38   Jesus rejoins, "You will give up your life for my sake? Amen, amen I tell you: the cock will never crow before you deny me three times!'"

As earlier the approach of certain God-fearing "Greeks" prompted the Johannine Jesus to announce the presence of his "hour" (12:23), so here the departure of Judas into the "night," symbol of his final alignment with "the darkness," prompts the same declaration, as the emphatic "now" indicates. Here however the evangelist underlines what is to become a major theme in his Passion-narrative: his innovative insight (mentioned in the Prologue through the community's credal statement, "We have beheld his glory!") that the Passion is the "glory" of Jesus. In a remarkable departure from the more traditional interpretation of Jesus' death (Phil 2:7-8; Mk 8:31; 9:31), John insists that it was only by "laying down his life for his friends" (15:13) that Jesus succeeded in revealing his self-identity as Son of God and exalted Son of Man. This writer had already made it clear that, despite all Jesus' repeated attempts during his ministry to disclose this great mystery to "the Jews," in a certain sense he had simply failed (12:37-41). Throughout the first great section of his Gospel John had also insisted upon the impossibility for human beings of seeing God (1:18; 5:37; 6:46). Only by "seeing the Son" in Jesus (6:40) with the eyes of genuine faith (12:45) will it be possible to "see the Father" (14:9).

However for such a possibility to become real for those who accept Jesus, a whole series of events involving Jesus must first transpire: his Passion, resurrection, return to God, and the sending of the Spirit. Moreover, as Jesus' prayer to the Father upon entering "the hour" had implied (12:27), the Father's dynamic action is necessary to set all this in train. John will return to the reciprocal character of this mutual glorification in the great prayer Jesus makes just before his Passion begins, by pointing out that Jesus can only glorify the Father in virtue of the Father's glorification of himself. "Father, the hour has come: glorify your Son in order that the Son may glorify you . . . I have glorified you on earth by bringing to completion the work you have given me to carry out" (17:1, 3). In fact, the glorification of Jesus extends beyond this world to include his return home to God. "So now, glorify me, Father, in Your presence, with that glory I possessed with You before the world began to exist" (17:5). The reason for this appears towards the end of the prayer: it lies in the ongoing revelation of himself to his disciples, which is to transcend their earthly experience of their glorified Master by being finally crowned in heaven. "I have given to them the glory You have given to me, that they may be one inasmuch as we are one—I in them and You in me—in order that where I am there they too may be with me, that they may behold my glory, which You have given to me, because You loved me from before the creation of the world" (17:22-24). The prayer then reveals what one can only call the "altruism" of Jesus' request for his own glorification: it is wholly orientated to the Father first of all, and then also to his own faithful disciples.

Furthermore, it is to be noted that our evangelist's inspired insight into the "other-directed" nature of love, human as well as divine, enables him elsewhere to speak of this love of Jesus as a response to God's "command." Because "The Father loves the Son and has given everything into his power" (3:35), Jesus can claim to have "authority" to lay down his life, in order to take it up again. This outpouring of divine love upon Jesus is described by John, in that juridical terminology characteristic of him, as a *"command* I have received from my Father"* (see 10:17-18). And it is the efficacious love of Jesus "for his own in the world . . . to the end" (13:1) demonstrated by dying for them, which will shortly be seen to be expressed as "a new *command* . . . by virtue of the fact I have loved you" (v. 34).

These reflections help towards a better grasp of the meaning of Jesus' triumphant announcement (vv. 31-32) enunciating the principles which govern the development of the entire discourse. Accordingly, its careful structuring in five short lines is described by Schnackenburg as "a closed whole statement of refined and almost poetic value."[4] The first two lines speak of Jesus' "glorification" as "Son of Man"; and here the passive implies that this disclosure of the mystery of Jesus occurs by God's action. The last two verses set forth explicitly the divine involvement. The third and middle verse functions as a hinge linking the whole statement. Despite its omission by some important witnesses to the Greek text (hence it is here placed within brackets), it is obviously necessary to the progress of the thought.

---

4 Schnackenburg, *John,* III, 49.

"Now has the Son of Man become glorified,
And God has become glorified in him.
[If God has become glorified in him,]
God will also glorify him in Himself.
Indeed, He will glorify him at once."

The reader should not take the past tenses of the verbs in a strictly temporal sense, as they are intended to embrace the entire "hour," the "now," which as has been stated includes the entire process involved in Jesus' "passing from this world home to the Father" (13:1). The evangelist's main interest lies in the mutual "glorification" of Jesus by the Father, and of the Father by Jesus' revelation of his own true identity. What happens "now" in this world through Jesus' death is followed "at once" by what happens when Jesus' "lifting up" on the cross is brought to its fulfillment by the Father in endowing him with perfect communion in heaven with Himself. While this leave-taking by Jesus puts an end to the disciples' "following" him, as Jesus points out to Peter, it creates the possibility of a totally new "abiding" (14:2, 23)—which is mutual—of believer and the Father and Jesus in one another.

Jesus displays his great affection for his disciples by the term of endearment, "My little children," which occurs only here in the Gospel (see 1 Jn where it is used seven times). It is calculated to take the edge off any sadness the disciples may feel in realizing they are to lose Jesus' company in "a short while." More importantly, this reminder of Jesus' love for them should lead them to see that, in spite of his remark, "as I told the Jews," these faithful followers stand even now, notwithstanding their profound ignorance of Jesus and his destiny, in a very different relationship to their Master. The former, by their refusal to put faith in Jesus and his message, have become obdurate: the disciples remain always open, despite their obvious shortcomings, to ever new, as yet unimaginable experiences of him.

This appears to be implied in the insertion (whether by the evangelist or a subsequent editor) of the characteristically Johannine saying, "A new command I am giving you: you must love one another!" This had been acted out by Jesus through the "example" set for the little community in washing the disciples' feet (13:15). Jesus' chilling rebuke of Peter's refusal on that occasion (13:8b) was seen to imply an aspect of this "new command," perhaps not always perceived. This injunction of the Johannine Jesus requires not only the performing of acts of love for others, but also the gracious acceptance of others' loving actions—for many, a much more difficult obligation.

The novelty of the "command" here stands in striking contrast to those expressed in the Synoptic Gospels, each of which reports Jesus' saying concerning "the greatest commandment" (Mk 12:28-34; Mt 22:34-40; Lk 10:25-28), with its innovative combination of the demand to love God (Deut 6:4-5) with that regarding the neighbor (Lev 19:18). The Fourth Gospel moreover contains no command to love one's enemies (Mt 5:44; Lk 6:27); nor is a command to love God ever expressly mentioned, while the obligation to love Jesus himself is only implied (v. 21) in the disciples' duty to "keep my commands." Humanly speaking, of course, it is understandable that the somewhat isolated Johannine community, which not only suffers persecution from "the Jews," but also endures a certain alienation and disapproval on the part of other Jewish-Christians because of its anti-temple attitudes, its Samaritan membership, should be thrown in on itself. Yet, in the light of the passage where the command is repeated, a much deeper reason becomes evident, in which friendship with Jesus is characterized by knowledge of what he is doing, as well as of the revelation from the Father he communicates to the disciples. "This is my command: you must love one another by virtue of the fact I have loved you. Greater love than this no one can have than that a person lay down his life for the sake of his friends. You are my friends, if you carry out what I am enjoining on you. I am no longer calling you slaves, because the slave does not know what his master is doing. No! I have called you friends, because everything I have heard from my Father I have made known to you" (15:12-15).

I venture to suggest accordingly that the insistence in this Gospel upon the giving and accepting of acts of love within the community springs from the writer's conviction that such reciprocity is the essential prerequisite for the experience through faith of Jesus' promised manifestation of himself to each member (v. 21) and crucial to an awareness of the mutual abiding of Jesus and the Father in the believer (v. 23). Such Christian consciousness is the antithesis of that sinful lack of any such knowledge by "the world." It "cannot accept the Spirit of truth" since "it does not even know Him" (v. 17), and it will pursue the disciples with its hatred—its partisans "do not know the One Who sent me" (15:21). Such culpable ignorance will ultimately lead to a monstrous misconception: "anyone who kills you thinks he is offering an act of worship to God" (16:2b). It is then these painful memories of the tragic history of his own community, which have influenced our evangelist in formulating the "new command" as he has done.

It would appear however from the intervention Peter now makes that he has heard nothing of what Jesus has just said. His artless question exemplifies the plight of ignorance in which all his companions remain before Jesus' glorification. His query, "Master, where are you going?", echoes the same lack of comprehension he displayed earlier in refusing to permit Jesus to wash his feet (13:6-8). Indeed Peter's expressed desire to continue enjoying companionship with the earthly Jesus is simply a superficial, far too natural one. This explains the distinction Jesus introduces by saying, "You cannot follow me *now*; still, you will follow later on." This is a repetition of the earlier warning given to Peter: "What I am doing you cannot know for the present, but you will know by and by" (13:7). The evangelist desires his reader to understand that it is only by the power of Jesus' death and glorification that the following of Jesus to which Peter clings is to be transmuted into a completely new experience. It is instructive to observe that the old "following Jesus," prominent in the first great section of this Gospel, will henceforth be used but once—to introduce the account of Peter's denials of his Master: "Peter kept following Jesus" (18:15) into the house of Annas. The next occasion when the expression will be employed will occur in the peremptory command of the risen Lord to Peter, "If I wish him [the beloved disciple] to remain until I come, what is that to you? As for you, you must follow me" (21:22). By then, the word will have acquired a new meaning.

It may be observed also that John intends Jesus' present remark to Peter to alert the reader to the parabolic character of the discourse which will follow with its "topographical" imagery of "making a journey" and its references to a celestial "house."

At present Peter must be cured of his boastfulness ("I will give up my life for your sake!"), and in view of this he must be made to feel his utter helplessness without the saving presence of Jesus. Consequently, it is at this point John pictures Jesus as announcing his disciple's denials. For it is essential that Peter undergo the sense of deep desolation—as St. Ignatius will later observe—"to encourage and strengthen him for the future, by exposing him to the stratagems of the enemy of our human nature" (Annotation 7). Actually, of the reasons the Saint enumerates for God's permitting one to endure desolation, two are applicable to the present situation. "God wishes to try us, to see how much we are worth," and "God wishes to give us a true knowledge and understanding of ourselves, so that we may have an intimate perception of the truth that it is not within our capability to acquire and attain great devotion . . . or any other spiritual consolation, but that all this is the gift and grace of God our Lord" ([322]).

That Peter did actually learn such lessons and die a martyr's death as a witness to his genuine faith in the risen Jesus is pointed out by the editor(s) of the Epilogue to this Gospel. In the scene by the Sea of Tiberias, after Peter has thrice protested his love and affection for his Lord with deep humility and has been given pastoral charge of the sheep belonging to Jesus (21:15-17), Jesus predicts "the kind of death by which he would glorify God" (v. 19). "Amen, amen I tell you: when you were younger, you fastened your own belt and went off wherever you might choose. However, when you became old, you will stretch out your hands, and someone else will bind you and take you where you do not choose." (v. 18).

2. Jesus Is to Be Seen as the Unique Way to God (14:1-17)

At this juncture, Jesus' words within the intimate circle of his beloved followers take on the character of a "farewell discourse"—a form of literature very popular in the ancient world of letters, exemplified at various points in the Bible. One thinks at once of Jacob's death-bed scene (Gen 49:1-27), of Moses' last words to Israel (Deut 33:1-29), of Paul's address to the Ephesian elders (Acts 20:17-35). The whole of 2 Timothy is regarded as Paul's last will and testament.

Father Raymond Brown remarks of the passage we are considering that "The Last Discourse is Jesus' last testament: it is meant to be read after he has left the earth. Yet is is not like other last testaments . . . the recorded words of men who are dead and can speak no more; for whatever may be of *ipsissima verba* in the Last Discourse has been transformed in the light of the resurrection and through the coming of the Paraclete into a living discourse delivered, not by a dead man, but by the one who has life (v. 57), to all readers of the Gospel."[5]

> 14:1 "You must not let your hearts be troubled. You believe in God—believe also in me! 2 In my Father's house abodes are plentiful. Were it not so, should I have told you that I am making a journey to ready a place for you? 3 Now when I have made the journey and readied a place for you, I shall come again to receive you into my company, that you too may be where I am myself.
>
>   4 Of course, where I am going you know the way." 5 Thomas rejoined, "Master we do not know where you are going!—how can we know the way?" 6 Jesus tells him, "I am the Way, [that is] the truth and the life. No one can come to the Father except through me. 7 If you have

---

5   R. E. Brown, *John XIII–XXI*, p. 582.

come to know me, you will know my Father also. In fact, now you do know Him—you have seen Him!'' 8 Philip asks him, "Master, show us the Father, and it is enough for us.'' 9 Jesus says to him, "I have been with you such a long while, yet you, Philip, do not know me? The one who has seen me has seen the Father! How can you say, 'Show us the Father'? 10 Do you not believe that I am in the Father and the Father is in me? The utterances I make to you I do not speak by myself: rather, the Father abiding in me is doing His works. 11 Believe me! I am in the Father and the Father is in me. If not, then believe on account of the very works! 12 Amen, amen I tell you: the one believing in me will in his turn perform the works I am doing—even greater works will he perform, because I am journeying [home] to the Father. 13 Indeed, whatever you ask in my name I will carry it out, in order that the Father may be glorified by the Son. 14 If you ask anything at all of me in my name, I am the one who will do it. 15 If you do love me, you will keep my commands. 16 Then I, for my part, will ask the Father and He will give you another Paraclete, that He may remain with you forever— 17 the Spirit of truth that the world cannot accept, because it does not perceive Him nor even know Him. As for you, however, you *do* know Him, because He is abiding in your midst, and He is within you.''

Jesus' first words,"You must not let your hearts be troubled," constitute the theme of the ensuing discourse. This is clear from the repetition of the same admonition, when, after blessing the disciples with his gift of "peace," Jesus concludes his farewell to them by saying, "You must not let your heart be troubled, nor let it play the coward!" (v. 27b). The astute reader will have recalled that Jesus' own reaction in the face of his "hour" was described in similar terms: "Now my heart is deeply troubled!" (12:27). Thus it may well be that John is hinting at a deeper cause of the malaise of the disciples—the terrifying confrontation with death. Only genuine belief in Jesus can provide the necessary safeguard against succumbing to despair in the face of this dire threat. Jesus knows that his Jewish disciples have been gifted with the traditional faith of Israel: "You believe in God." Still, to keep such faith intact through the traumatic experience of Jesus' sufferings and death more is needed: "Believe also in me!"

Jesus begins now to re-assure his depressed followers, by hinting, through a parable about journeying, at the loving purpose behind his leaving them. "In my Father's house *abodes* are plentiful." This difficult statement becomes less obscure when it is observed that "abodes" *(monai)* is derived from the verb "abide" *(menein)*. Hence it is a figurative way of speaking of that mutual "abiding" of Jesus in the believer to be described more clearly later in terms of loving communion. "If any one loves me, he will keep my word, and my Father will love him, and we will come to him and take up our abode *(mone)* with him" (v. 23). That such abiding is permanent and leads to the experience of true freedom may be gathered from an earlier parable in which the image of house also figured. "The slave does not abide in the house permanently: the son abides permanently. If therefore the Son makes you free, you will in fact be free" (8:35-36). This parable probably evolved out of the story of Isaac and Ishmael (Gen 21:9). It will be recalled that Jesus had referred to the sanctuary in Jerusalem as "my Father's house" on the occasion of his symbolic-prophetic action of cleansing the sacred precincts (2:16), inasmuch as the holy place was the earthly sign of God's covenanted presence to Israel.

Jesus now introduces a new element into the parable by speaking of his death and glorification as a "journey." "Were it not so, should I have told you that I am making a journey to ready a place for you?" The obscure reference back to the first announcement of his departure (13:33) is characteristic of the Johannine Jesus (6:36 see 6:23; 11:40 see 11:4, 25). Once the symbolic use of house and journey is grasped, Jesus is seen to reveal further his purpose in leaving the disciples. And to alleviate the pain his friends feel, Jesus now adds the promise of a future reunion with himself. "Now when I have made the journey and readied a place for you, I shall come again to receive you into my company, that you too may be where I am myself." Once again it is important to see the parabolic nature of the promise. Jesus is not speaking of the parousia (his glorious presence at the end of history), as the Latin Fathers of the Church thought, nor of the post-resurrection meetings with the disciples (the view of the Greek Fathers). He speaks figuratively of the experience of his permanent abiding through the growing faith and love of the believer (St. Ignatius will call it "consolation" [316]). It is this experience that is to replace, even for his immediate disciples, the now outmoded following of himself.

To stimulate his slow-minded disciples, Jesus interjects a new provocative remark, "Of course, where I am going you know the way." This time it is the morose Thomas (see 11:16) who objects. "Master, we do not know where you are going!—how can we know the way?" This provides an opening for Jesus to describe himself by means of a new revelational statement, "I am the way, [that is] the truth and the life." The obscurity of this mysterious assertion is partly dissipated by his added remark, "No one can come to the Father except through me." Once more we are dealing with a symbol for the communion with the risen

Jesus. For anyone who accepts him as unique mediator of a message from the unseeable God ("the truth") and of a participation in God's own life ("the life"), Jesus becomes—already in this present existence—'*the* way." For this reason the final words of the Johannine Jesus will be presented as a beatitude, "Happy those who have come to believe without seeing [me]" (20:29b). Of the present revelatory formula Rudolf Schnackenburg says, "It forms a classical summary of the Johannine doctrine of salvation that is based entirely on Jesus Christ. In Jesus Christ . . the invisible and incomprehensible God has, in his will to save men, made himself so tangible and so comprehensible that they are able to reach the goal of their existence along this way, by accepting in faith the truth that has been revealed to them in Jesus Christ and by sharing in his life."[6]

Jesus goes on to clarify how, as "the way," he is "the truth," by a new promise, in which to "know" a person signifies full communion with him. "If you have come to know me, you will know my Father also." And immediately, as with Thomas, Jesus adds an almost off-hand remark, "In fact, now you do know Him—you have seen Him!" He thereby elicits a rejoinder from Philip, the man who has, from the beginning of this Gospel (1:43-47), displayed such readiness to believe in Jesus, and, in consort with his good friend Andrew, has shown zeal for bringing even God-fearing pagans to "see Jesus" (12:21-22). With that simple practicality he had evinced at the feeding of the huge Galilaean crowd (6:7), Philip in turn now intervenes, with a plea reminiscent of that by Moses, "Show me your glory!"(Ex 33:18). "Master, show us the Father, and it is enough for us." John possibly regards this last expression, "it is enough," as a salient feature of Philip's attitude. In the preparations for feeding the crowd, it was he who had remarked "Loaves costing two hundred denarii would not be enough for each to have a little" (6:7). Jesus' mighty deed on that occasion should have taught Philip to revise his estimate of what "is enough." He has yet to realize that to "know" Jesus is in reality a never ending process. "I have been with you such a long while, yet you, Philip, do not know me? The one who has seen me has seen the Father! How can you say, 'Show us the Father'?"

The interruption permits Jesus to explain that he is "the way," because he is "the life." In connection with the restoration of the cripple, Jesus spoke of the Father's gift of life to the Son. "Just as the Father possesses life in Himself, so He has given the Son to possess life in

6   Schnackenburg, *John*, III, 65.

himself" (5:26). In his explanation of the Eucharistic "bread from heaven," the evangelist represented Jesus as promising, "As the living Father sent me and I have life because of the Father, so the one feeding on me will in his turn have life because of me" (6:57). Jesus now catechizes Philip regarding this central truth of Christian faith. "Do you not believe that I am in the Father and the Father is in me?" The Johannine theme of "the poverty of the Son" is once more recalled. "The utterances I make to you I do not speak by myself: rather, the Father abiding in me is doing His works." From the mutual abiding in each other of Jesus and the Father there results a reciprocity of cooperation: Jesus' words are only those "I heard from Him Who sent me . . . Of myself I do nothing, but I speak these things, because of the fact that the Father taught me" (8:26, 28).

Jesus continues by insisting on this all-important lesson, "Believe me! I am in the Father and the Father is in me. If not, then believe on account of the very works!" In the Old Testament, the "wonderful works" of the God of the fathers had been revealed to Israel through her prophets as an imperious summons to believe in Him. In the new economy of salvation the same peremptory demand by God is being made—now that "the Word has become flesh"—through Jesus' actions and words. Later on, Jesus will return to this crucial theme by asserting, "If I had not come and spoken to them, they would not have any sin. Now however, they have no excuse for their sin. The one hating me also hates my Father. If I had not performed the works among them that no one else has done, they would not have sin. Now however they have seen and have hated both me and my Father!" (15:22-24). Refusal to put faith in Jesus is "the sin of the world" (1:29), of which the Paraclete "when he comes will convict the world" (16:8). In our present passage then, to "believe on account of the very works" is tantamount to belief in Jesus.[7]

In this context of "works," Jesus goes on to make an astounding promise to all believers. "Amen, amen I tell you: the one believing in me will in his turn perform the works I am doing—even greater works will he perform, because I am journeying [home] to the Father." This statement, which is in appearance so extraordinary, is not to be classed with those examples of hyperbole for which the Synoptic Jesus is famous (Mk 9:42-48; 14:21). This becomes clear once it is realized that the infallibility promised to the prayer of the disciples has to do with their future mission. John, it will be recalled, had carefully avoided any mention of

---

7 See my article "Believe the Works," *The Way* 18 (1978), 272-286.

Jesus' sending of the disciples during his own lifetime, as recorded in the Synoptic Gospels (see Mk 6:6-13; Mt 10:1-15; Lk 9:1-6). In the view of our evangelist, it is only after his glorification that Jesus "sends" the disciples by his gift to the entire community of the power of reconciliation (20:21-23).

It is to be noted, however, that the Fourth Gospel presents a precise and consistent notion of mission. It is to be nothing less than the continuation of Jesus' own mission committed to him by the Father, and it consists essentially in challenging "the world" to believe in himself. This challenge is clearly articulated in the controversy with the Jews at the feast of *Hanukkah,* "I and the Father are one" (10:30). Consequently, it is only by maintaining that complete oneness among themselves and with Jesus and the Father, for which Jesus would pray so earnestly on the eve of his death, that the disciples present at the Last Supper (17:11)—as also all future disciples (17:20-22)—can make this challenge effective. In short, it is not so much by achieving success by their "works," as by what they consistently *are,* that these believers carry on the mission confided to them.

This is made incontrovertibly clear by the parable-allegory of the vine and its branches, and the ensuing explanations of it which a later editor provides. There it is the "abiding in me" which is described as "bearing abundant fruit," "because apart from me you can do nothing" (15:1-5). Two further sayings of Jesus throw light upon this point. "By this is my Father glorified, that you bear abundant fruit and become my disciples" (v. 8). That the "fruit" is to be understood to refer primarily to the "election" of the disciples to Christian friendship, and an unmerited gift from Jesus, is carefully spelled out. "You for your part have not elected me: it is I who elected you to go and bear abundant fruit, and that your fruit may abide, so that whatever you ask the Father in my name He may give you. Here is what I am enjoining upon you: you must love one another" (vv. 16-17). Schnackenburg's observations on this text deserve to be quoted. "The terminology in this verse hardly entitles us to tie the bearing of fruit down to missionary activity. It is rather that the discourse turns back at this point to an appeal to remain united with Jesus and to bear fruit. The idea of bearing fruit is deliberately kept very open (see v. 4) and this means that . . . the dominant aspect is undoubtedly the fruitfulness of Christian life, especially demonstrated in brotherly love, as the following verse makes clear."[8]

8   Schnackenburg, *John,* III, 112.

Jesus' promise that the disciples will perform "even greater works" is made not despite, but because, "I am journeying [home] to the Father." For only when his true identity has been revealed as "God an only Son" (1:18b) can his continued, if invisible, activity in this world be "seen"by the disciples, as they invoke his name in prayer. "Indeed, whatever you ask in my name, I will carry it out, in order that the Father may be glorified by the Son." In his great prayer to the Father, Jesus will state, "I have glorified You on earth by completing the work You have given me to do" (17:4). Here we learn that this glorification (or revelation) of the Father is to be continued by the exalted Son, specifically through his response to the prayer of the disciples. The promise is immediately reformulated to indicate that such prayer is to be directed to Jesus and to emphasize that it is he who responds: "If you ask anything at all *of me* in my name, I am the one who will do it."

In preparation for the great promise Jesus is about to announce concerning the gift of "another Paraclete," he now explains the real nature of the disciples' love for himself. "If you do love me, you will keep my commands." Here again, as was observed earlier in this chapter, John's penchant for using juridical language must be understood correctly as a kind of symbol of the outpouring of Jesus' love upon his friends. Raymond Brown comments on this verse, "His commandments are not simply moral precepts: they involve a whole way of life in loving union with him."[9] Rudolf Schnackenburg also warns against "thinking in this context of moral precepts." He notes that Jesus' "commands" are synonymous with Jesus' "words" or "word" (vv. 23-24), "which is not mine but that of the Father who sent me," and concludes, "The statement means, in this context, that Jesus will do everything with his Father, but that he also expects his disciples to remain close to him in love and faithfulness."[10]

"Then I, for my part, will ask the Father and He will give you another Paraclete, to remain in your company forever—the Spirit of truth that the world cannot accept, because it does not perceive Him, nor even know Him. As for you, however, you do know Him, because He is abiding in your midst, and He is within you." In this first saying about the Paraclete (four will follow: 14:25-26; 15:26-27; 16:12-15), John implies that the *earthly* Jesus had in fact been already, for those who "followed" him, a first Paraclete. It is only in a later piece of writing

9   R. E. Brown, *John XIII–XXI*, p. 638.
10   Schnackenburg, *John*, III, 74.

from the Johannine school that the exalted Christ will be given the title as heavenly advocate for sinners who repent. "My children, I am writing this to you in order that you may not sin: if a person sin, we have a Paraclete with the Father, Jesus Christ who is just" (1 Jn 2:1).The evangelist has already pointed out by means of the shepherd parables that Jesus had already fulfilled this function for those who followed him personally. The true shepherd of the sheep is the one whose voice they hear, "when he calls his own sheep by name and leads them out. When he has got all his own outside, he marches at their head: his sheep follow him because they know his voice" (10:3-4). To the incredulous Jews Jesus asserts, "However, you on your part do not believe because you do not belong to my sheep. My sheep hear my voice: I know them and they follow me" (10:27). In his solemn prayer before his Passion, Jesus will once more advert to this same privileged period by saying, "While I was with them, I kept them with the name you have given me, and I have guarded them. Indeed, not one of them has been lost except him who is doomed to perish that the Scripture might be fulfilled" (17:21).

In this first promise by Jesus of the disciples' new experience, which is to replace that of "following" himself, the continuity between the old and the new mode of presence is prominent: it is by Jesus' prayer that "the Father will give you another Paraclete," just as Jesus in his lifetime had been "the gift of God" (4:10; 3:16). Jesus had once described himself as "a human being who have spoken the truth to you" (8:40), which was the whole purpose of his entry into the world—"that I might bear witness to the truth" (18:37). In future, the Paraclete is to be known in the Johannine community as "the Spirit of truth," Who is to bear witness to Jesus (15:26). Like Jesus also, the Spirit is "to be in your company" in the world; and a hint is given of a confrontation with "the world," as had happened to Jesus himself. The second Paraclete is "to abide among you" in the community "forever," and give inner strength to each, since "He will be within you." From this initial description, it would seem probable that John employs "Paraclete" in an analogous sense to that used in Greek law-courts. The Holy Spirit is to act as a kind of counsellor for the defense.

3. At Jesus' Glorification "Abiding" Replaces "Following" (14:18-26)

While Jesus' announcement of his departure signalled the end of "following" him for the first disciples, his promise of "another Paraclete" intimates that, while seemingly absent, Jesus remains the unique "way" to the Father along which the disciples are now being called to walk. If however he has in reality been "the way" even while on earth, because as "the truth" and "the life" he has provided a mysterious glimpse of the unseeable God, still that vision must be more sharply focused by the gift of Christian faith through "the Spirit of truth," Who is "the life-giver" (6:63a). Still, since the Father will bestow the Spirit at the intercession of the glorified Christ (v. 16), the task of the Spirit is to further, *not* replace, the mission of the earthly Jesus, who when glorified is also to be present though not visible. This is the burden of the new development, in which a new "coming" of Jesus is to be understood, in the light of his promise of "another Paraclete," as an "abiding" of the Father and himself with the disciples. Such intentional triadic structuring by the evangelist will find an echo in the Trinitarian orientation of Ignatian spirituality.

18   "I shall not leave you [behind] as orphans: I am coming back to you.
19   Yet a little while and the world will no longer see me, but you for your part, *will* see me, because I live, and you will live!   20   On that day, you yourselves will know that I am in my Father and you are in me, and I in you.
21   The one having my commands and keeping them is he who loves me. Now the one loving me will be loved by my Father, and I in turn will love him, and I will manifest myself to him."
22   Judas (not the Iscariot) asks him, "Master, what has happened that you mean to manifest yourself to us, yet by no means to the world?"
23   In reply Jesus told him, "If any one loves me, he will keep my word, and my Father will love him, and we will come to him, and take up our abode with him.   24   The one who does not love me does not keep my words: yet the word you are hearing is not mine, but that of the Father Who sent me.
25   These things I have told you while abiding among you.   26   But the Paraclete, the Holy Spirit, Whom the Father will send in my name—*He* will teach you everything and make you remember all I have told you."

Jesus begins by relieving the desolation felt by his disciples through the announcement of his death (v. 1; 13:33) with a renewal of his earlier promise (v. 3) to come again. "I shall not leave you [behind] as orphans: I am coming back to you." Now however, this new presence of Jesus is explained in contrast with that "seeing" of the external circumstances of his death by "the world," which because of unfaith can only judge "from appearances" (7:24) and "by worldly standards" (8:15). Such superficial "seeing" is set down as the antithesis of the new "seeing" to be given the disciples through their communion in life, faith, and love with the risen Jesus: both experiences are to begin in "a little while." "Yet a little while and the world will no longer see me, but you, for your part, *will* see me, because I live and you will live!" Jesus further specifies when this is to occur. "On that day, you yourselves will know that I am in my Father and you are in me, and I in you." Like "the hour," the phrase "on that day" indicates the completion of Jesus' "lifting up" through death, resurrection, and return home to the Father, when with their new faith the disciples will "know" of Jesus' communion with the Father, as well as their communion with Him, through their mutual and permanent union with the exalted One. This divine gift of a "sense of family," as St. Ignatius later describes it *(familiaritas cum Deo)*, comes only through the mediation of the glorified Jesus.

Jesus continues by noting the essential conditions upon which such awareness depends: faith and love. "The one having my commands and keeping them is the one who loves me." And as a result, "The one loving me will be loved by my Father, and I in turn will love him, and I will manifest myself to him."

Now it is "Judas (not the Iscariot)" who shows surprise at the exclusion of "the world" from this new "sense of family." "Master, what has happened that you mean to manifest yourself to us, yet by no means to the world?" The question anticipates a difficulty often felt in later Christian apologetics: why did the risen Lord manifest himself (Acts 10:41) only to his friends (even indeed to women, who could not qualify as official witnesses), never to his enemies (Annas, Pilate)?

The intervention permits Jesus to elucidate further the promise in v. 21, which spoke only of a manifestation of "myself to him." His reply moreover discloses the reality earlier pictured in parabolic language (vv. 2-4). "If any one loves me, he will keep my word, and my Father will love him, and we will come to him, and take up our *abode* with him." "Abode" once again designates that mutual "abiding" or communion that will exist between the Father, Jesus, and the believer.

Again this experience of faith and love is set in contrast with "the sin of the world" (1:29). "The one who does not love me does not keep my words: yet the word you are hearing is not mine, but that of the Father who sent me." Once more, in the second half of this verse, the theme of the "poverty of the Son" makes its appearance, where it sets in relief the enormity of "the sin of the world" (15:22). The saying also serves to introduce a new promise, which forms the conclusion and climax of this section of the instruction. Since Jesus' words express in fact the word of God Himself, his disciples will be enabled by the Paraclete to "remember" them—a word freighted with meaning for John.

"These things I have told you while abiding among you." The teaching of the historical Jesus is to be treasured always by the community: it is to be regarded as the basis of genuine faith (1:38-39; 2:5, 19; 4:26, 42, 50). Rejection of Jesus' teaching characterizes "the world" (7:17; 8:37). Indeed, the word of the earthly Jesus contains the entire revelation of God; hence it is that word alone whose meaning the Spirit of truth will "unveil" (16:13), since it is His role exclusively to "testify concerning me" (15:26).

Yet while the word of Jesus is so personal to himself that he is "the Word of God" (1:1), still only with the coming of the Paraclete will the disciples begin to realize that "The words I have spoken to you are Spirit, and they are life" (6:63b). "But the Paraclete, the Holy Spirit, Whom the Father will send in my name—*He* will teach you everything and *make you remember* all I have told you." With the opening words of this verse, Jesus announces to his own that the period of their instruction during his lifetime is at an end. However, the promise which accompanies that announcement contrasts sharply with the comment by the evangelist (noted earlier) indicating the conclusion of the public ministry: "Thus Jesus spoke, and going off he hid himself from them" (12:36b). Here John makes it clear that in a very real sense the formation of the disciples (whose ignorance of Jesus' meaning at the Last Supper he repeatedly emphasized) is not entirely finished. For that, the coming of the Paraclete is crucial, since "*He* will teach you everything and make you remember all I have told you." As has been pointed out earlier, "remembering" is of paramount interest to the Gospel-writer, who inserted it into his narrative of the cleansing of the temple precincts, with which he began his account of the public ministry, and into the story of the final entry by Jesus into Jerusalem, which led to the closure of his "speaking openly to the world" (18:20). As has been seen, the significant term figured twice in the inaugural scene, where John drew his reader's attention to the casual link between Jesus' prophetic, symbolic action and his future death. "His disciples were to recall that it was written, 'Zeal for Your house will devour me' [Ps 69:10]" (2:17). John ended the narrative by pointing out that such "remembering" belongs in the post-resurrection period. "So when he was raised from death, his disciples remembered that he had said this, and they believed the Scripture and the word Jesus had uttered" (v. 22). John, no less than Paul, is aware that "God raised the Lord . . . through His dynamic power *(dynamis)*" (1 Cor 6:14)—even though the evangelist never employs that term in his book. Like Paul, he knows that "the gospel is God's dynamic power leading to salvation" (Rom 1:16): John refers to those future Christians, whose faith springs from acceptance of the apostolic preaching, as "those who come to believe in me through their word" (17:20). He is quite as aware as the Apostle that the goal of Christian living is "to know him [Christ] and the power of his resurrection" (Phil 3:10): "This is eternal life that they know You the only genuine God and him You sent, Jesus Christ" (17:3).

In his gloss on the symbolic action taken by Jesus on his own initiative as he enters Jerusalem for the last time, John observed, "All this his disciples did not understand at first. But when Jesus had been glorified, then they remembered that they had done those things to him, which had been written concerning him" (12:16). It will be recalled that our evangelist had introduced into the acclamation of the crowds on this occasion the phrase "the King of Israel" (Zeph 3:15), thus pointing ahead to the theme that will dominate his Passion-narrative.

While John had thus alerted his reader to the Christian significance of "remembering," which vitalizes faith in Jesus' word and reveals the true meaning of what had been written of him in the Scriptures of Israel, with the present text he now points to the Paraclete as the divine source of this all-important spiritual activity. It is our author's keen sensitivity to this dynamic, creative presence of the Holy Spirit in the community of faith, as was said previously, which leads him to picture Jesus as pronouncing his last-spoken beatitude on its members, "those who have come to believe without seeing" (20:29b).

Accordingly, John has, through this precious discourse, given his solution to the question of what has replaced the personal "following" of Jesus in the lives of future Christians: it is "remembering," inaugurated by the activity of the Paraclete in the community. Raymond Brown has remarked, "The thesis can be defended that the concept of the Paraclete took shape precisely against the background of the death of those who had been eyewitnesses to Jesus and as an answer to the dilemma of how to interpret Jesus' words in the face of new problems now that the apostolic guides were dead."[11]

For the one making the Spiritual Exercises, it is in the discernment of spirits, as she or he contemplates "the genuine grounds of the history" (Annotation 2) found in the Gospel-texts, that the experience which replaces the immediate following of Jesus by the original disciples is to be sought.

4. *With His Parting Blessing Jesus Attests His Love of the Father (14:27-31)*

---

11   R. E. Brown, "The Kerygma of the Gospel According to the Johannine View of Jesus in Modern Studies," *Interpretation* 21 (1967), 391.

27 "I am leaving you peace, a peace that is mine I give you—not the kind
the world gives am I giving you. You must not let your heart be troubled, nor
let it play the coward! 28 You have heard me tell you, 'I am going away,
and I shall come back again to you.' If you really loved me, you would rejoice that I am journeying [home] to the Father—because the Father is
greater than I. 29 In fact, I have told you now before it happens, in
order that when it happens you will believe. 30 I have no longer much to
tell you. The prince of this world is coming, yet he can have no claim against
me. 31 Still, that the world may know that I love the Father, and that I
act in accordance with what the Father has commanded me—get up! let us go
away from here.''

The blessing Jesus now imparts to these intimate friends is reminiscent of that beautiful prayer-wish in the Old Testament, which the priest
on leaving the sacred shrine of Israel imparted to the worshippers who
stood outside (Num 6:24-26). Yet in Jesus' mouth "peace" has been
given a new meaning. It is a *permanent* gift, as the present tenses, "I am
leaving . . . I am giving" imply.[12] It is a symbol of the sum total of all the
messianic blessings proclaimed by Israel's prophets and now realized in
the salvation brought by Jesus and the Father. Finally the fact that it is
"not the kind the world gives" implies that this peace is not simply to remain a hidden reality in the hearts of Jesus' followers, but is, in some
mysterious way, to pervade the earthly ambience in which the disciples
will carry out their mission of *reconciliation* through the power imparted
to them by the risen Lord (20:21-23).

With the blessing, Jesus repeats the admonition with which he began
his farewell-discourse, "You must not let your heart be troubled, nor let
it play the coward!"—an indication that the entire instruction has come
to its conclusion. In the appendage affixed to John's original discourse
by an editor, Jesus predicts candidly the terrible trials to be experienced
by believers in their journey through the world (16:1-4); and he terminates this speech by announcing the dispersion of the community (16:32),
adding, "I have told you these things in order that you may preserve
peace by communion with me *(en emoi)*. In the world you will experience
tribulation, but take heart! I have won the victory over the world"
(16:33).

"If you really loved me, you would rejoice that I am journeying
[home] to the Father." These faithful, intimate friends do in fact love
Jesus, as their presence here attests; yet their love for him is still too
human and possessive. Only in the crucible of the Passion can their "love

---

12 Schnackenburg, *John*, III. 84.

of enlightened self-interest" *(amor concupiscentiae)* evolve under the impact of Jesus' death for them into that "love of friendship" *(amor benevolentiae)*, the goal towards which the Christian life is meant to lead all Jesus' followers. In the *Spiritual Exercises* it is made clear that this is the aim of the contemplations of the Third [195] and of the Fourth [230-231] Weeks.

The reason here assigned as motive for acquiring this new, unselfish love for Jesus has perplexed generations of readers for centuries. "The Father is greater than I." Arianist subordinationism is irrelevant here, as are also the views expressed by the Greek Fathers within the framework of a metaphysical theology. So too is Cyril of Alexandria's invocation of the *kenōsis* of the Redeemer (Phil 2:7-8). The Johannine Jesus claims to have a "command" from the Father (10:18-19), which as has been seen symbolizes the Father's love poured out upon him. In this Gospel the economy of the redemption is governed by the initiative of the Father, Who sends His Son, the Word become flesh, and enables the Son to "glorify Him" by being "glorified" by God (13:31-32). John pictures the dying Jesus on the cross as being fully aware that the entire enterprise has been carried to its consummation by God (19:28). His final utterance is articulated by this evangelist as "It has been brought to perfect fulfillment" (19:30), that is, (as the passive indicates) the agency is God's alone.

Jesus next explains his reason in predicting his return home to God: "in order that when it happens you will believe." The issue of believing which underlies the entire Gospel of John is present continually in this final discourse. Jesus alerts his disciples to the "coming of the prince of this world" in the person of his betrayer (already at 6:70 called "a devil"), of whom "Satan" has already taken possession (13:27). John finds the descriptive title "the prince of this world," more meaningful than "the devil" (8:44, 13:2) or "Satan", which he employs only this once. In his turn, St. Ignatius prefers "the enemy of our human nature." This embodiment of evil, John has Jesus declare, "can have no claim against me." He had earlier attested his sinlessness in controversy with the Jews: "Which of you can convict me of sin?" (8:46). Here however it is rather the evangelist's intention to underscore Jesus' complete freedom from any external coercion in carrying out God's designs for the salvation of the world.

The discourse closes with a command by Jesus, "Get up! let us go away from here," which is almost identical with that used by Mark to end his account of Jesus' struggle through prayer in Gethsemane with the approach of Judas, "Get up! let us go: see my betrayer has drawn near" (Mk 14:42),—an indication that John was familiar, if not with the Marcan text, at least with the Greek version of the tradition behind it. The motive assigned to Jesus' action however seems at first sight surprising: "that the world may *know* that I love the Father, and that I act in accordance with what the Father has commanded me." John has consistently referred to the guilty ignorance of Jesus on the part of "the world" (1:10; 17:25) and "the Jews" (8:43; 16:3). At the same time, the evangelist has asserted God's love for "the world" (3:16), and he is aware that, as late as Jesus' final prayer before his Passion, he does not give up hope "that the world may know" (17:23). Schnackenburg's answer to this puzzle is helpful. "It is clear that the world of men still know, on the basis of the event of the cross, that Jesus is the one who was sent to save it (cf. 12:32)."[13]

Some Parallels Between Johannine and Ignatian Discernment

In the two chapters which follow the original discourse by the evangelist, a later editor has contributed three further Paraclete-sayings, which faithfully develop John's original insights into the role of the Holy Spirit. We shall find, particularly in these additions, some reflections that will help our understanding of the discernment of spirits, which St. Ignatius insisted upon as central to the project of seeing the will of God, indeed of "finding God in all things."

The first of these statements echoes sayings already attributed to Jesus in the Synoptic Gospels concerning the assistance of the Spirit in the testimony by the apostles when arraigned before Jewish or pagan courts of law (Mk 13:9-11). It is actually part of the "remembering" (14:26) carried on with the assistance of the Paraclete, now however directed to those outside the community. "When the Paraclete, Whom I shall send to you from the Father, comes, *He* will bear witness concerning me; but you yourselves also bear witness, because you have been in my company from the beginning" (16:26-27). During the public ministry, the Father had borne witness to Jesus through the "works" he had performed (5:36-38). Such testimony however, as John confesses, has not been entirely successful (12:37-40). Once embarked upon the service of the risen Lord, the disciples will find "their word" (17:20) efficacious, because their personal experience "from the beginning" of Jesus' public ministry will be supported by the Paraclete. It is this intuition into the real nature of an apostolic vocation by Ignatius (who, as will shortly be

---

13   Ibid., 87.

noted, almost never mentions the Holy Spirit in the *Exercises*), which convinced him there cannot be any real dichotomy between an active and a contemplative vocation.

The next statement concerning the role of the Paraclete transmutes his role as "defense-counsel" to that of plaintiff or accuser in imparting the Christian understanding of the trial of Jesus. As the evangelist will shortly make clear in the narrative of the Roman trial, Jesus is in reality judge, while his accusers have judgment passed upon them. "But now I am telling you the truth: it is for your [spiritual] profit that I am going away. For if I do not go away, the Paraclete will not come to you. Yet, if I make the journey, I will send Him to you. And when He comes, He on His part will convict the world of sin and convince it of justice and judgment: with regard to sin first of all, that they have not believed in me; with regard to justice, that I am going home to the Father and you no longer see me; and concerning judgment that the prince of this world has been definitively judged" (16:7-11). Jesus' departure is described as necessary for the disciples' "[spiritual] profit," because the coming of the Paraclete is contingent upon his journeying home to God. In this further delineation of the role of the Paraclete, the single verb has a double meaning, "to convict" and "to convince." It is within the believing community, to which the Paraclete is present that the conviction of the world can be rightly grasped: The disciples are brought to understand that "the sin of the world" is "that they have not believed in me." The Paraclete, testifying through the preaching of the disciples to the "justice" of the cause of Jesus (which they have made their own), empowers them to convince the world that he has returned to the Father, since they "no longer see" Jesus. Finally, the Paraclete supports the claim by the disciples before the world that their Master's "lifting up" on the cross, the inauguration of his return to God, is *ipso facto* the overthrow of "the prince of this world" (12:31). One might say that here we have an instance of apostolic "remembering" applied to the trial of Jesus and to the community's sense of victory over the world promised by Jesus (16:33).

The struggle of the Johannine community was in the next few centuries to be repeated in the history of the Fourth Gospel itself. George MacRae observes of this book that it "could lend itself to misunderstanding. It did so early in the history of interpretation, for two of its first known interpreters in the second century were Gnostic heretics, Ptolemaeus and Heracleon, who saw in it a justification of their totally anti-worldly dualist approach."[14]

14 G. W. MacRae, *Faith in the Word*, p. 9.

There is an interesting parallel in the early history of the *Spiritual Exercises*. Ignatius was hauled before the Spanish Inquisition on charges of belonging to the sect of "enlightened ones" *(Alumbrados)* in Alcalá and Salamanca. Indeed, Thomas of Villanova, saintly archbishop of Valencia, voiced the same suspicion in 1535 after Ignatius had given the Exercises in his see-city.[15]

I mention this here since one of the Spanish inquisitors, Tomás Pedroche, "was accurate in pin-pointing those places in the Exercises that seemed to smack of illuminism . . . [which], if you add the remaining guidelines on discernment, are the heart of the *Exercises* and of Ignatian teaching on apostolic life."[16] As has already been stated, the practice of discernment in the contemplation of the Gospels was the saint's highly original substitution for the "following" of Jesus by the first disciples in the case of future generations of believers.

The fifth and final saying defines more precisely the Paraclete's activity within the community by pointing to two areas in which it is deployed, each accorded prominence in Ignatian discernment: guidance in the continuing quest of the will of God and direction of the believer's attention to the earthly life of Jesus as unique source of the definitive revelation of the invisible Father. "I still have much to tell you, but you cannot bear it now. However, when *He,* the Spirit of truth, will come, He will guide you along the way by the entire truth. For He will not speak on His own, but will speak what He hears, and He will unveil to you the meaning of what is coming. He will in fact glorify me, because He will take what is mine and unveil its meaning to you. All the Father has is mine: that is why I said, 'He will take what is mine and unveil its meaning to you' " (16:12-15).

The first statement at first may appear to be an admission that the content of the revelation, which constitutes Jesus' mission to the world, still remains lacunary. But this impression will be carefully corrected in the sequel. The term "bear" in the saying, "You cannot bear it now," may well imply a contrast between the disciples' "following" Jesus with its obvious limitations and what will become after Easter their future way of life. For Jesus' saving act in "bearing the cross by himself" (19:7) influenced the evangelical tradition regarding discipleship as "bearing one's own cross" (Lk 14:27). It is to this tradition that Paul appears to

---

15   For a summary of Ignatius' struggles in defense of his orthodoxy, see H. Rahner, *Ignatius the Theologian*, pp. 156-165.

16   Joseph Veale, S.J., "Ignatian Prayer or Jesuit Spirituality," *The Way: Supplement* no. 27 (1976), 5.

allude in writing to the Galatians. "Each person must bear his own proper burden" (Gal 6:5). And in this same description of the Christian way of life he urges, "Help one another to bear these heavy burdens, and in this way you fulfil the law of Christ" (v. 2). This evangelical teaching appears throughout the *Exercises*. It is first hinted at in the Principle and Foundation ([23]), and articulated more clearly in the suggested response to the Call of the King ([98]), and in Two Standards ([147-148]). It reaches its apex in "the true teaching of Christ our Lord" with the third "manner of humility" (164, 167]).

The precise role of the Paraclete is next disclosed: "He will guide you along the way by the entire truth." Jesus himself is and remains "the Way" *(hodos)*—the unique way to the Father (14:6): "the Spirit of truth" acts as "guide along the way" *(hodogēsei)*, directing the life of the believer unerringly by means of "the entire truth." However "He will not speak on His own"—the Paraclete's role is not to bring any new or additional revelation. As "the Spirit of truth," He will only "speak what He hears," the truth contained in the mission of Jesus. Nor is it his function to provide apocalyptic visions of the future: rather He will reveal to the community in every age how Jesus' message is to be lived out faithfully no matter what may occur. Consequently, "He will glorify me" by disclosing more profoundly Jesus' identity as the Son of God by elucidating the true meaning of "what is mine,"—the earthly, human life of Jesus. This ultimately means the disclosure of the unseen God—"All the Father has is mine"—the ultimate reason why "the Word became flesh."

This crucially important teaching on discernment is exemplified in the great care taken by Ignatius to remind the exercitant, who (he confidently expects) will be "embraced by the creator and Lord in his love" for such a one, so as to "work immediately" with her or him (Annotation 15), to measure such spiritual experiences against certain objective norms. In the first place, there is "the genuine grounds of the history" which is, as has been repeatedly said, the earthly life of Jesus as reported in the Gospels. For these contain that "true teaching of Christ our Lord," with which the retreatant must be "inflamed before entering upon the elections" ([164]). For this reason too he counsels that the practice of discernment be carried out "at the same time as we contemplate his [Jesus'] life" ([135]). The fragmentary Directory from the saint's own hand insists on this for the second time of the Election: "while proceeding with one's meditations on Christ our Lord a person must observe, when experiencing consolation, in what direction God is moving her or him, and similarly for desolation" ([377]).

Secondly, the choice of a state of life must be kept within the parameters of "holy mother the hierarchical Church" ([170]). For to "the Spouse of Christ our Lord, our holy mother the hierarchical Church" one must be prompt to render complete obedience ([353]). It was Ignatius' unwavering belief "that between Christ our Lord the bridegroom and the Church his bride the same spirit holds sway. Because our holy mother the Church is ruled and governed by the same Spirit and Lord, who gave the ten commandments" ([365]). This text, curiously enough, is the single place (apart from references or allusions to the New Testament in the additional contemplations, where "the Holy Spirit" appears some six times) in the entire book of the *Spiritual Exercises*, in which the term "Spirit" is expressly named. It has been a matter of reproach that the saint, with his manifest concern about various "spirits," should have seemingly ignored the Holy Spirit, apart from mentioning "the three divine Persons" ([102, 106-109]). If one be permitted to hazard a guess, I venture the surmise that Ignatius, whose spirituality bears such a remarkable trinitarian stamp, sought to avoid any appearance of being influenced by the holy, yet eccentric Cistercian Abbot Joachim of Fiore (ca 1132-1202), whose apocalyptic, if trinitarian, interpretation of history had for long captured the imagination of the Middle Ages. The memory of the struggles between the papacy and the fourteenth century Franciscan "spirituals," who only succeeded in making Joachim's views on the Holy Spirit more outrageous, would have brought under suspicion of heresy any devotion centering on "the forgotten Paraclete."[17] However that may be, the Middle Ages were deeply devoted to the humanity of our Lord, and Ignatius was the rightful heir to that devotion, whose foundations were so solidly laid by the author of the Fourth Gospel.

Hugo Rahner has called Ignatian spirituality "a theology of visibility," which he explains as follows. "The decisions taken during the

---

17   Richard H. Roos in a monograph, *Saint Ignatius Loyola and the Holy Spirit in the Spiritual Exercises* (Jersey City: Program to Adapt the Spiritual Exercises, no date), remarks that "Somewhere along the way the Holy Spirit became implicit to Ignatius' theology. . . . In fact, the *Spiritual Exercises* are all but devoid of mention of the Holy Spirit as a distinct person of the Trinity" (p. 1). Father Roos assigns as explanation of this phenomenon the several occasions when the Saint had been accused by the Spanish Inquisition of being an *Alumbrado*. The basis for such denunciations lay chiefly in his Rules for the Election and in those for the Discernment of Spirits (pp. 2-4). It is the view of Roos that this explains the remarkably few allusions to the Holy Spirit in the text, and he states, "The role of the Holy Spirit in the Spiritual Exercises is that of 'God the divine Majesty' " (p. 10). Roos appears to view this phrase as a reference to the Father. I prefer the view of Hugo Rahner that it is used to designate the glorified Jesus.

Spiritual Exercises—the Election—will always have what might be called an incarnational or hypostatic structure: They originate *inconfuse et indivise* (Chalcedon) from the Spirit of God, who puts into the exercitant's soul what he ought to do; they are, however, equally *indivise* from the flesh—so much so, indeed, that visibility becomes a means of testing the spiritually authentic.''[18] The Paraclete-sayings in the Fourth Gospel (particularly the fifth) would appear to support the same point of view.

---

18   H. Rahner, *Ignatius the Theologian*, p. 214.

Chapter 15

JESUS "KING OF ISRAEL":
FROM THE GARDEN TO PILATE (18:1-19:16a)

In a very real sense the Passion and resurrection of Jesus has been on the horizon of the exercitant's consciousness almost from the moment he or she began the Spiritual Exercises. The colloquy of the first two exercises of the First Week brings one before the Crucified who has already "come to death in time by dying for my sins" ([53]). Yet, by the suggestion that the retreatant is to *speak* to him "as friend speaks to friend" ([54]), Ignatius presumably has the glorified Jesus in mind, in whom (as our evangelist will indicate) the mystery of the Passion now remains a contemporary reality (20:20). The offering of oneself which is proposed at the conclusion of the Consideration of the King specifies that the "imitation" one prays for is a participation of the sufferings of the crucified "Lord of all things" ([98]). When a detailed example of how all the contemplations are to be carried out during the Second Week is given in the text of the *Exercises*, St. Ignatius emphasizes that the Passion is an integral part of the earthly life and mission of Jesus ([116]). Thus it is taken for granted that even the contemplations on the childhood of Jesus are to take their direction from the perspective of the Cross. The meditation-contemplation on Two Standards points to one's sharing the sufferings of "Christ our Lord" as the source of any efficacious apostolic calling ([146]); and the consideration of The Three Degrees of Humility, particularly the third ([167-168]), is set down as a necessary preamble to "the Elections" ([164]). The most significant exercises of the Second Week are, in the mind of the Saint, a preparation for the contemplation of the Passion.

The Pre-Gospel Passion Narratives

Scholars tell us that the first pre-Gospel essays set down in writing early in the life of the Church were Passion-narratives, created for use in the public worship of the community. Such a concatenation of stories recounting and interpreting the sufferings of the risen Lord developed naturally from the ancient, Palestinian formula of faith, which Paul cites in writing to Corinth. "Christ died for our sins according to the Scriptures; he was buried; he has been raised the third day according to the Scriptures; and he let himself be seen . . ." (1 Cor 15:3-5). Indeed it is the opinion of Dr. R. H. Fuller that "This soteriological interpretation of Christ's death was achieved . . . probably at the first Christian passover in A.D. 31,"[1] that is, within a year of the death of Jesus. The same distinguished New Testament critic agrees with Ferdinand Hahn that "the Palestinian earliest church's distinctive interpretation of the death of Jesus . . . is the rejection of Jesus as the eschatological bringer of salvation by 'men' and the vindication of his *exousia* by God. At a very early date the Palestinian earliest church sought scriptural confirmation for this idea in Ps. 118:22. This is the earliest interpretation of Christ's death and resurrection."[2] The passage in question, the reader will recall, is cited repeatedly by New Testament writers (Mk 12:10-11; Mt 21:42; Lk 20:17; Acts 4:11; 1 Pet 2:4): it runs as follows, "That stone which the builders rejected has become the cornerstone. This is the Lord's doing, and it is a wonder in our eyes!" It may be of interest to note that the application of this conception to Jesus is nowhere alluded to by the fourth evangelist, since it does not fit into his innovative portrayal of Jesus' Passion and death as his "glory."

"According to the Scriptures"

Even a cursory reading of the *Spiritual Exercises* will indicate that practically no use is made of the Old Testament. In St. Ignatius' time copies of the Bible were not easily procurable. Nowadays (and most appropriately), considerable use is made of the inspired literature of Israel, in giving the Exercises, a practice which is very much in the spirit of St. Ignatius. It is important that the exercitant be aware of the relationship of Old to New Testament, and perhaps nowhere is this so useful as in the contemplation of the Passion. Indeed, in all the Passion-narratives in our Gospels passages from the psalms and the prophets are more frequently cited or alluded to than in the accounts of Jesus' public life. The fourth Servant Song (Is 52:13–53:12), which depicts the sufferings and the ultimate vindication of His Servant by God has exercised a preponderant influence upon all the evangelists. The Marcan account of Jesus' sufferings and death stresses his solitariness and his silence: the Servant's redemptive death is vicarious (Is 53:4, 12); during his sufferings, "He opened

1 Reginald H. Fuller, *The Foundations of New Testament Christology*, p. 161.
2 Ibid., pp. 152-153.

not his mouth" (Is 53:7). The fourth evangelist, in his reflection upon the failure of Jesus' public ministry, uses two Isaian passages (Is 53:1; 6:10).

Three psalms in particular were very early invoked to explain how what happened to Jesus was in accordance with the pre-ordained divine will, already announced by Israel's sages. Our Gospel-writer cites Psalm 69:9 (2:17) and 69:21 (19:28), the refrain of Psalms 42-43 (12:27), and Psalm 22:18 (19:24).

New Testament authors quote or allude to the Old Testament because they have observed a consistent pattern in God's dealings with Israel, which they discern continuing into the life of Jesus himself and the history of their Christian communities. C. H. Dodd has written a perceptive essay on how the inspired writers have appealed to the interpretations by the prophets of events contemporary with themselves and to their insight into the way in which the processes of history with great "variations of plot" are leading on to its consummation. "Thus, in interpreting the passion of Christ the New Testament writers find . . . not only the undeserved persecution of God's faithful Servant; they find also the element of judgment upon human sin (Jn 12:31) . . . the element of discipline (Heb 5:8) . . . the element of vicarious self-sacrifice, of which the classical expression is the fifty-third chapter of Isaiah. It is the drawing together of these separate strands, and others, all derived from the Old Testament, that provides the basis for the Christian theology of the atonement."[3]

The author of the Fourth Gospel appears to have meditated deeply on the Old Testament. His assimilation of its meaning in relation to Jesus, the Word of God made flesh, is exhibited in the bold and creative ways in which he cites or alludes to it.

1. Jesus' Triumphant Self-surrender in a Garden (18:1-12)

18:1   Upon saying this, Jesus went out with his disciples across the winter-torrent of Kedron, where there was a garden, into which he himself and his disciples entered.   2   But Judas his betrayer also knew the place because Jesus often met there with his disciples.   3   So Judas taking the military detachment and the temple-police from the high priests and the Pharisees, equipped with lanterns, torches, and weapons, arrives there. 4   Then Jesus knowing all that would befall him went out; and he says to them, "Whom are you looking for?"   5   They answered him, "Jesus the Nazorean." He replies to them, "I AM!" Now Judas his betrayer was also

---

3   C. H. Dodd, *The Old Testament in the New* (Philadelphia, 1963), pp. 28-29.

standing with them.   6   So when he told them, "I AM," they drew away and fell to the ground.   7   Accordingly he put the question to them a second time, "Whom are you looking for?", while they replied, "Jesus the Nazorean."   8   "I told you that I AM," Jesus responded, "If indeed then you are looking for me, allow these men to go away."   9   (This, in order that the word he had uttered might find fulfillment, "Of those You have given me I have not lost a single one.")   10   Now Simon Peter, armed with a sword, drew it, and struck the high priest's slave, and cut off his right ear. Malchus was the slave's name.   11   Thereupon Jesus said to Peter, "Put the sword back into the scabbard! Is it not inconceivable that I should not drink the cup the Father has given me?"   12   Then the detachment with its military tribune and the Jewish police arrested Jesus and secured him.

It is the view of most modern scholars that the primitive Passion-narratives began with the arrest of Jesus. We observed earlier that Mark, followed by his two Synoptic colleagues, had prefixed a series of stories by way of introduction, of which the most important was the story of the Last Supper (Mk 14:12-26) into which he had inserted a liturgical account of Eucharistic institution (vv. 22-24). In order to link this event with Jesus' arrest, Mark had created the dramatic story of Jesus' struggle and prayer in Gethsemane (vv. 27-42). John omits here any suggestion of this episode, which he incorporated briefly into his story of Jesus and the Greeks (12:27-33). Indeed, it is worthy of note that our evangelist does not represent Jesus as praying during the entire account of the Passion. As he engages in these critical moments of his hour, Jesus is serenely confident that the Father has already answered his prayer, "Keep me safe throughout this hour!" (12:27).

The introductory phrase, "Upon saying this," now refers in the present Gospel-context to the prayer of Jesus; originally however, before certain later editorial insertions (chs. 15–17) it pointed to the evangelist's carefully constructed discourse, which we have just considered (13:31–14:31).

John pictures Jesus as taking the same route followed by David as he fled at the rebellion of Absalom (2 Sam 15:23). David has been mentioned only once in this Gospel (7:42), where reference was made to the Davidic lineage of the Messiah. The name of "the garden," (Gethsemane, "olive-press") is not mentioned. In the Marcan story it was a suitable symbol for Jesus' agonized struggle (Mk 14:32-39). Our evangelist has imaginatively constructed the scene in strikingly different fashion as a prelude to Jesus' exaltation. George MacRae comments, "In the story of the arrest of Jesus in the garden Jesus plays a dominant role—anything but that of a helpless victim—even to the point of reducing the betrayal on Judas' part to merely pointing out where the garden was."[4]

The entry of Jesus with what appears to be a large Roman "detachment" is noted immediately (a "cohort" consisted of six hundred men; even if the word denotes a maniple, there would be two hundred). Historically, such collaboration by the Roman army is impossible—particularly as Jesus is led by these men under a military tribune to the Jewish ex-high priest, Annas. John probably wished to suggest that these pagans, no less than the Jewish religious authorities, are dominated by "the darkness," and so in need of salvation. Ironically, the two groups are presented as looking for "the light of the world" with "lanterns and torches."

Jesus, "knowing all that would befall him," steps forward to make a query similar to that he had put to the two disciples of John who were following him at the beginning of the Gospel (1:39), "Whom are you looking for?" This is the evangelist's way of reminding the reader of the central question, "Where is the risen Jesus for me now?" In reply to his would-be captors, Jesus pronounces the divine name, "I AM." That this is intentional on John's part seems indicated, if one recalls Jesus' earlier remark to the disciples at the Last Supper, "From now on, I shall tell you things before they occur, in order that when they occur you may believe that I AM!" (13:19). John's dramatic portrayal of the reaction of Jesus' enemies ("They drew away and fell to the ground") alerts the reader to a theological, rather than historical intention.

This appears to run counter to the Ignatian suggestion for contemplating the Passion, "to consider how the divinity hides itself" ([196]). However, the Saint includes this Johannine incident in his own "history" of the arrest ([201]); and we shall note the presence of this motif of Jesus' hidden divinity in the Roman trial.

Our evangelist proceeds to show Jesus' domination of the scene by having him issue orders to his enemies regarding the safety of his disciples, "Allow these men to go away." This is a variant on the Marcan description of Jesus as "the Shepherd" (Mk 14:27), who twice interrupts his prayer (vv. 37, 40) to ensure the safety of his "sheep." The Johannine Jesus has told the Jews during the confrontation on the feast of *Hanukkah*, "No one can snatch them out of my hand" (10:28b). Schnackenburg, who rejects Barnabas Lindar's suggestion that the physical safety

4   G. W. MacRae, *Invitation to John*, p. 203.

of the disciples is a "symbolic anticipation" of their ultimate salvation, explains this incident in somewhat similar fashion. "No one can tear the believers away from Jesus, that is, can separate them from his Church."[5]

The intervention of Simon Peter (identified here only by John) which occurs in the Marcan story *after* Jesus' arrest (Mk 14:46), had probably been intended by Mark as a note of comic relief—a ridiculously ineffectual act of bravado. In the present narrative, it affords Jesus the opportunity for a rebuke to such simple-minded violence, which runs counter to the will of the Father. "Is it not inconceivable that I should not drink the cup the Father has given me?" John thereby indicates his knowledge of the evangelical tradition behind the Marcan Gethsemane-scene.

It is only at this point in the story that Jesus submits to his enemies, who "arrested Jesus and secured Him." One recalls Ignatius' instruction for the Third Week, "to consider . . . according to the passage contemplated what he [our Lord] desires to suffer" ([195]). Nor should the exercitant fail to note the Saint's insistence (in the same point) upon the necessity "to begin with considerable effort to compel myself to grieve, feel sad, and weep, so as to *labor* through all the points which follow." Two experienced directors, Marian Cowan, C.S.J., and John Carroll Futrell, S.J., warn that extreme dryness in prayer is frequently experienced in the Third Week. Sister Marian feels that "the prayer of Christ himself was extremely dry at this time;" and she makes the keen observation, when commenting on the "for my sins," that "It is much more difficult to be with someone in true compassion when we are aware of being the cause of the suffering."[6] Father Futrell notes that "The compassion prayed for is that coming from passionate personal love of the suffering Jesus. It is *not* comprehension, which is so far beyond us." He cites the analogy suggested by Jean Laplace, S.J. of the reactions of a child who sees his parents grieving. "The child does not understand the world of sorrow of adults . . . This is probably what compassion with Jesus' suffering means for us. Remaining near this suffering will break something in our hearts."[7]

2. *Jesus Arraigned before Annas, while Peter Denies Him (18:13-27)*

John has replaced the official trial of Jesus before the Sanhedrin

---

5   Schnackenburg, *John,* III, 226.
6   Marian Cowan, C.S.J., and John Carroll Futrell, S.J., *The Spiritual Exercises of St. Ignatius of Loyola: A Handbook for Directors* (New York, 1981), pp. 119-120.
7   Ibid., pp. 112-113.

with an unofficial inquiry on the part of the former high priest, removed from that office by the Roman overlords for his cruelty and avarice. The notice of this interrogation by Annas, forgotten or ignored by Mark and Matthew, provides a plausible solution to three anomalies in the stories of the Sanhedrin-trial by those evangelists: it is conducted at night against everything we know about meetings of the supreme tribunal of Judaism—a nocturnal trial on a capital charge contravenes the legalities of all civilized peoples; abuse of a prisoner already "condemned as deserving of death" (Mk 15:64) is unthinkable (Mt 27:67-68 attributes such conduct to Jesus' judges!); finally, while both these writers mention a *second* session of the Sanhedrin "as soon as it was daylight" (Mk 15:1; Mt 27:1), they provide no plausible explanation for it. Luke 22:66-71 depicts but a single session, "when day broke." He presents it however, not as a formal trial, but simply as an occasion for Jesus to testify to his identity as Messiah and "the Son of God" before these religious leaders. Moreover, this evangelist imputes the mockery and abuse of Jesus to "the men guarding Jesus" immediately after his arrest and *before* the arraignment by the Sanhedrin (Lk 22:65-66). He assigns the three denials by Peter to this same night-period.[8]

> 13   And they marched him off first to Annas. For he was father-in-law to Caiaphas, who was high priest that particular year.   14   (Caiaphas was the man who had given the advice to the Jews, "It is in our interest that one man die on behalf of the people.")   15   But Simon Peter kept following Jesus, as did another disciple. Now that disciple was an acquaintance of the high priest, so he went in with Jesus as far as the high priest's courtyard;   16   but Peter was left standing at the gate outside. So the other disciple, the acquaintance of the high priest, went out, spoke to the woman at the gate, and led Peter inside.   17   Then the slave-girl on duty at the gate says to Peter, "Surely you're not also one of that man's disciples, are you?" He for his part said, "I'm not!"   18   Now the slaves and police, having made a fire with charcoal, were standing around warming themselves. So Peter was also standing in their company, warming himself.
>
> 19   Now the high priest began questioning Jesus about his disciples and about his teaching.   20   Jesus said to him in reply, "For my part, I have spoken openly to the world. I have in fact taught in synagogue and temple-precincts, where all the Jews gather, but in secret I have said nothing.   21   Why are you asking me? Ask those who listened to me what I told them. They indeed know what I said."   22   On his saying this, one of the

---

8   For a satisfactory discussion of these problems, see Pierre Benoit, O.P., *The Passion and Resurrection of Jesus Christ* (New York, London, 1969), pp. 74-114.

police struck Jesus a blow exclaiming, "Is that any way to answer to a high priest?"   23   Jesus came back at him, "If I have spoke impertinently, state it in evidence; but if correctly, why strike me?"   24   Then Annas sent him in bonds to Caiaphas the high priest.

25   Meantime Simon Peter was standing, warming himself. So people put the question to him, "Surely you're not also one of his disciples, are you?" He for his part denied it, "I'm not!"   26   One of the high priest's slaves, relative of him whose ear Peter had cut off, inquires, "Didn't I see you in the garden in his company?"   27   So once again Peter denied it, and just then a cock crowed.

This story of an interrogation by Annas has presented serious problems to commentators today; and even ancient copyists tried their hand at re-arranging the text (by moving v. 24 up to follow v. 13). Why, one asks, "*first* to Annas"? This unscrupulous, adept politician held the high priestly office ten years, then managed to have five of his sons, as well as his son-in-law, succeed him. As has been remarked, notice of such a preliminary hearing appears to solve some of the questions arising from the Marcan and Matthean accounts of the Jewish trial. The evangelist (or a later editor) wishes the reader to bear in mind the unconscious prophecy by the actual incumbent of the high priestly office, Caiaphas (11:51), introduced here somewhat awkwardly.

"Simon Peter kept *following Jesus*"—an interesting remark in view of Jesus' earlier warning to him at the Last Supper, "Where I am going you cannot follow me now" (13:46). Jesus had made clear that the announcement of his own departure meant the termination of all personal "following" of himself. The cryptic mention of "another disciple" as Peter's companion has also raised questions: is this "the disciple whom Jesus dearly loved" (13:23)? Is he in fact that anonymous disciple of John who had accompanied Andrew to follow Jesus in the beginning (1:40)? The characterization of this man as "an acquaintance of the high priest" might possibly mean that he was a citizen of Jerusalem. Puzzlingly enough, no more is heard of him after he "went out, spoke to the woman at the gate, and led Peter inside." Speculation on any of these conundrums can only prove a distraction to the prayer of the exercitant.

The evangelist employs Peter's triple denial of Jesus as a frame for the hearing before Annas, thus suggesting the disciple's weakness as a foil for the courage Jesus is meanwhile displaying before Annas. The ex-high priest had no right even to an informal interrogation: Peter had no business entering the courtyard and remaining in the company of the minions of this enemy of Jesus "warming himself."

An ominous note is immediately struck from the start in the account of the illegal inquiry: "the high priest began questioning Jesus about his disciples and about his teaching." Since conjecture about Annas' motivation would only go beyond the evidence provided by the text, one is invited to concentrate upon the candor and courage Jesus here evinces: it is he, not Annas, who remains in command. Moreover, the evangelist is suggesting that the reader recall that in his public ministry Jesus was described as "speaking openly" (7:26), especially in his challenging reply to the Jews in the portico of Solomon (10:24-30). He had moreover testified to his hostile hearers, "The One Who sent me can be relied on, and for my part I announce *to the world* what I have heard from Him" (8:26). And Jesus will shortly inform Pilate, "Here is why I was born and why I came into the world—to bear witness to the truth" (19:37b). During his public life his was no esoteric teaching restricted only to a few initiates: "in secret I have said nothing." Whatever may have prompted Annas to pursue this line of inquiry, Jesus tells him equivalently that the period of his mission to "the Jews" is now closed. This is his main reason for refusing to answer. Yet even now he does not give up hope for this malevolent inquisitor, and hence counsels him, "Ask those audiences what I told them. They in fact know what I said."

At the outrage perpetrated by "one of the police," Jesus does not "turn the other cheek" (Mt 5:39), but demands that anything reprehensible in his attitude be "stated in evidence." Or, if it be shown that he spoke "correctly," he demands redress for the insult before the bar of justice. Annas' only reaction was to "send him in bonds to Caiaphas the high priest."

In place of any account of this second hearing, the evangelist completes his story of Peter by quickly relating that disciple's second and third denials. These are told without any of the bluster and cursing which Mark had described (Mk 14:71). Nor does John refer to Peter's subsequent tears of repentance, as do all the Synoptics. In this Gospel it will be only at the prompting of the risen One that Peter will humbly confess his greater love (21:15-18).

3. *The Drama of the Roman Trial: Revelation of Jesus' Kingship (28-19:6a)*

John passes over the hearing before Caiaphas: he presupposes the reader's knowledge of it from the Synoptic tradition; and he has already dealt with the issues raised at it, as we have seen earlier (10:22-30). He does not wish anything to detract from the proceedings conducted by

Pilate, which he presents as a superb drama according to the best canons of ancient Greek tragedy. As George MacRae points out, it "is clearly the center-piece of the Johannine passion narrative. It brings the theme of judgment that has pervaded the Gospel to a startling climax with fine dramatic power and the most biting irony in the Gospel."[9] Rudolf Schnackenburg concurs: "It is the heart of the entire account. . . . It is Jesus' witness and self-confession as the hidden king, in another sense than the accusation intends, and yet in a real, deep sense (18:37)."[10] Following the lead of these two Johannine scholars, we divide the drama into seven scenes, commenting on each in its turn.

Scene One: Jesus Arraigned before Pilate (18:28-32)

> 28   So they march Jesus off from Caiaphas to Roman headquarters. It was early morning. Now they did not themselves enter headquarters, so that they might not incur defilement, and so could eat the Passover supper.   29   Thereupon Pilate came outside to them with the question, "What charge do you prefer against this fellow?"   30   They retorted, "If this were not an habitual criminal, we'd not have handed him over to you!"   31   At this Pilate rejoined, "Take him away and try him yourselves according to your own Law!" The Jews admitted to him, "We are not allowed to put anyone to death."   32   (This, in order that the word Jesus had spoken might be fulfilled, when indicating what kind of death he was to die.)

The Roman procurator had his residence in Caesarea, but came at Passover to Jerusalem to prevent riots. Whether Pilate was actually housed in the Hasmonean palace or in the fortress Antonia is not known. Roman judiciary tribunals began at "early morning." It may not be irrelevant to draw attention to the fact that in John's entire presentation there is no "crowd" present (as in the Marcan account, Mk 15:8). The entire drama is played out between Jesus, Pilate, and the Jewish religious leaders: the attendant temple-police (19:8) and Roman soldiery (19:2-3) play only minor roles.

Jesus' Jewish enemies "did not themselves enter headquarters"— that is, the (temporary) *praetorium*, where Pilate for the moment resided. The reason for this Jewish refusal to enter a Gentile establishment is important in the eyes of the evangelist: "that they might not incur defilement, and so could eat the Passover supper"—that same evening *after* Jesus' death. John's dating of this central event in open contradic-

9   G. W. MacRae, *Invitation to John,* p. 207.
10   Schnackenburg, *John,* III, 241.

tion to that (at least) implied in the Synoptic accounts has never been satisfactorily explained. Our evangelist will later (19:14, 36) make it clear
that Jesus' death as the new paschal lamb (1:29) has abrogated the traditional Jewish celebration.

This first scene is played "outside"—Pilate's first concession to the
accusers of Jesus. "What charge do you prefer against this fellow?"
Roman jurisprudence required that such a court-case open with a formal
statement such as this by the plaintiffs. In order to arrange the hearing,
the Jews would have undoubtedly informed the procurator previously of
the reason they sought a trial. The charge that Jesus has been "an habitual criminal" is simply a piece of political chicanery shortly to be exposed by Pilate. The Jews are forced to admit, "We are not allowed to
put anyone to death." In the provinces of the Empire the Romans reserved the *ius gladii* (death-sentence) to their own officials. An explanatory gloss by the evangelist or a later editor draws attention to his
earlier predictions (8:28; 12:32).

Scene Two: Pilate Interrogates Jesus about Kingship (18:33-38a)

The scene now shifts to the hall inside the praetorium where Jesus
had been conducted under guard. Pilate is known in history to have been
contemptuous of the Jewish people; for his repeated acts of cruelty to
them he was later recalled (36 AD) by the imperial government to answer
for crimes against Samaritans.

> 33   So again Pilate went back into his headquarters, summoned Jesus, and
> asked him, "Is it you who are the king of the Jews?"   34   Jesus asked in
> his turn, "Are you saying this on your own, or did others tell you this about
> me?"   35   Pilate retorted, "I'm no Jew, am I?—It is your own nation and
> high priests who handed you over to me! What crime have you committed?"
> 36   Jesus made an answer, "My kingship does not take its origin from this
> world. If it were from this world that my kingship derived, my troops would
> now be fighting to prevent my being handed over to the Jews. As it is, my
> kingship has no origin here."   37   Then Pilate asked him, "So then you
> are a king?" Jesus answered, "It is you yourself who say I am king! Here is
> why I was born and why I came into the world—to bear witness to the truth.
> Everyone who is on the side of truth can hear my voice."   38a   Pilate
> asked him, "What is truth?"

The judge comes at once to the principal indictment, Jesus' alleged
claim to be "king of the Jews." While the Synoptics appear to represent
Jesus as giving a simple, undifferentiated assent to the question, the
Johannine Jesus makes a distinction before giving his answer. Is the poli-

tically dangerous title employed by Pilate the result of Jewish trickery, or merely the result of confusion on the part of an ignorant pagan between this incriminating title and "King of Israel" (1:49; 12:13)?

At Pilate's testy rejoinder, Jesus explains his kingship in terms of its *origin*—a question of supreme significance to John (3:31; 8:23). It is important to recall that the Greek term *basileia* here signifies kingship, *not* kingdom. Jesus proposes an argument that even a non-believing Roman bureaucrat can grasp: he is no revolutionary, has caused no insurrection to threaten the *pax Romana.*

Pilate, seemingly impressed, appears to accept Jesus as some kind of king, and Jesus at once points that out to him, "It is you yourself who say I am king!" He proceeds by defining the meaning of his kingship: he is emissary from his Father, to whose "truth"—disclosure of the divine plan of salvation—he continues to testify. Belief in Jesus' pre-existence as eternal "Word of God" and in his Incarnation are necessary presuppositions for the most fundamental insight into what Jesus says here. The abstract given by the evangelist (3:31-36) of the preaching of the Johannine community has already said it all.

"Everyone who is on the side of the truth can hear my voice." Jesus has castigated his Jewish adversaries because "You do not believe me when I speak the truth . . . The person on God's side listens to God's words: here is why you do not listen to me—because you are not on God's side!" (8:45, 47). The shepherd-parable had pointed out that the shepherd's own sheep "follow him because they recognize his voice" (10:4; 10:27). It will be remembered that in Israelite tradition the king, God's human viceregent was, by analogy with the unique King of Israel, known as "Shepherd" (also of David: 2 Sam 5:2; Ps 78:70-71). Ezekiel presents the messianic promise from God as the supreme Shepherd (Ez 34:11-16) to appoint "David my servant" as "the one shepherd," and "prince among them" (vv. 23-24).

At this point, Pilate, apparently at a loss and also perhaps experiencing fear (see 19:8) for the first time in the interview, is made to ask a question, which John has been putting to his reader throughout his entire book, "What is truth?" Schnackenburg has a telling comment, "Pilate's famous question . . . is meant to express . . . neither philosophical scepticism nor cold irony . . . certainly not a serious search for truth . . . With that [question], the Roman judge has already decided against Jesus."[11]

---

11   Ibid., 251.

Scene Three: Pilate Attests the Innocence of Jesus (18:38b-40)

Once more the scene shifts to the "outside," where Pilate again addresses the Jews.

> 38b   On saying this, he again went outside to the Jews to say to them, "For myself, I can find no case against him.   39   Now you have a custom that I am to free one prisoner for you at Passover. So do you want me to release for you this king of the Jews?"   40   So they again shouted, "Not this fellow, but Barabbas!" (Barabbas was in fact a bandit.)

Pilate's verdict that Jesus is innocent is to be taken as his response to the earlier accusation, "This man [is] . . . an habitual criminal" (v. 30). The Roman is prepared to release Jesus, but unfortunately he now proposes a barter. The Synoptics present the initiative regarding the release of Barabbas as coming from the crowd, not Pilate. The "custom" referred to here is possibly supported historically by a Mishnah text. The importance of the Barabbas-incident (awkwardly introduced into some accounts) for all the evangelists, I suggest, lies in their effort to show that Pilate's eventual condemnation of Jesus was his own free act, not simply the result of Jewish pressure or mere vacillation on his part. Jesus' death was no mere accident: it was the result of deliberate choice on the part of the Roman judge.

The curious expression "they *again* shouted" (no mention of this has been made previously) may be a relic from the source which our writer used. John noted that this man, not Jesus, was in fact "an habitual criminal"—"a bandit," no mere robber.

Scene Four: Mockery of Jesus as King (19:1-3)

The insertion of this episode at this point in the trial by the evangelist is clearly contrived for dramatic effect. Set in the very center of the whole drama, this action sets forth the principal motif of the entire narrative: rejected by his own nation, Jesus, albeit in mockery, is proclaimed king by Roman soldiers.

> 19:1   At that point, Pilate took Jesus and had him flogged.   2   In addition, the soldiers plaited a crown out of thorns, and set it on his head; and they threw a purple cloak round him,   3   and time and again, they would come up to him, as they kept shouting, "Long live the king of the Jews!" And they rained blows upon him.

Luke with his sensitivity to scenes of violence implies that Pilate despite his threat to do so (Lk 23:16), does not have Jesus flogged. Moreover, that evangelist omits entirely the crowning with thorns. John's account comes close to the Marcan narrative (Mk 15:16-20), but omits the detail of the reed, with which the guards struck Jesus. The chief difference in John's presentation is that the flogging is no longer a preliminary to crucifixion: it is the preparation for the scene which immediately follows—Pilate's public presentation of Jesus as king.

Origen appears to have been the first of the patristic writers to interpret the crowning with thorns as torture. In all the Gospel-accounts the primary meaning is mockery. On the coinage of Hellenistic rulers of the period, the king is represented as wearing what is known to numismatologists as a "radiant crown" *(corona radiata)*,—the emanating rays were a symbol of deity. The best known example perhaps is seen on the head of the statue of Liberty in New York City harbor. While it is no longer possible to know whether this symbol was sensed by the soldiers on this occasion, it should be noted that no evangelist ever dwells on the physical torments inflicted on Jesus in his Passion.

Scene Five: Pilate Presents the King to the Jews (19:4-8)

4 And again Pilate went outside to say to them, "Look, I am bringing him outside to you, in order that you may know I find no case against him."
5 Thereupon Jesus came outside, wearing the thorny crown and the purple cloak. Then he [Pilate] says to them, "Look at the [poor] human being!"
6 Now when the high priests and the police saw him, they began to shout, "Crucify! crucify!" Pilate retorts, "Take him and crucify him yourselves. For my part, I can find no case against him." 7 The Jews rejoined, "We have a Law, and by that Law he ought to die, because he has made himself out a Son of God!" 8 Now when Pilate heard this charge, he became more filled with fear.

Pilate in somewhat melodramatic fashion now emphasizes his conviction that Jesus is not a revolutionary. He puts Jesus on display—shabby and beaten, no more than a caricature of kingship. He does this (in the context of the second declaration of innocence) to demonstrate his conviction that Jesus is no threat to Roman rule. His very appearance in the tattered robe of mock-royalty with a "thorny crown" is surely proof of that! He is nothing more than "a [poor] human being." There is not any question here of the *anthrōpos*-myth, nor of an abbreviated "Son of Man." The Word become flesh has been reduced to this. In the evangelist's eyes (and those of the believing reader) the hidden divinity of Jesus is still an object of belief and love. St. Ignatius tells the exercitant to keep this great truth in mind always when contemplating the Passion ([196]).

The evangelist describes Pilate's reaction to this by saying "he became more afraid." John has not to this point mentioned any fear on Pilate's part, unless he implied it in the question, "What is truth?" (18:38a) as was suggested. It is possible John simply took this idea from his source, but more probably he sees this fear as the awe, even terror, in a human heart confronted with the numinous.

Scene Six: Pilate Returns to the Question of Jesus' Origin (19:9-12)

9 So he re-entered headquarters to interrogate Jesus, "Where do you come from?" But Jesus made him no reply. 10 Accordingly, Pilate tells him, "You refuse to speak to me? Don't you know I have authority to let you go, and I have authority to crucify you?" 11 Jesus said to him, "You would have no authority over me, were it not given you from above. That is why the one who handed me over to you is guilty of greater sin." 12 From then on, Pilate kept trying to let him go; but the Jews went on shouting, "If you let this fellow go, you are no friend of the Emperor! Any man who makes himself king is defying the Emperor."

Pilate now returns to speak to Jesus for the last time: he poses the question which is central to the message of the entire Gospel, "Where do you come from?" The query manifests the insecurity and fear of Pilate, but since he has demonstrated by his query "What is truth?", that he has closed himself to Jesus and his message, he receives no answer—at least not for the moment. The silence of Jesus as the Servant of God (Is 53:7) is a theme, as has been observed, prominent in the Synoptics. Here it is implied that there is nothing more Jesus has to say to his would-be judge. Like the insecure person he is Pilate now underlines his administrative authority *(imperium)*, and his question, "Don't you know I have authority to let you go, and I have authority to crucify you?", elicits a response from Jesus which also implies the answer to Pilate's original query, "Where do you come from?" Jesus, as the reader well knows, is "from above" (8:23a). He had been characterized thus in the Johannine kerygma: "The One coming from above stands above all men" (3:31). John had borne witness to Jesus before his own disciples, "No human being can take even a single thing unless it has been given him from above" (3:27). If then Pilate could only comprehend that it is God who has *only in this instance* permitted him the choice "to let you go or to crucify you," he would see that Jesus "comes from above," and hence is the one truly endowed with "authority" from God.

Jesus' last word to Pilate is mysterious: "the one who handed me over to you is guilty of greater sin." The "sin of the world" is of course to refuse to accept Jesus as "the One coming from above." But who is the guilty one? Is it "the Jews," or Caiaphas, or Judas? The Prologue had declared, with reference to the struggle between the light and the darkness continuing in history, "The darkness has never mastered it" (1:5). I venture to suggest that here behind the historical figures in this drama played out in the Roman trial it is the evil power-structures contrived by "the prince of this world" (14:30), which are indicated.

Pilate is pictured as still "trying to let him go." However, the shouting of the Jews penetrates to the court-room; and they now play their last card. "If you let this fellow go, you are no friend of the Emperor." *Amicus Caesaris* (Emperor's friend) was a prerogative of those of senatorial rank. Pilate, a member only of the equestrian order, was well aware that his only hope of being granted this title rested precariously on the favor of the suspicious Tiberius, who—he also was well aware—reacted brutally to any hint of high treason. The Jews also were not ignorant of this facet of the Emperor's character, and so began to shout, "Any man who makes himself king is defying the Emperor!" The procurator had indeed left himself open to an accusation of being accessory to the fact by his dramatic presentation of Jesus as mock-king. The case is as good as finished: there remains only the official sentence of death.

Scene Seven: Sentence of Death is Passed on Jesus (19:13-16a)

13 Overhearing these insinuations, Pilate had Jesus led outside, and took his seat on the judge's bench at the place called "The Pavement" (or in Aramaic, Gabbatha). 14 It was the day for Passover-preparation, and the time about noon. Then he says to the Jews, "Take a look at your king!" 15 For their part, however, they shouted, "Off with him, off with him, crucify him!" Pilate asks them, "Am I to crucify your king?" The high priests retorted, "We have no king but the Emperor!" 16a At that point he handed him over to them to be crucified.

At this crucial moment in the hearing the evangelist carefully draws the reader's attention to place—"outside" on "The Pavement." The procurator's capitulation to Jesus' enemies is symbolized by his having the *sella curulis* (magistrate's chair) moved out of the courtroom to the courtyard where the Jews had remained. The time is, however, much more significant in John's eyes: at "noon" on "the day for Passover-preparation" when the inferior Jewish clergy began the ceremonial slaughter of the paschal lambs. Jesus "the Lamb of God" (1:29, 35) is now through death to replace such old, outmoded rites.

The trenchant dialogue between Pilate and the Jews places emphasis on the word "king"—the theme which dominates the entire Passion-story as conceived by our evangelist. Here it reaches a climax in the apostasy of the religious leaders, "We have no king but the Emperor!" The traditional faith of Israel proclaimed almighty God as the unique King of His people. By closing themselves to belief in Jesus, his bitter antagonists have denied their faith in God. For as Jesus had taught the disciples at the Last Supper, the single way of maintaining faith in the God of Israel is by believing in himself: "You believe in God—believe also in me" (14:1). For as he had also told them, "No one can come to the Father except through me" (14:6b).

Chapter 16

"THE CRUCIFIED MAJESTY OF GOD" (19:16b-42)

T he very distinctive interpretation of the Passion as the "glory" of Jesus, which is so very far from the Synoptic presentation of this central mystery, may raise some questions in the mind of the exercitant, accustomed to the Ignatian approach with its stress upon how the divinity of our Lord "leaves the most sacred humanity to suffer so cruelly" ([196]). It may therefore be helpful to recall the view of Gil Gonzalez Dávila, president of the commission which produced the official *Directory* of 1599. He is quoted by Hugo Rahner[1] as stating that the Third Week is calculated "to find the heart of Christ amid the turmoils of the Passion, and to rouse us to enter into communion with the crucified Christ, that we may declare, *amor meus crucifixus est*—my love has been crucified!" And indeed our evangelist (as has been seen) has in his Gospel, beginning with chapter thirteen, laid repeated emphasis upon love, about which he said very little in the early section of his book. In his view, the mystery surrounding Jesus can only be revealed to his most intimate followers when "he lays down his life for his friends" (15:13). He pointed out through a saying of Jesus the magnetic attractiveness of the Crucified: "As for myself, when I am lifted up, I will draw all mankind to myself" (12:32). Jesus' gift of "life to the world" (6:51b), most profound proof of his love, will, as John is about to indicate (19:30), only become possible when he successfully carries out the "mandate" of the Father. And having once passed through death, the risen Lord, who in this Gospel manifests his identity to his disciples by "showing them his hands and his side" (20:20), will forever display the stigmata of his sufferings. For John, as for Ignatius, Jesus remains "the crucified Majesty of God."

Anyone at all familiar with the contemplations on the Passion in the Third Week of the Spiritual Exercises will have observed certain notable changes in the author's strategy. In the Second Week, at least from the

---

1   H. Rahner, *Ignatius the Theologian,* p. 132.

fifth to the twelfth day ([158-160]), a single mystery was proposed for contemplation. Moreover, these were obviously the result of a kind of eclecticism, chosen from the vast range of materials that lie to hand in the Gospels with no discernible connection one with another (except for a vague chronological arrangement, also characteristic of the Gospel-accounts of Jesus' public ministry.) The impression of concentrating on discrete pieces in a mosaic is heightened by the first remark in the Notes for the exercitant during this week to the effect that "I should read only the mysteries of the contemplation which I am immediately to make; so that, for the time being, I do not read any mystery which I am not to make that day or at that hour, in order that the consideration of one mystery may not disturb the consideration of another" ([127]). Now however, attention to *continuity* between the mysteries contemplated is perceptible in the change made for this Week in the sixth Addition: "to bring to mind frequently the life and mysteries of Christ our Lord, beginning with his Incarnation up to the point or mystery which I am going to contemplate" ([130]).

In the Second Week also one senses a certain peaceful, almost static quality in the approach to somewhat disparate, unconnected units, whereas by contrast in the Third Week there is, from the first contemplation, a decided emphasis upon movement from one locale to another and an obvious concern to link the various mysteries of the Passion each to the other ([see 190-191 and 201]). Moreover, the headings of the brief abstracts given as subjects for contemplation from the second to sixth day ([208]) underline the progress of Jesus from one place to another. And this sense for the sequential character in the ongoing contemplations of the Passion is reinforced by a further change in the sixth Addition: the exercitant is now bid "induce in oneself grief, sorrow, anguish by bringing frequently to mind the labor, fatigue, and sorrow of Christ our Lord, which he has endured from the moment he was born up to the mystery of the Passion in which I find myself at present" ([206]). Finally, the seventh day is devoted expressly to the unity of the whole Passion-story, to be contemplated twice. Then in place of repetitions and Application of the Senses "one is to consider all that day as frequently as possible how the sacred body of Christ our Lord remained separated apart from his soul, and one will call to mind where and how it was buried; and in the same way one is to consider the loneliness of our Lady, afflicted with such great sorrow and fatigue—then in addition the loneliness of the disciples" ([208]). It is only on this final day, when his ceaseless "labor" has been replaced by the repose of death for Jesus, that he no longer is the almost unique subject of all activity (Ignatius even remarks of Jesus that "he made the supper," as later, "he made a prayer to the Father" ([201]). And now finally attention is called to our Lady and to the disciples. All these details appear to point to the Saint's conviction that for the kind of unitive prayer desired in the Third and Fourth Weeks it is of paramount importance to acquire a profound sense of the unity of the Passion.

1. Jesus' Enthronement in the Glory of the Cross (19:16b-27)

16b   They now took Jesus in charge;   17   and carrying his own cross he went out to Skull Place, as it is called (its Aramaic name is Golgotha),   18 where they crucified him and with him two others, one on either side with Jesus in the center.
19   Moreover, Pilate had a placard inscribed to be put at the top of the cross. It ran, "Jesus the Nazorean the king of the Jews."   20   Thus many of the Jews read the placard, since the place where Jesus was crucified was close to the city. It was in fact inscribed in Aramaic, Latin, Greek. 21   Consequently, the Jewish high priests tried to influence Pilate, "Do not leave it to read 'The king of the Jews,' but 'This fellow claimed, "I am king of the Jews" '."   22   Pilate rejoined, "What I have had written stands written!"
23   Now when the soldiers had crucified Jesus, they took his clothes, and divided them in four parts, a share for each soldier—which left the tunic. The tunic however was without seam, being woven in one piece.   24   So they said to one another, "Let's not tear it, but toss dice for it, to see who gets it." (This, in order that the Scriptures might find fulfillment, which read, "They divided my clothes among them: for my tunic they rolled dice.") So much for what the soldiers did.
25   Now there stood, near the cross of Jesus, his mother with his mother's sister, and Mary of Cleophas with Mary of Magdala.   26   On seeing his mother with the disciple he dearly loved standing by, Jesus says to his mother, "Lady, that is your son!"   27   Then he says to the disciple, "That is your mother!" And from that very hour the disciple received her into his home.

It is reasonable to suppose that the vague "they," which introduces the very brief account of the *via crucis,* indicates the Roman soldiers. Our evangelist dispenses with Simon of Cyrene (Mk 15:21; Mt. 27:32), whom Luke pictures as the ideal disciple by his acceptance of the task laid on him "to carry the cross behind Jesus" (Lk 23:23). That evangelist continues the same theme of the cost of discipleship in Jesus' warning issued to the "daughters of Jerusalem" (vv. 27-31). Luke alone mentions that the sad procession included two criminals destined to be executed with Jesus (v. 32). John characteristically focuses on Jesus' "carrying his own cross." It is probable that the evangelist may be thinking of the terrible tale of the "binding of Isaac," where Abraham laid the wood needed for the sacrifice on the little boy's shoulders (Gen 22:6). We have already seen a hint of the story of Isaac and Ishmael (Gen 21:9) behind the parable at 8:35.

Like his earlier colleagues, John notes the exact place of the crucifixion, while not delaying on the gruesome details of the torment suffered by Jesus. Such historical circumstances of the central act of salvation are of supreme importance in John's eyes. Thus he also indicates "two others" crucified with Jesus, who (as befits his majesty) is seen "in the center." For this reason the evangelist does not name these men "bandits," as do Mark and Matthew, or "criminals" (Luke). Everything which might distract from the glory of this "lifting up" of Jesus is passed over in silence by John.

For the same reason our evangelist has created a little drama out of the incident of the title above Jesus' head. The "placard" was read by "many of the Jews," since the proclamation of Jesus' kingship is meant first of all for them. Moreover, it is intended for the information of all the inhabitants of the entire Mediterranean world being written in the language of Palestine, of the Roman overlords, and of all peoples of Hellenistic culture. Pilate, by refusing to alter the wording of his "placard," not only humiliates the Jews, but testifies before the world the honorific nature of this royal title.

The Synoptic evangelists had made allusion to the division of Jesus' garments as well as to the title on the cross. It is John however who fills out the reference to the great psalm of the Passion (Ps 22:19) with additional detail—in particular, concerning "the tunic without seam." It was probably not John's intention to present this as a symbol of Jesus' high priestly character, or of the unity of the Church. In addition to finding this "tunic" as part of the announcement in "the Scripture" of the divine plan concerning Jesus, Rudolf Schnackenburg suggests what he calls "a sensible explanation."[2] As later with the piercing of Jesus' side, John sees here, despite the complete spoliation of all his earthly possessions, a sign of God's providential protection of Jesus in the soldiers' agreement to leave the tunic intact. "So much for what the soldiers did;" the remark indicates the evangelist's intention to contrast this scene with

2   Schnackenburg, *John*, III, 274.

what immediately follows.

As an aid to our understanding of the meaning of this episode involving the mother of Jesus and "the disciple he dearly loved," it is to be observed that John has set this narrative in place of the mockery of the Crucified recorded by all three Synoptics (Mk 15:29-32; Mt 27:39-44; Lk 23:35-37). Also to be noted is John's remark following the scene that Jesus realized "that all had already been brought to perfect fulfillment" (v. 27).

Mark had mentioned the presence of women at the death of Jesus "looking on from afar" (Mk 15:40). John alone expressly mentions that "his mother stood near the cross." At the wedding in Cana, the mother of Jesus with her unerring instinct in perceiving the importance, for genuine faith, of the word of Jesus ("Do whatsoever he tells you.") was disclosed as representative of the true "Israel," to which John came "baptizing with water that he [Jesus] may be manifested" (1:31).

The mention of the beloved disciple here is as abrupt as his first appearance at the Last Supper (13:23-26), where he was cast in the role of intimate and confidant of Jesus. After the discovery of the empty tomb, it is he, who "saw and began to believe" (20:8). It is this disciple who, as the future founder of the evangelist's community, will transmit and interpret the genuine sense of Jesus' message to his community, under the guidance of the Paraclete.

Jesus may be thought of as adding a "codicil" to that "last will and testament," which, as has been seen, was his farewell discourse at the Last Supper. He first says to his mother, "Lady, that is your son!" Father Schnackenburg comments, "Jesus' mother represents the section of the population which was open to the 'King of Israel' (see 12:13). In the scene at the cross, it is not to be overlooked that not only is Jesus' mother handed over to the disciple, but also that the disciple is entrusted to Mary as his mother. The intention behind this can be to remind the Christian community of the mother from whom both Jesus and the Church originated."[3]

Jesus' last words to the disciple, "That is your mother," would appear to indicate that, as his last significant act in this world, Jesus means, in the person of his mother confided to the beloved disciple, to ensure effectively that "the Israel of God" (Gal 6:16) will continue to receive "the truth" which constituted his mission on earth from the "God no one has ever seen" (1:18). The statement employed to conclude the incident is

3   Ibid., 278.

seen to be of some significance, when it is remembered that Jesus had used the same term, "receive," in the promise made to the disciples as he took his leave of them. "Now when I have made the journey and readied a place for you, I shall come again to receive you into my company, that you too may be where I am myself" (14:2). If the mother of Jesus is to become mother of the beloved disciple, he in his turn as her adopted son is to give more than mere shelter to her. He is to share with her his privileged insights into the meaning of Jesus' life and mission. Thus one might, without exaggeration, consider that for our evangelist Mary is the charter-member of the Johannine church.

2. As the Glorified Son of Man, the Dying Jesus Imparts the Spirit (19:28-37)

It is of considerable importance, as one contemplates the Passion and death of Jesus, to keep in mind the unity of the entire Paschal mystery.[4] Our evangelist had reminded his reader of that by a brief parable, nowhere included in the collections of the Synoptics, but quite in character with Jesus' practice of using the mystery of growth in nature to illustrate his teaching. "Amen, amen I tell you: unless a grain of wheat die when sown in the earth, it remains by itself in isolation; but if it dies, it produces a rich harvest" (12:24). Jesus' resurrection no less than his death forms an integral part of his redemptive activity. Paul had stressed this again and again (1 Thes 1:10; 2 Cor 5:15; Rom 4:25; 7:4; 8:34; 14:9). So had the Church prior to his conversion, as Paul's citations from earlier formulae of faith indicate (1 Thess 4:14; 1 Cor 15:3-5).

Each of the Synoptic evangelists, in his own distinctive way, attests his belief that Jesus' glorification constitutes, with his death, the crowning phase of the central event of man's salvation. Even Mark, whose story of the Passion approaches nearest to stark tragedy, depicts the dying Jesus as "uttering a mighty cry" (Mk 15:37). This inarticulate shout is immediately interpreted as one of victory—a presage of the resurrection—by two subjoined symbolic happenings. "Then the curtain before the sanctuary split in two from top to bottom" (v. 38): this signifies the de-sacralization of the old, now outmoded sign of God's presence to save His people, and the good news that access to the divine presence is henceforth open to all (see Heb 10:19-22). The second conse-

---

4   "We have to anticipate the fourth week in order fully to understand the third week, especially in its closing phase": W. Peters, *The Spiritual Exercises of St. Ignatius*, p. 142.

quence is the extraordinary reaction of a pagan Roman soldier, which anticipates the Gentiles' response to the gospel. "But the centurion stationed nearby to face him, on seeing that he expired crying out as he did, declared, 'In very truth this fellow was God's Son!' " (v. 38).

Matthew, by a most creative adaptation of the Marcan narrative which he has followed almost verbatim in describing the last hours of Jesus' life (Mt 27:45-50), links the death of Jesus to an apocalyptic description of the Lord's triumphant second coming at the end of history. "And lo! the curtain in the sanctuary was rent in two from top to bottom: and there was an earthquake, and rocks were torn asunder; tombs yawned open, and many bodies of the sleeping saints were raised. Then emerging from their tombs after his resurrection, they entered the holy city and were manifested to many persons" (vv. 51-53). For this sacred writer the death of Jesus issues in the completion of man's redemption through the general resurrection of all believers.

The sophisticated Luke, in order to present his idea of the unity of Jesus' death with his glorification (an anticipation of John's characteristic insight into the Passion as the glory of Jesus) rearranges the materials received from tradition by placing the rending of the curtain hanging before the holy of holies *before* Jesus dies. "The sun suffered eclipse, while the curtain in the sanctuary was torn down the middle, and uttering a mighty cry, Jesus said, 'Father into your hands I commend my life' " [Ps 31:6] (Lk 23:45-46). By his articulation of the shout of the dying Jesus with the help of a psalm, Luke appears to represent him as greeting the Father at his entry into heaven. This points to Jesus' "assumption" (Lk 9:51; 24:51), the sequel to his death—an interpretation which the author of Hebrews would seem to have adopted. "Consequently, my brothers, since we now possess freedom of entry, by means of the blood of Jesus, into the [heavenly] sanctuary—that new and living way through the *curtain*, I mean, his flesh—let us draw near with a sincere heart in the assurance of faith" (Heb 10:19-21).

In his day, St. Ignatius when arranging the sequence of the *Spiritual Exercises* makes no perceptible division between the Third and the Fourth Weeks. William Peters calls attention to the fact that, "The first day of the Fourth Week might just as well be called the eighth day of the Third Week, or the last day of the Third Week might be called the beginning of the Fourth Week."[5] This becomes evident as soon as one compares the instructions for the seventh day of the Third Week with the

---

5   Ibid.

"history" of the first contemplation of the Fourth Week. In his suggestions for the repetition of the entire Passion, St. Ignatius urges that "the exercitant consider as often as he or she can throughout the whole day, how the sacred body of Christ our Lord remained detached and separated from the soul; and one is to call to mind where and how it was buried" ([208]). The first prelude of the first contemplation in the Fourth Week reads, "how after Christ had died on the cross, and his body remained separated from the soul, but united to the divinity, his blessed soul, likewise united to the divinity, descended into 'hell,' from which it freed the souls of the just; then on returning to the tomb, he rose and appeared in body and soul to his blessed mother" ([219]). We must now turn to the Fourth Gospel, to see how its author justifies his insight into the Passion as the exaltation of Jesus.

> 28   After this, Jesus—knowing that all had already been brought to perfect fulfillment—said, "I thirst" (in order that Scripture might be completed [Ps 69:21]).   29   A jar stood there full of sour wine; so fixing a sponge soaked with the wine on a piece of hyssop, they reached it to his mouth.   30 Then when he had taken the sour wine, Jesus declared, "It has been brought to perfect fulfillment!"; and bowing his head, he handed over the Spirit.
>
> 31   Now since it fell on Sabbath-preparation, in order that the bodies should not remain on the cross for Sabbath—moreover that Sabbath was a high holiday—the Jews made petition to Pilate to have the legs broken and the bodies taken down.   32   Accordingly, the soldiers came and broke the legs of the first man, then of the second, who had been crucified with him. 33   However, on coming to Jesus, as they saw he had already died, they did not break his legs.   34   Instead, one of the soldiers plunged his lance into his side, and at once blood and water gushed forth.   35   (Note that the eyewitness has testified [to this], and his testimony is trustworthy. Moreover, *he* knows that he is telling the truth, in order that you also in turn may come to believe.)   36   This took place so that Scripture might find fulfillment— which reads, "No bone of his must be broken" [Ex 12:46];   37   and still another text runs, "They will look on the One they have pierced" [Zech 12:10].

The last of Jesus' tasks in accomplishing the mission entrusted to him by his Father, as John here remarks, was carefully indicated in the scene immediately preceding. Accordingly, it seems strange that now "in order that Scripture might be completed" Jesus is represented as expressing a desire to drink, "I thirst," a brief allusion to the Greek words found in the Septuagintal version of Psalm 69:21: "For my thirst they made me drink sour wine." This appendage to John's advertence to Jesus' awareness "that all had already been brought to perfect fulfillment" appears as something of an anticlimax, and is probably to be explained by what had appeared in the source John employed. More appropriately perhaps one may divine a particular purpose on the part of this evangelist for whom his Passion means Jesus' glorification. It is, I feel, significant that John represents Jesus as himself taking the initiative in asking for some drink—in the earlier Gospels, drink was offered out of compassion (Mk 15:36) or in mockery (Lk 23:36). It will be remembered that in the garden scene Jesus had emphatically announced his desire to fulfill his Father's will in terms of drinking. "Is it not inconceivable that I should not drink the cup the Father has given me?" (18:11). Earlier, when addressing his incomprehending disciples during the visit to Samaria, Jesus had stated his resolve to carry out the Father's will in terms of eating. "I have food to eat you do not suspect . . . My food is to do the will of Him Who sent me, and to carry through His work to its completion" (4:32, 34). Schnackenburg has an apt comment, "the bitter drink which Jesus takes is an image for the knowingly accepted pain of death."[6]

The inexplicable action of "fixing a sponge soaked with the wine on a piece of *hyssop*"—a tiny bushy plant used sometimes for sprinkling—is of no great consequence. It had been used to smear lintels and doorposts during the preparations for the exodus of the Hebrews from Egypt (Ex 12:22).

The very last utterance of Jesus is of paramount significance to John, as it was also to his colleagues. The great solemnity of these final words is not to be missed as "Jesus declared, 'It has been brought to perfect fulfillment!' " The passive indicates that the agency is that of the Father, to Whom the Johannine Jesus had twice prayed (see 12:27), "Glorify Your Son that the Son may glorify You" (17:1). By his completely voluntary act of "laying down his life for his friends" (15:13), Jesus has revealed the identity of his Father as the compassionate, loving source of the world's salvation. It had been his single task to make the Father visible, audible—above all, lovable, through his own human life and his mission. All this has now been accomplished by the divine action to which Jesus' last gesture gives full assent by "bowing his head." After all the indignities Jesus has endured at the hands of his enemies and a vacillating Roman judge, he takes his leave of this world with incomparable dignity.

"He handed over the Spirit." By this deliberately chosen expression the evangelist interprets the last breath of the dying Jesus as symbol for

6   Schnackenburg, *John*, III, 284.

his crowning gift to mankind. "The Spirit is the life-giver" (6:63), and Jesus had promised to "give his flesh for the life of the world" (6:51b). The evangelist himself has been seen to comment on Jesus' invitation to the believer to come to himself to slake his thirst for life (7:37-38), "He said this concerning the Spirit, Whom those believing in him were to receive: for the Spirit did not yet exist, since Jesus was not yet glorified" (v. 39). The moment of Jesus' death is in truth the moment of his "glorification"—his self-revelation, when he discloses his own identity as source of the Spirit, and so source of life. Accordingly, the paradox towards the unravelling of which John has been working since it was announced in the Prologue ("The Word became flesh") is now resolved. The very humanity of Jesus, exalted on the cross, has become source of life and salvation.

A final episode, which—like the drama involving Jesus, his mother, and his dearly loved disciple—is mentioned by no other Gospel-writer forms a solemn conclusion to the events on Golgotha—the piercing of Jesus' side by a soldier to ensure the reality of his death. The incident is explained as the result of a religious scruple by Jesus' Jewish enemies. Since he had been crucified on a Friday, a day devoted to various preparations dictated by Sabbath-observance, which would begin at sundown, and since in addition on that particular Sabbath, Passover, "a high holiday" occurred, the Jews won their request to Pilate to have the legs of all three crucified men smashed with clubs to hasten death and accelerate the burial of the corpses. The soldiers in charge of the crucifixion carry out their grisly task on the two men on either side of Jesus. However, discovering Jesus "had already died," one of their number plunged his lance into his heart in order to make certain of death, "and at once blood and water gushed forth." That this occurrence, no matter what explanation (medical or other) be advanced for it, is intended to be taken in a profound sense seems clear from the affidavit cited immediately from "the eyewitness," who is the beloved disciple. "Blood" in biblical usage signifies the life of any living being; "water," particularly "living water," that is, water that "gushes forth" has been used in this Gospel as a symbol of the Spirit, "the life-giver" (6:63). And in view especially of the statement by the Johannine Jesus, "As Scripture says, 'Rivers of living water will flow from his heart'" (7:38b), this phenomenon, obviously of consummate significance for the evangelist, emphasizes dramatically what was stated in the description of Jesus' death: once he is glorified in death, Jesus becomes the unique source of life and salvation for all who are given grace to believe.

The solemn corroboration of the testimony given to his community by "the eyewitness" acknowledges his unique authority because of what he personally experienced near the cross.[7] It is on his testimony that, after the gift of faith by God, those who belong to the beloved disciple "have come to believe." And to this affidavit two scriptural citations are appended—although it must be confessed that their significance here is not entirely clear.

The source of the first citation is debated, "No bone of his must be broken." It can be taken from the rubrics for the celebration of Passover by eating the paschal lamb (Ex 12:46c; or 12:10 LXX; or Num 9:12b). This would fit into the evangelist's presentation of Jesus as the new paschal lamb (19:14; 1:29, 35). It may be an echo of the prayer of the persecuted Israelite, who counts on divine help, where it is stated that God "watches over all his bones; not one of them shall be broken" (Ps 34:21). In this Gospel Jesus had been portrayed as both God's suffering and glorified Servant and as "the lamb of God."

The second Old Testament quotation comes from Zechariah, in a context reminiscent of the fourth Servant Song (Is 52:13–53:12). It seems to be a divine oracle promising conversion to God's People, who have been involved in the murdering of an unidentifiable holy man. "I will pour out on the house of David and on the inhabitants of Jerusalem a spirit of compassion and supplication; and they will look on him whom they have pierced, and will mourn for him as people mourn an only son, and will grieve over him as one grieves for a first-born" (Zech 12:10). The general tone of the passage suggests a promise of salvation rather than a judgment of condemnation, on condition of repentance for such a grievous wrong. The brevity of the evangelist's citation suggests that his attention has been caught by two elements, "look on" and be "pierced." That the second feature applies to the dead Jesus is clear from the incident John has just narrated. The one who "looked on" Jesus, "the eyewitness" to his death, is made prominent because of his reliable testimony. If one recalls certain earlier statements by the Johannine Jesus with reference to his death, the "looking on" assumes a deeper sense. The first prediction of his "lifting up' by Jesus had boldly made use of the serpent Moses had lifted up in the desert (3:14). As we had occasion

---

7   In the second half of v. 35, it is possible that the phrase "he knows" is a reference to Jesus or the Father or the Holy Spirit, each being designated as "that one" *(ekeinos)* by John fairly often, particularly in a context of salvation. For this usage to denote Jesus, see 1:18; 2:21; 3:28, 30; 4:25; 5:11; 19:21. It refers to God the Father at 1:33; 5:19, 37; 6:29; 8:42; and to the Holy Spirit at 14:26; 15:26; 16:8, 13, 14. See also 1 Jn 2:6; 3:3, 5, 7, 16; 4:17, which indicate Jesus.

to remark in our presentation of the First Week, this had been called by the author of the Wisdom of Solomon, "a sign of salvation . . . for he who turned towards it was saved—not by what he saw, but by You the Savior of all!" (Wis 16:5-7). And in beginning the present chapter, we had occasion to cite John's version of Jesus' third prediction of his Passion and exaltation, "Yet, as for myself, when I am lifted up from earth, I will draw all mankind to myself" (12:32). Through his contemplation of the Crucified, John has discovered the fascination he can exert for the eyes of faith.

3. The Dignified Burying of the King (19:38-42)

Perhaps no incident in the Passion-narratives displays such variations and discrepancies as the accounts of the burial of Jesus. This is an important observation, since it indicates the prominence of this final act of loving devotion in the ongoing reflection of the earliest believers. It will be remembered that the burial is enumerated among the four articles of faith in the most ancient creed that has come down to us (1 Cor 15:3-5). This not only points to the liturgical cultus paid to Jesus' tomb from the very early days of the Church (which ensures the historical authenticity of the site), but it also explains the inclusion in the creeds of the *descensus ad inferos*, the descent of the glorified Lord into the abode of the dead announcing his lordship "also of the dead as of the living" (Rom 14:9). Nor has St. Ignatius neglected this article of faith ([219]). In John's brief account of this important event, the intended ministration of the women (Mk 16:1) is ignored. He moreover introduces Nicodemus, a secret disciple who at last, like Joseph, makes a public declaration of his faith.

> 38 When all was over however Joseph from Arimathea—he was a disciple of Jesus, remaining incognito however for fear of the Jews—petitioned Pilate that he might take down the body of Jesus; so Pilate gave permission. So he came and took down his body. 39 Now Nicodemus—the man who came the first time to him at night—also came, bringing along a mixture of myrrh and aloes, about one hundred [Roman] pounds in weight. 40 Accordingly, they took Jesus' body and wrapped it with the spices in linen strips, according to Jewish burial-customs. 41 Now at the place where he had been crucified, there was a garden, and in the garden a new tomb, in which no one had been laid. 42 It was there consequently, on account of the Jewish preparation-day (since the tomb was close by), they laid Jesus.

Joseph, originally from the village of Arimathea but by this time a citizen of Jerusalem, is the principal figure in all four Gospel-accounts of the burial. Mark characterizes him as "an influential member of the Council," the Sanhedrin—like Nicodemus according to our Gospel (3:1; 7:50). In the Marcan story, he "actually was himself a man looking out for the Kingdom of God." Matthew describes him as "a rich man, who was also a disciple of Jesus" (Mt 27:57). In Luke he appears as "a member of the Council, and a humane and holy man—he was not party to their plot and stratagems. He was also looking out for the Kingdom of God" (Lk 23:50-51). In his turn, the author of the *Spiritual Exercises* includes a tale of Jesus' appearance to this attractive personage ([130])—taken, according to Pedro de Leturia,[8] from the *Flos Sanctorum* of the Cistercian Vagad. All the evangelists credit Joseph with successfully obtaining Pilate's assent to his demand to bury Jesus.

John's interest in Joseph and Nicodemus—both crypto-believers—is connected with his concern to make an appeal to those Jews, who despite true faith in Jesus were afraid to identify themselves as Christians towards the end of the century.

The contribution by Nicodemus—"a mixture of myrrh and aloes, about one hundred [Roman] pounds in weight"—is an impressive one, and consonant with his status in Jerusalem. By his cooperation with Joseph, Nicodemus finally justifies the title conferred on him by Jesus at their first meeting, "You are the teacher in Israel" (3:10)—he now is part of the true "Israel."

The two men, in the absence of women, "took Jesus' body and wrapped it with the spices in linen strips." The three Synoptics speak of "a linen shroud," which Joseph had bought according to Mark (Mk 15:46). John, who had described the corpse of Lazarus in a similar way (11:44), asserts—to the discomfiture of the partisans of the holy shroud of Turin—of "linen strips." Much more significant than this variant detail however is the remark that Jesus was buried "according to Jewish burial-customs." Where the Romans normally cremated, and Egyptians mummified a corpse, which involved the evisceration of the cadaver, the Jews simply entombed their dead after washing the body and surrounding it with spices. The body of Jesus, John seems to insist, must remain inviolate in view of the resurrection.

Only our evangelist mentions the proximity of "a garden." John alone explains the reason for choosing this pleasant place—"on account of the Jewish preparation-day (since the tomb was close by)". It may well be, by this repetition of the notice about "the *Jewish* preparation-day," that John implies that all was done by the two men who buried Jesus ac-

---

8   Pedro de Leturia, *Iñigo de Loyola*, p. 112.

cording to God's intended plan. For the Jews' demand for the barbarous method of hastening death by brutally smashing the legs of the crucified men had been motivated by this same prescription thought to be based in the divine will. Accordingly, despite the need for haste in carrying out the entombment of Jesus, all was done as God himself desired with dignity in accordance with the honor to be paid to him who had been declared by the Roman procurator—at the trial and through the multilingual "placard" on the cross—as the King.

John, who had begun his story of the Passion in "a garden" (18:1), brings it all to a serene conclusion "in a garden" (19:41). After the "labor" of his Passion ([206]) and of his earthly life ([116]), which Ignatius depicted also as a salient feature of the career of "the earthly king" ([93]), as also of the "life of the eternal King" ([95-96]), the King now enjoys repose. It was pointed out in the beginning of this chapter how the exercises of the Third Week, dominated throughout by ceaseless movement on the part of Jesus and unremitting "labor through all the points" ([195]) by the exercitant, terminate in a seventh day of quite unstructured contemplation of the whole Passion ([209]). The next occasion on which the term "labor" will appear will be in the Contemplation to Attain Love. There in the third point one is "to consider how God toils and labors for me" ([236])—in a quite different sense however, as the Latin phrase *"id est, habet se ad modum laborantis"* would seem to suggest.

Chapter 17

THE RISEN JESUS IN THE LIFE OF CHRISTIAN FAITH
(20:1-31)

In the *Spiritual Exercises* St. Ignatius is seen to present the events of the risen life as so many epiphanies. In the contemplations he proposes, he instructs the exercitant "to consider how the divinity, which appeared to hide itself during the Passion, now appears and manifests itself so miraculously in the most sacred resurrection through its genuine and most sacred effects" ([223]). A glance at the mysteries of the risen life shows that no less than thirteen post-resurrection appearances are set down as possible contemplations ([299-311]). Indeed, with his inveterate habit of harmonizing differing narratives, the saint has even managed to transform Mark's eerie story of the empty tomb (the grand finale of that Gospel) into "the second appearance" by mixing in the Johannine account of the appearance to Mary Magdalene ([300]).

As a fifth point in these contemplations, the exercitant is bid "consider his role of consoling which Christ our Lord displays, comparing it with the way certain friends habitually console others" ([224]). It seems clear that the saint has taken this facet of the risen Jesus from the writings of the Johannine school: from the Gospel, where Jesus implies that he is the original "Paraclete" (14:16); and also from the First Epistle, in which the exalted Christ has become "a Paraclete we have with the Father" (1 Jn 2:1). "Comforter" or "consoler" as well as "advocate" is the meaning sometimes given to "Paraclete." As has already been seen, Jesus acted the part of "consoler" in his parting instructions to his own at the Last Supper. In John's eyes, the Jesus who uttered the final discourse is already the risen Lord.

George MacRae remarks on the paradoxical nature of the popularity of the Fourth Gospel among present-day Christians. "Consider the portrayal of Jesus. At a time when the emphasis of piety and of theology is on the humanity of Jesus, the Gospel of John presents him as frankly divine and other-worldly."[1] Yet for all that, as we have often observed,

1   G. W. MacRae, *Faith in the Word,* p. 7.

271

the chief theme of this book is the truth that only through the human, earthly life of Jesus can the unseen God be seen and heard. And, for my part, I wish to suggest that the concern of our evangelist to resolve the paradox of his statement, "The Word became flesh," should alert the reader to the consoling fact that throughout this Gospel John has directed her or his attention to the growth in humanity by the One, who is always "God, an only Son." A moment's reflection on the series of "signs" which have been narrated will disclose an ever deepening emphasis upon the compassion of Jesus—from Cana I, where only at the plea of his mother does he relieve the embarrassment of an obscure bride and groom, through the raising of Lazarus, one can discern such an evolution in the attitude of Jesus. But it is even more evident in the farewell-address to his intimate disciples, where love within the community of faith is dwelt on, where "the disciple whom Jesus dearly loved" makes his first entry on the scene, and where the promise of a new "Advocate" or "Consoler" is announced.

In the first large section of this Gospel the reader learns that "God so loved the world as to give his only Son, in order that everyone believing in him may not perish, but may possess eternal life" (3:16). And Jesus will explain, "This is why the Father loves me: because I lay down my life, in order to take it up again" (10:17). The tender affection entertained by Jesus for the family in Bethany was dwelt on: in the sisters' note to Jesus with a discreet plea for help, "Master he whom you hold in affection is ill" (11:3); in John's comment, "Jesus loved Martha and her sister, and Lazarus" (v. 5); in Jesus' allusion to Lazarus, "our dear friend" (v. 11); in the Jews' remark, "How dearly he must have loved him!" (v. 36).

It is, however, in the second section of this Gospel that the evangelist dwells insistently on the theme of Jesus' love for his disciples: "Jesus—who had loved his own who were in the world—showed his love for them to the last" (13:1); it is "by reason of the fact I have loved you" (13:34) that Jesus issues his "new command" to give and accept offers of love in the community; "Now the one loving me will be loved by my Father, and I in turn will love him, and I will manifest myself to him" (14:21); "If any one loves me, he will keep my word, and my Father will love him, and we will come to him and take up our abode with him" (14:23). And Jesus brings his long prayer to his Father to its climax and conclusion with the words, "I have made known to them Your name, and I will make it known, that the love with which You have loved me may exist in them, even as I exist in them" (17:26).

We may better appreciate John's interest in showing how Jesus becomes progressively more human, if we recall how inextricably intermeshed he regards the Incarnation and the Passion and glorification of Jesus to be. "Incarnation" (a theological, not scriptural term) denotes the central truth of Christian faith by prescinding from the human development of the Son of God. For John, that humanness attains perfection in the risen Lord.[2]

The Mystery of the Resurrection

If as we have been implying throughout this study, one is to read John's Gospel as a dialogue between himself and his reader, *not* so much as a biography of Jesus as an autobiography of the evangelist, not as history but as good news, we shall gain new insights into the mystery of Jesus' raising by God to a new, unprecedented existence—"a life lived unto God" (Rom 6:10).

Dr. Krister Stendahl, distinguished New Testament professor of Harvard Divinity School, once remarked to me that the most striking feature of our Gospels is the astonishing lack of nostalgia for 'the good old days' of Jesus' earthly life, which their authors display. They nowhere give any grounds for the suspicion that they wish their readers to return to the earthly life of Jesus as to a vanished golden age. But then, one may well ask, why did Mark, who was originator of this unique *Gattung* we call a "Gospel," choose to wrap his "good news of victory" by the ever-contemporary Christ, now exalted in power at God's right hand, in the winding-sheet of Jesus' past and mortal life. For Mark, as has been already remarked, gives no account of the appearance of the risen Lord to his friends. And even Mark's colleagues, the later evangelists, who do include these beautiful stories of the disciples' confrontations by the risen One, devote but a tiny part of their Gospels to the risen life. Why, if these writers wished to make their presentation of the Christian mystery relevant to the concerns and problems of their communities, did they not write letters in the creative manner of Paul? Why not, as did the seer of Patmos, compose a message of consolation from the stuff of their own profound experiences of the dynamic presence to history of the risen Lord? The answer to such questions is a simple one, though its meaning is elusive, except to Christian faith: the resurrection of Jesus. If one is to grasp what one can of this central mystery, it is imperative to put oneself

---

2   D. M. Stanley, *The Call to Discipleship: The Spiritual Exercises with the Gospel of St. Mark*, pp. 176-177.

to school to Paul and to our Gospel-writers.

In the first place, it is striking that none of these authors make any attempt to portray the event itself. It is in fact not to be imagined (as later apocryphal Gospels would do) simplistically as the resuscitation of a corpse. That type of occurrence does find a place in the Gospel-stories: Jesus' raising to life of the little daughter of Jairus (Mk 5:35-42), of the only son of a widow in the village of Naim (Lk 7:1-17), of Lazarus of Bethany even after his corpse had begun to decay (Jn 11:8-44). It is crucial to realize that these remarkable acts of divine power enabled such privileged beneficiaries to return to this present, mortal existence. These people, however, did not escape the inevitable necessity imposed on all human beings of facing death a second time.

As for Jesus, "raised from death through the glory of the Father" (Rom 6:4), he has *not* come back to this life with its restricted freedom ("the flesh is useless," 6:63). Paul has made that unmistakably clear, "You know that Christ raised from death can no longer die: death has no more power over him. The death he died was a death once for all to sin: the life he now leads is one lived unto God" (Rom 6:9-10). That is why Paul agrees with the early credal statement already cited, which had declared Jesus to have been "constituted Son of God in Power" (Rom 1:4). For the astounding truth is that the risen Jesus is more dynamically present to each of his own and to the community of faith than ever he was "in the days of his flesh."

In the second place, the unanimous testimony of Paul and our evangelists insists that this mighty event was in truth a *bodily* resurrection. Paul leaves his Corinthians in no doubt concerning this quintessential truth by his remark, quoted earlier in connection with the Johannine parable of the grain of wheat (12:24). "Now someone will ask, 'How do dead men rise? with what sort of body will they come back?'—You fool! what you sow does not come to life except it die. Yet, as for what you sow, you do not sow the body that will evolve, but a naked seed, say, of wheat or of some other grains. It is God Who gives it a body as He decided—indeed to each seed its own body" (1 Cor 15:35-38).

This same conviction is to be seen to operate in the stories of Jesus' post-resurrection meetings with his own. It will be recalled that what the Church preserved in her memory, which is tradition, was originally a simple *list* of these appearances (1 Cor 15:5-7). In the course of time certain anonymous Christians appear to have developed *stories* from such an itemized series. This is now evident from the half-evolved narratives of some of the post-resurrection occurrences to be found in the canonical ending of the Marcan Gospel. Today there is a gradually growing consensus among scholars that Mark 16:9-20 is actually earlier than any of the Gospels, and thus represents a precious development in the pre-Gospel tradition. The passage was once thought to be an abridged version of Easter-stories in Luke and John added to the seemingly unsatisfactory ending of Mark's Gospel. Nowadays, scholars take the view that this canonical ending to Mark is older than our Gospels. They have come to see that the accounts by Matthew, Luke, and John of how the risen One appeared to his friends were created by these writers in order to express certain significant features of the resurrection. A prayerful examination of these lovely stories will disclose that each of the three evangelists put them together in the light of his personal image of Jesus and with a view to the particular needs of his own community.

It is helpful to be aware how conscious each of these writers is of certain dangers in describing Jesus' appearance after his resurrection. On the one hand, they are concerned to inculcate the reality of the bodily presence of the risen Lord. Luke even pictures him as eating with the disciples from Emmaus (Lk 24:30-35) and in Jerusalem before "The Eleven and those with them" (v. 33, 41-43). Moreover he draws attention to the fact he is not a "ghost" (v. 39). In the first recognition-scene John recounts, which we shall shortly discuss in detail, Mary of Magdala has to be ordered to "Stop touching me!" (20:17), while in the second scene the ten disciples recognize "the Lord" from the wounds in hands and side (v. 20), and the compassionate Jesus invites Thomas to overcome his doubts by exploring his pierced side with his hand (v. 27).

On the other hand, however, the evangelists manifestly wish to avoid giving the impression that the risen One has simply returned to his former manner of life. This may well be one reason why Mark refused to provide any stories of these momentous meetings. Those other evangelists, who do depict them, draw attention to the significant fact that the old familiarity with Jesus during the public ministry by his disciples has now disappeared. They are, in these scenes, prey to doubts and fears. "They doubt for joy, and they are filled with wonder," says Luke by way of extenuation (Lk 24:41). "Some doubted," remarks Matthew in describing the happy reunion in Galilee (Mt 28:17b). In the epilogue to John's Gospel, the disciples at the sight of Jesus by the lake remain silent in embarrassment, too inhibited to ask "Who are you?" (21:12). By contrast, the risen Lord is presented as the one totally liberated human being. No Gospel-writer attempts to explain how the risen One came to the disciples, or how he took leave of them. The use of the Greek verb employed in the early list of appearances, taken over from the Septuagintal account of theophanies in the Old Testament, should consequently be rendered, "He allowed himself to be seen." The untrammeled freedom of the exalted Jesus is a most significant feature of these scenes after his resurrection. In fact, it also vindicates the truth of the terse statement of St. Thomas Aquinas, "After his resurrection the disciples saw the living Christ, whom they knew to have died, with the eyes of faith."[3] The saintly theologian does not here call in question the bodily presence of Jesus on these occasions. He merely points out that it is not sufficient to have one's eyes open to see the glorified Lord. And in fact, as Jesus will be seen to warn Mary of Magdala, any desire merely to return to the dead past is a barrier to the insight of Christian faith. One can see the truth of Aquinas' remark in the failure of the two disciples to recognize the Lord on the road to Emmaus (Lk 24:16), and in Mary's mistaking Jesus for "the gardener" (20:14-15). These devoted followers are described as being yet without the gift of Christian faith, shortly to be communicated to them by the bodily presence of Jesus, through which he will communicate the Holy Spirit.

In the third place and finally, the great good news announced in the gospel of the earliest Church is that the glorified Son of God has chosen to remain human forever. This conviction is voiced in the ancient creed, "Jesus is Lord!" The name "Jesus" is a designation for "the historical Jesus," while "Lord" is the customary post-resurrection title. Thus is affirmed the continuity between his earthly existence and his new status as "Christ of faith." Paul repeatedly evinces his belief that the Lord who now speaks is one with the Jesus who spoke, as can be seen by his references to the words of the earthly Jesus preserved in the traditions as "a saying of the Lord" (1 Thes 4:2, 15; 1 Cor 7:10; 9:14; Rom 14:14). And we have already noted how Luke and John present the risen One (so also the seer of Patmos, Apoc 5:1-6) as conserving in his body the marks of his Passion. Indeed, it is the contemporary reality of the Passion which enables the doubting disciples to recognize their now transformed Master.

Thus it becomes clear that Jesus, now "raised by the glory of the Father" to an unprecedented existence, has carried all his human experiences into his new life with God. He has indeed taken into glory his very "historicity." Not only has Jesus become a "new creation" in the bodily, material aspect of his personality. This transformation has actually imparted a perennial contemporaneity to all those human experiences

---

3 *Summa Theologiae,* III, q. 55, a. 2, ad 1.

that went into what is called the life of Jesus on earth. Now one can better appreciate why our evangelists have devoted by far the greater proportion of their books to that earthly life. They have come to realize that these accounts of what Jesus said and did can become so many avenues of approach to that personal relationship to our Lord which is of the essence of faith. For otherwise in his present state he so transcends all our human resources of mind and heart, as to make such a relationship impossible. It is because we believe that the kind of Lord he now is has to a degree been specified by those human, earthly experiences, it has become possible for us to enter into communion with him by means of the contemplation of that "genuine history" found in the Gospels.

1. The Empty Tomb (20:1-10)

1 On the first day of the week, Mary of Magdala arrives at the tomb very early in the morning while it is still dark, and she notices that the stone has been removed from the entry to the tomb. 2 So she runs off and comes to Simon Peter and the other disciple, whom Jesus dearly loved, to tell them, "They took the Master out of the tomb, and we don't know where they put him!" 3 Accordingly, Peter and that other disciple went off and made for the tomb. 4 But while they both started running side by side, the other disciple outran Peter, and he arrived first at the tomb. 5 Then stooping down he observed the linen strips lying there, but he did not enter. 6 Now Simon Peter also arrived in his wake. He entered the tomb, and took note moreover of the linen strips where they were lying, 7 and of the cloth which had covered his head, not lying with the strips of linen, but in another spot, rolled up by itself. 8 Whereupon the other disciple—the one who had reached the tomb first—entered in turn, and took a look, and began to believe. 9 As yet of course they did not know of the scriptural passage telling that it was God's will he should rise from death. 10 Then the disciples went back home again.

As the exercitant enters the Fourth Week of the Exercises he or she is allowed unprecedented freedom, somewhat out of character for the author, who otherwise displays concern for meticulous detail. He suggests that "it is more suitable to have four exercises, not five" ([227]). Indeed, the saint is vague (not to say confusing) with his reference ([226]) to "repetitions" which he proceeds to eliminate ([227]) in the sequel. He does clearly presuppose that each day three contemplations on different appearances of the risen Christ are to be made. Having set out five "points" ([222-225; see 226]), he later remarks that "the person who is contemplating can take fewer or more points as he finds better" ([228]). Ignatius is obviously concerned that the retreatant not permit himself to become bogged down in details that might inhibit freedom. Hence the remark that I "avail myself of light, pleasant temperature—for instance, coolness in spring, in winter, the sun or a fire, to the extent a person thinks or surmises these can be of aid to rejoicing in his creator and redeemer" ([229]).

The single contemplation presented in detail for the Fourth Week is the risen Jesus' appearance to his mother ([218-225]); and the Saint feels it necessary to make an apology for this, "Although this is not mentioned in Scripture, it is as good as stated by the remark that he appeared to so many others." This may well be a reference to the "upwards of five hundred brothers" (and sisters) in the early credal formula cited by Paul (1 Cor 15:6). Ignatius defends this selection of a non-scriptural experience of the risen One—"since Scripture presumes we have intelligence, as it is written, 'Are you people also without understanding?' " ([299]). Presumably this is an allusion to Mark 7:18, or to Matthew 15:16.

Some years ago the interesting suggestion was made that the Lucan story of the raising to life of "an only son *(monogenēs)* of his mother" (Lk 7:11-17) was originally an account in the tradition of Jesus' appearance after the resurrection to his own mother. Subsequently the extraordinary occurrence was judged to have been retrojected back into the public ministry. The hypothesis was supported by Luke's use (for the first time) of the resurrection-title, "the Lord" (v. 13) for the earthly Jesus, and by the way the story is told chiefly in terms of the interaction between "the Lord" and the bereaved mother, who "was a widow" (v. 12). Jesus is described as "being moved to compassion for her" and saying "Stop weeping!" (v. 13). His command to the dead son employs (v. 14) the resurrection-word "be raised up" (by God). The young man is of secondary interest in the account, which simply states, "the corpse sat up and began to speak" (v. 15), without disclosing what he said. It must be admitted however that while the interpretation is ingenious, it is highly implausible.

John begins his account of the visits to the empty tomb by a reference to "the first day of the week," and not, as in Luke, to "the third day" (Lk 24:7, 21, 46), although our evangelist appears to have known the significance of "the third day" (2:1) for the resurrection. The change suggests the importance in Christian worship of what had for some years become known as "the Lord's day" (Apoc 1:10) on which "the Lord's supper" was celebrated (1 Cor 11:20). Earlier in John's account of the public life, certain major events were associated with the Jewish liturgical feasts. With the resurrection of Jesus a new order has been introduced.

"Mary of Magdala" first appeared in this Gospel when she took her place at Jesus' cross with his mother, the other Mary, and the beloved disciple (19:25). In the Lucan Gospel she was mentioned as one of those wealthy women, who out of gratitude to Jesus for deliverance from evil spirits or disease had provided for him and his disciples "out of their own means" (Lk 8:1-3). Mary is there described as a woman out of whom "seven demons" had been driven by Jesus—a remark all too frequently misconstrued as the result of her personal sinfulness. Since the time of Pope Gregory the great, she has suffered further damage by being confused with Mary of Bethany and some public sinner (unnamed in Luke) in a town in Galilee (Lk 7:36-50). The present narrative, in which Mary forms the link between the first two scenes of the risen life, should serve to "rehabilitate" a faithful disciple, whom the risen Lord will honor by making her (in a happy phrase of St. Bernard) *apostola apostolorum*, a woman entrusted with announcing to his "brothers" the joyous news of Easter.

John pictures Mary as making for the tomb unaccompanied "while it is still dark,"—a symbol of the desolation felt at the loss of Jesus. Upon discovering "that the stone has been removed from the entry to the tomb," and without inspecting it, Mary "runs off" to bring the terrible news to "Simon Peter and the other disciple, whom Jesus dearly loved, 'They took the Master out of the tomb, and we don't know where they put him!' " The "we" is a relic from the tradition, in which three women had visited the empty tomb (Mk 16:1). Mary will repeat the remark to the angels later, "I don't know where . . . ," which thus becomes a significant motif in both scenes involving Mary. It reflects the evangelist's concern (to which reference has been made before) that his reader ask the crucial question, "Where is the risen Jesus now for me?"

The two disciples "made for the tomb" at once, and Peter is outrun by his companion, who however awaits Peter's arrival to permit him to be first to enter the empty tomb. He had time however to "stoop down and observe the linen strips lying there." Inside the tomb, Peter could observe not only the position of "the linen strips;" he also discovered that "the cloth which had covered his head" was "rolled up by itself" some distance away. What all this evidence meant to Peter we are not told by John, who does not record the puzzled attitude of Peter indicated by Luke. "Peter got up, ran to the tomb, and stooping down he observes the linen strips by themselves; and he went off home wondering at what had happened" (Lk 24:12). In the Johannine story, it seems to be implied that Peter's inspection was sufficient to show the error in Mary's deduction that someone had taken away the body.

John's remark that "the other disciple," once inside the tomb, observed enough that "he began to believe," remains a conundrum, to which no contemporary scholar has produced an entirely satisfactory solution. Whatever be made of the comment immediately following that these disciples were ignorant of "any scriptural passage telling that it was God's will that he should rise from death," the concluding remark that the two simply "went back home again" would seem to hint that from their silence at their discovery they had as yet no inkling of the glorious truth of Easter. Possibly, apart from his obvious interest in the beloved disciple, John wished to make Mary first to receive Christian faith from the risen Lord and the herald to the other disciples of the resurrection. It is quite possible that the evangelist wished to underscore the mystery surrounding Jesus' resurrection. The questions concerning it raised in Paul's day (1 Cor 15:35) and in Mark's community (Mk 9:10) remain always with the Church.

2. The Risen Jesus Reveals His Identity to Mary (20:11-18)

One receives the distinct impression, on reading the various stories of post-resurrection meetings between Jesus and his followers, that it was to women—despite the fact that they did not qualify in the eyes of the early Church as official witnesses—that the risen Lord first appeared. The canonical ending of Mark's Gospel, which as has been observed antedated any of our Gospels, states, "Rising early the first day of the week he appeared first of all to Mary of Magdala" (Mk 16:9). It is interesting to recall that Luke, despite his manifest interest in women, omits any appearance to them by Jesus. Because of his overarching theme regarding "the original eyewitnesses" (Lk 1:2)—all of them men—he can be seen to have altered notably (especially in his Passion-narrative) certain data preserved in the evangelical traditions. It is then strikingly significant that the fourth evangelist, in the story we are about to consider, depicts Mary of Magdala as the first person to be favored by the glorified Jesus, who gives her Christian faith and assigns her a special role in announcing the Easter tidings to the men who followed him. John's surprising departure from the official attitude towards women may well be explained by their special status in the community of the beloved disciple.

11   As for Mary, she took her stand just outside the tomb and was weeping. Now as she wept she stooped down to peer into the tomb.   12   And she sees two angels in shining apparel sitting where Jesus' body once lay, one where his head, the other where his feet [had been].   13   Those two ask

her, "Woman, why do you weep?" She answers, "They took my Master away, and I don't know where they put him." 14 On saying this, she turned round the other way, and sees Jesus standing there. (She did not know however that it was Jesus.) 15 Jesus asks her, "Woman, why do you weep? Whom are you looking for?" She in turn, supposing him to be the gardener, says to him, "Sir, if it was you who carried him away, tell me where you put him, and I will myself take him." 16 Jesus calls her by name, "Mary!" She turns round to greet him in Aramaic, "Rabbouni!" (which translates as Teacher). 17 Jesus tells her, "Stop touching me! I have not yet ascended to the Father. Off with you to my brothers, and tell them, 'I am ascending to my Father and your Father, to my God and your God.' " 18 Mary of Magdala goes off to announce to the disciples, "I have seen the Lord!" and what it was he told her.

After the departure of the two disciples, Mary remains at the tomb without entering, inconsolable at the disappearance of the body of the dead Master. For some unexplained reason, "as she wept she stooped down to peer into the tomb." She expresses no emotion at the sight of the "two angels"—an indication that their intervention (probably contained in the tradition John made use of) is of little importance. The pair of heavenly visitors offer Mary no consolation, but simply wish to satisfy their own curiosity, "Woman, why do you weep?" After answering their unfeeling query, Mary rightly (one feels) ignores them by turning her back to them.

It is however Mary's response that is of great interest to the evangelist (and the reason he includes this inconsequential episode from tradition). Mary repeats the statement she had made to the two disciples, "They took my Master away, and I don't know where they put him." It is this thematic assertion which the evangelist wishes to keep before his reader: it is Mary's (as yet) deficient faith which keeps her ignorant of where the now risen Jesus is. Accordingly, it is probably best to translate the term *Kyrios,* the normal designation of the risen Lord, as "Master." In fact, the evangelist underlines this absence of genuine faith in Mary, who now turns to "see Jesus standing there." "She did not know . . . it was Jesus." In fact, she mistakes him for "the gardener" in charge of this lovely place.

However, if faith is as yet lacking in Mary, her love for her dead Master is made clear by her disclosed determination to take on the impossible task of carrying the corpse away unaided. She says to the unrecognized Jesus, "Sir, if it was you who carried him away, tell me where you put him, and I will myself take him!" Her ingenuous manifestation of such deep affection shows her readiness to accept the gift of new faith in the risen One, which Jesus bestows at once by simply calling her by her own name, "Mary!" It will be recalled how our evangelist, especially in the opening chapters of this Gospel, repeatedly insisted on the word of Jesus as the unique basis for Christian faith. At the sound of her name, Mary now recognizes Jesus in the person standing before her, and (it may be presumed) at once throws herself at his feet, embracing him with loving adoration like the women in Matthew's Easter-story (Mt 28:9b).

Jesus however issues a warning to her, "Stop touching me!" It is, in John's intention, actually an admonition to his reader not to cling to the dear, dead past—even that of Jesus' earthly life. Real faith is to be based upon a relationship with the risen Lord. In the story, Jesus is represented as having a further reason for telling Mary to stop clinging to his feet. She is now entrusted with the privileged duty of bearing the gospel-message of Easter to "my brothers." This affectionate designation of his disciples takes on a deeper sense when it is recalled that, just before dying, Jesus had told his mother to accept "the disciple he loved" as son in place of himself (19:26). In virtue of this final action as testator, Jesus had, in the person of this disciple, accepted all his faithful followers as brothers and sisters. Rudolf Schnackenburg suggests that when Jesus here calls the disciples "my brothers," this is the result of the evangelist's reflection. "Then (so the evangelist reflects) he also wants to place them in a new and special relationship to his Father . . . This corresponds to Jesus' promises to his disciples at the time of his leave-taking."[4]

This observation has the merit of throwing considerable light on the two puzzling references to his ascension by the Johannine Jesus. "I have not yet ascended to the Father" and "I am ascending to my Father and your Father, to my God and your God." The first mention of the ascension in this Gospel occurred in the first summary of the kerygma of the Johannine community, where it is a kind of definition of "the Son of Man" in the distinctly Johannine sense. "No one has ascended into heaven except the One who descended from heaven—the Son of Man" (3:13). In this Gospel Jesus becomes "the Son of Man" through his "lifting up on the cross"—the initial step in his return home to the Father, from whence he sends the Spirit to his own. A second reference to the ascension was seen in the context of the disenchantment of some of the disciples as a result of Jesus' promise of the Eucharist. He countered their objections with the remark, "Does this cause you to lose faith? Then what if you behold the Son of Man mounting to where he formerly

---

4 Schnackenburg, *John,* III, 320.

existed?" (6:61-62). John is well aware that the Eucharist, as the Easter-sacrament is "the food that abides unto eternal life, which the Son of Man *will give* you" (6:27b). It is, as we have frequently had occasion to note, through his "hour" that Jesus evolves, so to say, into "the Son of Man," and while the "hour" can be seen to consist of various events leading to salvation, still "the hour" often ceases to have any relation to past, present, or future. When one bears this in mind, it becomes clear that the "not yet" in "I have not yet ascended to the Father" cannot be meant in any temporal sense; and the same is true of the "I am ascending" in the fuller explanation which follows.

What then is the thrust of these statements? They announce the fulfilling by Jesus of the promise he had made to his own at the Last Supper, where he had employed "journey" and "house" (as we saw) somewhat as parables to picture that permanent "abiding" with himself and the Father. "In my Father's house abodes are plentiful. Were it not so, should I have told you that I am making a journey to ready a place for you? Now when I have made the journey and readied a place for you, I shall come again to receive you into my company, that you too may be where I am myself" (14:2-3). Father Schnackenburg points back to this prophecy as "the main reason why the evangelist added to his source those two interpretive sayings about Jesus' 'ascent' . . . with that, the Easter event is brought into the theological line of the gospel and, on the other side, the announcements of the farewell discourse find their Easter confirmation and realization."[5]

3. The Reunion of the Risen Lord with His Desolate Disciples (20:19-23)

The last story ended with the grand climax of Mary's mission to the disciples with the joyous disclosure, "I have seen the Lord!", to which John adds how she faithfully relayed to these men Jesus' revelation of a great promise now fulfilled. As the new scene opens however one receives the distinct impression that Mary's "gospel" had had little or no effect upon the grieving disciples. It may be that John here takes into account the tradition Luke and the anonymous author of the Marcan canonical ending had put in writing. The latter, who had asserted that Mary was first to experience the joyous reunion with the Lord, also reported Mary's failure to convince the sceptical men. "That woman went and reported the news to his grieving, tearful companions. Yet they, for their part, on hearing he was alive and had been seen by her, refused to

---

5   Ibid., 319.

believe'' (Mk 16:10-11). Luke states this even more colorfully as a report by the disciples from Emmaus. "And moreover certain women of our company caused us excitement: visiting the tomb very early in the morning and failing to find his body, they came back with the news they had even seen a vision of angels, who claim he is alive. Now some men from our group went off to the tomb and discovered things just as the women had also reported, but himself they did not see" (Lk 24:22-24). The first evangelist, Mark, had terminated his whole book with this disappointing discovery, while including a formulation of the Easter proclamation by the ancient Church (which he put in the mouth of the angel), "You seek Jesus the Nazarene, the One who has been crucified. He has been raised!" (Mk 16:1-8). Only Matthew of the Synoptic writers inserted into the story of the empty tomb the encounter by the women with the risen Jesus (Mt 24:8-10). Such remarkable divergences among the four presentations lead to the conclusion that in composing their narratives of the risen life our evangelists are guided by theological, rather than by historical considerations. In this respect, these stories are similar to the Infancy episodes which Matthew and Luke have employed as prologues to their Gospels. There as here the sacred writers are influenced by their distinctive image of Jesus and by their concern for the needs of their own communities.

> 19   Now early in the evening on that first day of the week, with the doors to the place where the disciples took refuge locked for fear of the Jews, Jesus came and stood before them. And he greets them, "Peace to you!"   20 On saying this, he showed them his hands and his side; and so the disciples rejoiced at seeing the Lord.   21   Then he again said to them, "Peace to you! By virtue of the fact that the Father sent me, so I in turn am sending you."   22   While saying this, he breathed upon them, and he tells them, "Receive a Holy Spirit.   23   If you remit anyone's sins, they are remitted for them: if you retain anyone's sins, they stand retained."

This dramatic confrontation of his disciples by the risen Jesus is as noteworthy for what it does *not* say as for what it does. John does not state (nor even imply) that the glorified Lord came through the locked doors; and I venture to suggest that the assumption by certain theologians that in his risen state Jesus was endowed with *agilitas,* the capability of passing through solid walls, is based on a false inference. Such a conclusion contradicts the conviction of the sacred writers that Jesus' body, though transformed so as to be recognizable only with the eyes of faith, had been assumed into glory. In contemplating these beautiful scenes the exercitant should be conscious that our evangelists are bravely attempting to convey in human words what is in fact ineffable.

Accordingly, after renewing his prayer for "peace," which he used in blessing the disciples at his departure from them at the Last Supper (14:27; see 16:33), John represents Jesus as permitting his disciples to inspect "his hands and his side"—which still bear the marks of crucifixion. It is through these ineradicable signs of his Passion that the risen One is now recognized: "and so the disciples rejoiced at seeing the Lord." Another inspired writer of the Johannine school, the seer of Patmos, had earlier set forth this important truth when presenting his vision of the court of heaven in the book of Revelation. Through his tears of frustration at his failure to find one "worthy to open the scroll and read it," this visionary beholds "immediately before the throne [of God], in the center of the four living creatures and the ancients, One standing like a lamb with the marks of his slaying still upon him" (Apoc 5:1-6). It is the exalted Jesus, risen to become Lord of history. For these writers, as also for Luke as we have seen in our reflections on the mystery of the resurrection (Lk 24:39), the unity of the paschal mystery is a truth of incomparable depth. In the glorified Lord the Passion remains a living reality, as do also those human experiences which formed part of his "life in the flesh." It will be recalled that the Johannine Jesus had declared to his followers that he is the unique "way" to God, even in his mortal existence (14:6b). Accordingly, "The one who has seen me has seen the Father" (14:9), since "I am in the Father and the Father is in me" (14:11).

It is this intuition of the continuity which obtains between the earthly and the risen life of Jesus which endows the Christian "remembering" with its efficacy in the eyes of our evangelist. In fact, it makes "remembering" imperative for Christian prayer, which is nothing but "keeping Jesus in mind"—as he himself enjoined through the words of Eucharistic institution. We have observed how well aware of this unbroken continuity St. Ignatius shows himself in the *Spiritual Exercises* ([116, 206]). Indeed, we have earlier observed his insistence that for an effective Election discernment must be practiced "while continuing to contemplate his [Jesus'] life" ([135]). Like the fourth evangelist before him, the Saint is convinced of the perennial reality of "the mysteries of the life of our Lord." Christian contemplation is then no mere exercise of pious imagination: it is the quintessential means of relating in faith to "the crucified Majesty of God."

And here one may raise a problem in prayer often deeply felt by the contemporary believer. "Can one pray to Jesus *now*, as he *was* during his mortal life in this world?" Specifically, is it realistic to pray to the agonizing Jesus depicted so poignantly in the garden of Gethsemane? Is one guilty of sentimentality in attempting to pray to the infant Jesus? If there is any validity in what has been said previously about the mystery of the resurrection, that is, our Lord would not be Lord of history in the way he actually is, were it not for the human experiences of his earthly life, then it is not only possible or useful, but in fact necessary to pray to the risen One through these mysteries of his earthly existence, which transfigured by his glorification are very much part of his dynamic presence to the life of the Church and to the life of each Christian. The words of the Lucan Jesus to his doubting followers on the first Easter evening are addressed to each believer who desires to learn how to pray: "Why are you so deeply disturbed? Why do objections arise in your hearts? Look at my hands and my feet—it is I myself!" (Lk 24:38-39).

In John's version of this post-resurrection meeting, Jesus now moves to the commissioning of these disciples, "By virtue of the fact that the Father sent me, so I in turn am sending you." The mission of these "apostles" is to be a continuation of the mission of the earthly Jesus himself. His challenge to "the world" when he flung down the gauntlet to the Jews by declaring "The Father and I are one" (10:30) is to be kept alive through the undivided fellowship he desires preserved in the community of faith. The Jesus of the Fourth Gospel has been seen never to lose hope for the conversion of the world. This was the burden of his great prayer before the Passion: "that all of them may be one, inasmuch as You, Father, are in me and I am in You, that they in turn may be one in us, so that the world may believe You have sent me" (17:21).

John, through an allusion to the second creation-account in Genesis, pictures the risen Lord communicating the "Holy Spirit" to his disciples by "breathing upon them." The priestly editor has made use of the Yahwist account of the creation of the human race. "The Lord God created Adam [human kind] out of the clay of the ground and He breathed into his nostrils the breath of life; and so the Man became a living being" (Gen 2:7). The evangelist has selected the same Greek verb found in the Septuagint version of the passage. Thus he presents the enablement of the ten disciples present on this occasion as a "new creation" by the glorified Lord.

"Receive a Holy Spirit. If you remit anyone's sins, they are remitted for them; if you retain anyone's sins, they stand retained."

Each of the Gospel-writers reports the commission given to the disciples in his own fashion. In the several accounts of this all-important action by the exalted Jesus each author interprets it with a view to the particular problem or concern besetting his own community. Matthew deals in his Gospel with a divided community, one still debating the validity or irrelevance of the Mosaic Law for Christians and so he pictures Jesus, on whom "All authority in heaven and on earth" has been conferred by God, as defining the missionary mandate by three significant features. His followers are (1) "to make disciples of *all* nations," (2) through Christian baptism in the name of the Trinity, and (3) by "teaching them to observe everything I enjoined upon you" (Mt 28:18-20). Matthew had insisted by means of the Sermon on the Mount that the Christian code to be observed in his community was "the Law and the prophets" as "brought to fulfillment" through the teaching and the life of Jesus (Mt 5:17). The Lucan Jesus is seen to have conferred their apostolic mandate on the "apostles" by appointing them "witnesses" to his entire life through "my Father's promised gift" of "power from above" (Lk 24:48-49). Thus it was that "the eyewitnesses from the beginning" actually "became servants of the word" (Lk 1:2), the Christian proclamation.

In the scene we are considering from the Fourth Gospel, two special features are noteworthy: (1) the gift of the Spirit by the risen One is specified as a power to be used for the forgiveness of sins; and (2) this mission of reconciliation is entrusted to ten disciples (in Thomas' absence) as representatives of the future Church.

To underscore the completeness of this authority over sin, the evangelist employs forensic terminology in his characteristic manner through what is known as a "totality conception" typical of semitic language. Aramaic and Hebrew are notoriously concrete languages (by contrast, for instance, with Greek): thus any abstract notion such as universality can be expressed only by means of antithetic expressions. Matthew chose to employ the rabbinic expressions "bind—loose" (Mt 16:19; 18:18) to present the new power over sin given to the community, as well as to Peter. Consequently, it would be a misunderstanding of this peculiarly semitic idiomatic usage to think of "binding sins" as a function distinct from remitting them.

Our reading of the Fourth Gospel has by this time clearly indicated that unity, communion, abiding, mutual love in act and by word is a prominent theme in John's conception of Christian life. Accordingly the function of reconciliation is in his view an essential characteristic of his community's role in the world. "Here is how everyone will know you are my disciples: if you preserve love one for another" (14:35). It is not accidental then that John, in order to draw his reader's attention to this all-important feature of the community's life, has represented the Lord as twice blessing his disciples with the wish for peace.

Finally, when it is recalled that in this Gospel the disciples (who are never called apostles) represent the new community of faith, which springs to life from the bestowal by Jesus of the Paraclete, one begins to see that the universal power to forgive sins is not committed simply to the ten disciples, who happen to be together when Jesus visits them on the first Easter evening. In the closing scene with Thomas nothing is said to imply that this authority over sin had to be imparted to him.

A further reason for concluding that the power to forgive sins is given to the Church as a whole is perceptible from the "sending" by the risen Lord to continue Jesus' mission to the world. As Schnackenburg comments on verse 21, "any restriction to the disciples who are present is not apparent and scarcely intended; John nowhere calls them 'apostles' in the specific sense. They represent for him the entire community of believers."[6] The same scholar's observations on the conferral of the power to forgive sins is consistent with that view just quoted. "It was thought in the Johannine community that forgiveness of sins was mediated (through baptism, confession of sins, supplication, intercession, cf. on 1 Jn 1:9), it happens through the blood of Jesus (1 Jn 1:7) in the bosom of the Church. The authoritative saying of the risen One which the evangelist found is for him the fundamental and axiomatic promise, that forgiveness of sins occurs and will continue to occur within the Church. A limitation of the authority to the disciples present or to later office-holders, is far from the evangelist's mind; as up till now the disciples represent the Church, and in 1 Jn office-holders are not mentioned in connection with ecclesiastical practice."[7]

When at the Council of Trent appeal was made to the final verse of this narrative (v. 23) in order to show that Christ instituted the sacrament of Penance or Reconciliation, the intention was to exclude the Reformers' view that it meant only authority to proclaim the Gospel. Trent did not imply that it was giving the first or the only sense of the passage. Our evangelist teaches that the chief work of the Church, empowered by the Spirit, is a work of reconciling. This would seem therefore to include a bestowal of new power on any gesture of forgiveness that any member extends towards another. Such a view in no way contravenes the prerogative of the later Church, by whose authority the ministerial priesthood would be deputed to confer the sacrament of Reconciliation, which, as a

6   Ibid., 324.
7   Ibid., 327.

matter of history, evolved only gradually in the life of the Church. A helpful parallel may be suggested with the charism of infallibility, bestowed by Christ on his Church. The Pope under certain carefully defined conditions may personally exercise this power, but so also, in her degree, does any mother who teaches her child the Our Father.

4. With Jesus' Confrontation of Thomas John Ends His Gospel (20:24-31)

There is universal agreement amongst Gospel-critics that what is now the twenty-first chapter of John is an epilogue appended by later editors for reasons that are not entirely clear. As will be seen shortly, our evangelist selected his closing scene with great care with a view to coping with certain concerns of believers, who had never seen or known Jesus personally during his life in this world, by representing the risen Lord as bestowing a special beatitude on them. In this way, the inspired writer prepares future readers for what we termed, in the initial chapter of this book, his "startling pledge," so similar to that made by Ignatius of Loyola in his *Spiritual Exercises*.

> 24 However, Thomas, one of the Twelve (his name means Twin) was not in their company when Jesus came. 25 Accordingly, the other disciples kept telling him, "We have seen the Lord!" But he informed them, "Unless I can see the marks from the nails in his hands, and can thrust my hand into his side, I refuse to believe!" 26 Then eight days later his disciples were once again at home, with Thomas in their company. Jesus came, though the doors were locked, stood before them, and said "Peace to you!" 27 He then bids Thomas, "Put your finger here and examine my hands: reach out your hand, and thrust it into my side, and stop being incredulous—become believing!" 28 In response Thomas declares to him, "My Lord and my God!" 29 Jesus tells him, "You have come to believe because you have seen me. Happy those who become believers without ever seeing!"
>
> 30 Actually, Jesus performed many other signs in the presence of his disciples, which are not set down in this book. 31 These however have been recorded in order that you may believe that Jesus is the Messiah, the Son of God, and that by believing you may possess life in his name.

The reader is familiar with Thomas, a faithful if incomprehending follower, inclined to expect the worst—as when Jesus decides to return from Transjordanian Bethany to that other Bethany where Lazarus had dwelt with his sisters (11:16). He is one of those "practical" people, who points out to Jesus at the Last Supper that he can hardly expect his followers to know "the way" when they are ignorant of his destination

(14:5). Such features of the man's character prepare the reader for what now occurs. John offers no explanation for Thomas' absence from the circle of disciples "on the first day of the week," and is in consequence able to introduce this appearance-story that is without parallel in the other Gospels. Our evangelist is also the only Gospel-writer to point out the Greek meaning of the Aramaic name; in all lists of the Twelve this disciple is simply called Thomas.

Thomas reacts to the joyous Easter message, "We have seen the Lord!" (see v. 18; Lk 24:34), by insisting upon "seeing." One is reminded of the desire on the part of certain "Greeks" which they expressed to Philip, "Sir, we wish to see Jesus"(12:21). By highlighting "seeing" in this story, John is preparing for the closing reference by Jesus to those who subsequently will find faith without seeing Jesus whether during his mortal life or through any post-resurrection meeting.

The incredulity of Thomas is dramatized by the evangelist: the disciple demands not only to see, but to touch, depicted in an almost brutal way. It comes then as a surprise to the reader that when Jesus once again joins his disciples and orders Thomas to verify such harshly voiced conditions for becoming a believer, Thomas is *never* said to *touch* Jesus! John has consistently, if tacitly, criticized as defective any faith based merely on "seeing the signs Jesus performed" (2:23; 3:2; 4:48; 6:2; 11:47). Mary of Magdala had been reprehended by the risen Lord for continuing to touch him. As was observed in the opening chapter of this book, it is only those sense-experiences "remembered" with the help of the Paraclete (14:25-26) that John deems of any consequence to Christian living. That such are of great value can be seen by the Johannine writer of 1 John in his description of his own personal reception of the evangelical traditions (1 Jn 1:1-4) in sensory terms. In his turn St. Ignatius' directions for the Application of the Senses as the climax of each day of contemplation in the Second and Third Weeks are proof of his high regard for the use of the "spiritual senses" in the exercitant's advance towards the prayer of union.

As a consequence then of the word of Jesus (and not by seeing or touching) spoken to Thomas, "Stop being incredulous—become believing," that disciple makes his fervent act of faith.

"My Lord and my God!" forms the climax in a series of such confessions in the Fourth Gospel (1:49; 4:42; 6:68-69; 11:27). The risen Jesus himself had employed the expression "My God" in the message to the disciples entrusted to Mary (v. 17). Paul had effectively, if rarely, used this very personal, tender phrase in the thanksgiving of two of his most intimate letters (Phil 1:3; Phlmn 4), in what amounts to a prayer (Phil 4:19), and in a deeply emotional passage addressed to Corinth. "(I fear) that when I come again my God may humiliate me" (2 Cor 12:21). This usage ("my God") is striking in view of Paul's reticence about his religious feelings towards God the Father.

Thomas then makes his final commitment to the risen Jesus by confessing himself to be servant to "My Lord" with a devout and dedicated faith in "My God." And for his part, Jesus accepts this loving dedication by affirming the completeness of Thomas' declared belief, "You have come to believe because you have seen me." Schnackenburg's suggestion that this be read as a statement, not a query, has been accepted in my own version.[8]

Our evangelist now terminates this encounter by having Jesus pronounce a beatitude—rare in this Gospel (13:17)—on successive generations of believers. "Happy those who become believers without ever seeing!" John by this striking conclusion manifests his great concern for those who never knew the earthly Jesus, which was seen as the burden of the discourse at the Last Supper. I drew attention at the beginning of this chapter to St. Ignatius' concern to present the contemplations of the Fourth Week as so many epiphanies, and also to his wish to have the exercitant contemplate a proportionately large number of these accounts of the risen life. I venture to suggest that this is another of the Ignatian ways of remedying the exercitant's lack of personal experience in these formative encounters with the risen Jesus.

John is the only evangelist to add a formal, literary conclusion to his book. Mark gave his Gospel a title (Mk 1:1); Luke prefixed an elegant periodic sentence as introduction to his Gospel (Lk 1:1-4). Our evangelist's manner of ending his work gives rise to a number of questions. "Actually, Jesus performed many other signs in the presence of his disciples, which are not set down in this book." The seemingly belated remark about "signs," which were apparently recounted only in the first half of the Gospel, appearing as it does immediately after the stories of the risen life, would indicate that these important experiences by the disciples are to be included under the rubric of the Johannine "sign." Schnackenburg has now adopted this view in the last volume of his commentary: he has come to realize that, by deepening the meaning of "sign" through the inclusion of the post-resurrection appearances in this category, John draws

---

8   Ibid., 334 for the persuasive reasons given for the view.

attention to the "revelatory quality" he assigns to it.[9] This brings the exercises of the Fourth Week with their epiphany-character into close relationship with the final scenes in the Fourth Gospel.

"These, however, have been recorded in order that you may believe that Jesus is the Messiah, the Son of God, and that by believing you may possess life in his name." Two features of this statement of purpose may be noted: (1) it seems more probable that our evangelist did not write primarily to bring nonbelievers to faith in Jesus. The aorist tense of the Greek verb, believe, is to be understood of those who already believe; and so John's intention is rather to deepen that faith "in his name," that is, in his person. For Jesus in the course of this Gospel has been disclosed as the answer to the messianic expectations voiced by Israel's prophets, but in a transcendent sense—he is to be accepted by the genuine believer as "the Son of God." And here the exercitant cannot fail to be struck by that "startling pledge" by the evangelist—so similar to the claim made by St. Ignatius for the making of the *Spiritual Exercises*—that through reading his book the man or woman of faith will be helped to grow into a richer relationship with Jesus, so that "by believing you may possess life in his name."

---

9   Ibid., 337; see also I, 515 and 520, where a different interpretation of "sign" was put forward, which excluded the post-resurrection appearances.

Chapter 18

"IF YOU REALLY LOVED ME, YOU WOULD REJOICE . . ."
(14:28b)

At the conclusion of the Fourth Week, one finds a kind of epilogue to the entire course of the Spiritual Exercises designated Contemplación para alcanzar Amor. The verb *alcanzar* has a twofold meaning—to "obtain" (as a grace through prayer) and to "attain" love (by transcending one's self-concern and self-interest). Accordingly this exercise functions as a profound deepening of one's awareness, intended to transform our relationship with God, with the whole creation, and with ourselves. Thus it is a crown for the Exercises by leading the exercitant to embark on an exodus that is at once the heart of the gospel-message (Mk 8:34) and the final step towards maturity as a human being. Michael Buckley observes that "Love cannot be forced. It emerges spontaneously from consciousness. An elevation of consciousness gives way naturally to a heightening of love. One has only to realize what God is doing to love him, and this recognition itself constitutes a new power within a man. . . . Love is not forced; it is evoked. A man is drawn to God."[1] Thus by the title he gives this contemplation the saint seems to suggest that by "obtaining" a deeper awareness of the manifold ways God has in Christ demonstrated His love for oneself, the exercitant will be led at the conclusion of the Exercises to make a deeply personal response of love to "God our Lord" ([232, 234])—the risen Jesus now become Lord of the universe.

It may be noted further that by categorizing this exercise as a contemplation, St. Ignatius contributes to the development of the traditional way of prayer for attaining communion with God, which we have seen set out in medieval times by Guigo II, once prior-general of the Carthusians.[2] That time-honored method however took its rise from the "divine reading" *(lectio divina)* of the Book of Scripture: the author of the *Exer-*

---

1 M. J. Buckley, S.J., "The Contemplation to Attain Love," *The Way: Supplement* no. 24 (1975), 96.
2 For the English version of Guigo's "Letter on the Interior Life," see *The Way* 5 (1965), 333-444.

cises directs the retreatant to "consider" the "book" of the entire cosmos and its testimony to the never-ending love of its "creator and Lord," thereby orientating Christian contemplation to the apostolic life. Ignacio Iparraguirre perceptively notes that, "the Contemplation for Love is a bridge linking the Exercises with the reality of one's everyday life."[3] Accordingly, just as the Principle and Foundation ([23]) was a "presupposition" to the entering into the Spiritual Exercises comparable to the Prologue of the Fourth Gospel, so this final contemplation assists the exercitant to channel all the newly acquired energies which have graced the retreat into a dynamic living of the gospel.

It is then of some moment to take cognizance of the unusual arrangement under four points instead of the customary three. Thereby this exercise is meant to be seen as a recapitulation of the four weeks of the Exercises. As a result, because from the colloquy of the very first meditation ([53]) to the end of the contemplations on the appearance of the risen Lord the exercitant has been confronted with the person of Jesus in his mysteries, it is helpful to consider a remark by Hugo Rahner regarding this final exercise. "The actual text (just like that of the Foundation) would seem not to refer to Christ at all, and its wording has at least a touch of scholasticism about it. But . . . every word must be interpreted exclusively in terms of the christology of the *Exercises* as a whole. In full accordance with Ignatian theology, the 'creator and Lord' of this contemplation is Christ, the incarnate Word, who in virtue both of what he is and of what he does, dwells in all creatures and 'behaves as one who works' ([236]) . . . The creator and Lord, to love of whom the grateful soul is inflamed, is the 'crucified majesty of God.' To find all creatures in God is to find all creation in Christ."[4] With due respect however to the celebrated Ignatian *Fachmann,* while agreeing that Christ is intended by Ignatius in the first three points, I should incline to the view of William Peters that in the fourth point one is given the impression "that in Ignatius' vision, the risen life of Christ merges into that of the Blessed Trinity."[5] My own reason for this is the appearance of the Johannine term "from above" *(anōthen)* in place of "God our Lord," which strikes Father Peters as "almost . . . a pagan phrase in the mouth of Ignatius."[6] He seems to have forgotten that *de arriba* (from above) is characteristic of Ignatian mysticism.

3   I. Iparraguirre, S.J., "Introduction to the Spiritual Exercises," *Woodstock Letters* 84 (1955), 257.
4   H. Rahner, *Ignatius the Theologian*, pp. 134-135.
5   W. Peters, *The Spiritual Exercises of St. Ignatius*, p. 157.
6   Ibid., p. 166.

Presentation of Divine Love in the Exercises

After reviewing the places in the *Spiritual Exercises* where divine love is explicitly mentioned, Ignacio Iparraguirre remarks, "As can be seen, St. Ignatius very rarely employs the expression . . . This is a consequence of his strongly realistic attitude. He prefers to put before the exercitant *the manner in which God keeps loving him,* rather than to use general terms."[7] As has been seen earlier, divine love is not mentioned in the Principle and Foundation ([23]). Ignatius, who does refer to it in the astonishing assumption of Annotation 15 ("It is more appropriate . . . that the creator and Lord give himself to the open-hearted exercitant, inflame him with his love and praise"), mentions "the love of the eternal Lord" but once in the First Week ([65]) (see however the *tanta piedad y misericordia* [71]). Surprisingly, the text for the Second Week has also only one instance: "that love which motivates me and leads me to elect a specific thing must descend from above *(de arriba)* from God's love" ([184]). Nor is divine love explicitly named in the comments on the Third or the Fourth Weeks, apart from the description (in the supplementary contemplations) of "the most holy sacrifice of the Eucharist as the greatest proof of his love" ([289]).

Ignatian Pedagogy for Response to Divine Love

Father Iparraguirre remarks that it is "The style of divine love which determines the exercitant's response. His or her love forms part of the divine love."[8] This is clear from the second manner of making a good Election in the text partly cited above where it is stated that the love motivating the exercitant "must descend from above, from God's love, so that the one making the Election must first feel within himself or herself that the love, which he experiences to a greater or less degree for what he elects, is uniquely for his creator and Lord" ([184]). It is accordingly in the Rules of Discernment which guide the Election that St. Ignatius speaks of the arousing of love in the exercitant. He finds "consolation," when the soul elicits a certain interior movement by which it comes to be inflamed with love for its creator and Lord, and as a consequence can love no created thing on the face of the earth for itself, but only in the creator of them all" ([316]). Desolation, the antithesis of consolation, is simply being "without love" and "separated from its creator and Lord"

---

7 I. Iparraguirre, S.J., *Vocabulario de Ejercicios Espirituales: Ensayo de Hermenéutica Ignaciana,* 2d ed. (Rome, 1978), S.V. "Amor," pp. 11-27. I wish to acknowledge my indebtedness to the great Basque specialist for what is said in this section.
8 Ibid., p. 13.

([317]), "since the Lord has withdrawn his great fervor, increasing love, and intense grace" ([320]). The supreme example of consolation is that which comes "without any previous cause, since it is the exclusive role of the creator to enter, leave, cause a movement in the soul by drawing it in its entirety to love for his divine Majesty" ([330]). Iparraguirre asserts that "This vision of the continuous action of God constitutes, as in the Bible, the basis of the pedagogy of the Exercises,"[9]—a truth we shall verify now in our review of the Johannine texts which illustrate the four points of this Ignatian contemplation.

First Point: "If you only knew God's gift . . ." (4:10)

"The first point is to bring to my mind the benefits received of creation, redemption, and personal gifts; and to ponder with great love how much God our Lord has done for me, and how much he has given me of what he has, and further, how much the same Lord desires to give himself to me, so far as he can, in accordance with his divine design. And then I will reflect upon myself, by bringing to mind what, in all reason and justice, I ought, on my part, to offer and give to his divine Majesty: namely, all that I have, and myself as well, like one who makes a gift with all his heart" ([234]).

From our reflections with the help of certain passages from the Gospel of John, we have been led to see the very positive function "the consideration and contemplation of sins" (Annotation 4) is designed to play in achieving the proposed results of the First Week. The immediate confrontation of the exercitant with the risen Christ as "crucified Majesty of God" led to consolation, gratitude, love for him who has turned my "sin-history" into a "graced history" by never leaving me "by myself" ([58]). Indeed, it is presumed I shall reach the point where I am almost compelled to utter "a cry of wonder" ([60]) at the realization that the entire cosmos has "preserved me in life" under the direction of the glorified Lord of history, who "has until now always treated me with such loving kindness and compassion" ([71]). The obvious conclusion from all this is the consoling truth that all is gift in Christ, himself the Father's supernal gift to the world. Michael Buckley sums up the fruit of the First Week by saying, "Even God and the man are gifts: God, longing to give himself; the man, able to give all that he possesses and himself along with this. The sweep is universal: God and man moving through all things towards each other."[10]

9   Ibid.
10   M. J. Buckley, "The Contemplation to Attain Love," 101.

A cursory review of the Fourth Gospel suffices to provide the impression that John's God is an endlessly giving God, that the Johannine Jesus, "God's gift" (4:10) to the world He so much loved (3:16), moves through his "hour" to become the glorified "Son of Man," the giver of the Spirit (19:30) Who in turn is "the life-giver" (6:63).

Already in Israel's history God revealed Himself as the donor of "the Law as a gift through Moses" (1:17). John however situates God's revelation of Himself as Father in the new dispensation first of all through the many gifts He has given to Jesus as "the Son." His community has been seen to proclaim how "the Father loves the Son and has given all into his power" (3:35), and the evangelist begins his account of Jesus' symbolic-prophetic action at the Last Supper by drawing attention to Jesus' awareness "that the Father had given all into his power" (13:3). The kerygma of the community had in fact dwelt particularly on two of God's gifts to the Son as significant of His love. "The Father dearly loves the Son and shows him everything He Himself is doing. . . . He has given all judgment to the Son" (5:20-22). "He has given him authority to pass judgment, because he is Son of Man" (v. 27). In the context, the Son's role as judge is meant to point to him as "the Savior of the world" (4:42). The other great gift to the Son by the Father indicates his function as the source of life. "As the Father possesses life of Himself so also He has given the Son to possess life in himself" (v. 26). The Johannine Jesus returns to this salient feature of himself in explaining the meaning of the mysterious "food that abides unto eternal life, which the Son of Man will give you" (6:27). "As the living Father sent me and I have life because of the Father, so the one feeding on me will in his turn have life because of me" (6:57).

John presents Jesus throughout his Gospel as tirelessly acknowledging that the determining factors of his life in this world are all gifts from his Father. "The One Who sent me as Father has Himself given me a command as to what I am to say and how I am to say it" (12:49). In his great prayer to the Father, Jesus gratefully enumerates these many gifts, "the human beings You have given me out of the world: they were Yours and You have given them to me. Now they know that all You have given me is from You" (17:6-7). It is the Father, Who "gave me the utterances I have given them" (v. 8). Jesus asks that "You guard them with the name You have given me, that they may be one even as we are" (v. 11). He prays for all disciples, present and future, that "they may behold the glory You have given me" (v. 24). In view of this constant, grateful insistence on the Father's many gifts to himself, it seems plausible to render the much debated verse in Jesus' speech to the Jews at *Hanukkah* as follows. "What the Father has given me is greatest of all!" (10:29a).

If the dominant trait in John's image of God is certainly that of the divine Giver, it is not surprising that gift-giving also features prominently in the evangelist's image of Jesus. In the poetic presentation of him in the Prologue, Jesus appears as the preexistent Word of God, the perfect expression of the Father. When he comes "to his own realm" to "his own folk," he "gave to such as did accept him the power to become children of God" (1:11-12). And indeed John depicts the story of Jesus' life as a series of unremitting acts of giving: abundant wine at a wedding, "living water" to a woman of Samaria, life to a child dying in Capharnaum, rehabilitation to a cripple, sight to a man born blind. John alone of the evangelists represents Jesus as himself giving out the food to a hungry Galilean crowd. "Jesus then took the loaves and, on giving thanks, distributed them *(diedōken)* to the people as they sat there. He did the same with the dried fish—as much as they wanted" (6:11). As the Good Shepherd Jesus asserts, "My sheep hear my voice, and I for my part know them, and they follow me. And I give them eternal life" (10:22-23). Within the circle of his intimate disciples at the Last Supper, he announces, "A new command I am giving you" (13:34). "I give you peace" (14:27). In his great prayer to the Father, Jesus states "I have given them Your word" (17:14); "I have given them the glory You have given me" (v. 22).

As a kind of preamble to his Contemplation to Attain Love, St. Ignatius sets down two observations about the nature of genuine love. "The first thing to be kept in mind is that love should express itself rather through actions than words" ([230]). The Johannine Jesus on two occasions points to the integrity that exists between his words and what he does. Firstly, to his adversaries, who take umbrage at his challenging claim, "The Father and I are one" (10:30), making the charge, "You blaspheme!"—because I said, "I am the Son of God"—the Johannine Jesus retorts, "If I am not doing my Father's works, do not believe me; but if I am doing them, even though you do not believe me, believe the works" (10:36-37). To his friends at the Last Supper he urgently insists, "Believe me! I am in the Father and the Father is in me. If not, then believe on account of the very works!" (14:11). Later in the course of these final instructions, Jesus endeavors to impress upon his disciples the imperative necessity of this same integrity he himself has displayed: "If you do love me, you will keep my commands" (14:15). Here, as we have already seen, Jesus is attempting to teach his own the secret of discipleship—a manner of life lived out in fidelity and love for him. He reiterates this in words that might have inspired the first Ignatian animadversion about love ([230]), "If any one loves me, he will keep my word" (14:23a). To demonstrate the importance of this teaching, Jesus repeats his promise that the Father will send the Paraclete: "He will teach you everything and make you remember all I have told you" (14:26).

In his second note, St. Ignatius asserts "that love consists in a mutual interchange between the two parties" ([231]). We have seen the Johannine Jesus in Samaria offer to share with his incomprehending followers what for him is his very "food." "My food is to do the will of the One Who sent me, and to carry through His work to its completion" (4:34). He then adds, "To this extent the proverb is correct, 'One sows—another reaps,' that it is I who sent you to reap where you have done no work. Others have done the hard work, while you have come in for the yield from their work" (4:37-38). We saw Jesus magnanimously associate his disciples with his mission of mercy in restoring sight to a blind man. "For our part, *we* must perform the works of Him Who sent me, while day lasts. Night is coming when no man can work" (9:4).

At the Last Supper, John draws the reader's attention to the foot-washing as a symbol of Jesus' saving death by having Jesus threaten Peter (unaware as he is of the meaning of the Master's offer of love), "If I cannot wash you, you cannot share anything with me!" (13:8b). In the supplementary discourse appended by a later editor, Jesus tells his own, "No longer do I address you as slaves, for the slave does not know what his master does. *You* I have called dear friends, because I have made known to you everything I heard from my Father" (15:15). In his final prayer, Jesus concludes by saying, "And I have made Your name known to them, and I shall make it known, in order that the love with which You have loved me may be in them, and I too may be in them" (17:26).

Second Point: *"I Am the Way. . . . No One Can Come to the Father except through Me" (14:6)*

"The second, to look at how God is dwelling in his creatures: in the elements, giving them existence, in plants by making them grow, in animals through sensation, in men by giving them intelligence; and he dwells in me by giving me being, life, sensation and intelligence—moreover, by making a temple of me, since I am created in the image and likeness of his divine Majesty. And again, in the way indicated in the first point or in some other that I feel to be better, I am to reflect upon myself." As José Calveras points out, St. Ignatius is intent upon directing the retreatant to become present to our Lord, to recognize one's dependence on him, to give thanks, to increase reverence for the self as made in the divine image, and to deepen apostolic zeal.[11] Michael Buckley comments: "The advance over the previous point is obvious: God not only gives, but he lives within his gift . . . Things are not only gifts, they are holy: for they contain God."[12]

It is clear from certain entries of St. Ignatius' Journal—those few pages that survived destruction at his hand—that a dominant feature of his mystical experiences was to regard the incarnate and glorified Christ as *the* point of entry into union with the Trinity. For the second day of Lent 1544, 28 February, a note reads, "Entering the chapel, fresh devotion, and as I knelt a revelation or vision of Jesus at the feet of the most holy Trinity . . ."[13] And for Sunday, 9 March of the same year, one finds the interesting observation: "Entering the chapel, greater feelings and tears, all terminating in the most holy Trinity, sometimes in Jesus, sometimes in all three Persons together, or nearly so, in such a way that the termination in Jesus did not lessen the devotion to the most holy Trinity nor contrariwise . . ."[14]

We have frequently drawn attention to the Johannine motif running through the Fourth Gospel, which I have termed "the poverty of the Son." This profound insight by John into the mystery of Jesus, the Word become flesh, discloses a mysticism similar to that just noted in Ignatius of Loyola, centered as it is in the insight that the revelation of the unseen God must come in the flesh of Jesus who has nothing he can call his own. "Amen, amen I tell you: the Son can do nothing by himself except what he sees the Father doing" (5:19); "I can do nothing by myself!" (5:30). "I have come down out of heaven, not to do my own will, but the will of the One Who sent me" (6:38). "My teaching is not mine, but His Who sent me. If a person chooses to do His will, he will know if the teaching is from God, or whether I am speaking on my own" (7:17). To the disciples at the Last Supper, Jesus declares, "The utterances I make to you I do not speak by myself: rather, the Father abiding in me is doing His works" (14:10b). The announcement by the (risen) Jesus which terminates the first great section of this Gospel reiterates the theme: "The person seeing me is seeing the One Who sent me" (12:45). "I have not spoken on my own. Rather the One Who sent me, the Father Himself,

11   José Calveras, S.J., *Ejercicios espirituales y Directorio,* pp. 156-157.
12   M. J. Buckley, "The Contemplation to Attain Love," 101-102.
13   William J. Young, S.J., *The Spiritual Journal of St. Ignatius Loyola: February, 1544-1545* (Woodstock, 1958), p. 20.
14   Ibid., p. 31.

300

has given me a command as to what I am to say and how I am to say it" (v. 49). The Johannine Jesus does nothing, says nothing, *is* nothing without the Father who acts, speaks, through him, exists in him. John's final comment in his Prologue discloses the similarity of his viewpoint to that of St. Ignatius. "No one has ever seen God. God an only Son, who [now] reposes on the Father's heart—*he* it is who revealed Him!" (1:18).

One might, without exaggeration, say that throughout the contemplations of the Second, Third, and Fourth Weeks the author of the *Spiritual Exercises* is guiding the retreatant to the great vision he will unveil in the fourth point of the present Contemplation to Attain Love, "to see how all good things and gifts come down from above" *(de arriba)* ([237]). Our evangelist in his narrative of the public life presents Jesus as "the One who descended from heaven—the Son of Man" (3:13). As has been noted, the Johannine Son of Man, through the trajectory of his descent into human history and his return home to the Father, is delineated as the link between God's world and our own. "Amen, amen I tell you all: you will see an opening in the sky, and the angels of God ascending and descending upon the Son of Man!" (1:51). The allusion here to the dream of the patriarch Jacob (Gen 28:10-22) indicates that in the evangelist's eyes "Jesus as the Son of Man has become the locus of divine glory"—a quote from Raymond Brown already referred to.[15]

Now it will be recalled from what was said about the sense of "sign" in Johannine usage, that the evangelist's choice of this term discloses his Christological interest in the actions of the Jesus of the public ministry. This "sign" terminology directs the believing reader by means of the concrete historical happening to contemplate the mystery of Jesus himself. These actions of Jesus are meant as a significant phase in the revelation of his own self-identity, so that he can reveal the unseen, unheard God, since "You have neither ever heard His voice, nor have you seen His form" (5:37b). John ends his account of Cana I by saying, "This was the first of his signs that Jesus performed at Cana in Galilee: he manifested his glory, and his disciples believed in him" (2:11). It will be remembered that "glory" in the Bible is a term for the divine manifestation of God's presence in power. It will also be recalled that in this Gospel only Jesus performs "signs" (see 10:41).

St. Ignatius' purpose in the second point of this contemplation we are considering is to heighten our awareness that Christ, "God our Lord," by his new, dynamic presence to creation and to history, presents

15   See chapter 4, n. 17.

himself to our love and faith as "the lover, giving and communicating with the beloved what he has or can give" ([231]). John the evangelist, as has been noted, in the conclusion of his Gospel has broadened the sense of "sign" to include also his narratives of the post-resurrection appearances. This deliberate deepening of meaning enables our Gospel-writer to assert that *what he has written* has become an effective means to such increase in faith that "You may possess life in his name" (20:31). This surprising conviction that the risen Jesus may actually be found by means of such "divine reading" reveals John's conviction—an even bolder one than that of Ignatius: that the person of faith can, by means of his book, become present to the contemporary reality with which Jesus' resurrection has imbued his words and actions once uttered and performed "in the days of his flesh."

Third Point: "My Father Is Working Even until Now, and I for My Part Am Still at Work!" (5:17)

"The third, is to consider how God works and labors for me in all created things upon the face of the earth—that is, conducts himself as one who labors *(habet se ad modum laborantis)*—as in the heavens, elements, plants, fruits, flocks and herds, and so forth, by giving existence, preserving it, giving growth and sensation, and so forth. In consequence, to reflect upon myself" ([236]).

Michael Buckley regards this third point as "critically Ignatian," and he comments, "Much metaphysical doctrine and religious teaching has found things as gifts of God, while religious and even mystical experience emphasizes his dwelling in all things. Either of these first two points can be documented from widely divergent traditions and even contradictory philosophies. But that God works, that he labors in all things, that he struggles when the galaxies move, that the rush of all life is indicative of his sacred toil, that all things are caught up in the redemptive workings of God: this is not so common a tradition . . . It is critically Ignatian because it stands as the foundation for discernment . . . This attempt to read, to interpret and to understand things as caught up in his labors and directions, bears upon any contemplative apostolic life."[16]

In the Consideration *Del Rey* (On the King), work or labor is prominent in the program announced by "Christ our Lord, the eternal King," who invites "the whole world" in these words. "Whoever consequently desires to come with me must labor with me, in order that by following

16   M. J. Buckley, 'The Contemplation to Attain Love," 102.

me in suffering he or she may also follow me in glory" ([95]). Indeed, so central is "labor" to the image of the Ignatian Christ that this characteristic appears in the idyll of the dream-king, "elected by direct designation of God our Lord, to whom all Christian princes and all Christian warriors render reverence and obedience" ([92]). "It is my design to conquer the entire territory of the infidel. Consequently the one who desires to come with me is to be content . . . to labor with me by day, and keep watch at night, and so forth, that afterwards he may share the victory with me as he shared in the hard work" ([93]).

Throughout the contemplations of the Second and Third Weeks attention is constantly drawn to the "labor" of Jesus. Even from their eternity "the three divine Persons" are pictured as "laboring over *(obrando)* the most holy Incarnation" ([108]). In contemplating the Nativity, one is "to look at and consider what they (our Lady, Joseph, and the servant girl) are doing, that is, the kind of journey and labor they carry out in order that the Lord may be born in the utmost poverty, and after such labors—hunger, thirst, heat, cold, insults and obloquy—die on a cross; and all this for me" ([116]). Ignatius reminds the exercitant how closely "labor" was associated with the earthly life of Jesus in the changes to be made in the sixth Addition during the Third Week "not trying to elicit joyful thoughts, but on the contrary rousing myself to sorrow and grief and affliction by the frequent recollection of the labors, weariness and sorrows of Christ our Lord, which he endured from the moment he was born to the mystery of the Passion in which at present I find myself" ([206]). Even after death, while his body reposes in the tomb, Jesus' "blessed soul . . . descended into the realms of death, whence he took out the souls of the just" ([219]). The Ignatian Christ, "God our Lord," thus illustrates throughout his life and death the necessary truth "that love should express itself rather through actions than words" ([230]).

The Johannine Jesus labors through his life after the manner of his Father (5:17)—Who is seen to be at work in the life of "the person who lives the truth" (3:21). John describes Jesus after the trek from Jerusalem to Samaria as "thoroughly tired out from his journey" (4:6b). Note was taken of his remark to the disciples before giving sight to the man blind from birth, "For our part, we must perform the works of Him Who sent me, while day lasts. Night is coming when no one can work" (9:4). Indeed, we have come in the course of our contemplations on the Fourth Gospel to realize how characteristic it is of the Johannine Jesus to describe his mission from his Father as "to carry through His work to its completion" (4:34). It is in all probability this joint labor which John refers to as "hard work" (4:38b).

In this Gospel Jesus appeals to his "works" as the authentication of his mission from God (5:36; 10:38). His claim that they are done "in the name of my Father" (10:25b) demonstrates that the Father is at work in him (14:10b). While the "signs" are insufficient without the word of Jesus as the basis of genuine faith, still his "works"—like those of the God of Israel—are an imperative summons to believe. They are also the diagnostic disclosing the sin of unbelief. "If I had not done the works among them which no one else did, they would not have sin: now however they have both seen and have hated me as well as my Father" (15:24). One might rightly say that for our evangelist, nothing reveals Jesus to be the Word of God, the perfect expression of the Father, quite so effectively as the works he carries out. They testify to the truth of his challenge to the Jews, "The Father and I are one!" (10:30). And it is no accident that John pictures Jesus at the moment of his death as solemnly declaring of his work in this world, "It has been brought to perfect fulfilment!" (19:30a).

Fourth Point: "Were it Not Given You from Above" (19:11a)
In this final point of the Contemplation to Attain Love,' as was remarked at the beginning of this chapter, the exercitant is led by the glorified Christ into communion with the tri-personal God Himself. It is here that the Saint's conviction, quoted earlier ("the termination in Jesus did not lessen the devotion to the most holy Trinity"), is manifestly operative. "The fourth, to look at how all good things and gifts come down from above *(de arriba)*, as for instance, my limited power from the supreme and infinite power from above *(de arriba)* so too justice, goodness, filial love, mercy, and so on—even as its rays descend from the sun, a cascade of water from the fountain, and so on. Then to end by reflecting upon myself, as has been said" ([237]).

Michael Buckley remarks, "This last point reached beyond my personal life, to recognize how things speak of him who has given them, who dwells in them, who works in them for the liberation of men. It reaches to a love of God responsive not simply to what he has done, but to what he is in himself. This does not oppose the previous considerations; it completes them."[17]

Throughout the contemplations of the Fourth Week, St. Ignatius, as we have seen, was almost uniquely concerned with "how the divinity . . . appears and manifests itself so miraculously in the most sacred resurrec-

17   Ibid., 104.

tion through its genuine and most sacred effects" ([223]). In this final point he selects certain of the most significant "effects"—"my power, justice, goodness, filial love, mercy"—for the purpose of assisting the retreatant to acquire that "sense of family" *(familiaritas cum Deo)*—the deep awareness of communion through the risen Jesus with the Trinity. It is to be noted that whereas in the first three points the contemplation ranged over the entire universe and every one of its "inhabitants"— mineral, vegetable, animal, rational—here one's gaze is directed upon those gifts which only I (apart from God) can be aware of. It is solely in the depths of my own graced self-awareness that I can effectively realize "how all good things and gifts come from above." It is uniquely in "the heart," the truest part of the self, that one can meet God, Who in Ignatian theology is so frequently indicated by the term, "above."

A little reflection on the Fourth Gospel will reveal how characteristic of its author's thought is this notion of "above" and "from above." First, however, to increase our sense of the harmony between the thought of John and Ignatius, it is helpful to recall that the two symbols used in the *Spiritual Exercises* to illustrate the reality "from above," light from the sun and water flowing from a fountain, are given a prominent place in John's image of Jesus. These are moreover set in relation with each other against the background of the ancient feast of *Sukkōth.*

"On the last, great day of the feast Jesus took his stand and cried out, 'If anyone thirsts, he must come to me. Then let him drink—the one believing in me. As Scripture says, "Rivers of living water will flow from his heart." ' (He said this concerning the Spirit, Whom those believing in him were to receive: for the Spirit did not yet exist, since Jesus was not yet glorified)" (7:37-39). To the woman of Samaria Jesus had disclosed his identity as the source of "living water." "If you only knew God's gift, and who it is who asks you, 'Give me a drink,' you for your part would have asked him, and he would have given you living water" (4:10). The water which "gushed forth" from Jesus' side as the soldier "plunged his lance" into it (as we have seen) is probably also an allusion to this "living water" (see 19:34).

As the liturgy for rain (adopted from an earlier Canaanite rainmaking ritual) on the seventh day of *Sukkōth* was a significant feature of this happy festival, so also was the nightly illumination of the temple-area. When a little later in his narrative John refers to this background for Jesus' other important announcement at the feast, he deliberately links this second self-revelation by Jesus with the first by the use of "again." "Again therefore Jesus announced to them, 'I am the light of the world: the one following me will not walk in darkness, but will have the light of life!'' (8:12). This image of Jesus is prominent in the Fourth Gospel: he was represented as referring to it as he ended his public ministry. ''Yet but a short while light is with you: walk while you have light, for fear darkness overtake you. One who walks in darkness does not know where he is going. While you have the light, believe in the light, that you may become sons of light!'' (12:35-36). The characterization had already formed a prominent facet of the creator-Word in the Prologue. ''What came to be found life in him—and that life was the light of mankind. Indeed this light is still shining through the darkness, for the darkness has never mastered it'' (1:4-5).

With his Christological concentration, our evangelist has dwelt repeatedly upon Jesus, sent by the Father, as ''the One from above.'' It is central to John's distinctive interpretation of ''Son of Man.'' ''No one has ascended into heaven except the One who descended from heaven— the Son of Man'' (3:13). ''The One coming from above stands above all men'' (3:31). In his angry retort at the diabolical insinuation by the Jews that he is going to commit suicide, Jesus says, ''You are from below: for my part, I am from above!'' (8:23a). The idea also forms an important part of John (the Baptist's) testimony to Jesus. ''No human being can take even a single thing, unless it has been given him from heaven'' (3:27). This idea dominates the great discourse on the ''bread of life,'' in which Jesus is first presented as divine wisdom incarnate—''the one who comes down out of heaven and is giving life to the world'' (6:33; see vv. 32, 41, 50). In the Eucharistic section of this instruction one sees the same emphasis. ''This is the Bread come down out of heaven—not such as the fathers ate, and still died. The person feeding on this Bread will live forever'' (v. 58; see v. 15).

It was suggested earlier that this conception of Jesus as the One coming from the Father presides over the first twelve chapters of John's Gospel—the idea already present in the Prologue. The evangelist had there commented on the statement that the Word incarnate ''empowered such as did accept him to become children of God'' (1:12) by explaining that the reference was to ''those who believe in his name, who were . . . begotten from God'' (v. 13). The theme is taken up in the dialogue between Jesus and Nicodemus, where to ''be begotten over again *(anō-then)*'' (3:13) is interpreted as being ''begotten of Spirit'' (v. 6). And Jesus concludes by remarking, ''Do not wonder at my saying to you, 'It is necessary that all of you be begotten from above!' '' (*anōthen*, v. 7). We had occasion earlier to cite the suggestion by Hugo Rahner that the

Ignatian *de arriba* "may perhaps have been an echo of the *anōthen* in John."[18] The author of the Fourth Gospel employs the idea of rebirth (see 16:21) from above in much the same way as Paul speaks of "the new creation" (2 Cor 5:17; Gal 6:15) to describe "all good things and gifts come down from above."

"So now, Father, glorify me in Your presence" (17:5a)

For the first (and I believe the single) time in the *Exercises,* no suggestions for the colloquy are given here nor is the exercitant directed to pray to any particular person ([237]). One is left with the feeling of something unfinished—or better, open-ended. As John in the final chapter of his Gospel implies that the life of Christian faith has begun for the immediate disciples and for "those who through their word will believe in me" (17:20), so Ignatius of Loyola at the close of this sublime contemplation leaves the retreatant to enter upon a life of prayer and faith.

He has, however, at the end of each of the four points suggested an offering to be made to "God our Lord," the *Sume ac suscipe,* a kind of recapitulation of this recapitulation of the entire course of the Exercises. "Take, Lord, and receive!" This oblation exemplifies that "mutual exchange" in which love consists ([231]). It is expected to flow from that "interior awareness of such great good received *(recibido),* in order that, by acknowledging it to the full, I may in everything love and serve his divine Majesty" ([233]). It is then through this newly acquired self-definition in terms of my utter poverty (I consist only "of such great good received") that I now ask the risen Lord, not only to "take," but also "receive" *(recibid).* This use of the two imperatives is more than rhetorical expansion: the request that God "take" expresses one's willingness to share what has been given by the risen Lord, while "receive" is a plea that the divine Giver graciously confirm the offer by accepting it. Father Peters finds here "a certain playfulness," which returns in the request, "You have given it to me, to you Lord I return it."[19]

The offering in a real sense looks back over the entire experience of making the Exercises. As the exercitant began this spiritual journey, it was said to be "highly advantageous to enter on the Exercises with a great heart and liberty with his creator and Lord" (Annotation 5). Now the retreatant offers "my entire liberty," and also those "three powers of the soul" ([45]) employed constantly in meditation, consideration, ap-

---

18   H. Rahner, *Ignatius the Theologian,* p. 61.
19   W. Peters, *The Spiritual Exercises of St. Ignatius,* p. 161.

plication of the senses, contemplation during the entire course of the Exercises. And "because all is yours," the risen Christ is asked to "dispose it [that is, restore order to it][20] in complete accord with your will." This was said to be the very purpose of making the Exercises, "to prepare and dispose the soul to rid oneself of all disordered loves, and once rid of them to seek and find the divine will in [God's] disposition of one's life" (Annotation 1). The reader cannot help recalling that this was the single-hearted quest of the Johannine Jesus throughout his earthly life.

"Keep giving me your love and your grace—for that is enough for me." The present imperative used here implies that this divine giving is, in this life, always a piece of unfinished business. "That is enough" reminds one of Philip's pre-occupation (14:8; 6:7) with that idea. More importantly, it reminds one of the constant theme of the prayer of Jesus in the Fourth Gospel, "Father, save me throughout this hour . . . Father, glorify Your Name!" (12:27). "Father, the hour has come: glorify Your Son, that the Son may glorify You" (17:1). "So now, Father, glorify me in Your presence" (17:5a).

We began this study of the feasibility of making the Spiritual Exercises with help from the fourth evangelist by suggesting that there is a perceptible harmony between the encounter with God granted to these two specially privileged Christian writers. John wrote his Gospel with the avowed purpose of leading his readers along the unique "way," Jesus Christ, to that "abiding" in the triune God, which means "life in his name" (20:31). We found such astonishing boldness to be justified by that writer's confidence in the attractiveness of the Crucified, who promised when once "lifted up from the earth" to "draw all people to myself" (12:32). It was seen to be justified also by John's unshakeable faith in the guidance of the Paraclete "to teach you everything and make you remember all I have told you" (14:26). One might rightly characterize the Fourth Gospel as the classic example of such Christian "remembering." Consequently, it can provide an assured and assuring point of departure for Christian contemplation, which—like the Eucharist—is part of the believer's obedient response to the command, "Do this in memory of me."

In its own way, the little book of the *Spiritual Exercises* has been discovered through the experiences of numberless retreatants to possess a similar power to produce the grateful conviction, "I encountered God!" Admittedly the starkly worded, matter-of-fact pragmatism of the Igna-

20   Ibid., p. 5.

tian composition reads more like a recipe-book than a treatise on the spiritual life. It contains none of the poetry, nor of the sublime diction found in the Gospel by John. Indeed, it rarely offers anything like the moving drama so often found in the Fourth Gospel. Yet, written as it was out of the singularly precious experiences of Ignatius at Loyola, at Manresa by the river Cardoner, at LaStorta, it can, if faithfully followed in making the Spiritual Exercises, accomplish those marvels of grace in a similar—if not indeed the identical—manner once produced in its author. The exercitant comes to sense, as she or he is directed along the path on which Ignatius once encountered God in Christ, the devotion and love for "the crucified Majesty of God" so reminiscent of that attested by John the evangelist. One can then catch a glimpse of the happy truth, which Mary Magdalene de' Pazzi's mystical insight expressed. "The spirit of John and of Ignatius is one and the same! That spirit consists totally in love and in bringing others to love."[21]

---

21   Cited by D. Mollat, "St. John's Gospel and the Exercises of St. Ignatius," *Communications*, no. 5, pp. 1-2.

APPENDIX

A SUGGESTED APPROACH TO *LECTIO DIVINA*

Since the approach to the Gospel of St. John adopted in this book is
closely related to the time-honored practice traditionally known as Lectio
divina *('prayerful reading'), the author adds here his earlier article which*
appeared in The American Benedictine Review *23 (1972), 439-455—with a*
few small changes merely editorial. This is done with the permission of the
editor, Father Terrence Kardong, O.S.B.

The article was originally given as a conference at the annual meeting of
the Benedictine abbots and priors of the United States, held March 13-17,
1972, in the Abbey of New Subiaco in Arkansas, at which the general
theme was prayer. The writer makes bold to add that the generous praise of
the study by the distinguished scholar, Father Godfrey Diekmann, O.S.B.,
provided an additional reason for its inclusion here.

The resonances and similarities between the *lectio divina* of St.
Benedict and the Ignatian *contemplatio* in the *Spiritual Exercises* have
led this son of St. Ignatius to venture a closer examination of the earlier
monastic practice.[1] That in fact the Jesuits of the mid-twentieth century
have officially recognized such a relationship to exist may be gauged by a
statement in the decree on Prayer issued in 1966 by the Thirty-first
General Congregation of the Society of Jesus.

In each of us, as the whole tradition of the Church attests, Holy Scripture becomes our saving word only when heard in prayer that leads to the
submission of faith. *Lectio divina,* a practice dating back to the earliest days
of religious life in the Church, supposes that the reader surrenders to God
who is speaking and granting him a change of heart under the action of the
two-edged sword of Scripture continually challenging to a conversion. Truly

---

1 See David M. Stanley, S.J., *A Modern Scriptural Approach to the Spiritual Exercises*
(Chicago and St. Louis, 1967), p. 85: "We have become accustomed to represent
divine revelation as a conversation between persons (God and man), with all that implies of interpersonal reaction . . . By means of what St. Benedict in the Rule has called *lectio divina,* or Ignatius in the *Exercises* calls *contemplation,* I attempt to live my
'spiritual' life, that is, existence under the divine domination of the Holy Spirit, by in-
tegrating myself into this conversation or dialogue."

we can expect from the prayerful reading of Scripture a renewal of our ministry of the word and of the Spiritual Exercises . . .[2]

Perhaps some readers may be moved to reflect that it is about time the Jesuits were catching up with the renaissance of biblical spirituality in the church that has now for some decades had a deep and revitalizing effect upon so many religious families. Yet, if one who has been engaged in biblical studies for some years may be permitted a personal impression, it has appeared to the writer that, after the first flush of enthusiasm for the renewed reading of the Bible and praying from the Scriptures, not a few religious have experienced a sense of frustration and disillusionment. This is not the occasion to analyze the many possible factors contributing to this state of affairs. Yet I venture to suggest one that is germane to the subject which here concerns us: a lack of clarity about the aim and scope of this ancient Christian and monastic preoccupation with the Bible. In the mind of the author of *The Holy Rule,* as will shortly become evident, the principal purpose is to have a spiritual experience, in other words, to be united with God through Christ in prayer.[3]

The distinguished authority on the religious and cultural history of twelfth-century Western Europe, Dom Jean Leclercq, who has thrown such light on the distinction between monastic and scholastic theology, has convincingly shown that the former is a development of *lectio divina.* "Monastic theology is a *confessio*; it is an act of faith and of recognition; it involves a 're-cognition' in a deep and living manner by means of prayer and the *lectio divina* of the mysteries which are known in a conceptual way; explicit perhaps, but superficial. 'To understand' is not

---

2   No. 6 in decree 14, On Prayer, in *Documents of the 31st and 32nd General Congregations of the Society of Jesus* (St. Louis, 1977), 139-140. [The term *lectio divina,* used in ch. 48 of *Regula Sancti Benedicti,* is appropriately translated "prayerful reading" in the scholarly *RB 1980: The Rule of St. Benedict in Latin and English with Notes,* ed. Timothy Fry, O.S.B. (Collegeville, 1981), p. 249. The translators point out that in the literal translation "divine reading," the adjective refers to the quality of the text read rather than to the action of reading or the reader. This action has traditionally been understood as a meditative, reflective reading of the Bible, the Fathers of the Church, or some other spiritual writing. Editor.]

3   See Jean Leclercq, O.S.B., *The Love of Learning and the Desire for God: a Study of Monastic Culture* (New York, 1960), p. 264. "A certain experience of the realities of faith . . . is at one and the same time the condition for and the result of monastic theology. The word experience, which has become equivocal in meaning because it has been abused in a certain recent period, should not, in this context, imply anything esoteric. It simply means that, in study and in reflection, importance was granted to . . . that grace of intimate prayer, that *affectus* as it is called by St. Benedict, that manner of savoring and relishing the Divine realities which is constantly taught in the patristic tradition."

necessarily 'to explain' through causality; it can also mean the acquiring of a general view: *comprehendere.'*[4] Angelo Pantoni has made a similar point in an article not immediately available to the present writer. *"Lectio* is . . . oriented towards prayer and life, not towards a *quaestio."*[5]

The Cistercian abbot, André Louf, has discerningly remarked, "Not only is the spiritual reading of the bible not identified with its scientific study, but one might even say in a certain sense it goes in the opposite direction. Scientific study reconstructs the past from the starting point of the present. The Christian with faith . . . listens day by day to what the Eternal Word wants to make known to him here and now, though he does this through that letter which comes to him from the past, clarified, prudently restored, illuminated with its original light . . . replaced finally in its own context by the efforts of biblical science."[6]

This remark of Dom André Louf is significant because it draws attention to the important truth that if *lectio divina* is not "scientific study," it most assuredly was never intended to be cultivated in any spirit of anti-intellectualism. To be specific, it cannot be expected to flourish in a mind-set dominated by bibical fundamentalism, that misguided refusal to employ man's God-given spirit of inquiry (out of a fallacious sense of reverence for the divine origins of the Bible), in order to discover what the inspired human writer meant to say, that is, the 'literal' sense of Scripture.[7] The long and imposing intellectual tradition which is an integral part of the Benedictine heritage must surely derive its inspiration from the man who was author of *The Holy Rule.* "If the painter Spinello

4   Ibid., pp. 267-268. [Some of the Latin terms here require comment. *Confessio,* "confession, acknowledgement" in classical Latin, took on many new meanings by the age of Augustine and monasticism, such as avowal of faith, profession of faith, praise of God. *Comprehendere,* "to take together, to unite" in classical Latin, came to mean "to take a synthesizing view." Ed.]

5   Angelo Pantoni, "La lectio divina en suoi rapporti con la Bibbia e la Liturgia," *Vita Monastica,* 14 (1960), 167-174.

6   André Louf, O.C.S.O., "Exegèse scientifique ou Lectio monastique," *Collectanea O.C.R., 22* (1960), 225-247.

7   Perhaps the greatest achievement of Pius XII's encyclical *Divino afflante Spiritu,* published September 30, 1943, is its insistence upon the primacy of the *sensus litteralis* of Scripture, with its consequent rejection of biblical fundamentalism. See John L. McKenzie, "Problems of Hermeneutics in Roman Catholic Exegesis," *Journal of Biblical Literature, 77 (1958), 198:* "The sword of central authority is two-edged; if it could halt the entire Modernist discussion, it can also, as it has done, unequivocally repudiate fundamentalism in Catholic exegesis."

Aretino six times shows St. Benedict either holding or reading a book, it is not because the artist's imagination failed to find anything better to put instead. Since Aretino is to the Dialogues what Giotto is to the life of St. Francis, we can assume that he has caught, in his Florentine murals, the authentic spirit of St. Benedict. The wonder-worker, the father, the judge, the man of prayer—he is there as each—and, as suggested, the reader and student."[8]

Lectio Divina *in* The Rule of St. Benedict

When one is aware of the importance attaching to *lectio divina* in Benedictine spirituality, one is astonished to discover how relatively rare are the references to it in *The Holy Rule*. It first appears among the "tools for good works" (*instrumenta bonorum operum*), in conjunction—most significantly—with prayer."[9] Dom Hubert Van Zeller in his commentary has rightly seized on the significance of this juxtaposition. "Prayer rises out of reading as song rises out of music. Reading is the most appropriate prelude to prayer. To the degree that 'faith is from hearing', prayer is from reading. Just as hearing does not complete the work of faith, so neither does reading complete the work of prayer."[10]

The next mention, oddly enough at first sight, occurs in the chapter dealing with daily manual work.[11] Yet its situation in such a context reminds us that *"lectio divina,* like manual labour, is an ascesis."[12] The fact that it is, together with physical work, proposed as a remedy for idleness (*otiositas*) indicates how much this exercise demands the full at-

8   Dom Hubert Van Zeller, *The Holy Rule: Notes on St. Benedict's Legislation for Monks* (New York, 1958), p. 75.

9   See the discerning comment of Dom Odilon M. Cunill on "Lectiones sanctas libenter audire" in *San Benito y Su Regla* (Madrid, 1954), pp.351-352. His passage, translated into English, reads: "The study and penetration of things supernatural is a monk's occupation of predilection. His renuntiation of temporal things is not enough; his mind is eager to be nourished with eternal truths, to be sated with them. The holy readings have an important function in St. Benedict's plan, and that in a manner supremely noteworthy."

10   Van Zeller, p. 75

11   Chapter XLVIII: "Idleness is the enemy of the soul. Therefore, the brothers should have specified periods for manual labor as well as for prayerful reading." [Translation from *RB 1980;* for full reference, see fn. 2 above. Ed.] This combination of manual work and reading would not seem so strange to St. Benedict's contemporaries, who normally read aloud; see Leclercq, p. 19.

12   Van Zeller, p. 305; see the comment of Cunill, p. 253. His passage, in translation, reads: "Although this *lectio* could have been the source of the many activities and studies of an intellectual character which the monks of successive generations have taken up, St. Benedict's own thought seems to be that this reading constitutes the soundings which the soul takes in supernatural truth, with light from God himself."

tention and energetic application of the monk. Moreover, "it is probable that in addition to the energy involved in the study of the sacred books, *lectio divina* in the mind of St. Benedict embraces unrestricted access to prayer and contemplation."[13] It will in fact be recalled that the last paragraph of this same chapter of the *Rule* describes this religious activity as "to study or to read" (*meditare aut legere*).[14] Indeed, as has been suggested by Dom Anscari Mundo,[15] the phrase indicating the object of Lenten reading, :"to receive each one a book from the library" (*accipiant omnes singulos codices de bibliotheca*), may refer to those manuscript volumes which contained a certain number of bibilical books. Further proof of the sacred and prayerful character of this *lectio* may be deduced from its special cultivation during sacred times, viz., Lent and Sunday (*Quadragesima* and *Dominico die*).

Among the principal Lenten observances listed in chapter XLIX we find application "to prayer with tears, to reading and compunction of heart" (*orationi cum fletibus, lectioni et compunctioni cordis*). The stress upon affectivity is instructive; in particular, St. Benedict's use of the ancient Latin medical term *compunctio* – [16] in conjunction with *lectio*. The passage, perhaps more than any other in *The Holy Rule,* reveals the intimate connection in its author's mind between prayer and *lectio divina.*[17] St. Benedict would appear to presuppose as an essential compo-

---

13   Cunill, p. 564. Van Zeller, p. 306, observes in this connection that "nothing so destroys the prayerfulness of spiritual study as rush and fuss. Tension is the enemy of *lectio* as St. Benedict conceived it."

14   Leclercq, pp. 89-91, remarks: "The monastic *lectio* is orientated toward the *meditatio* and the *oratio* . . . The *meditatio* consists in applying oneself with attention to this exercise in total memorization: it is, therefore, inseparable from the *lectio* . . . This way of uniting reading, meditation and prayer, this 'meditative prayer' as William of St. Thierry calls it, had great influence on religious psychology. It occupies and engages the whole person in whom the Scripture takes root, later on to bear fruit."

15   Dom Anscari Mundó, " 'Bibliotheca.' Bible et lecture du Carême d'après saint Benoît," *Revue Bénédictine, 60 (1950),* 65-92; the conclusions 3 and 5 on p. 89 are particularly noteworthy.

16   Cf. Joseph Pegon, art. "Componction," *Dictionnaire de Spiritualité,* tome II, 2ᵉ partie (Paris, 1953), 1312-1321.

17   See William Yeomans, S.J., "St. Bernard of Clairvaux," *The Month N.S., 23 (1960),* 273: "This enables us to see why Bernard attaches importance to the reading of Scripture, the *lectio divina* of St. Benedict, that reverent, prayerful search for the Word in the word. Reading the Scriptures is not merely an exercise of the memory and in-

nent of this exercise that warming experience of being "under the inspiration of divine grace" (*affectus inspirationis divinae gratiae*) mentioned in chapter XX. The superlative value he ascribed to the reading of the Scriptures as *the* rule of Christian living is abundantly clear from his remark in the concluding chapter LXXIII: "What page, what passage of the books of the Old and New Testaments is not the truest of guides for human life?"

An Approach to Lectio Divina

If we have correctly grasped the nature of *lectio divina* as it is understood by the author of *The Holy Rule,* it becomes plain that its proper functioning comprises (1) an inquiry with a mind illumined by Christian faith into the meaning which the inspired author has expressed through the sacred text (2) in order to comprehend[18] what the risen Christ is saying to me *here and now* and (3) to submit through "the obedience of faith" (Rom 4:5) my entire person to God my Father in filial love and hope. Because I believe God "has spoken through the prophets" of Old and New Testaments, whose intuition of the divine activity from within the historical process has been recorded upon the sacred page, it becomes imperative that I endeavor to *understand* the message. At a far deeper level, that of faith, it is crucial that I also strive to comprehend (as far as that is possible) the mystery which confronts me in all its contemporaneity and relevance for myself. *Lectio divina* is no mere academic exercise: it must issue in affection, in bringing "ourselves to prayer with tears, to reading, to compunction of heart" *(orationi cum fletibus, lectioni et compunctioni cordis). It must be engaged in "with the utmost humility and sincere devotion" (devotione).*[19]

tellect, though it implies a careful study of the text and of the patristic commentaries on it. It is a work which engages the whole man, all his faculties and all his affective powers. The Scriptures are known only when they are lived, when they are translated into terms of one's own experience."

18   Pius XII in the encyclical *Divino afflante Spiritu* insisted repeatedly upon the crucial importance of recovering the 'literal sense' of Sacred Scripture, because "it is evident that the chief law of interpretation is that which enables us to discover and determine what the writer meant to say . . . " Tr. Canon G.D. Smith (London, 1963), no. 38.

19   *The Holy Rule,* ch. XX, Reverence in Prayer; also, chs. XLVIII, XLIX; and G. Penco, O.S.B., *S. Benedicti Regula, Introduzione, Testo, Apparati, Traduzione e Commento* (Florence, 1958), who in ch. XX translates *ex affectu inspirationis gratiae divinae* by "per l'infervorante ispiratione della grazia divina."

I venture to suggest that it is by reflecting upon the manner in which the Scriptures were created that we can discern how to conduct this spiritual exercise fruitfully. The procedure will appear to recommend itself at once if we ask ourselves why, from the viewpoint of Christian faith, the Bible was written.

We believe that the incarnate Son of God, Jesus Christ, was sent into our world by the Father to assist us in making that response of faith and love and hope to the divine activity in history (at once infallible and infinitely efficacious) in which our salvation lies. For our redemption is not an impersonal, automatic process—even though it remains true that Jesus Christ through his death and resurrection accomplished in place of us what we ourselves, because of sin, were incapable of realizing. What was the nature of this human predicament in which by the sin of Adam and its own consequent personal sins the human race found itself inextricably enmeshed? It was, very simply and briefly, mankind's culpable loss of self-identity. Men and women through sin lost the awareness of who they were, viz., the adoptive sons and daughters of God. Jesus Christ's mission was to reveal to all that "God no man has ever seen" (Jn 1:18), "in order that we might receive the adoptive sonship" (Gal 4:5). It was through the gift of that most filial attitude, "the obedience of faith," that humanity recovered its lost identity as sons or daughters in the Son. For it had been by his total acceptance of obedience to the Father in all the concrete circumstances of his life, death, and resurrection that Jesus Christ effected what men and women through Adam had made themselves incapable of accomplishing, that is, offering a single act of filial love to the Father whereby we would acknowledge who we most truly are.

There is another aspect of our redemption which comes into consideration here. Jesus Christ died and rose for all, not to excuse or exclude men and women from participating personally in this redemptive experience of dying and rising. In fact, Jesus died and rose to create the possibility of our dying and rising with him. Thus the mysteries of Jesus' earthly life have been recorded in the New Testament to teach the believer how in his or her own life one can collaborate with this process of one's own redemption (Jn 20:31). And what is true of the Gospel narratives holds true also (when they are read in the light of Christ with Christian faith) of the Old Testament books, since in them also is to be found that "truth which God has chosen to consign to the Sacred Books for the sake of our salvation."[20]

20   See *Dei Verbum* no. 11 " . . . veritatem, quam Deus nostrae salutis causa Litteris

Why then was the Bible written? In order to make available to the man of faith that truth, which is not historical truth, nor scientific truth, nor philosophical truth, by the assimilation of which alone we can be saved. One traditionally Christian method of assimilating this saving truth is *lectio divina*. Hence by reflection upon the dialectical process through which the Scriptures have come into existence, we may hope to perceive more clearly how to employ this ancient Christian approach to prayer.

This dialectical process consists of three moments which may be simply stated as (1) experience, (2) reflection, (3) articulation, or verbalization, first orally, then in writing. While the process will presently be exemplified from the history of Israel and particularly from the earthly life of Jesus Christ, it may be useful at this point to explain the precise import of each of the three stages for the creation of sacred literature.

All authentic Scripture takes its origins from a real experience of God by a 'seer' or prophet. It is the privilege of such a man to be granted an intuition of the divine activity through some concrete historical event, for example, the Babylonian captivity, the Maccabean wars of independence. A prophet may be described as a man who has been accorded the great grace of looking at happenings in our sublunary world from the divine viewpoint.

For this experience, of course, faith is essential: the faith of Israel in the Old Testament, Christian faith after the resurrection of Jesus. It is through this faith the seer grasps what he or she has experienced of God's activity through which he has deigned to reveal himself to us. Only by our reflection with faith can the implications of the prophet's experience be grasped.

Because he realizes that this precious self-revelation on the part of God has been committed to him for the instruction of the community, the prophet accepts as a sacred duty the commission to proclaim the message. He is impelled to announce his experience 'in the spirit' to those to whom he is sent. Ultimately, in the case with which we are concerned—the sacred books of the Bible—the message is set forth in writing, by the prophet himself or some other author guided by the Spirit of God. It becomes "scripture" (it is written down) under the divine impulse because the seer has come to see its value for future members of the community, its "usefulness for right teaching, for the correction of er-

Sacris consignari voluit . . . " —A fuller discussion by the present writer of the character of the redemption proclaimed in the Gospel may be found in *Faith and Religious Life: a New Testament Perspective* (New York, 1971), pp. 6-30.

ror, for the reform of manners, and discipline in right living'' (2 Tim 3:16).

By way of anticipating what we shall suggest further on about finding a formula for *lectio divina,* we may state here that it is a matter of reversing this threefold process by which our biblical books were produced. The believer must begin with the sacred text, endeavoring with an intelligence enlightened by faith to comprehend the message of the sacred author. He or she must then react with faith, reflect with faith, upon what one has grasped of the message for oneself here and now. Finally, through being "under the inspiration of divine grace" (*affectus inspirationis divinae gratiae*) one is given an experience in prayer of what God in Christ is saying to her or him.

God's Election of Israel

It may be helpful, before turning to the Gospels, to sketch rapidly the manner in which Israel's sacred literature came to be written, in order to provide a concrete illustration of the dialectical process (experience, reflection of faith, articulation) which we already indicated to have presided over the composition of the Bible. Since it is obviously only possible to deal summarily with such a vast body of literature, I have chosen to review the way in which the record of Israel's birth as a people, as *the* people of God, gradually came into existence.

Somewhere about the beginning of the thirteenth century B.C. a group of Hebrews under the skillful leadership of a man named Moses succeeded in escaping from their adopted country of Egypt (where their forebears had dwelt for generations) and from the galling slave-labor of the Pharaoh by eluding the task-force dispatched to recapture them. After their remarkable getaway they found a hideout to the east of the Red Sea in the Sinai peninsula, where they were granted, in the person of Moses, a mysterious experience of a God they had not previously known, or at any rate, whose covenant with their remote ancestor Abraham they had forgotten.

After living as nomads during the next two or three generations (the period of the Judges), these Hebrews managed, by infiltration, border forays, and guerilla warfare to wrest the strip of territory at the eastern extreme of the Mediterranean from the Canaanites, and settle down as the people of Israel in what their new-found faith had told them was the land Yahweh had promised them.

This series of events, rather insignificant no doubt within the political, economic, cultural history of the ancient Near East, gave these Hebrews their sense of identity as a nation. From the viewpoint of the religion of Israel and (ultimately) of Christianity, however, this historical phenomenon, reacted to with faith in a unique, all-powerful God who had chosen them as his "acquisition," was comprehended as the vehicle of that God's self-revelation of his special relationship to his people, Israel, and eventually, through them, to the entire human race. It was thus in history that God "spoke through the prophets," those "seers" who intuited and interpreted the meaning of the divine activity in the world.

The priests and prophets and wisemen of Israel through many centuries articulated their beliefs by means of creedal formulae, the cultus, legislation. These were preserved in large part, if not entirely, by oral transmission for countless generations, being modified and reformulated in the light of subsequent experiences in the national history (interpreted in their turn by Israelite faith). The monarchy arose with Saul, to be split in two after Solomon's death and irreparably destroyed at the Babylonian exile. And during these half dozen centuries, it must not be forgotten, the Bible *as we know it,* specifically, the collection of Israel's inspired writings, had not begun in any proper sense to be written. One element essential to its creation was missing: the eschatological hope in Yahweh's definitive intervention in his people's history. This key tenet of faith was hammered out under the cruel experience of the Babylonian captivity through the indomitable belief in their God by the great Israelite prophets. Only at this point in her national history, when Israel had learned that the divine election of herself and the covenant God had made with her was a responsibility as well as a privilege, did the composition of the Old Testament under the guidance of the Spirit of God become possible. For, as Roderick MacKenzie has discerningly remarked, these sacred writings present a unique phenomenon: "it is a national literature that does *not* glorify the nation," but that nation's God.[21]

The Composition of the Gospels

Before turning our attention to the creation of the four canonical Gospels,[22] it may not be inappropriate to remind ourselves that these

---

21   R.A.F. MacKenzie, S.J., *Faith and History in the Old Testament* (Minneapolis, 1963), p. 35. The writer adds: "With extraordinary consistency and heroic honesty, Israel glorifies its God at the cost of belittling herself."

22   The reader might find it helpful to study the decree of the Pontifical Biblical Commission, issued April 21, 1964 on *The Historical Truth of the Gospels.* The text is available in Catholic Biblical Quarterly, 26 (1964), 299-312; a discerning commentary on the document by Joseph A. Fitzmyer, S.J., "The Biblical Commission's Instruc-

were not the first books of the New Testament to be written. They were preceded, at least, by the entire collection of St. Paul's letters. This chronological anteriority was, I suggest, no mere coincidence,[23] but a necessary stage in the effort of the apostolic Church to articulate, through its privileged representatives, the unprecedented experience of God's definitive act of salvation in Jesus Christ. It fell to Paul particularly, with his unique mystical gifts and powerful religious genius, to provide the theological expression of his profound insights into the Christian mystery with the aid of "the Scriptures" and his acquaintance with the world view that inspired contemporary Hellenistic culture. The outcome of Paul's struggle to assist the young Christian communities of non-Semitic provenance to apply the gospel to the concrete circumstances of their daily living, his persistent effort to press into service the popular Greek language as a medium of articulating the apostolic kerygma, originally expressed in Aramaic thought-patterns, made possible the writing of our Gospels, which despite their seeming artlessness constitute unquestionably the supreme literary and theological achievement of the apostolic age.

In any discussion of the experience by "the Twelve" of the earthly career of Jesus Christ which underlies the composition of the Gospels, it is crucial to recall that this experience occurred at two distinct chronological moments and at two very disparate levels. There is firstly the disciples' immediate involvement in what happened during Jesus' public ministry "in the days of his flesh" (Heb 5:7): they were, in Luke's phrase, "the original eyewitnesses" (Lk 1:2), personally and collectively engaged in what Jesus did and said during his preaching career in Galilee and Jerusalem and through his passion. Secondly, this same group was privileged, with the women devoted to Jesus, to share in the post-resurrection appearances of the glorified Christ. What gives these latter experiences their singular quality is the fact that through them *for the first time* Christian faith was created in the hearts of those who had been disciples of Jesus of Nazareth during his mortal life.

At that earlier period, as the Gospel record attests, these men were

---

tion on the Historical Truth of the Gospels" may be found in *Theological Studies, 25 (1964), 386-408;* a briefer treatment by the same author, "The Gospel Truth" was published in *America, 110 (1964), 844-846.* An Anglican New Testament scholar, Dr. F.W. Beare, presents his view of the decree, "The Historical Truth of the Gospels: an Official Pronouncement of the Pontifical Biblical Commission," *Canadian Journal of Theology, II (1965), 231-237.* "The Historicity of the Gospels" by Msgr. Myles M. Bourke is to be highly recommended; it appeared in *Thought, 39 (1964), 37-56.*

23   "Contemplation of the Gospels, Ignatius Loyola, and the Contemporary Christian," *Theological Studies, 29 (1958), 417-443.*

attracted to Jesus by some winning, mysterious quality (Jn 1:38-39). They were struck indeed by the original and independent traits perspicuous in his manner of teaching (Mk 1:27), so transcendently different from that of all other rabbis. As they lived with him, listened to his doctrine, witnessed his mighty "acts of power" (Mt 13:54) or "signs" (Jn 9:16), they came to realize he was a prophet (Lk 7:16) like those of old (Lk 9:8). At a privileged moment during the public ministry, which the Synoptic tradition has linked with Caesarea Philippi (Mk 8:27-29) they began to see in him the historical verification of the ancient messianic hope of Israel: he was in fact "the Christ," the annointed of the Lord. This was the peak point of the disciples' understanding of the mystery surrounding Jesus prior to his resurrection.[24]

This knowledge and attachment to Jesus, only acquired by the Twelve, in the course of his public life, was not merely human. It was a reaction of faith, the traditional faith of Israel. Yet such faith was not sufficient, it would appear, to sustain the disciples through the traumatic disillusionment of Jesus' sufferings and death. Indeed, he himself had predicted this tragic denouement: "All of you will lose faith in me" (Mk 14:27). This eclipse of his followers' expectations is confessed by two disciples as they walk with the risen Jesus towards Emmaus, "We had been hoping he was the one who is to redeem Israel" (Lk 24:21). The author of the fourth Gospel in the discourse after the Last Supper delineates the ineffectiveness of this pre-resurrection faith in the Master they knew so superficially (Jn 14:8-10).

St. Paul perhaps more than any other New Testament author has underscored the truth that the "Jesus of history" is *not the adequate object* of Christian faith. "Even if we had known Christ in a merely human way, we now know him so no longer" (2 Cor 5:16). The Apostle insists that his entire knowledge of Jesus, including his earthly career, was given to himself by "a revelation of Jesus Christ" (Gal 1:12. It is instructive to observe that when Paul alludes to a saying of Jesus he invariably speaks of them as "a saying of the Lord," i.e., the glorified Christ (1 Thes 4:15; 1 Cor 7:10). The authority of this teaching, for Paul, derives not immediately from its emanation from Jesus of Nazareth, but from Paul's awareness that it was the confrontation with the risen Christ on the Damascus road upon which he based his claim to be an apostle (1 Cor 9:1; 15:8), despite his never having enjoyed the experience of the Twelve of Jesus' public life.

24 See "The Divinity of Christ in Hymns of the New Testament," *Proceedings: Fourth Annual Convention of the Society of Catholic College Teachers of Sacred Doctrine,* 4 (1958), 17.

Basis in Faith

This all-important fact must be borne in mind in any attempt to assess the authority of the four Gospels, whose canonization by the Church was from earliest times based upon their apostolic origin. Modern critical studies of the Gospels have made it clear that none of these books was actually penned by any one of the Twelve; and in fact from the earliest days the Church was well aware that neither Mark nor Luke was among "the original eyewitnesses." Accordingly, the authority of the Gospels derives principally from the fact that their inspired authors (while they had no personal experience of the "Jesus of history") did experience his words and actions "in the spirit." It is for this reason, and not for any mere historical accuracy, that these sacred books have always been treasured as a privileged locus for Christian contemplation.

What was the nature of the second moment in the experience of the first disciples? The post-resurrection appearances made Christians of the Twelve. The Gospel narratives of this supremely important event are intended chiefly to describe this genesis of Christian faith, and, in addition (where such appearances to the Twelve are recorded, for example, Mt 28:16-20; Lk 24:16-20; Jn 20:19-29; 21:1-25), to record the risen Lord's commission to "preach the gospel to all nations." St. Thomas Aquinas has expressed with his usual admirable clarity the character of these experiences. "After his resurrection the apostles saw the living Christ, whom they had known to have died, with the eyes of faith *(oculata fide),*" he observes in the *Summa Theologica.*[25] The post-resurrection appearances were in the most profound sense an *experience of faith,* Christian faith, for the Twelve. This in no way implies that these appearances were merely a subjective phenomenon induced by some kind of group hysteria. And the comment in Jn 20:9 categorically excludes possibility of any explanation in terms of an expectancy based upon "the Scriptures." Nor can St. Thomas' remark be taken to imply that the risen Lord was not bodily present on these occasions. It does mean, however, that any natural explanation of these experiences in terms of mere sense perception is inadequate. It was not enough to have one's eyes open in order to see the risen Jesus: Christian faith was a *sine qua non.* Whatever Mary Magdalene may be thought to have seen when she mistook Jesus after his resurrection for a gardener (Jn 20:14-15), she did

---

25   "Apostoli potuerunt testificari Christi resurrectionem etiam de visu: quia Christum post resurrectionem viventem oculata fide viderunt, quem mortuum sciverant," *Summa Theologica, III,* q. 55, 2, ad 1.

not yet see the glorified Lord, because she had not, at that moment, been given the grace of Christian faith. She was only able to recognize the risen Master when, through his own gracious intervention (5:16), she was given the great grace of faith.

While these post-resurrection appearances were of a unique character (cf. 1 Cor 15:4-8)—since it is upon the apostolic testimony arising out of them that our faith reposes (Jn 20:31)—still, for all that, they remain experiences of Christian faith, in some way analogous to our own faith-experiences of the presence of the risen Lord in our own lives (Jn 20:29). They were also similar, in a very real sense, to the experiences by the inspired evangelists (who had received the data concerning Jesus' earthly life from apostolic tradition) of the words and deeds of Jesus "in the Spirit." For through the gift of Christian faith these writers received the Holy Spirit "to lead them into the whole range of truth (Jn 16:13). Indeed, as Jesus had promised the disciples, it was for this purpose that the Spirit was sent to them. "Everything he makes known to you, he will draw from what is mine" (Jn 17:24).

I should like to direct attention to another aspect of this question. It was only when the Twelve, in the light of their new Christian faith, reflected upon the words Jesus had uttered, the deeds he had performed in their presence during his earthly life, that they came to perceive their true, saving significance. The author of the fourth Gospel is aware of the crucial relevance of this apostolic reflection, which he denominates as *remembering*. Jesus had promised that the Paraclete "will teach you everything and cause you to remember all that I have said to you" (Jn 14:26). "When therefore he was risen from death, his disciples remembered that he had said this, and they believed the Scripture and the word which Jesus had spoken" (Jn 2:22); "these things his disciples did not understand at first, but when Jesus had been glorified, then they remembered that what had been written concerning him had been done to him" (Jn 12:16).

I have dwelt upon this point at some length because it is of paramount importance for distinguishing this manner of comprehending Jesus' words and deeds "in the Spirit" from the previous "eyewitness" experience accorded the Twelve of these words and deeds during Jesus' public ministry. In the case of our evangelists, who (like Paul) did not have the immediate, personal, collective experience of Jesus in his earthly life, these data had been transmitted to them by "the original eyewitnesses." Through the inspiration of the Holy Spirit, these writers enjoyed a specially privileged experience, of what Jesus had said and done, "in the Spirit." And it is this Spirit-filled experience that they have intended to record in their Gospels. Because of this, each of the four evangelists has presented in his book his personal approach to the risen Lord, his own "spirituality." Accordingly, it becomes necessary (as we shall now attempt to show) that in the practice of *lectio divina* the reader attend to the very individual manner, characteristic of each Gospel-writer, in which he depicts the mysteries—for these accounts are of far greater significance than mere historical narratives—of the earthly life of Jesus.

A Formula for Lectio Divina

It remains to describe the suggested approach to *lectio divina* which, as was stated earlier, amounts to a reversal of the process through which the Bible came into being. One begins with the inspired text, the sacred writer's articulation of his experience which issued from his reflection with faith (the faith of Israel for the Old Testament, Christian faith for the New). And here perhaps it may not be inappropriate to remind ourselves that the desired experience in which *lectio divina* is calculated to issue is one of Christian faith. The believing Christian does not read the sacred text of the Gospels, for instance, in order to be able by some effort of the imagination to reproduce in himself the "eyewitness" experience of the Twelve. *Lectio divina* has little, if anything, to do with historical reminiscence of the past. One of the salient features of our Gospels is their perspicuous lack of nostalgia for "the good old days" of Jesus' earthly life—notwithstanding their almost exclusive character as the record of what Jesus said and did "in the days of his flesh." The Gospel narratives, far from representing any mere return to the past as a vanished golden age, are orientated to the present and the future. This is to say that their authors' primary aim and concern is to foster and fortify the interpersonal relationship with the risen Lord Jesus, which constitutes the life of Christian faith. "These things have been written," says the author of the Fourth Gospel, "in order that you may deepen your faith that Jesus is the Messiah, the son of God, and that through this belief you may have life in his name" (Jn 20:31). Luke in his dedicatory preface gives the convert Theophilus as his reason for writing, "that you may gain a profound knowledge of the sound basis for those things that you heard in the catechesis" (Lk 1:4). Paul has exposed his "gospel" to the Roman community in his letter for a similar purpose. "I have written to you somewhat boldly at times in order to recall to your memory the favor bestowed on me by God, that is, my role as a minister of Christ Jesus to the pagans, my function as a priest [in preaching] the gospel of God, in order that the oblation of the pagans be an acceptable sacrifice, made holy by the Holy Spirit'' (Rom 15:15-16). It is the deepening of this same Christian faith which is the purpose of the *lectio divina* of the Old Testament, those books (as Vatican II has declared) ''which express a lively sense of God, contain sublime teaching about God and salutary wisdom about man's existence . . . in which finally the mystery of our salvation lies hidden.''[26]

As one begins the exercise of *lectio divina,* the first concern must be the comprehension of the sacred text insofar as that is possible. The point of departure for any sound and fruitful reading of the Bible remains always the understanding of the meaning which the words are intended to express. To approach the text with a fundamentalist mentality is to imperil the whole enterprise. One must make an effort to grasp what the inspired author is saying by discerning the type of literature in which he enshrines his message, by acquiring some sense of his idiom, of the historical and cultural background out of which he speaks. All this however is but the point of departure for the man of faith. He seeks above all to become impregnated with that ''truth which God has chosen to consign to the sacred books for the sake of our salvation.''[27]

Accordingly (and this is the second step) one must reflect *with faith* upon the literal sense already uncovered, in order to hear what the risen Christ is saying through his Spirit as one reads a particular passage at a given moment. St. Paul has asserted that ''faith comes by hearing, while hearing comes through the utterance of Christ'' (Rom 10:17). The assimilation of the Gospel is not a matter of communications, rhetoric, or philosophy (see 1 Cor 2:4; 1 Thes 1:5) in the mind of Paul. He employs auditory sensation as an image of the opening of man in his innermost, truest self to that divine dynamism effecting man's salvation, which is the Gospel (Rom 1:16). Such ''hearing'' signifies the ''obedience of your faith'' (Rom 7:5; see also 15:18).

The practice of *lectio divina* is calculated to effect my confrontation by God in Christ, and my response implies that I confront my God in Christ. What is God saying to me today in this passage of Holy Scripture?—that is the question I must endeavor, with the grace of Christ, to answer. ''Let us open our eyes to the light that comes from God,'' St. Benedict urges in the prologue to the holy *Rule,* ''and our ears to the

---

26   *Dei Verbum,* no. 15: ''Unde iidem libri, qui vivum sensum Dei exprimunt, in quibus sublimes de Deo doctrinae ac salutaris de vita hominis sapientia mirabilesque precum thesauri reconduntur, in quibus tandem latet mysterium salutis nostrae, a christifidelibus devote accipiendi sunt.''

27   Ibid., no. 11

voice from heaven that every day calls out this charge: 'If you hear his voice today, do not harden your hearts' " (Ps 94[95]:8).

God's dynamic power, unleashed through the prayerful reading of the sacred text, elicits my cooperation in producing the experience of the mystery symbolized by the text. Through my reaction of faith and love and hope the mystery becomes an event for me. It happens to me. This experience is described in an ancient Christian document, which speaks of Christ as "he who appears as new, is discovered to be from of old, is daily born anew in the hearts of the faithful."[28] The goal of *lectio divina* is actually what St. Ignatius has called "an interior knowledge of our Lord, who has become man *for me,* that I may love him more and follow him more closely."[29] Israel's deep sense of how through the Scriptures the event of the past becomes a contemporary experience has been articulated in a striking way by the author of Deuteronomy. This writer composed his book five or six hundred years after the striking of the covenant on Mount Sinai. Yet he can represent Moses as speaking through the centuries to his own (the author's) contemporaries: "Hear, O Israel, the statutes and ordinances which I am delivering in your hearing *today* . . . The Lord our God made a covenant *with us* at Horeb. It was not with our forefathers that the Lord made this covenant, but *but with ourselves, who are all here alive today"* (Deut 5:1-3).

It is just such a contemporary experience, personal to me as a member of the people of God, that *lectio divina* was designed to create.

Regis College
Toronto, Ontario

---

28   "Ille est qui novus apparet, qui vetus invenitur, et denuo cotidie nascitur in cordibus fidelium," *Epistula ad Diognetum,* II, 4.

29   *The Spiritual Exercises,* [105].

---

on the Term "Spiritual Exercises"

Throughout this book, as was pointed out in footnote 1 (one) on page ix above, *Spiritual Exercises* (in italics) refers chiefly to Ignatius' book, and Spiritual Exercises (in roman type) to the activities of an exercitant within a retreat. The term "Spiritual Exercises" gives rise to many editorial problems. The procedures by which they are handled are shown by exemplification in the following paragraph.

Long before Ignatius various spiritual exercises, such as attendance at Mass or recitation of the Office, were common. He gradually composed directives for a sequence of such exercises. Before 1535 his companions Xavier and Favre made his Spiritual Exercises for a period of thirty days. Ignatius assembled his notes in his book *Spiritual Exercises,* which was (or were) published at Rome in 1548. To make references easier, in modern editions since that at Turin in 1928 a number in square brackets has been added to each paragraph of the text; for example, the purpose of the Exercises is stated in *Spiritual Exercises,* [21] or, in our abbreviation, *SpEx,* [21]. The Introductory Observations *(Anotaciones)* are in [1-20]. Important meditations or other exercises in his book are the First Principle and Foundation ([23]), the Call of the King ([91]), which is an introduction to the Second Week or division of the *Exercises,* the Three Modes of Humility ([238-260]). In references run into the text—for example, to the Call of the Temporal King ([91-100])—the parentheses ( ) indicate that the numbers are a reference, and the square brackets [ ] show that the numbers themselves are a modern addition to Ignatius' text. Since 1548 the *Spiritual Exercises* have been read or made by many persons. These Exercises are often a stirring spiritual experience.